Simon

D1642555

THE EARL.

Simon Gray was born in 1936. He began his writing career with *Colmain* (1963), the first of five novels, all published by Faber. He was the author of many plays for TV and radio, also films, including the 1987 adaptation of J. L. Carr's *A Month in the Country*, and TV films including *Running Late*, *After Pilkington* (winner of the Prix Italia) and the Emmy Award-winning *Unnatural Pursuits*. He wrote more than thirty stage plays, among them *Butley* and *Otherwise Engaged* (which both received *Evening Standard* Awards for Best Play), *Close of Play*, *The Rear Column*, *Quartermaine's Terms*, *The Common Pursuit*, *Hidden Laughter*, *The Late Middle Classes* (winner of the Barclay's Best Play Award), *Japes*, *The Old Masters* (his ninth play to be directed by Harold Pinter) and *Little Nell*, which premiered at the Theatre Royal, Bath, in 2007, directed by Peter Hall. *Little Nell* was first broadcast on BBC Radio 4 in 2006, and *Missing Dates* in 2008. In 1991 he was made BAFTA Writer of the Year. His acclaimed works of non-fiction are *An Unnatural Pursuit*, *How's That for Telling 'Em, Fat Lady?*, *Fat Chance*, *Enter a Fox*, *The Smoking Diaries*, *The Year of the Jouncer*, *The Last Cigarette* and *Coda*. With Hugh Whitemore he adapted his *Smoking Diaries* for the stage: *The Last Cigarette* was directed by Richard Eyre in 2009. Simon Gray was appointed CBE in the 2005 New Year's Honours for his services to Drama and Literature. He died in August 2008.

For more information please visit
www.simongray.org.uk

also by Simon Gray

collected editions

PLAYS ONE
(*Butley, Wise Child, Dutch Uncle, Spoiled,
The Caramel Crisis, Sleeping Dog*)

PLAYS TWO
(*Otherwise Engaged, Dog Days, Molly,
Pig in a Poke, Man in a Sidecar, Plaintiffs and Defendants,
Two Sundays, Simply Disconnected*)

PLAYS THREE
(*Quartermaine's Terms, The Rear Column, Close of Play,
Stage Struck, Tartuffe, A Month in the Country, The Idiot*)

PLAYS FOUR
(*Hidden Laughter, The Common Pursuit, The Holy Terror,
They Never Slept, After Pilkington, Old Flames*)

PLAYS FIVE
(*Cell Mates, Life Support, Just the Three of Us, Japes,
Little Nell, The Old Masters, The Late Middle Classes*)

stage plays
MELON, MICHAEL, SEPARATELY AND TOGETHER, JAPES TOO, THE PIG TRADE,
HULLABALOO, THE LAST CIGARETTE (with Hugh Whitemore)

television plays
DEATH OF A TEDDY BEAR, THE PRINCESS, A WAY WITH THE LADIES,
SPOILED, THE DIRT ON LUCY LANE, THE STYLE OF THE COUNTESS

radio plays
THE HOLY TERROR, THE RECTOR'S DAUGHTER, WITH A NOD AND A BOW,
SUFFER THE LITTLE CHILDREN, LITTLE NELL, MISSING DATES

television films
THE REAR COLUMN, QUARTERMAINE'S TERMS, THE COMMON PURSUIT,
RUNNING LATE, FEMME FATALE, UNNATURAL PURSUITS

non-fiction
FAT CHANCE, ENTER A FOX, THE SMOKING DIARIES,
THE YEAR OF THE JOUNCER, THE LAST CIGARETTE, CODA

fiction
SIMPLE PEOPLE, COLMAIN, A COMEBACK FOR STARK,
LITTLE PORTIA, BREAKING HEARTS

films
BUTLEY, A MONTH IN THE COUNTRY

audio books
THE SMOKING DIARIES, THE YEAR OF THE JOUNCER,
THE LAST CIGARETTE, CODA

SIMON GRAY

The Early Diaries

*An Unnatural Pursuit
and other pieces*

&

How's That for Telling 'Em, Fat Lady?

faber and faber

First published in this collected edition 2010
by Faber and Faber Limited
74–77 Great Russell Street
London WC1B 3DA

An Unnatural Pusuit and Other Pieces first published in 1985
by Faber and Faber Ltd
Copyright © Simon Gray 1985

How's That for Telling 'Em, Fat Lady? first published in 1988
by Faber and Faber Ltd
Copyright © Simon Gray 1988

Foreword © Harold Pinter 1985

Typeset by Country Setting, Kingsdown, Kent CT14 8ES
Printed in England by CPI Bookmarque, Croydon, Surrey

A CIP record for this book
is available from the British Library

978–0–571–25491–0

2 4 6 8 10 9 7 5 3 1

Contents

AN UNNATURAL PURSUIT
AND OTHER PIECES

This book is dedicated to the cast and
company of the Lyric, Hammersmith,
production of *The Common Pursuit*,
without whom it could not have appeared.

Acknowledgements

I should like to thank Sarah Moorehead, without whose efficiency, constructive contributions and moral support this book would probably not have appeared.

For permission to reproduce extracts and reviews the publishers gratefully acknowledge the following:

Methuen London Ltd for 'Flops and Other Fragments' from *A Night at the Theatre*, edited by Ronald Harwood (1982) and 'Memories of Lopez' from *Summer Days: Writers on Cricket*, edited by Michael Meyer (1981), and for extracts from *The Common Pursuit* by Simon Gray (1984); Robson Books for 'My Cambridge' from *My Cambridge*, edited by Ronald Hayman (1977); the *Sunday Times* for 'The Pursuit of F. R. Leavis' by Simon Gray (21 October 1984); *The Times Literary Supplement* for 'Confessions of a TV Playwright' (19 September 1968) by Simon Gray; and to *Wisden Cricket Monthly* for 'My Place in Cricket History' by Simon Gray (October 1979).

Foreword

Harold Pinter

How I managed to get through this book without a fag I don't know.

The author did mention that he intended to keep a diary of the production, but I hadn't taken it seriously. In fact I had forgotten all about it. We got on with the rehearsals, put the play on the stage, threw it at various audiences, discussed its future with the management, watched the last performance, had a few drinks, had supper at the Trattoo. I was just about to sit back and reflect upon the whole damn thing when this manuscript arrived, saving me the trouble of reflection. Well . . . not really.

Our perceptions of the endeavour, while closely allied, could never be identical. The author stands alone on a sheer cliff. Others can sympathise, but none can share his unique brand of vertigo. Certainly I had no idea that, after a day's hard labour, Simon would be up until all hours speaking into a machine. No wonder he looked like a particularly rough night on so many mornings.

However, he's got it right; even if some of it makes uncomfortable reading. In setting down what is often referred to as 'the naked truth', he shows himself no mercy. (In the light of this, it seems to me, none of the other protagonists can complain of harsh treatment.) Actually he's not nearly such a pain as his self-portrait would have you believe. In the course of our association on *The Common Pursuit*, I sometimes heard him offer the most extraordinarily helpful observations on subjects like life, putting on plays, and death.

This journal is a remarkable account of a remarkable experience.

Introduction

About a year ago, I had lunch with a friend who asked me why I didn't write a book about my experiences in the theatre along the lines of a short article I'd once done called *Flops and Other Fragments*. (The title surely defines the nature of the piece.)* I replied that I'd now and then yearned to do a diary of a production from the playwright's point of view – or, at least, from this playwright's point of view – from the moment the play was finished through to the play's opening and its critical and public reception. (The two aren't necessarily the same.) He said, well, why don't you? I said I wasn't sure that I'd ever write another play, or at least a play that would be thought worth producing, but agreed that if I did and it was, I would. I did write another play; it was thought worth producing, and I did keep a diary – if reporting into a tape recorder counts as keeping a diary. What follows isn't a transcript of the tapes – there were nearly twenty hours of me talking to myself after all, much of it incomprehensible to anyone except me, some of it incomprehensible to me as well. I've therefore used the tapes as a kind of *aide-mémoire*, amending the grammar of almost every sentence I've included, condensing passages that contained more information than anyone could possibly want, cutting out details that even I could see were boring. Nevertheless, I've done my best to follow the story of the production accurately. I don't believe that any of my reconstruction has distorted the nature of the experience itself – a view corroborated by my wishing, on reading it through, that the experience had been different. I haven't altered, in other words, except for the sake of coherence and speed. Now

* It was published in a collection of essays edited by Ronald Harwood, called *A Night in the Theatre*, published by Methuen, and is reprinted here on page 173.

and then – and on one occasion particularly – I have left a passage exactly as I spoke it, on the grounds that a truer truth was communicated by a lunatic or drunken syntax than would have been communicated by rendering it merely comprehensible.

For me, the main revelation of the transcripts is that I habitually speak in a language that makes only partial sense. From which I gather that I am mainly understood in conversation through my gestures, and the play of my features. If I *am* understood, that is, by any except those closest to me, who probably understand me only too well, even when I'm silent.

1

An Unnatural Pursuit

The Play

A few days after I'd finished the last draft I made the following notes on the characters, the plot and the structure. Realising that in their original context they tended to hold up the story of the production, but still thinking it might nevertheless be helpful to give the reader some sense of *The Common Pursuit* (and for easy reference), I have decided to place them here. I have kept them as written, and also left in some further commentary from the transcripts.

26 November 1983

Spent the day reading the play, making revisions, testing it scene by scene. Like a pudding? But one doesn't test a pudding scene by scene. Also tried to find out what it's about. I never know until after the last draft, after the *first* version of the last draft, and then I'm not always sure. Not that it matters, there are lots of others, critics, etc., around to tell one what it's about. If anything at all, of course.* I think it's a play about friendship, though. English, middle-class, Cambridge-educated friendship. Which might well be, from several points of view, a play about nothing at all. If I'd set it in a working-man's club, a factory, an insurance office or possibly even a green room† (I'm less sure about that) it would

---

* The Most Influential Critic in San Francisco began his radio review of one of my plays – rather a poignant one too, I thought – by bawling out, 'Ladies and gentlemen, the play's the thing, as Shakespeare put it. But ladies and gentlemen, there isn't a play here! No play at all, ladies and gentlemen.' (I quote from memory so may have got a phrase or two wrong.)

† The 'green room' is the room backstage to which the actors can retire when not performing, or between the acts, for cups of coffee and tea. It isn't unlike a university common room, except that the conversation tends to be of a higher intellectual standard.

clearly be about something – i.e. real life. But middle-class and Cambridge-educated is unreal, or anyway impermissible life, elitist, incestuous, who-cares kind of life. Why should theatre-goers, theatre critics, want to know about privileged undergraduates – especially ones who become literary careerists, involve themselves in small-scale magazines, tangle with the Arts Council, commit adultery, become impotent, get divorced and even, in one case, end up butchered by a bit of rough trade in elitist rooms in Trinity? All this is liable to be found a trifle remote, at least by theatre critics and London audiences, who hunger for reality as they know it. But we are, I console myself, what we are. Which is why we write what we write. A bit of a conundrum, that. I think I've only just scratched its surface here. But I mustn't get paranoid about the reviews before the play hits the boards. Time enough for that afterwards. One of the offstage characters, rather an endearing one, ends up as a theatre critic. Another instance of the play's unreality. Nobody ever does *that*, as we all know.

But the characters seem OK to me. At least I believe in them all. This afternoon I made the following notes about them.

Stuart

The spine of the play, serious about literature, prepared to suffer for it – up to a point. A Cambridge johnnie, all right. In love with Marigold. Genuinely in love, genuinely loving. An astringent and passionate man, with the strength and charm to hold his friends to him – almost. Finally, as it turns out, easy to deceive. An egoist, too vain, as he admitted in an earlier draft, to run a literary magazine successfully, even a small one. Even a small one demands efficiency, a respect for money, crude calculations, etc.

Martin

The rich orphan. Shy, loving, loyal, adorer of cats, desperate for friends, a traitor. A traitor precisely because he comes to understand (the only one of the group to do so) what precisely he wants from life, and who he's prepared to sacrifice to get it. He burrows into other lives from within, probably unconsciously, at first. He ends triumphant, matter-of-factly and ruefully so. A man finally at ease in the world. With the usual shadows. I believe I've seen lots like him all my life, but most particularly in the early stages at my public school, Westminster, where I always felt like an outsider – to do with my being an evacuee during the war, coming back to a middle-class education as a jug-eared, nasal-accented Canadian, envious particularly of the shyly charming Martins who ended up as monitors, and who were occasionally and therefore reluctantly compelled to inflict pain on one.

Humphry

Two of my friends, both homosexuals, have been murdered by casual pick-ups. Humphry is based on neither, although I used facts from both their lives (and other lives) in tracing his career. The important fact about Humphry is not his homosexuality but his over-developed critical (and self-critical) faculty which grows into contempt (and above all self-contempt), destroying whatever creative powers he might have. His murder is really a form of suicide. A man capable of deep affection, which he can show only critically. Almost wilfully unhappy. Brave.

Nick

Again a very *English* type, buoyantly and humorously on the make, a kind of (self-aware) mascot of the others, coarsely unlike Martin – devious, always expecting, no, assuming, that he'll be forgiven. The most overtly ambitious, though for nothing (as he really recognises) of value. Simply getting on and on in the literary world, then no doubt in the television world, just as he would have got on in any world, selling cars perhaps, or as a lawyer. His compulsive smoking is, I presume, an indication of his active, minute-by-minute self-waste. Is he the first character in theatre history to smoke himself to death (well, almost) on stage? A substantial claim. Although all Nick's friends are the ones we see on stage, his natural companion through life is his offstage rival, Harrop, nicknamed 'Nappies', a balding, homosexless derivative poet who is as competitive as Nick (ending up, or middling out, as theatre critic on the *Sunday Times*). So perhaps Nick, who is, I suspect, heterosexless, is a perpetual adolescent, looking for someone to play bloodless competitive sports with.

Peter

Devoted to the sexual act. (Why? Perhaps because he enjoys it.

Then why with so many different women?) Begins his sexual career at Cambridge, with pick-ups, easy lays, etc., which becomes as much a habit, really, as Nick's chain-smoking until he falls in love at last (or thinks he does) and wrecks a marriage no better or worse than the one he replaces it with. A generous, hopeless, extravagant soul, doomed to a lifetime of academic self-peddling. A polar opposite of Humphry, who therefore loves him. Like Humphry, he also despises and destroys his own intelligence. Not based on anyone specifically, though I've known one or two people of his sort. I wish more academics had his sweetness of nature, his endless tolerance. There was an exchange in one of the early drafts that went something like this:

> PETER (*having described the mess he's in the middle of making of his life, marriage, etc.*) I don't blame anyone. Not even myself.
> STUART (*I think*) You've always been remarkably tolerant.

(But Stuart – if it was Stuart who said that – would have meant it ironically, and would nevertheless have missed the point. A truly tolerant man doesn't blame himself either.)

McTavish

A rowdily self-righteous Scot, who has rooms above Stuart's at Cambridge. His function is to interrupt. In the play's first scene, he bursts into the room to demand something back, though it's not clear what, as Stuart isn't there. He returns in Act Two, the Epilogue in fact, just after Stuart's return, to demand it again. What he wants, making a magnificent and moralising fuss about it, is his butter back, having lent it to Stuart a few days before. He is referred to at various other points in the play by his nickname, or rather nicknames: 'McButterback', 'McButtocks', 'McButterbum', etc., although nobody can remember how he came by them. So he has a bit of an intervening offstage life. He once, in a long-ago but not completely forgotten draft, had a scene in the middle of the first act with Stuart and Martin, which I enjoyed writing. But I finally forced myself to cut it. It had no real purpose. Or at least discernible purpose. So there he is, in the first and last scenes, ferociously self-important, ferociously recriminating, ferociously Scots.

[*Marigold*]

The absence of information about Marigold is explained in the diary.

Plot

There isn't one. Lots of *incidents*, of course. Stuart struggling to save his magazine; Stuart renouncing his magazine to marry Marigold, who is pregnant. Marigold, not realising Stuart's intentions, having an abortion. Then Stuart married, constantly in one kind of debt or another to Martin, being rendered impotent (by circumstances or merely by me?), getting cuckolded, getting divorced, ending up as a successful literary biographer only too willing to plug his book on Nick's programme. Martin, the old friend and humble ally, being virtually responsible for everything that happens to Stuart. Peter working away at his infidelities, being (an irony intended here) saviour of the magazine that Stuart anyway relinquishes, while betraying his own career, his marriage, etc. Humphry, provoking himself into getting hit by Peter, getting himself murdered. Old Nick, scrambling up the greasy pole into an early grave. I suppose all these people are talented in a way, but in the end their talent doesn't amount to much, i.e. Dr Johnson on Levett: 'To see that single talent well employed.' But no – Martin has a distinct talent for business; Stuart possibly finding and employing his real talent at the play's end, has written 'a good book' – but how good a book?

But let's face it, there really isn't a plot. Simply happenings. Love affairs, abortions, adulteries, treacheries, compromises, lingering deaths, sudden deaths. The routine stuff of English social comedy, in fact.

Further thoughts. The beginning and the ending are crucial to the play's structure. The last scene (the Epilogue) goes back to the first scene, a few minutes on, the rest of the play covering some fifteen or is it seventeen? – can't quite work it out – years of the characters' lives. The first scene ends with a gramophone playing Wagner. The Epilogue opens with the gramophone still playing the same piece of Wagner, a bit further into it. The thought of seeing people as they were; then seeing them as they become; and finally seeing them as they had been; and the image of a gramophone playing the same piece of music; were the source of the play. Both the idea and the image have haunted me, pestered might be a better word, for years.

Another source is an old friend, Ian Hamilton, editor twenty years ago of that small but potent Oxford literary magazine, *The Review*, and subsequently editor of the much grander, more cosmopolitan *The New Review*. He suggested I write a play about his editorial experiences, and furnished me with useful details once I got started. A further source was a television piece I wrote years ago called *Two Sundays*, which alternated scenes between two boys at a public school on a specific Sunday with the same two men in their forties, on a Sunday therefore some twenty-five years on, a gramophone being one of the devices that connected the two couples. The audience wasn't meant to know, I was never quite sure myself, which boy became which man. The real point, though, was time, change, lack of change. When I finished *Two Sundays*, I suspected I hadn't quite finished with it, there was something else there. Which is what we've got now. This is probably of no interest to anyone except myself. But then one likes to be got right. Up to a point, of course. Never to be got *completely* right – otherwise who would 'scape whipping and so forth?* (See *Hamlet*.)

---

* I didn't escape whipping on this one. Several reviewers claimed that I'd stolen the revolving-time effect from Harold Pinter's *Betrayal*, which was written quite a few years after *Two Sundays*.

The Journal

I finished the play at six this morning, having worked through half the night. I'd also worked through three packages of cigarettes and half a bottle of malt whisky. But the main thing is that it's finished. Olé!

Of course when I say finished, I don't actually mean *finished*. What I mean, actually, is that I've finished the first version of the last draft. If this one goes as the others went, I'll be correcting and revising from about tomorrow night through to the first public performance, or even through to the official first night. This isn't because I'm a perfectionist, but because I get so many things wrong that it takes me the length of rehearsals to notice them all. I wish I wrote plays as Harold does, complete as texts when the ink is still wet on the last words. Or had the panache of Tom Stoppard, who virtually writes his plays in rehearsal, so I'm told. I suppose I'm one of the routine ones. What inspiration I have goes into getting it not quite right in the first place. Still, for the time being I've finished to this extent: the play has a first and a second act. They seem to belong to each other. So olé! Olé with reservations. Let's put it that way.

So at six this morning I numbered the pages, packed and shaped them into a completed-looking pile, toasted myself with a further gulp of whisky and a few more cigarettes, gloated. This, for me, is the only moment of pure happiness I ever experience in the playwriting business. I wish there was some ceremony, some physical ceremony, to express it – picking it up, turning it upside down, slapping its rump, dishing out cigars. But then there'd also be the alternatives, like having to rush it straight into an oxygen tent, or wrapping up its still little form and handing it back to myself, with a muttered: 'Believe me, it's better this way.'

Outside was the dawn and a bit more. Birds knocking about, light, no doubt dew, so forth. I called Hazel from under my desk, where she'd spent the night at my feet, and got up to fetch her lead. I fell over, not quite to the floor full stretch, but to my hands and knees. For a few seconds, or minutes even, Hazel and I were snout to snout. She hates it when this happens, the main distinction between us being, from her point of view, that I'm meant to be upright on two, she's meant to be down there on four. I clambered to my feet by means of the desk and the chair, took a few uncertain steps. (This is beginning to sound like Dick Francis.) Very odd, being so clear-headed, so exhilarated, so triumphant, and yet to have one's knees buckle under one. When I got my balance about right, we went out.

A middle-aged woman was coming up the pavement towards me, full of early-morning virtue and business ahead. A matron in a hospital? A policewoman? What, at six in the morning? Or had *she* just finished a play? They're all over the place these days, playwrights, and there's no knowing what they look like, what sex even. I prepared to give her a salute, spirit to spirit abroad in the dawn, but as I raised my arm she tacked quickly away, to the other side of the street. I suppose that as I was unshaven, my clothes shapeless, my gait unsteady, I looked a bit like a tramp. A tramp who'd just stolen a dog. But nobody would want to steal Hazel except somebody who already loved her. Perhaps we looked as if we were eloping.

Walked through Highgate woods. Very beautiful. Made it home. Went to bed an hour or so before everybody else started getting up.

27 November

Oh Christ. Just noticed I left Marigold off my list of characters. (For list of characters see previous section.) The only woman in the play, and what in lit. crit. essays they call 'the catalyst'. And yet Grahame McTavish, two brief scenes and about five lines, got on my list. What does this mean? It reminds me of *The Rear Column*. Five men who occupy the stage all evening and one woman, a Black girl, who has two minutes or so at the beginning of the third act, stripped to the waist, tied to a post, no dialogue. One afternoon in the New York rehearsal, as she was being tethered by the neck, I heard myself crying out, 'And they say I can't write parts for women!' As a matter of fact, I've written quite a few parts for women. My first television play, *Death of a Teddy Bear*, was about a woman entirely, really; so was *Molly* – actually *Death of a Teddy Bear* transformed into a stage play, and not nearly as good as the original. So I suppose that doesn't count. But *Man in a Side-Car* was also about a woman. And lots of other women, in all my plays. *Close of Play* has a woman in the lead, originally to be played by Peggy Ashcroft.* And yet, resist the accusation though I will, the fact remains that I completely forgot Marigold, the only woman in the new play. What shall I say about her?†

28 November

Read through the play again. Made one or two corrections. Worry a bit about Stuart's revelation of impotence (Act Two, Scene One). Speech seems laboured, the conclusion too set up. Pleased, though, with the cats motif, Martin's love of them, ownership of them, cheerful dispatching of them when they become inconvenient. On the whole felt OK. Decided to telephone Harold, let him know that 'something' was on the way, but stressed that it was only work in progress, wouldn't mind some advice. This ploy fooled neither of us. He knows I mean business, or at least want it.

Evening A few hours after phoning Harold I read through the play again. Still felt OK, if a trifle tremulous. Tonight I'd like to go out in a top hat, my nose reddened, and swivel around the lampposts. This may be my last chance to celebrate. Soon somebody

---

* *Close of Play* was done at the National. Rehearsals were interrupted by a series of illnesses and accidents, so that at one point it seemed that we ought to be running a shuttle service between the theatre and the hospital. Then there was the six weeks' strike. And then, as a kind of afterthought, just when we were poised to go ahead, Peggy Ashcroft, who had begun rehearsals with a broken ankle, had to have an emergency operation on her knee, and was forced to withdraw from the production. Almost the greatest regret of my professional life is that she didn't perform in *Close of Play*, a part I would have written especially for her if I'd had the nerve.

† I didn't say anything about her. I think the reason becomes clear further on, during my first conversation about the play with Harold Pinter.

else (Harold) will have read it and it'll be on its way – perhaps to nowhere in particular.

A few hours later   Didn't read through the play again, but dipped into it, reading a few pages, jumping, reading a few more. Saw urgent need, on every page I looked at, for revision. Began to make corrections but gave it up, as tomorrow I have to make photocopies, one of which will go to Harold. I'd like it to look spruce. Some of the dialogue is distinctly leaden. Made me think yearningly of the chap once known on Broadway as 'Doc', because he began his career doctoring other people's plays. Always a bad moment for the playwright when he came into rehearsal and found 'Doc' ensconced in an aisle seat, a pad on his knees, working on some salvaging one-liners. Or was it really a good moment, knowing that his play was receiving the best medical attention? 'Doc' must have picked up a few tips in his turn, as he went on to become Neil Simon, most successful living American playwright. Is anyone called in to doctor his plays, I wonder, now that he writes them instead of doctoring them?

28–29 November

Read the play through again after all. See further problems, notably Grahame McTavish, Marigold, great sections of speeches here and there. But cling to the view that it's OK. That is, taken as a whole.

30 November

I spent the day correcting and amending little passages, typing out the pages to keep them neat, then getting the play photocopied. I didn't go into College (Queen Mary, down the Mile End Road), although I was meant to be teaching. In the evening I took the play around to Harold's. I was in a highly sensitive state, possibly even hysterical.

I had arranged to meet him in his studio at the bottom of the garden of his Holland Park house, which has a separate entrance on a parallel street. For some reason I still can't fathom, I went to the main house and was received by Antonia. I met her surprise with an attempt at insouciance, made the usual enquiries, answered the usual enquiries, and then allowed myself to be gestured towards the studio. I have made this journey many times before, in both directions. How, then, did I manage to walk straight into the trellis gate that separates the house garden from the studio patio, virtually straight through it in fact, kicking out a lump or two of wood in the process? Harold, alerted (with good reason) by Antonia that I was on my way, came out to greet me as I was bent double, trying to pack some of the wood back. I expect he wondered what I was up to. I didn't try to explain, except with half-gestures and a grunt. We went into the studio, had a few drinks. I talked almost all the time, my mind ranging freely over the play in the blue shoulder bag, my tongue dealing with quite other topics, many other topics. When I decided the time had come to leave, I swung the blue shoulder bag back over my shoulder, and made for the door. I suppose I would have left without handing the play over if Harold hadn't asked for it. He said he would read it tomorrow. We would meet in the evening, at L'Epicure, to discuss it. So that's that.

Friday, 1 December

Had lunch with David Jones, to consider approaches to a film version of *The Rector's Daughter*, which I've been longing to do for years. David Jones, who likes the book as much as I do, wants to direct it. It was a useful lunch, even though a lot of the time my attention was straying to images of Harold – at that very moment reading the play; or sitting glumly with it on his lap, having read it. I went home and hung about waiting for our dinner date, feeling slightly sick. I was also worried about our having chosen L'Epicure, because traditionally that's where we go to celebrate after (a) he's liked a play, and (b) made it clear that he'd like to direct it. In this case, it seemed to me, we'd taken a serious risk. Challenged the gods. So forth. Just before I left to meet him, he telephoned, sensitive to the kind of state I'd be in. One of the advantages of working with a fellow playwright is that he knows about the vanities, the timidities, the sheer terror attendant on sending a play out for the first time. He said that he was very excited, loved its structure, be of good cheer, only had four points to discuss. I set off for L'Epicure in highish spirits, that sank a bit on the tube, as I began to wonder what the four points were.

It occurred to me that there are only five scenes in the play. Perhaps he really meant that four of them were wrong. But would he actually say, 'Be of good cheer. Only four of your five scenes are wrong'? By the time I got to the restaurant I'd worked myself into a bit of a frenzy, made worse by his being, for almost the first time in my long experience of him, late. He is almost obsessively punctual. I had to wait for twenty extremely bad minutes, chain-smoking, staring towards the door, checking my watch, starting to my feet, had I got the restaurant wrong, had he funked it, made the mistake of rereading it, etc.

When he arrived, having been delayed by a protracted meeting to do with his cricket club, the Gaieties, we got off to a sensational start by his proclaiming that he was delighted with the play. He already seemed to have grasped it. Grasped, I mean, not only its structure, what it was about, that sort of thing, but lots of its details, even to remembering quite a few of the lines. All on one reading. I kept him lingering around the compliments for as long as I decently could, then let him get to the four points. Which were as follows:

1   *Old Grahame McTavish*. An intrusion, one that doesn't belong within the play's world. Also he doesn't think that the part, whittled down to a few lines of Scots bluster, justified hiring an actor. He also feels that the idea embodied in McTavish is already done in various offstage characters. The name seems to him a giveaway: farcical and unconvincing. Or was it I who made that point? Anyway, McTavish's got to go. I knew it.

2   *Marigold*. Or specifically, the scene in which she tells Stuart she's had an abortion. In Harold's view, too portentously a 'scene', signalling itself as a solemn piece of theatre instead of maintaining the tone already established, which is not, I hope, at all solemn.

3   *Marigold again*. This time the later scene, in which she tells Stuart and Martin that she's pregnant. Harold feels the same about this as about the earlier scene, in other words, portentous. This led us on to a discussion of her character as a whole. He feels

that she has more life, individual life, in the first short scene than in her two major ones, where she is being rather ceremonially presented as 'woman', with her 'womanly' nature, 'womanly' virtues. I admitted that I'd always had a slightly numb feeling about those two scenes, but didn't admit that I had actually forgotten her when drawing up my list of characters the other evening. He tried to persuade me to have another look at her, to find her in the particular rather than in the general. I put up some resistance, not because I didn't think he was right, but because I wasn't sure I could face going back to a section of the play on such large terms. He said they weren't large, that the structure of the scenes was fine, it was really just a question of finding a slightly different line in the dialogue. In the end I agreed to give it a go. What worries me is that I might go on to rewrite the whole play, drafts on drafts of it. I'm a compulsive. He knows that. Anyway, I reminded him that I was.

4 *Stuart*. Act Two, Scene One. Really, Stuart's explanation to Martin as to why he wants to quit Martin's publishing firm. Harold feels that Stuart has thought his speeches out too clearly, which therefore makes them seem rehearsed. My defence was that the speech actually has been rehearsed. There's a line, I pointed out, in which Stuart says he's 'thought it all out' while sitting on the hospital steps after his visit to the dying poet, Hubert Parkin (an offstage figure who dogs Stuart's life). Harold looked suddenly alert. 'Where is this line? I don't remember a line like that.' I showed him in my copy. He checked in his, where there wasn't a line, only a white smear, where a line might have been. Of course I realise it doesn't matter whether the line was there or not. The fact that Stuart says that he's 'thought out' what he wants to say doesn't mean that he's rehearsed his speech cadence by cadence. The truth is, I realised, looking at it with Harold then and looking at it several times since, that it's a rather dead, or more likely, overwritten exchange, in which nothing is left to chance, no unexpected thought, no uncertainty. The wrong pulse in the rhythms. He ended rather oddly by drawing attention to Stuart's long speech about Martina, the cat, but didn't amplify, perhaps because he's not yet sure what it is he's drawing my attention to. There's nothing wrong with the speech itself, as far as I can see.

So there were the four points, none of them involving many hours' work, all of them crucial. In making them, Harold had already begun to direct the play. So there we were, halfway through dinner, beaming away at each other, about to embark on a new production. This fairly prolonged lyrical passage ended when we began to discuss dates, his availability and mine. When it comes to putting a play of mine on, I'm always available, but he's committed to writing a film for Joe Losey,* so can't begin until the late summer of next year. Suits me perfectly, apart from not being anything like soon enough. Then we discussed a producer.

I was slightly surprised that we should need to, having assumed that we would go, as we've always done (except once, when we went to the National), to Michael Codron, who after all has produced all my West End plays. But Harold's view was that Michael *wouldn't* want to do it. He would love the play but would find it uncommercial. First of all he would think its world too enclosed and secondly it isn't a vehicle for stars, and Michael, like most West End producers these days, prefers to go into a theatre with a star or two.† Everything Harold said made sense, but I still felt I had an obligation to offer the play to Michael anyway, both because of our past association; and because he's the best producer in the West End. Also, as I pointed out to Harold, if it weren't for Michael, I would never have written stage plays at all, which perhaps means that he has a lot to answer for, and deserves all he gets; even a crack at my latest. We left it that I'd get in touch with Michael tomorrow – today – tomorrow, depending on what time it is. Today. Later today. Also that we'd ask him to decide quickly. Within a week would be nice. Harold asked me, by the way, to report to Michael his prediction of Michael's response.

Saturday, 3 December

I phoned Michael up – he was in the country – to tell him that I'd written a new play and that I'd bring it around on Monday. He said he was going to Boston on Tuesday for Tom Stoppard's *The Real Thing*, and that he would read it on the plane. He would

---

* Joe Losey became ill just before we began rehearsals and died during them.

† But not more. Too expensive.

phone me soon after he arrived. He sounded quite excited, I thought, until I passed on Harold's prediction. Then he sounded apprehensive.

Sunday, 4 December

Beryl (my wife) has ricked her back, and is confined to bed. Every movement hurts. We decided that I shouldn't take Lucy back to school (she is a weekly boarder just outside Haslemere) as it would mean leaving Beryl on her own for four hours or so, immobile. I'll take Lucy back tomorrow, then go straight on to Michael's office.

Monday, 5 December

Sitting on the train on my way back from delivering Lucy to Haslemere, with Michael's copy of the play in my shoulder bag, I suddenly noticed an elderly man in the seat diametrically opposite. He reminded me of my father, although in every respect except one quite unlike him. The central character of *Close of Play*, Jasper, was based on my father. Jasper is in fact dead (my father died a year or so before I wrote the play) but is forced to endure, as if alive, a traditional English Sunday, helpless in his favourite armchair as his three sons and their wives fall to pieces in the usual English middle-class style, sometimes blaming him, sometimes appealing to him for help and sobbing at his feet for forgiveness, but basically ignoring him as they squabble around him. In other words I'd stuck him in Hell, which turns out to be 'life, old life itself'.*

When I went in on the first day of rehearsal Michael Redgrave, who was playing Jasper, was sitting in a chair, his jaw out-thrust, which gave me a slight chill as I had been going to suggest that he thrust his jaw out in performance, this being my father's most striking characteristic. I'd remembered it all the way through writing the play. My son thrusts his jaw out, by the way; so do both my brothers. I do it myself. All the male Grays do it, when tired. Sometimes, when we're all together in a room, we look like a gang of antique simians, particularly if our right hands are also, as they

---

* This phrase, which recurs throughout the diaries, is a quotation from *The Common Pursuit* (Stuart to Marigold, Act One, Scene Two).

frequently are, resting in our left armpits. The point I'm coming to is that the elderly man sitting diametrically opposite was doing both these things, sitting with his jaw stuck out, his right hand tucked into his left armpit, thus taking me back through Michael Redgrave to the image of my father, especially in the last months of his life, his jaw almost permanently thrust out in fatigue, despair, defeat. The elderly man on the train looked as if he, too, were in some state of despair or defeat. He had cheap rings on his fingers, but his shoes weren't properly laced and his trousers were stained. When we got into Waterloo, I passed him on the platform, and glanced casually down at his large, brown, almost empty, from the way he was carrying it, suitcase. The name 'James Gray' (my father's name was James) was painted on it in bold white letters, which gave me one of those hair-raising moments in life that I'm on the whole sure no one actually wants to be without, but never particularly wants at the moments when they come.

Michael Codron had just got back from an Equity meeting when I arrived. He came out of his office to greet me, then escorted me into it. I took out of my blue shoulder bag the large brown envelope and handed it to him. He received it gingerly, almost as if puzzled, seeming to weigh it in his hands, putting it on his desk, picking it up again, putting it down. All the time he kept saying, in a slightly strangled voice, 'Well, I very much *want* to like it. I do *want* to like it. I do *hope* I like it.' The accumulation of repetitions, along with his peculiar physical relationship with the envelope, as if it contained a relic both sacred and disgusting, had a rather pole-axing effect on me. I felt that he'd already lost his preliminary skirmish with attempting to like it. We had a briefish conversation about this and that, with both this and that seeming to lead us back to mild recriminations from both sides about our behaviour to each other in past productions. Michael said he sometimes felt that we (Harold and I) didn't sufficiently realise that as producer he very much wanted to produce. That is, to take part in the casting, the discussions on set design, all that kind of thing. In short, that's why he was in the business of producing. What Americans would call the 'creative' part of producing.* 'But why didn't you

* Though, unlike Michael, most American producers' idea of 'creative' producing is to fire people, preferably actors. They can't think of anything else to do with them once they've hired them. My first experience of this came during a Broadway

tell me this before?' I asked at one point. He gave me the look that I suppose the question deserved, and took me in to see David, his partner, whom I've known over many years, and who had previously never failed to give me a cheery welcome. He was on the telephone. He greeted me by raising his hand and then turning his back on me.† I left with Michael promising to read the play on the plane to Boston, and to phone me as soon as he arrived, but really with the words, 'I do want to like it, do hope to like it' ringing hollowly in my ears.

I went home, put a hot-water bottle or two under Beryl's back, phoned Harold and gave him the facts and some of the flavour of my conversation with Michael. I explained, too, about Michael's wanting actively to be a producer, not simply to be the money behind an already designed package. Harold said, 'Well, he's never said anything like that to me,' and I said, remembering Michael's look when I'd said much the same, that I suspected Michael assumed that he shouldn't have had to say it, we ought to have known.

Tuesday

Michael now ensconced in Boston. Hasn't phoned.

Wednesday

Spent the day working on the text, along the lines discussed with Harold. Finally killed off Grahame McTavish. Minded a *bit*. Nothing from Michael in Boston. Hate waiting for the telephone to ring. I think I can work out what its silence means.

---

production of one of my early plays. I was driven straight from the airport to the rehearsal room, where, jet-lagged and slightly drunk, I sat through the first act. The producer, who actually was short and squat and smoking a cigar, sat down beside me and asked me what I thought. Lacking any thought, having been mainly comatose, I said vaguely that perhaps one of the actors, looking at a cluster of them in a corner and arbitrarily indicating the one who was closest, possibly needed a bit of attention. 'Want me to fire him?' he asked, rising eagerly to his feet. What he was trying to do, of course, was to resolve his professional identity crisis creatively.

† I learnt later from Michael that David was having a most difficult conversation, and didn't even take in whoever it was Michael had brought into his office.

Thursday

Had a *nuit blanche* fuming at Michael for not having phoned, then attempted to exonerate him on comforting grounds, i.e. his plane had crashed, he'd been mugged, *The Real Thing* was a disaster, etc., before finally making it to sleep at about 9 a.m. Michael then phoned. Not from Boston, but from London. He'd postponed his Boston trip because he'd been ill, was leaving for Boston in an hour or so. His first words were, 'Harold's quite right. I like it hugely, *hugely*, but I don't think it's commercial.' Not because the world of the play's too confined, but because he doesn't see how, given six equal parts, we could attract any stars. He doesn't want to be part of it if we insist on starting it off in the West End, but would like to be part of it if we'll consider going with a young and unstarry cast to the Lyric, Hammersmith, or Greenwich, from which we might get ourselves wooed or invited into the West End. What did I feel? I said I'd think about it and discuss it with Harold, but could see his point, and trusted his judgement.

My real feelings were, actually, mainly of resentment that he hadn't (a) insisted on buying the play immediately, on any terms; with a view to putting it on at any theatre of my choice, on any terms; (b) which amounts to the same thing, that he hadn't talked about the play at length, analysing its structure, revelling in its characters and dialogue, and generally showering it (me) with compliments. Nevertheless, I suspect Michael's right. We probably won't get a star or two, of the kind that people will pay to see whatever the reviews are like. And unspoken between Michael and myself is the knowledge that my plays generally get bad reviews,* with the probability that this one will fare worse than usual.

I telephoned Harold to give him a summary of my talk with Michael. We agreed to meet very shortly and consider it properly. He's not opposed to Greenwich or Hammersmith in principle. He wasn't of course surprised by Michael's rather ambivalent reaction – as it conformed precisely to his prediction.

---

* *Butley*, for instance, got mainly poor reviews, but had Alan Bates in the lead, and did very well. It's now generally assumed that it got good reviews, an assumption that I do nothing to discourage, especially as it's now actually beginning to get some.

Friday

Beryl has at last read the play, having put off doing so until she'd finished a piece of work of her own – or until she could actually face up to the months ahead, the obsessiveness, the bouts of paranoia concluding in grim, denunciatory post-mortems. I was out when she read it, and she was out when I got back, so she left her views on the telephone answering machine. She has a number of what she calls 'wifely worries' to do with the literary world as the play presents it, and of how 'they'll' take it. She's particularly concerned over the joke about 'Nappies' Harrop being appointed theatre critic on the *Sunday Times* because of his 'lack of qualifications'. She felt I was asking for trouble. When she got back, I assured her that it was such a minor part of the evening, really coming down to one line, and that line *en passant* – and besides, reverting to a traditional tack, I wrote what I wrote and had to stand by it, the whole kit and caboodle – we'd wait and see how it went in previews – one could always adjust it.

Weekend

Nothing of interest. Several desultory conversations with Harold. We're meeting before Michael gets back from Boston.

Monday, Tuesday, Wednesday

Mainly working on a draft of *The Rector's Daughter*, but also looked at the play, going over the scenes discussed with Harold. Grahame McTavish gone. (Actually a few days ago. I think I've recorded that butchery.) Stuart's resignation speeches to Martin rewritten. I've encouraged Marigold to take me by surprise in her dialogue.

Thursday

Creepy. Creepy, creepy, creepy. I give two long seminars at Queen Mary on Thursday afternoons, one on something called 'Practical Criticism', which in effect means reading a poem or a passage from a poem or a piece of prose with students, and then going through it to find out what we think about it. Who likes it, why? I always try to do something I've forgotten, or best of all, don't know, so that I'm as new to it as they are, which helps us both.

I've often found myself liking or, if not liking, admiring poetry I've got into the comfortable habit of assuming I hate. This afternoon it was a lump from *Paradise Lost*. My established view of *Paradise Lost* is that it's a gigantic and exhausting bluff, reminding me of that Scots preacher who used to write in the margins of his sermons, 'Weak point here. Shout like hell.' But this afternoon I happened to hit on a passage from Book 2 – I can't be bothered to go on with this. Because what I really want to talk about is what happened after the seminar. No, it was after the *second* seminar, when we read bits of plays, examine them as if they were being rehearsed for production, so that students begin to get the idea that in Shakespeare, for instance, there's a lot of (frequently very interesting) life going on among the characters who aren't speaking. Anyway, I gave the two seminars, and was sitting in my office, jaded and irritable, wondering who to phone up and what excuse to offer, and also eyeing my typewriter and contemplating an attempt at *The Rector's Daughter*, when there was a knock on the door. A student, a girl, put her head in. I worked up one of those welcoming smiles that means, 'Don't move another inch.' She said, 'Oh, I don't want to disturb you, but I forgot to tell you earlier. Grahame McTavish sends his regards.' The hair on the back of my neck did what hair is reported to do on these occasions. 'Who?' 'Grahame McTavish. Don't you remember Grahame? He was in the drama seminar last year.' Upon which I remembered Grahame McTavish, a tall, limber, authoritative, and very English youth, with a powerful voice and strong bone structure.

The fact is that I've always had a problem remembering names, and connecting them to faces. I wonder who all the other names in the play belong to, and also what Grahame McTavish would have felt if I'd sent a message back saying that I couldn't accept his regards as I'd eliminated him a few days ago on the grounds that he's too coarse and farcical a figure, with too bogus a name, to be allowed to inhabit my refined fictional world.

9 December

I've thrown out all the previous versions, drafts, etc., of the play. I don't know if that's of interest to anyone but myself, but the fact is I had trouble lifting this dreadful accumulation of scenes, half-scenes, drafts. There were pages of the play that simply haven't changed very much and pages that I'd rejected, and scenes written pointlessly again and again because I was making no progress with them and kept thinking that if I wrote them through from the beginning they'd decide out of sheer boredom to end up somewhere differently. Anyway, there they all were, unliftable in a wastepaper basket. Although the wastepaper basket is actually an enormous wicker basket, not easily liftable in itself. Perhaps the rubbish men will refuse it. They're very choosy around here. What if I were to be confronted with a container holding all the ends of the cigarettes I'd smoked during the writing of the play? And another holding all the empty bottles?

I've pretty well decided to call the play *Partners*. And subtitle it 'Scenes from the Literary Life'.

I've been meditating on and off about something Harold said at the dinner after he'd just read the play. That I keep all my characters on a tight rein. I suppose that's one of the many differences between us. Harold can have a perfectly appropriate, or he makes it seem appropriate, monologue on, for example, the location of Bolsover Street (in *No Man's Land*) which is nevertheless apropos of nothing, and to which there may well be no further reference after no previous reference. I can't do that. My characters live within a precise, probably over-precise, world, and everything they say is in some way or another to do with it. There's scarcely a line in *The Rear Column* that doesn't arise from the practical problems of being marooned in the Congo. The same is true of this play. I must get into the habit of calling it *Partners*. The same is true of *Partners*. All of it is life in practice. The characters are mired in it. Harold's characters, though seemingly locked in habits and circumstances, always have an ultimate freedom from thisness or thatness which is likely to express itself in an aria of free-wheeling lunacy, sometimes comic, sometimes frightening, but never needing justification. Perhaps Charlie Peake, Professor of English at Queen Mary College, and a great admirer of Harold's, would like to add some notes to all this.

On the question of Queen Mary College. When I mentioned to some of my colleagues last Thursday that I had finished a new play, they immediately and adroitly changed the subject to something vastly more interesting, from their point of view.

12 December

9 p.m.   Had lunch with Harold. The main issue was, of course, how to proceed with Michael. Or without him. Harold's view, which he came to over the meal, was that Michael had already signalled that he didn't want to produce the play, and that perhaps therefore we should let him off the hook by looking for another producer. This seems sensible, although depressing. I find it difficult to contemplate Michael not being involved in some way. We went on to consider alternatives. I should say that Harold, having just completed the film script of *Turtle Diary*, was in a state of exhilarated clear-headedness. My own head was stuffed with half-realised apprehensions, most of the exhilaration of having finished *Partners* having worn off. The main alternative was UBA (United British Artists), a consortium got together by the actor Richard Johnson with a board consisting entirely, apart from an accountant and/or lawyer, of actors – Glenda Jackson, John Hurt, Albert Finney, Maggie Smith, etc. – with the intention of making films and producing plays. As Harold had just accepted an invitation to join the board, and they were about to commission me to write the film script of *The Rector's Daughter*, we decided that Harold should show the play – offer it, really – to Richard Johnson. This has another advantage in that, given Harold's imminent connection with UBA, and my own imminent connection, Michael and I should be able to extricate ourselves from each other without distress to either side.

And yet. And yet. Beryl being out, I had a meal at a Chinese restaurant up in the village (Highgate). I have an odd relationship with the owner there. Years ago, when I went in with a friend for lunch, I asked him, quite politely, to turn the music either down or preferably off altogether. His response was to tell me to fuck off. Which I did, with appropriately dignified gestures and exclamations. Nevertheless, I've started going back there, and he's started treating me with great civility, now and then bringing to the table a free brandy. I've no idea why either of us behaved as we did, or are now behaving as we are. Except that I love Chinese food, and there isn't another Chinese restaurant for miles; and he needs as much custom as he can get. Perhaps that's the explanation.* As I sat brooding over my duck, I suddenly remembered that I hadn't reported to Judy Daish, who is agent to both Harold and myself, what we'd decided about UBA. I phoned her from the restaurant, got her at the office, and inevitably found myself unleashing all my worries about Michael. She was very calming, certain that we would end up with a producer who would do well by the play – 'and that's all that matters'. True. The problem for me is, after so many productions with Michael, it's no longer just business. Somewhere between personal and business, which is exactly the wrong spot, according to *The Godfather*.

But I'm not the only one in a stew about producers. Arnold Wesker phoned this morning to ask me about Ken Frankel, who directed the American production of *Quartermaine's Terms*, and is about to do Arnold's *Love Letters on Blue Paper* for the Hudson Guild in New York. Or was about to, Arnold having withdrawn the play when told that the Hudson Guild could pay him only a five-hundred-dollar fee, and no royalties. He's just received a letter from Ken Frankel telling him he's mad to withdraw the play, what matters is to give it an airing in a showcase, get along the critics, work for a transfer to another theatre, which will pay royalties on a (with luck) decent run. Arnold was sure I'd be on his side. Five hundred dollars is a miserable amount, after all. But I argued passionately for Ken Frankel's position. What matters in New York these days is not where you open but where you move to. I think I managed to change his mind. I hope so, as I know I'm right. I always know I'm right when deciding other people's destinies. Partly, I suppose, because I don't have to worry too much about the consequences. In my own case, the consequences being so serious, I worry continuously, and therefore usually make the wrong decision. Which brings me back to worrying about Michael Codron on the one hand, UBA on the other.

13 December

Michael back from Boston previews of *The Real Thing*. I told him that we'd decided to approach UBA. He sounded first surprised; then dignified; finally fed up. It was agreed that he should have further discussions with Judy. I hung up feeling that I'd been a shit. I put the matter cogently but objectively to Beryl, pointing

---

* But he still hasn't turned the music off.

her carefully to the right conclusion, that it's really all Michael's fault for not having been more enthusiastic when he received the play. Beryl, however, let me down yet again by pointing out that all Michael had done was to agree with Harold that the play was uncommercial, and offer to do the best for it by going to Greenwich or Hammersmith or wherever, where we might well end up doing it anyway but without Michael, and what would be the advantage of *that*, she asked? In other words, she suggested that I was being impatient, and possibly even paranoid. She's possibly right, which seems to me even more unfair.

(There followed various conversations between Michael and Judy, Judy and Harold, Michael and me, Judy and me, Harold and me, the upshot of which was that (a) Michael felt the whole affair had become too muddied, and didn't want to be involved, and (b) that we shouldn't consider that the door between us was closed, as he'd like to read the play again, with a view to making an offer. Could we please get him a copy of the play before he went to New York for the opening of *The Real Thing*? In the meanwhile, between conversations with Michael, at a point when he appeared definitively to have withdrawn, Judy sent the play to Richard Johnson who promised to read it before the launching party for his newly founded company. I had been invited to the party. So, of course, had Harold. In fact, the party was being given on the day on which Harold was to become a member of the DBA board.)

Monday, 19 December

The DBA launch party, a lunchtime affair. I went along in a fairly smouldering state, not having heard a word from Richard Johnson, although Judy had left him numerous messages. I took my shoulder bag with me, with nothing in it except, I think, a handkerchief. I had an idea the bag would make me look distinctive – I might at least succeed in getting myself searched.* I wasn't searched at the launch although I'd packed the bag *en route* with

---

* The only time I've ever had my bag searched was in a seedy cinema below Leicester Square. The Irish-looking chap who went in ahead of me, who was carrying several carrier bags and had a brown paper parcel tucked under his arm, didn't have anything searched.

a *Standard* and a few other newspapers to give it purpose and me an air of intent. It was being held in a restaurant off Wardour Street, new and in the American mode, with an upstairs, large and airy for ordinary lunches, and a downstairs, large and airless for DBA. The room was full of journalists, film directors, actors, theatre directors, and more journalists, a covey of whom were gathered around Harold, in black as usual. The journalists seemed to be in pinks or light blues, pastel, and crouching slightly as if they were taking pictures, though I didn't see any cameras. I think this was an illusion on my part, both the crouching and the colours, but that was the effect. Harold standing blackly upright in a little circle of crouching pastels. I ploughed my way shyly through to him, nudging the pastels out of the way and him into a corner. He asked me whether I'd spoken to Richard Johnson. I said I hadn't. He gestured to a circle of about nine people, in the midst of whom Richard Johnson was standing, fluently outlining his plans for DBA. 'Well,' Harold said, 'he loves the play. Bowled over by it. Mentioned it at the board meeting this morning.' We collected some champagne from a passing tray, talked a little longer, separated.

On my way towards Richard Johnson, who was now outlining his plans to about four journalists, I bumped into David Jones, who will, I hope, be directing *The Rector's Daughter* if the script gets written, the money raised, the film made. But all the time I was keeping a track on Richard Johnson who was now down to two journalists. I left David Jones and went up to him. His eye, I might say, completely failed to take me in. Perhaps because it was a trifle bleary. Or perhaps because, in spite of being six feet *and* sporting a blue shoulder bag, I don't cut much visual ice. I waited until the two journalists were down to one, a humble-looking grey-haired woman with a squint, who's probably ruined more reputations than I've had hot dinners, then scooped up another glass of champagne and interposed myself between them. He outlined some of his plans for DBA before taking in that I wasn't one of the journalists, but one of his plans. I told him I gathered he'd read *Partners*, and so got him into our talk.

He began promisingly by being immensely enthusiastic, describing it as wonderful, terrific, wonderful, moving, tragic, funny, just what UBA needed, a new play to announce at the launch, before extending the same sentence into a couple of provisos, the first of these being that *Partners* would have to be read by all the other members of the board – John Hurt, Maggie Smith, Glenda Jackson, Diana Rigg, Albert Finney, Uncle Tom Cobblers and all – which struck me as preposterous because what actor wants to read a play in which there is no conceivable part for him- or herself. But he was adamant, his sentence running on well above my protests, that this protocol would have to be observed, not, *not* that it mattered what they thought because the actors almost certainly wouldn't get around to it, why should they bother with a play they couldn't possibly be in, but on the other hand, *the other hand*, did I know that Harold wouldn't be free to do the play until the autumn, he had a previous commitment? I said I wasn't sure that that was the case. It depended rather, didn't it, on whether the film he was currently discussing with Joe Losey actually happened or not. If it didn't happen then Harold would want to do it in the spring, wouldn't he? 'But one should assume the autumn, shouldn't we?' Richard Johnson asked firmly. I should admit here, confidentially, that Richard Johnson, in the conversation so far, was striking off a very good impersonation of a chap who is keen on champagne, with a lot of it to hand. I wasn't altogether sober myself, being now on my fourth or fifth glass with an empty stomach waiting to receive it. He reverted briefly to the play, still finding it wonderful, terrific, wonderful, and then moved on to the question of how much I was going to be paid by UBA for *The Rector's Daughter* (my doing of which he'd apparently announced to the press), and his feeling that Judy (my agent) ought perhaps to discuss the matter with him yet again. He mentioned this in terms that clearly indicated a downgrading of what I'd been offered so far, which was nothing, as far as I knew. So the rest of the conversation was not to do with *Partners*, but to do with how much less money than the money he hadn't so far offered me he could get me to do *The Rector's Daughter* for. He then clutched my shoulder firmly, business satisfactorily concluded, from which, in retrospect, I deduce that he wasn't at all drunk, just practising producing, and went off to outline his plans for DBA to a cluster of journalists who had probably innocently thought their day's work was done, and that they could get down to the champagne and canapés at last.

I rocked about on uncertain feet, watching the board being photographed: Finney, Glenda Jackson, Harold, Richard Johnson, Tom Cobbler, and an enigma I took to be the solicitor and/or accountant. Taken individually they were pretty glamorous. But forced by the press photographers into a homogeneous group, they suddenly looked like a gang of corrupt prep-school teachers. Group photography is like group therapy, it exposes the worst in people, even if it isn't there. Harold detached himself as rapidly as he could, and told me to stop worrying. Richard Johnson wanted very much to do the play. We'd meet soon with Judy to discuss the next move.

Having thought about the above for several hours, I have come to realise that all my sourness really stems from Richard Johnson's forcing me to come to his party to find out what he thought about my play, instead of phoning when he said he would. Surely people understand that when one hands them a script, one expects them to read it within minutes, and comment on it both profoundly and favourably for weeks afterwards.

21 December

This afternoon I went to Harold's studio, where he and Judy had already had a long talk. Harold began by telling me that the projected film with Joe Losey was off for the foreseeable future, and that he therefore wanted to get on with *Partners* as soon as possible. Judy then said that she'd informed Richard Johnson of Harold's changed schedule and that Richard Johnson was aghast, UBA being committed to other projects until late summer. Nevertheless he was sure he could raise the money for a spring production,* and would phone in at four o'clock to confirm that he had.

We mulled over the situation and came firmly to the following conclusion: that we would wait for Richard Johnson's call. We did. It didn't come. Judy tried to contact him. He wasn't to be found. An hour and a half after he was supposed to call, we turned back to the Michael Codron question. I put the case for going ahead with Michael fairly passionately, my heart always having been in it. We agreed to send the script around to him immediately. I

---

* From a Greek producer of his acquaintance. Of everybody's acquaintance, in fact.

phoned Michael to tell him it was on its way. He'd left for New York half an hour before. We mulled. And mulled. It suddenly struck Judy that as we all really wanted the play to be done outside the West End, and that as the Lyric, Hammersmith, was our first choice, why didn't we settle that part of it, at least? Especially as she knew the theatre was available during the weeks that Harold was now free to rehearse in. If the Lyric wanted to do it, we could turn to Michael Codron, to DBA, or to a third producer, whom we could invite to participate in the subsequent West End production. We agreed that Judy should send a script around to Peter James, the artistic director of the Lyric, Hammersmith.

What this means, I now realise, is that owing to the muddle of the last few weeks we have somehow contrived to have the play on offer to three managements at the same time – to Michael, to DBA, and to the Lyric. This doesn't seem to me an altogether distinguished moral position.

The other matter we discussed was the designer. Actually, there wasn't much discussion because every play of mine that Harold's directed has been designed by Eileen Diss, with whom we both feel comfortable, mainly because she's a superb designer, and also a kindly and intelligent woman. Also she's beautiful. I can't see what other qualifications a designer needs, when it comes down to it. So we agreed to send the play to Eileen, Harold having already checked on her availability.

When I got home, I thought about the design. There are two sets: Stuart's rooms in Cambridge, then Stuart's office in London (which becomes Martin's office), then, in the Epilogue, Stuart's rooms in Cambridge again. The transitions from Cambridge to London, then back to Cambridge, have got to be effected very quickly, as they both come mid-act. That seems to me the major technical consideration. But there's a gap of years between the other scenes, when the set doesn't change, though time (a lot of it) goes by. I'm quite proud of the way in which I've worked this out, arranging the characters so that the ones who start a scene are always off before the end of the previous scene, giving them time to change, put on moustaches, wigs, whatever. Tonight, flicking through the play, I noticed that in one scene I've left a character (Nick) on stage, though he initiates the next scene, which takes place years later, thus giving him no time offstage to change costume, and to age. I've had to do some rewriting, getting him off earlier, while keeping the other characters on stage. I hope it works. It seems to me a more serious matter, at least right now, than who is to produce the play.

I have another little problem. I'm meant to be writing a film script of *The Rector's Daughter*, which I'm failing to write because I'm talking into a tape and worrying about *Partners*, and its future.

23 December

11 a.m. Judy sent a copy of *Partners* to Peter James at the Lyric, Hammersmith. He is going to phone her back at 5 p.m. to let her know whether he wants to do it.

5.30 p.m. I've just phoned Judy to find out whether Peter James has phoned her. He hasn't. These people and their attitudes to people who write plays seem to me beyond belief.

7 p.m. Judy still hasn't phoned me, from which I deduce that Peter James still hasn't phoned her. You'd think he could at least phone her to apologise for not being able to phone her.

8 p.m. Judy phoned to say that Peter James had just phoned to say that he wants to do the play. Furthermore, that he wants the Lyric to produce it subsequently in the West End. Apparently they (who?) have just set up an investment company. *Partners* will be their first commercial venture. Thus at a stroke we have not only our theatre, but our long-term producer. Terrific. No more problems. Except that the play is still on offer to Michael and DBA.

25 December

Harold phoned to exchange Christmas whatsits. He goes to New York on Tuesday to have a look at Ken Frankel's production of *Old Times*. We arranged that I should go around to his studio tomorrow to get on with casting. He's very pleased about the Lyric. He's already discussed dates with Peter James. The play will open some time in June, rehearsals therefore in May, if that's all right with me.

(This was where we ended up – at the Lyric, Hammersmith, with the management of the Lyric as producers. But it wasn't, of course, quite the end of the matter. I phoned Michael when he got back from New York, where he'd gone for the first night of Michael Frayn's *Noises Off*. He sounded very glum about his successes – *The Real Thing* as well as *Noises Off* being the two biggest hits for years, with lashings of money all around. When I asked him why he was glum, he said it was because he kept having to go to New York. I told him we'd decided to shack up with the Lyric, and that they didn't want another producer involved. He said that he was sure that the Lyric was the right theatre for the play, was glad that Peter James had finally taken the step into producing, and wished us well. He also said that if we *did* need a producer, to let him know. So that was nice. Richard Johnson, however, who had only got around to phoning Judy days after his four o'clock deadline, knew only that we'd decided to send the play to the Lyric (which he also thought the right theatre to start from) but not that the management had set up its own production company and wanted to produce the play themselves. He had spent an intensely active Christmas, raising the money to produce the play, then phoned Judy up to announce triumphantly that DBA was ready to go ahead – first at the Lyric, then on to the West End. Inevitably, there was a lot of trouble between Judy, Richard Johnson and the Lyric, accusations and counter-accusations on the telephone, and dignified summaries in letters, until all the parties concerned realised that nobody meant to deceive anybody, and Richard Johnson withdrew gracefully. I don't go into any of this in detail because it was tedious to report into the machine as it was happening; was tedious and expensive to have transcribed; was tedious to read when transcribed; and would be tedious to edit into a coherent narrative, which it would still be tedious to read. My own feeling, though, which, persisted throughout the subsequent weeks and through to the end of the production, was that we'd got off, through nobody's fault, to a poisoned start. And that in our beginnings are our ends. Or some such.)

28 December

Beryl and I went to a party at Martin and Judith Bax's, just down the road, an annual Christmas event. Martin is a paediatrician, a novelist, and the editor of the literary magazine *Ambit*. One of his advisers on *Ambit* is Irving Wardle, theatre critic of *The Times*. We met up at the party, as we annually do, and had a perfectly pleasant conversation, as we annually have. At least until about one in the morning, when overcome by drink, I suppose, I rounded on him about a play I'd seen some months ago. It concerns a young man going blind from diabetes. He takes back to his house a girl who is completely blind, in order to examine her blindness in close-up. It turns out that she wants to examine him in close-up too, and asks him therefore to undress. He does. She strokes him gently, sightlessly, all over, until she comes to his penis, which she fondles. On the evening we saw it, his penis continued to dangle limply when fondled, but I can't, of course, speak for its behaviour on other evenings. It might have done any number of things, and it's clearly unreasonable to expect a consistent performance from a fondled penis when it might well have all kinds of business off-stage. Anyway, on the night we saw it, it hung there, not only lazily and unflatteringly, but against the run of the plot, as we had been led to understand that both these young people, the blind girl and the boy-going-blind, were strongly attracted to each other. There was, however, a complication in the form of another girl, the young man's established girlfriend, who, while able to see, had her own serious disabilities, among them a foul temper, and a pretty scathing attitude to sex. One couldn't work out why, even when going blind, a normal chap would want her in the same room as himself. The fact of the matter is that I didn't care for this play very much and certainly nothing like as much as Irving did, but instead of commenting lightly on our difference of opinion, and passing on to another subject, or better still, exchanging good-nights and slipping away, I insisted on conducting him through my memory of his review, challenging virtually every sentence in it. Irving defended himself with obstinate reasonableness and stubborn courtesy, until able to slip away himself, leaving behind him the very image, I suspect, of a drunken, envious and spiteful playwright. In *The Times* this morning, in his round-up of the year's theatre, he singled the play out – in a piece he must of course have written before the party – for special commendations. I decided to phone him up to continue our debate in a different spirit, relaxed, sober and confiding, but fortunately he wasn't in. Or had decided against answering the telephone.

We're off to dinner tonight with friends who are going to introduce us to a Greenham Common woman.*

3 January 1984

I'm going to Paris later today, to hole up in a hotel and take a crack at a first draft of *The Rector's Daughter*. Harold has just phoned from New York, where he's been working hard on the production of *Old Times*, to wish us a happy New Year and to discuss possible casting. I'm looking forward to Paris, no telephone calls except crucial ones, with lots of work, punctuated by food, wine and films.

10 January

Filthy time in Paris. My typewriter broke before I left. I had to take a pen and an exercise book. For four days I sat staring dolefully down at the exercise book, my pen held in an awkward posture in my hand, my hand sensing it was back at school, unable to write. The last three days were spent writhing from gastric flu, or possibly from too much champagne on an empty stomach. The only bright spot was the appearance of Peter James, artistic director of the Lyric Theatre, Hammersmith, who was holidaying with his wife. We had a celebration lunch, a convivial occasion. His wife is Irish and an actress, very charming. Peter James has long grey hair, a beard, a gentle, solicitous voice, an easy manner, likes wine, good food. Reminds me of someone. Out of the New Testament? Or the sixties? Is it a trick of memory, or was he wearing a cape and sandals? Not sandals, surely, in Paris in January. Anyway, doesn't look at all like one's idea of a producer (i.e. Michael Codron) but could correspond to one's idea of the artistic director of a theatre in Hammersmith, I suppose. He said that the reason the Lyric had decided to go into West End productions was that

---

* She wasn't. Merely a woman who'd met a Greenham Common woman.

they were tired of trying out plays for other managements, who transferred them if they were successful and made a great deal of money, while the Lyric, who paid for the original production, ended up making very little. It was time, he said, that the Lyric forced its way into the real commercial world. So here, raising his glass, to *Partners*, their first venture.

Friday 13 January

Had lunch with Ian Hamilton, to whom I mentioned that various people – Harold, Michael Codron among them – hadn't been too taken with *Partners* as a title. He said he wasn't either. We discussed alternatives in a desultory sort of way until he suggested, out of nothing, *The Common Pursuit*, which with all its Cambridge associations, and Leavis* associations, of 'the common pursuit of true judgement', on the one hand, and its simple human associations, or the common pursuit of money, fame, sex, happiness, survival on the other, struck an immediate chord. He went on to talk about his days as literary editor, first of the small but influential *The Review*, and then the plushier version, which involved him in negotiations with the Arts Council, who first graciously set him up with money, and then righteously cast him down by withdrawing promises of more. I told him that I'd recently seen on television the author of one of the articles in *The Review* I'd most admired. He was quipping smartly away on a variety of irrelevant topics. His eyes were shiny with self-satisfaction, though the shine might have been from the studio lights, come to think of it. I suppose, given the way the world goes, it isn't necessarily depressing or wrong that a man who once wrote interestingly about literature and life should end up parading himself on television, as a kind of intellectual clown, but the history there, the professional and personal history, is one of the things *The Common Pursuit* is intended to be about. Ian and I reflected rather astringently on the old contributor's wasted promise, before moving on to a relaxed and tolerant discussion of our own lives, their strange reversals. Ian is recently remarried, to an Egyptian writer. He mentioned

* Two essays later in this book give some account of my relationship with, and feelings about, Dr Leavis.

that she was pregnant, which made him very happy. This was one of the reversals we were talking about, as for the last ten years he's been pretty miserable.

When I got home, I phoned Harold and offered him *The Common Pursuit* as a title. He thinks it's appropriate. As does Beryl, to whom I offered it, in lieu of supper and a bit of cosseting, when she came home tired and hungry from teaching. I've now got to stop thinking of the play as *Partners* and start thinking of it as *The Common Pursuit.*

16 January

Harold's written a new play, *One for the Road.* It's a crisp and brutal study of an interrogator/torturer going about his business in an un-named country. (South Africa? Turkey? Albania? Almost anywhere in South America today. And probably anywhere else tomorrow.) The chap's name is Nicholas, and we see him having professional chats with three of his victims – a hideously tortured dissident; the dissident's wife who has been subjected to all kinds of brutal-ity, including gang rape, to which she will be further subjected; and their eight-year-old son whom Nicholas finally has put to death, a fact he slips to the father in the last line or two of the play. Its running time is about half an hour, I'd guess, which is pretty short in terms of time, but quite long enough in terms of subject. What I like best about it is the ghastly richness of Harold's mon-ster, the seemingly unmotivated switches of mood from bantering playfulness to self-righteous rage followed by a joke that he genu-inely wants to share with whichever victim is immediately in his presence.* In fact, it's a study in the absolute power of someone who's gone beyond absolute corruption on to complete freedom of spirit. Which is also complete vacancy. Nicholas isn't simply good at his job, but was positively born to it. I suppose in some ways Nicholas is a relation of Max, Davis, Goldberg and McCann. He'd also find congenial company in Dickens's world – Fagin, Dennis the hangman, Bounderby, the murdering Chuzzlewit. But

---

* Exactly like one of my teachers at prep school, now I come to think of it, although unlike Harold's monster he did the torturing as well as the interrogating. An all-rounder, in other words. I still dream of meeting up with him one day, especially if he's become enfeebled by time.

then Harold's always been a very English writer, rather than the enigmatic European intellectual (Beckett, Kafka, etc.) that academics and critics would like to turn him into. Like Dickens, he can make one laugh in panic.

Harold himself, of course, loves laughter in the theatre, especially when it's provoked by his own plays. The cathedral reverence with which they're sometimes received (thanks mainly to the industrious spade-work of English departments and literary journals) must be exasperating. I remember being told to stop laughing during the first run of *The Homecoming* by a member of an audience (it was at the RSC) that looked as if it were composed entirely of British Council pamphlet writers far too busy, I suppose, working out the diagrammatic patterns of the territorial imperative, or making mental jottings of the symbols, myths, paradigms, emblems, to catch the life going on on the stage. That was the first Pinter I'd seen, having been put off his previous stuff by the language of the reviews (the favourable ones, I mean) but Beryl insisted that she'd had a *terrific* time at *The Caretaker*. When I booked the tickets, I told the box office that I was accompanying an elderly relative with a game leg, could we have two on the aisle, please, and reminded Beryl that if by any unlikely chance we stuck it through the first act, we were to treat the interval as the first polite opportunity for returning us to the streets. The highest tribute I can pay the evening is that we spent the interval in the theatre bar, listening quite good-humouredly to the guttural decodings going on all about us.*

* The trouble with the RSC, I suspect, is not that the company has a house style (though at its worst, it has, and I don't mean the tendency of the actors to curl up in your lap both metaphorically and sometimes actually both before – when they do it actually, and during, when they do it, thank God, only metaphorically – the performance; or the inability of their stars to speak a single line without vocal curlicues, loops and other lingerings; or their determination to point either their faces or their buttocks – remembering even as I write this, the recent Hal delivering one of the great speeches with his back to the audience, sword or crown – I can't remember which – held aloft as his buttocks jiggled and jounced to what purpose I still can't grasp; or – but I'm temperamentally unsuited to comment fairly on the RSC at their worst, being the only person I know to have left after a mere three hours or so of *Nicholas Nickleby*, still shaking at the recollection of the actors who'd impeded my progress to my seat with insolent assurances that I was about to have a good time, thus guaranteeing that I didn't; I didn't like the play much either, thinking it would probably work better as a novel), but that the audience has a

I suppose, finding myself unexpectedly back at my first Pinter play after all these years, that this is an opportune moment to work in an account of my first meeting with him. It was at his then house in Regent's Park, to which Michael Codron, David Sutton and I had been invited after Michael had sent him the script of *Butley*, with the suggestion that he might like to direct it. We were taken up to his eyrie by, I believe – my memory's not at all clear on this – a housekeeper. Harold was lying on a chaise longue in a black silk shirt (and other garments, like boots and trousers, etc.), a dandy at first glimpse, or something worse even. That was the only time I've seen Harold as if he were posing for the *Yellow Book*, the only time I've seen him stretched on a chaise longue, indeed stretched anywhere.* Normally he stands or sits bolt upright. The only other thing I remember from that first meeting, apart from the incisiveness with which he talked about the play, was his new car, a Mercedes Benz, which had just been delivered, and which fifteen years later he still drives. Michael and David stood on the pavement eyeing it with reverence as he pointed out its body tone, its sultry panelling, its classical this and that. To me, a non-driver, it was a car, if not exactly like any other, not significantly different. In the days when we owned a car (Beryl used to drive), I could never remember its make, let alone its licence number. In fact we have owned at various stages three cars. One was small; one was red; the last one was black. That's as far as I can go. So Harold's passion for his machine was quite foreign to me. The first subject about which we really began to talk (apart from the play itself) was cricket. I count the intensely companionable summer of 1970 in which we took *Butley* through rehearsals in London, previews

house style to match it, being the kind of people who admire, even encourage, the kind of thing outlined in the bracket above, which I inserted as an act of revenge on Bernard Levin, whose name, I've just learned, has appeared above a review published in the *South China Morning Post* originally written by me and published in the London *Sunday Times*. (Actually I was quite happy to have the review attributed to Bernard Levin, as it was so severely mangled that it might have damaged my reputation in the China Seas.)

* Harold has disputed this version of our meeting – denying that he's ever stretched out full-length in black silk on a chaise longue. I am inclined to believe him, though I am quite unable to understand why my memory has presented me with this image, so uncharacteristic except for the *colour* of the shirt, as to be virtually a contradiction.

in Oxford, and into the West End, as one of the happiest of my life. Harold insisted that I attend all the casting sessions, all the rehearsals, all the previews, and so he released in me the obsessive, which I suspect from time to time he has had reason to regret.

(It was about this time, mid-January, that we began casting. We nailed our last actor on 19 May, three days before rehearsals began. Some of our difficulties arose because we'd decided to cast to the age of the characters in the last scene, when they are in their late thirties, early forties, rather than to the first scene and the Epilogue, when they are all in their twenties. Once our first actor – a name actor, something of a star – had accepted, we were stuck with his age group, and furthermore wanted actors of equivalent authority and reputation to balance against him, our feeling being that as *The Common Pursuit* is an *ensemble* piece, we wanted six names *ensemble*. If we had cast younger at the beginning, the question of a name would have been irrelevant. All the actors would have been equally unknown. Perhaps, in retrospect, we fell into the trap of casting for Hammersmith as if we were casting for the West End. I don't mean by this that I was dissatisfied with the actors we ended up with. Far from it. I'm only attempting to account for the endless difficulties and frustrations as the months dwindled to weeks, the weeks to days. But it was, as they say, invaluable experience.* For one thing, I had never been engaged in so much of the nitty-gritty of casting before. Among the things I had to learn was that agents love their actors to be offered parts almost as much as actors love being offered parts, even if there's really no question of the actors being free to do them. It presumably confirms, or even enhances, an actor's status to be able to say that he's turned a part down, especially when talking to the actor to whom the part is currently on offer. The phrase that tips the wink is *technically* available, which usually means that the contract for the part he really intends to do has been drawn up, is probably indeed in the post, but hasn't yet been actually signed. Sometimes, however, the phrase means what it ought to mean – that the actor has been offered a part that he's thinking about but hasn't yet committed himself to, or that he's *almost* certain to take his

---

* Meaning, as it usually does, that I hope I never have to go through it again.

children by his first wife on holiday at last, or that he thinks he *ought* to spend more time at the bedside of his disabled mother. But on the other hand he really is technically available to do your part and, if he finds it interesting enough, might drop the other part, the children, the disabled mother, and do it. Therefore one has to send scripts to all the 'technically available' on the off chance that both they and their agents have scruples in such matters.

I have spared everyone, including myself, the boredom of going through the whole process detail by detail; I've also included events not directly connected to casting, when they seem to be part of the texture of that fraught period. I begin by giving five examples of the kind of thing we encountered regularly. As a matter of fact, they are five actual cases, but as they occurred right at the beginning, I wasn't aware until I read through the transcript that they were models of numerous cases to come.)

Actor One

(Wanted for Humphry.) His agent told us he would be available. We had a script sent around to him immediately, but still managed to hear, before it reached him, that he wouldn't be available, as he was planning to go out of town to star in a revival that he was also helping to produce, and of course expecting to transfer to the West End. If it didn't transfer he'd be available, but by then we'd either be on the brink of, or into, rehearsals.

Actor Two

(Offered Stuart.) Was available, but in fact wasn't. He was desperate to get out of the play he was currently in in the West End, in order to do a major television film that was scheduled to start immediately. If he couldn't get out, he'd be free in May to do *The Common Pursuit*, which he liked. (He got out, the producer of the West End play taking an exasperatingly decent attitude to his plight.)

Actor Three

(For Nick.) Was, according to his agent, available. According to the actor, however – Harold, who knows him, phoned him up – he wasn't available, as he was going to be doing something big at the

RSC. The agent then phoned to say that the actor was mistaken, he was available, could we send around a script? The script was sent. The agent then phoned to say that the actor wasn't available, as he was going to be doing something big at the RSC. (The second time the agent had got it right.) It's difficult to determine what exactly was going on, though there are two obvious possibilities: (1) that the agent genuinely thought a leading part in a new play might be a better career move than 'something big' at the RSC; (2) that he wanted another positive offer to use in his bargaining with the RSC. There are about nine other possibilities, less clear, that I'd better not examine here. As it turned out, it was all quite irrelevant as the actor felt that the part of Nick offered him too much time in the dressing room, not enough on stage.

Actor Four

(For Martin.) Might have been available if the film he was working on (he was on location) finished on time. As the film was being directed by someone who is famous for running over schedule, there was little chance that he'd be back in London when we needed him.

Actor Five

(For Peter, or for Nick.) This was a complicated and interminable piece of nonsense. The actor was on holiday in Los Angeles (could this be true, one speculated? Would any sane man holiday in Los Angeles, and if not, did one want an insane one in the cast?) and sometimes could be traced, and sometimes not, by his agent, who sometimes phoned us back when he said he would, but usually didn't. On one occasion, David Porter, the casting director of the Lyric, was left 'holding' on the line while the agent took several other calls, and was still 'holding' on the line when the agent left his office, I can't remember whether for lunch, or for home in the evening. This sort of thing went on until we eventually gave up, my own suspicion being that the actor was in Hollywood to get a film, and didn't want to make a decision until he knew whether he'd got it; and of course not getting one film leads to staying on in California and not getting another, and another . . .

20 *January*

Peter James, who has had flu, telephoned Harold and confessed to being surprised that we were going ahead offering parts without clearing it with him first. On reflection, I suppose it is rather brazen of the author and director to be casting away without consulting the producer. So we agreed to meet Peter James, the artistic director; Robert Cogo-Fawcett, the administrative director; David Porter, the casting director, for lunch, and to go through our list with them, adding to it names generally agreed to be worth pursuing.

21 *January*

This morning I phoned up Irving Wardle to comment on his recent review of *Masterclass,* or rather on the last sentence of his review, which said in effect that the play raises the question of whether a tyrannical society (i.e. the USSR) that takes music seriously is any worse than a free society (I suppose he means ours) which takes music as a mere entertainment. He was rather surprised by my call in the first place, and my tone, although I tried to keep it moderate, in the second. He was nevertheless courteous, *gallantly* courteous. I don't know myself quite why I phoned him, except that I vaguely believe that reviewers should now and then be called to account, even decent ones like Irving. And there *was* something chillingly bland in his rumination, especially as a last sentence. Irving was sure that he can't actually have meant that murder and repression were justified by a serious interest in music. Nor that a lack of serious interest in music was too high a price to pay for comparative political freedom. He was no longer sure what he did mean precisely, but explained that reviews had to be written on the wing, after all, and were subject to editorial cuts, and half-thoughts were converted by circumstance into emphatic statements, and so forth; and anyway he'd forgotten the review, having reviewed one or two things since, and didn't have it to hand. All of which, being excuses rather than arguments, seemed to me utterly reasonable. The conversation ended on a rather unsatisfactory exchange of good wishes up and down the line. Given our little fracas at Christmas over the blind play, I've obviously made it my aim to unmask myself to Irving as a dangerous paranoid, desperate to turn friendly encounters into conversational brawls, phoning up unexpectedly to engage in political debate. Should I extend this tactic to other reviewers, or reverse it, and start sending playful and affectionate postcards and notes to Irving, or would this unnerve him further? I hope he doesn't get anonymous phone calls, though. He'll certainly assume they're from me.

23 January

I went to Harold's for a drink, and then the two of us went on to the Lyric, to see Peter James, Robert Cogo-Fawcett and David Porter, who is also in charge of the Studio theatre, where *One for the Road* is to be produced a couple of months before *The Common Pursuit* opens in the main theatre. We did a tour of the Studio, a natty little place, capable of more versatility than most studios, and then went on to the main house. It's both lovely and anomalous, having been pulled down while a hideous urban complex, with a high-rise car park attached, was constructed, and then rebuilt exactly as it was, inside the complex. If you approach it from the tube, you pass an odd little patch of benches and bushes where winos, tramps and drug addicts sit in clusters, or lie full-length, semi-conscious. Then on around the concrete into a downstairs foyer, where you can buy your ticket for the show. On up the stairs into a large and comfortable modern bar and cafeteria, out of which, through sliding glass doors, you can step on to a terrace. There, on a fine day, you can eat your lunch, or drink your drinks, peering over the wall at the human debris below. Then, as the curtain is about to rise, you go up further stairs, through a corridor of offices, into a late Victorian auditorium that corresponds exactly to your sense of what a theatre should be, if you're my age or older, a theatre of one's childhood, cosy and elegant. Nobody who loves theatres, or the theatre, could possibly wish it any different, but the contradictions that surround it provoke questions about how seriously we take, and ought to take, theatre in a free society, which lays waste to our cities, and to so many human lives, and compensates with little pockets of luxury and nostalgia here and there.

Perhaps I should get on the blower to Irving and ask him what he makes of all this.

After our tour of the two theatres, the five of us went to an Italian restaurant down the road, and discussed casting. We confirmed that we were all agreed on the actors to whom the play had been sent, that offers should be made in the cases where we hadn't yet made offers, and then went on to consider other names. The lunch passed pleasantly, with wine and quite a few jokes, and there was a point when looking affectionately around the table I took in an astonishing fact. Two astonishing facts. Five chaps, all working in the theatre, all heterosexual, all smoking. The odds against that combination these days must be pretty high. Even outside the theatre. By the time we'd finished lunch we had compiled a list of two and even three names for each part, on the understanding that if our first choices turned us down, we'd move straight on to offer the part to the next choice, and so forth.

After lunch, Harold and I had a very peculiar return journey to Holland Park, being rejected by one taxi driver after another, I think on grounds of appearance. I suspect that I looked like Harold's minder, as he was very smartly dressed in a black raincoat and a sort of semi-suit and always walks very stiffly and upright, like a key figure in the Mafia or a prosperous undertaker. While I was in a sloppy raincoat, with my blue shoulder bag which I suppose might well look as if it contains a knife and knuckledusters – my whole effect being seedy and rough. Anyway, the taxis kept passing us by except one that stopped, then refused point blank to take us to Holland Park or even to explain why, the driver just whisking himself off with a mumble. It was hideously cold, as well, late January weather all right. We got one in the end, but it was an unpleasant business. I always seem to have a lot of trouble with taxis. Probably my most disagreeable experience was after a Test match at Lord's. I saw one on the other side of the road, and signalled him. He saw me, signalled back, stopped, gestured me over. Whereupon a youngish, city-dressed member of the MCC, who had witnessed all this – I'd seen him witnessing it – climbed in. I ran across the road, across the fronts of cars and buses, flung myself at the door and wrenched it open. The MCC bounder was reclining in the corner, one hand resting meditatively on his member's tie, a uniquely disgusting tie, I always think, of red and yellow stripes. I gestured him out. He shook his head. I appealed to the taxi driver, who agreed that he'd stopped for me but otherwise wanted to 'stay out of it'. I returned to the bounder, who was now smirking defiantly. I turned back to the driver. The bounder closed the door. The driver drove off. Whereupon another taxi drew up beside me, and a face full of sympathy and outrage bent through the window. 'I saw all that,' it said. 'I thought it was very bad. Very bad indeed. Gives cabs a bad name, that sort of thing does. Now where do you want to go, Guv?' I said I wanted to go to Highgate. 'Highgate? Sorry, that's right out of my way,' he said, and drove off.

3 February

I have had a thought as I sit here, swooning softly from too much Scotch, that the best solution to the problem of the first scene change, when we go from Stuart's rooms in Cambridge to Stuart's office in London, is a revolve. All the people who are waiting for Stuart in his rooms would be carried off to the Wagner Humphry puts on the gramophone, as simultaneously Stuart, seven years later, seated at his desk, is revolved on. Then when we come to the set change from the last scene of the play to the Epilogue, the reverse would happen: Stuart, sitting at what is now Martin's desk to read Humphry's posthumous poems, would revolve off and all the people waiting for Stuart some fifteen years before would revolve on in the positions we'd left them in, the gramophone still playing Wagner, of course.

4 February

I put the possibility of the revolve to Harold over lunch. He was very keen on it, and suggested I put it to Eileen Diss when we meet her on Friday. We then discussed casting, which is becoming increasingly complicated, as Harold is going to direct One for the Road at the Studio three weeks earlier than was originally planned. The fact is we're still nowhere on the casting, still waiting to hear from some agents, having been turned down by others. Now that Actor One is out for Humphry, we've decided to offer the part to Ian Charleson, who lives just around the corner from the Lyric, and who will therefore receive a script in an hour or two. We're going to offer the part of Nick to Jack Shepherd,* who is currently at the National. We're waiting to hear from Ian Ogilvy for the part of Martin, but are currently at a loss about Peter as when we do make contact with Actor Four's agent, he claims he can't make contact with him in Los Angeles, and we're still wondering what to do about Jenny Agutter, who is also in Los Angeles, and would apparently like to do the part of Marigold, but only in Hammersmith, not in the West End, because she doesn't want to commit herself to a long run. We haven't really got a clue about Stuart, although we think Ian Charleson could also be a possible Stuart. Perhaps we ought to offer him both parts, let him decide. Of course, as everybody keeps saying, we have masses of time. Yes, but what is disconcerting is that we have offered the parts around a bit, and so far no takers.

6 February

Met Eileen and Harold at the Lyric. Eileen had brought along a design which she scrapped when I put forward my proposition about the revolve. The only problem she could see was that our two sets would be rather small, but she felt that the speed and visual effect of the changes would compensate for this. One of the things I found interesting about her discarded design was that she had faithfully reproduced redundant details that I had failed to eliminate in my last draft. In earlier drafts it was crucial that you should be able to see into the bedroom in Stuart's room in Cambridge, so in describing the set I'd made a point of the 'door opening on to the bedroom'. Later I'd cut all the action and dialogue involving the bedroom, but had forgotten to cut the stage direction. There, nevertheless, in Eileen's design, was the bedroom, brilliantly worked into the structure of the set. An example of the power of the written word.

A finer example comes to mind. Last year, at around Easter, I went to Germany to see a production of *Quartermaine's Terms*.

---

* For some reason I haven't followed the offer to Jack Shepherd up in the transcripts, but as I recall, he decided to stay at the National, where he continued to give a remarkable performance in *Glengarry Glen Ross*.

I sat listlessly through the last dress rehearsal, keeping my eyes mildly averted from a large, florid, and totally bald Quartermaine, not because he was bad, but because I have my own image of Quartermaine, to which he certainly didn't conform. As we reached the end of the play I prepared a few routine compliments, as my getaway to an early lunch. In the last scene, however, I was appalled to discover that a character, an accident-prone North Country man, who was meant to turn up in a neck-brace, was bending his head easily this way and that, while a middle-aged spinster, who in the script was meant to be sitting hunched over a cigarette, was instead sitting bolt upright, locked in a neck-brace. I assumed German symbolism here, all right, this peculiar reversal of situations. When the director came up to me, I said smoothly that I had much enjoyed his production, but did find it odd, a trifle odd, that Melanie, not Mr Meadle, was wearing the neck-brace. Why? 'But that's what you have written,' he said. 'Nonsense,' I explained calmly. He handed me the English version of the text, and indeed it *was* written that Melanie was wearing the neck-brace, not Meadle. A typing error that I'd missed; a printing error that the editor had missed – but there it was. 'So it is *Meadle* who wears the neck-brace, good God!' he said. 'Good God! Of course. *That* makes sense! And to think – three days we spent in rehearsal talking about why Melanie is wearing a neck-brace, finally we worked it out that it was guilt from killing her mother' (she had) 'and so she'd possibly thrown herself down the stairs, like she'd thrown her mother down the stairs. You see?' I asked him why he hadn't phoned me, for clarification, and saved himself three days. 'But so it is written,' he said, pointing to the page again. I observed lightly that no harm had been done, all we had to do was to transfer the neck-brace from his Melanie to his Meadle, and then noticed that my German agent was looking rather drawn. 'So no need for any of us to worry, is there?' I added, making it clear that I didn't hold her responsible, even though she'd attended all the dress rehearsals. 'No,' she said. 'Well, you see it just happens that, well – in the production at Vienna also Melanie has been wearing the neck-brace.' The production in Vienna had been running for three months. 'It's in the script, you see. It's written in the script.' At such moments, I feel almost Godlike. Supposing I had written, 'Melanie in a neck-brace and naked. Meadle in a tweed skirt, blouse.' It might, of course, mean the director's losing five or six days of rehearsal to work out why, but that's his problem. 'So I have written.'

8 February

The hot news today is that Ian Charleson has said 'no' to both Humphry and Stuart. The precise message passed on by his agent was, 'Ian Charleson says no.' Harold and I are both rather wounded by this, as we cast him for the student in *Otherwise Engaged* and so tend to think of ourselves as the johnnies that gave the laddy his first real break (though probably people were queuing up to give it to him). We felt we deserved a more emollient message or even a little personal note or card. If he didn't like the play he didn't have to say so, there being so many formulae: 'Not quite right for me at this stage . . .' etc. In fact, the more we went into it together, the more wounded we became.

9 February

Clive Francis, offered Humphry, has asked to read the script again. This always worries me. But perhaps he just wants to check my grammar. Clive is one of my favourite actors, having been a superb Troup in the original production of *The Rear Column*, and in the television version; and a very funny Meadle in the touring production of *Quartermaine's Terms*. So I can look forward to a 'Clive Francis says no' tomorrow or the next day. I attribute my increasing bitterness to the exhaustion of maintaining confidence in a play that so far every actor except Ian Ogilvy has turned down.* It's true that several have been highly complimentary, but then they could afford to be, being safely engaged in something else.

---

* It's not clear in the transcripts exactly when Ian Ogilvy accepted the part of Martin, mainly because his name is entangled in conversations I had with Harold about Alan Bates (my fervent recommendation) as the lead in *One for the Road*. But I've recorded a conversation in which Harold announces 'good news' that I took to be Alan Bates's agreeing to play Nicholas, but on further scrutiny of the transcript, and closer listening to the tapes, might have been Ian Ogilvy agreeing to play Martin. Anyway, whenever it was, it was self-evidently before 9 February.

10 *February*

Late last night, stewing in Scotch and rancour, and feeling I'd played out the Wardle connection for a while, I wrote Ian Charleson a note that struck a perfect balance between affronted vanity and moralising self-righteousness. I concluded, I believe, by *nevertheless* wishing him well in his career. I posted this five minutes after sealing and stamping it. I brook no delay in these matters, aiming for the maximum amount of time for regret.*

12 *February*

Three more actors have said no to offers of Stuart, Nick, Marigold. Although they produced widely different reasons, I begin to suspect there is something more behind it. Could it be that they have started reading the scripts they're sent, instead of just counting the lines, as I've always hoped they do?

14 *February*

Clive Francis has said yes to the part of Humphry. Why? What's the matter with him?

15 *February, Wednesday*

I went up to Cambridge with Eileen Diss to look at various rooms in Trinity that might serve as models for Stuart's rooms. Of all the places in the world I hate going to, I hate going to Cambridge most. I was there for nine years, and almost all my memories are in some way associated with the train, sliding along the longest, I believe, platform in England, or the United Kingdom or even Europe, I can never remember which, either carrying me from loneliness to a sour love affair in London, or depositing me back from the sour love affair to loneliness in Cambridge. I seem to

---

* Ian Charleson replied in due course, a charming if slightly puzzled letter in which he explained that he left all professional communications to his agent, in order to avoid embarrassment. This strikes me as a sensible policy, that others might do well to adopt. He also wrote glowingly of our past association, ending with salutes to Harold, etc. I bore up well before such good manners, good sense and good feeling, and may in due course forgive him for them.

recall a train that left at about six in the morning, on Sundays, and arrived in London around lunchtime – which must be memory being true to the experience, but playing fast and loose with the facts as usual – and thinking, after a few hours without breakfast, the dust from the seats in my nose, and the heating on (so it was surely summer), my head aching, my tongue parched, that I'd at last found the perfect expression of all that was worst about my Cambridge life, my London life, appropriately achieved midway between the two. About the only time I've been back in the last twenty years was to see a production of one of my plays, which I'm happy to report provided me with a thoroughly shaming evening in the theatre. So I dreaded my trip up, even with Eileen.*

It therefore turned out to be exceptionally pleasant, perhaps because I'd managed to pick up a bottle of champagne at Liverpool Street Station. Eileen and I knocked it daintily off, in paper cups, the last swallow going down as we began the long slide along the longest platform. We met a young don who showed us over various rooms. Eileen took photographs, asked questions, made notes, until we found exactly the room I'd remembered in Great Court, which a friend of mine had occupied about a quarter of a century ago, and which I'd inhabited, imaginatively or in memory, when writing the first scene and the Epilogue of *The Common Pursuit*. It was eerily unchanged, except that the main room, the sitting room, seemed to be shared by a young man and a young woman, who allowed us to roam about with a courtesy that went against the grain, my natural inclination, which I don't like to have thwarted, being to find today's twenty-year-olds either unruly hopheads or cold-eyed sharks – after either my blood or my job. When Eileen had finished with the room, the three of us went to a pub that used to be called the Baron of Beef but is now, I think, called something else (but why?). On the way I saw posters advertising the touring production of *Butley*, which is coming to the Cambridge Arts Theatre in a few weeks. This rather pleased me. Over lunch, we talked vivaciously about a book on tragedy that the young don is writing (why?) and then, only moments (I'm convinced) before something was going to go wrong, as for example glimpsing, or even worse, being glimpsed by, some

* There is a piece on my Cambridge days on page 199.

long-forgotten figure from my past, I hustled Eileen back to the station, and on to the train. So *that* was all right.

6 March

Beryl and I went to see Donald Sinden, but most particularly Clive Francis, in *School for Scandal* at the Duke of York's. Enjoyed lumps of it very much, the men mostly. We had a little trouble with the older ladies, who were in fact rather older ladies than the text suggests they should be, and clearly had difficulty remembering their lines. One of them dealt with this, by substituting her own when she couldn't recall Sheridan's. All right if you're not Sheridan, or don't know the play, or don't mind the spectacle of other actors standing anxiously about wondering whether their own lines, to which hers sometimes led and sometimes didn't, would make sense. But there was an air of confident good humour on the stage that mostly got across the footlights and was shared by the audience. Clive Francis was, I'm relieved to report, in total command, effortlessly funny, effortlessly holding his silences to the second, and often triumphantly beyond. Donald Sinden boomed richly away, postured ripely away, and was delighted in by the audience, whose delight he delighted in. Who can resist Sheridan, when he's done half decently?

Afterwards we went around to see Clive. John McCallum, with whom he was sharing a dressing room, was getting out of his stage togs, and into his life togs, when we entered. He carried off having to pad about in pants and vest with sympathetic stateliness. Clive, on the other hand, was changing rapidly as he was having dinner with Sinden. He did say, though, as he unmade his face, that when he read *The Common Pursuit* the first time, he felt he didn't like any of the characters at all, and that Polly James, the actress with whom he has lived for many years, felt much the same. This, in one of Harold's phrases, 'stopped me dead in my tracks'. Could it be, I pondered to Beryl over dinner afterwards, that actors had been turning us down not only because none of the parts was a star part but also because they don't like the characters? Of course, I find this incomprehensible. Nevertheless I decided to pass Clive's comment on to Harold, with the recommendation that in future we ask actors to whom we offer parts either not to read the play at all, or to read it, as Clive has done, at least twice.

9 *March*

Been turned down by two more actors, one of whom was invited
to play Stuart, one of whom invited to play Nick. Usual reasons
given. On the one hand, a previous engagement; on the other, not
exactly what he wants to do at the moment. There was compensation in the form of a letter from a very old friend, to whom I'd
sent a copy of the play a month or two ago. He'd finally found
time to read it, though had very little to say about it. He attributes
his general lack of response to slowness of wit, absent-minded-
ness, an overall unfamiliarity with theatrical texts. I suppose he
means his slowness of wit, etc., but it's possible he means mine.
I've just checked. He means his. I find this quite reasonable, as
he's a university lecturer. I wish, though, that he'd stumbled into
one compliment. I could do with support from any source at the
moment. Meanwhile, I wait for comment from another friend,
mutual to the above and to myself, also a university lecturer, who
has been unable to read the play yet as he's been laid up in bed
with a damaged ankle.

13 *March*

No movement on casting. Harold is deep in rehearsals of *One for
the Road*.

21 *March*

Last Wednesday I saw a preview – the last preview, in fact – of
One for the Road. It's a concussive twenty-five minutes. Harold's
direction is impeccable, every movement of the actors informed
with meaning, not a detail left loose, not a gesture haphazard or
lacking in eloquence. I wonder though, my reaction to the play on
the page being what it was, whether the director hasn't slightly
straitjacketed the writer. The terrifying, sometimes exhilarating,
lunacy of the torturer has been subdued into a calculating sadism.
We don't want to share the life of *this* creature, watching him from
as far away as we can get, hypnotised, as if expecting to be his
next victims. A man who has complete power must surely love
his power now and then, just as now and then it fills him with
despair. On the page he himself doesn't seem to know what he's

going to feel next, and therefore what he's going to say next. On the stage he seems to be working to a plan, almost a habit, of repression. Not born to his job, in fact, merely practised in it. Alan (Bates), who I had thought a natural for the part in his easy extravagance, his charm, his gift for flirting dangerously with the audience, gives the most restrained and consequently the most violent and hateful performance of his career. This is clearly what both he and Harold intended, or came to during rehearsals, and perhaps they're right. Certainly some of the resulting visual patterns are extremely disturbing – in the scene with the wife/mother actually erotic – as if Harold had found formal means of signalling as director what he's otherwise shied away from in the writer. And of course the difference between reading on the stage and expressing on the stage is emphasised in this case by the fact that the victims scarcely speak. When I read *One for the Road*, I entered quite cheerfully into the torturer's world. But we can't simply revel in this moral monster, if we're also forced to *look at* the man he's had tortured, the woman he's had violated, their child whose murder he announces in the last line of the play. So when it comes to it, perhaps Harold's channelling of Nicholas's malevolent exuberance into merely lethal efficiency was the only possible solution. Anyway, I came out of the Studio as if I'd been violated myself. I had a brief drink with Harold at the bar, and noticed that Harold has set himself and others a social problem. He can hardly stand at the bar as if in celebration of a work achieved, given the intended effect of the work. And friends can hardly present themselves to him with grins of congratulations, slaps on the back and so forth. (Though I can't recall ever seeing anyone slap Harold on the back.) Mainly the procession was a glum one, respectful, anguished, as if at a funeral, although loosening into humdrum cheerfulness with a drink or two, nevertheless careful not to dishonour the horror of the event. I also wondered, as this is lunchtime theatre, when precisely the audience prefer to take their lunch. Before or after (I exclude the possibility of during) the show.

24 *March*

The reviews for *One for the Road* were mainly excellent, although I thought they concentrated too much on what they saw as the political statement of the piece. I can see that they were unlikely to emphasise its value as sheer entertainment, but I'm not sure what kind of political statement the play amounts to. It should hardly come as a surprise that Harold is (a) against torture, (b) against totalitarian regimes. What he's making is surely a demand. Look at this – this is what goes on, daily, in this country and that. Look, and see what it really means to be in the power of such people.

26 March

We've just been turned down by an actor for Stuart. That's not quite accurate. He is prepared to do the play at the Lyric, but not to go on with it into the West End, his point being that he's a star, and when he goes into the West End he wants to go as a star, not as a member of a company piece. I would have found this honesty refreshing if anything could refresh me at the moment, apart from a positive piece of casting. Robert Cogo-Fawcett, Harold and I (in Harold's studio) began to go through further names, not of what one might loosely (or even tightly) call stars, but of actors not familiar to us, of whom we've heard good things. It will mean meeting them, and reading them, perhaps several times. There is nothing wrong with that – it can be very exciting – but we've now been at it for months, time is getting short, Harold is off to New York any day for the American premiere of *One for the Road*, and I'm off to San Francisco shortly after that for a production of *Quartermaine's Terms*.

After the meeting, I went to see a rehearsal of a touring production of *Butley* at a church hall off Holborn, where, as it turns out, there is also a badminton club. I found out about the badminton club because, true to my current form, I arrived at the hall a few minutes after the *Butley* company had left, to make room for the badminton players. I went home, tried to work on *The Rector's Daughter*, while glaring at the telephone, waiting for news.

30 March

A last casting session with Harold, before he goes to New York. We met at our usual restaurant in Hammersmith, for lunch.* An odd lunch, an odd afternoon. For one thing, I *felt* odd, having a slight touch of flu, I think. We were mostly in reminiscent vein, talking of everything except the matter to hand, but finally came around to our new list for Stuart, deciding that the play should be sent to five or six actors, with a covering note to their agents making it clear that we're not making an offer and that we will have to see and probably read those that are interested. We then went to the theatre, arriving just as the cast of *One for the Road* was emerging into the bar. The actors, having now played the piece often enough to adjust their lives to horror at midday, are beginning to relax. In fact Alan looked quite jovial after twenty-five minutes of concentrated sadism, and Jenny Quayle looked very pretty and lively after having had quite a lot of the sadism concentrated on her. This seems to me healthy, the experience of the play not being one that one would want them to live with for a minute longer than is necessary. But Harold, who had had a fairly convivial lunch, found himself nevertheless in the situation I described earlier, having to find an appropriate manner when accosted by shell-shocked, distressed and respectful friends. When they'd cleared off, we suddenly found ourselves developing a small party, all tension released, as if the need to celebrate the success of *One for the Road* as a play had taken us unawares. I was in no state to drink much, so of course did, and finally left feeling distinctly woozy. I picked up a copy of the *Spectator* in the underground. In it I came across a review which compares *One for the Road* with 'a great rendition of *King Lear*', thus simultaneously missing the point of both plays, the one being about the triumph of innocence over evil, the other being about almost exactly the opposite. Reassuring, though, that sometimes the reviewers' little errors go in the playwright's favour. After a brief discussion with Beryl, when I got home, about my condition, which I attributed in a shaking voice to flu, to bed.

1 April

Where I remained most of yesterday.

---

* Usual while we were working in Hammersmith, I mean. Our usual usual restaurant is in Soho.

2 April

One of the actors to whom *The Common Pursuit* was sent, with a covering letter saying this didn't constitute an offer, phoned up the Lyric to say he was very excited, and was this an offer? On having the meaning of the letter explained to him, he said he'd phone back in the afternoon. Which he did, to say that on rereading the play he'd found himself less excited by it, and didn't want to be considered. Another actor phoned to say that he didn't really think the play was for him, really, as he didn't like it. How invigorating, I mendaciously cried, that at last *someone* has had the honesty . . . Another actor we thought was out of the running as he was in a West End play is back in the running as the play he's in is about to close early, though he doesn't know it yet. Judy, who represents the playwright concerned, passed the information on to us. The actor has been sent *The Common Pursuit* but not for Stuart, for Peter. It would be nice to get Peter fixed, but the problem of Stuart is the crucial one.*

11 April

Lunch with Harold, just back from New York. He was in good form, pleased with the production over there, which had been directed by Alan Schneider, an old friend and colleague, who directed not only the first of Harold's plays to be done in the States, but also many of the early Beckett plays.†

But he (Harold) was worried about his health. He has been advised to cut down on his drinking and smoking and I suppose all the things on which you have to cut down if you're not to cut down on life. After lunch we went to the Lyric to see two possible Stuarts. One of them has just finished in a long series on television. He gave an extremely accomplished and intelligent reading, but

---

* I don't know what happened with the actor to whom we offered Peter. I haven't followed it up on the tapes, so assume that he said no but that in my concern over Stuart I didn't take much notice.

† While we were rehearsing *The Common Pursuit*, Schneider came over to London to cast a play he was going to direct for the Hampstead Theatre Club. He was run over on the Finchley Road, when crossing back to the theatre after posting a card to Beckett. He died a few days later, in hospital.

worried me by closely resembling Ian Ogilvy, looking almost like a brother – not really a good idea. The other fellow – the Lyric is very keen on him – is immensely attractive. Extraordinary eyes, bluish violet; and very intelligent, I thought, in discussing the play (i.e. he liked it). But I detected something odd in his speech, especially in his reading. He sounded precious. *Slightly* precious. I decided that perhaps he was queer, but discovered afterwards from Harold that in fact he's South African. Then we saw a girl whose name escapes me.* She was very nervous, I think, arriving like a wounded bird, fluttering and gasping and struggling for breath, and gave a first reading that had a strong charge of the Dorothy Tutins about it – interesting, idiosyncratic and highly wrought, but (as she wasn't Dorothy Tutin) not completely convincing. Harold then took her through the scene, as reassuring and clinical as a doctor. No, as one's best idea of a doctor, mainly derived from old films. She read again, very much more naturally, and yet with an idiosyncrasy (not this time mannered or imitative) that lifted my spirits. I still feel, though I haven't looked at the part and its problems for ages, that the Marigold I've written needs special help from the actress: someone who's so *particular* that we don't notice how general, how functional my Marigold is. Of course I hope that my rewriting has given/found *some* particularity, but . . .

Harold, by the way, read all the other parts, as he's going to have to do through auditions. His instinctive grasp of where the conversational stress should fall was immensely helpful, I think, to our three actors, whom he constantly and gently nudged into a more considered response. It was invaluable for me, too – hearing my lines spoken for the first time, getting a whiff of almost forgotten intentions. In fact, Harold's reading reminded me of the enormous advantages of having a director who is also a playwright who is also an actor.[†]

---

* It was Nina Thomas, who was in fact to play the part.

† The first time I attended auditions, about twenty years ago, my eyes were fixed on the reader, not on the actors we had come to see. At the end of the session, I couldn't remember a single one of the candidates clearly, though I couldn't forget the reader, who had dominated the stage with uninhibited confidence. I would have cast him on the spot, even though Alec Guinness was already contracted to the part. Fortunately, the director, John Dexter, was looking in the other direction,

Afer the Marigold audition, we went up to the Lyric offices and compared reactions. The general feeling is that we have a Stuart in the violetish-blue-eyed actor, and a potential Marigold in the Dorothy Tutinish actress (although we intend to see a few other Marigolds). I'm still worried, though, about violetish-blue's accent, which, though not queer, merely South African, still seems to me prissy. A prissy Stuart isn't on the cards, at least not on my cards. Tomorrow we see another little crop of Stuarts, the best of them an actor called – called something French, Huguenot, I suppose, who was in *The Jewel in the Crown*, which I didn't see, but was much admired by everyone, including Beryl, who once called me in to admire an actor with a French, or Huguenot-sounding name. I remember that I thought he looked and sounded pretty good, without at all remembering what he looked like, the way he spoke.*

12 *April*

The actor whose name I couldn't remember from *The Jewel in the Crown* is Nicholas Le Prevost. He's very intelligent and attractive, saturnine, about thirty-seven, I'd guess. He was sporting a number of militant left badges on his shirt, but was otherwise both shy and composed, his eyes alert for professional complications. We

---

at the actors we were there to audition. Furthermore, he took notes. In the end we did well, casting Simon Ward.

* Beryl has a sharp eye for the coming actor. When Michael Codron, Harold and I were casting the part of Jameson in *The Rear Column*, she insisted that we go to see the RSC production of an eighteenth-century comedy called *Wild Oats*, written by an Irishman called O'Keeffe. (I've since heard that the Inland Revenue tried to make contact with O'Keeffe, with a view to getting a share of his royalties. I suppose an income tax inspector passed the theatre one day, saw O'Keefe's name on the hoarding, long queues at the box office, and struck like lightning, two centuries late.) Beryl wanted us to see Jeremy Irons, a young actor who was playing the second lead with the authority and glamour of a chap playing the starring role. As we were after glamour and authority in Jameson, we cast him forthwith. Although *The Rear Column* had only a brief run, Jeremy Irons won awards and critical praise for his Jameson, which led to his being auditioned for, and getting, the main part in *The French Lieutenant's Woman* on Harold's recommendation (he wrote the script), which led to his getting the main part in the film of *Betrayal* (a scrupulous version of Harold's play), which led to his getting the main part in the Broadway production of *The Real Thing*, more praise, Tony awards, etc. So from Jeremy Irons to Beryl a magnum of champagne at least, please, to share with her husband.

took him up to the second-floor lobby of the theatre for his audition, had scarcely got into a preliminary conversational skirmish
when Harold, seeing David Porter trekking up from the bar to his
office, rose abruptly and went over to him. All Harold wanted to
know was whether there was a quiet room we could use instead of
the lobby, but it looked – Harold gravely muttering, David Porter
nodding and whispering – as if something prime-ministerial were
taking place. Nicholas Le Prevost continued talking to me about
his early education – he seems to have had a bad time at schools
or to have given his schools a bad time – but his eyes kept rolling
towards Harold and the casting director, David Porter. We were
taken off to a quiet room a few flights up or down (at the Lyric
up often leads to down, down to up) and Nicholas Le Provost
launched himself into the reading proper. I felt almost at once that
he was the chap for me, but had to acknowledge that he was also
a trifle low-key, beginning quietly, and sliding from there down
the scale until in the end he was picking out a few syllables for
articulation, with noisy little smiles between. When he left, Harold
made it plain that he was the man for him too – a bit hard on the
violetish-blue-eyed South African but there we are. We went up,
or down, to the bar, bumped inevitably into David Porter, gave our
verdict. After Porter had agreed to set about contracting Le Prevost,
and had gone up to the office to do so, Harold and I noticed Le
Prevost out on the terrrace, standing with a friend, gazing com-
passionately down on the derelicts in the patch of shrubs and
benches beneath. We went over to him and offered him the part,
which he promptly accepted. So, we have a Stuart, unless of course
Le Provost's agent phones tomorrow with a rebuff, or Le Prevost
decides to reject the play for political reasons. Assuming he's fixed,
all we need now is a Nick, a Peter, a Marigold.

15 April

This afternoon, a Sunday, I went to Harold's studio to see an
actress for Marigold, recommended to me by someone who's
directed her in South Africa. She gave an interesting reading but
was too old. She wasn't unattractively too old, she simply had the
presence, the style, the movements, the body of an attractive
woman in her middle-to-late thirties, who would therefore work

well in the last scene, but would seem an imposter in the first scene, and in the Epilogue, when she has to be twenty-one or twenty-two at the most. Lesser actresses of the same age might be able to move convincingly from twenty to their late thirties, but she couldn't – nature having chosen to develop her in a strictly linear fashion, month by month, year on year, a perfect product, a classical example, at each stage, of growth, and change. I'm probably making my point even less urbanely than Harold did, who, when she had finished, and after passing her a few deserved compliments, found himself saying, 'Look here, I think it's better to be honest. I mean, let's face it, the thing is that you have a very attractive, no doubt are, unquestionably, a very attractive woman. Mature woman. You are a mature woman. But the part does call for somebody who can be nineteen or twenty and there is no doubt whatever, in my mind, that however – um – striking – uh – attractive you are; you are nevertheless too mature for that sort of part.' And looked at me for confirmation. Which I gave. She accepted all this – two blundering men bent on honesty – with as much grace as anyone could muster under the circumstances, and left. What was awful was that we both really did think she was (a) talented and (b) attractive, but between us must have given her the impression that we thought she was (a) over the hill as an actress and (b) over the hill as a woman. Harold and I drank a glass of champagne, to make it up to her, while acknowledging the fact that we still haven't cast Marigold (at least officially, but we talked enthusiastically again of Nina Thomas) and we haven't cast Peter, and we haven't cast Nick. In two days I go to San Francisco, for two weeks.

3 May

I'm back from San Francisco. I would prefer not to go into my experiences there in detail, except to say that at the end the production seemed to me OK although nobody in San Francisco seemed anxious to go to it.* It's a hick town, is my belief, except in sexual matters, where it has been making medical history for a decade or so. There was one small incident I'd rather leave un-

* See footnote on page 3 for the review of *Quartermaine's Terms* by the Most Influential Critic in San Francisco.

recorded, but recording it may help me to make it unremembered. I was peeing in the men's lavatory late in the interval during the last preview. From the booth beside me came the sounds of somebody also peeing. The bell rang audibly for the second act. We were the only two still at it. There was the sound of the main lavatory door opening, an elderly woman's voice calling out: 'Henry, Henry, are you all right!' Silence from the next booth. 'Henry! You there!' A non-committal moan from the next booth. 'Well, are you all right, Henry?' A brief pause this time, then, 'I'm all right, I'm all right, but I'm not going back in the theatre, you and Maureen go back in the theatre, but I'm not going back in the theatre.' There was the sound of the main door closing. Complete silence from the next booth as I went back in the theatre. But then I had no choice, while old Henry had a night of San Francisco at his feet. Or over them, I strongly hoped. Which brings me to an important question. Why do lavatories in the States, men's any-way, have such a big gap between the floor and the door, and such a quick cut-off on top, so that not only can you see a chap's feet and even ankles if you glance down, but if he's tall enough, also his face if you glance up?

But the fact is, this *is* 3 May, I'm back from San Francisco, and we still haven't got a Peter or a Nick. While I've been away we've had a number of top-class refusals for both parts, one, for Nick, by an actor who, after he'd enthusiastically accepted, explained that actually he'd morally committed himself to something else which he'd hoped wouldn't happen, but was after all and against the odds now about to happen. I can't be bothered to go into the reasons for the other refusals for Nick. Or for Peter, come to that.

10 May

We saw three actors for Peter. One of them was Simon Williams, whom we saw last. My observations about him were as follows.

Simon Williams had the edge. He brought a great deal of in-stinctive wit to the reading, and is also an extremely attractive and sympathetic man. One sensed an understanding of the deep daft-ness in the character, most importantly of Peter's habit of mean-ingless sexual conquest that would one day ambush him into causing pain to others without teaching him a single lesson about himself.* This Peter would always survive in the affection of his friends among whom, I trusted, would be the audience. He is, quite simply, very likeable. So let's hope that his agent doesn't, etc. . . .†

We decided to consider the two other actors who'd auditioned for Peter as possible Nicks tomorrow, then went upstairs to look at rough drafts of the poster. The designer is a glamorous Argentinian, Czech or Pole – half Czech/Pole, half Argentinian – called Carlos Sapochnik. Most of the images he'd worked on were strikingly inappropriate. There was one extraordinary vista of tree stumps in a desert, another of a withered but full-grown tree with a half-human skeleton lying beside it. They were all powerful, one particularly so: a man-baby erupting from a typewriter as if being born from it, his barely formed fingers aiming down towards the keys. We sensed a future in that image, if only we could find some way of making it – I don't mean to sound perverse – more cheerful. We suggested that he might make the head an adult head, a literary intellectual's head, or the conventional view of same – glasses, balding, undeveloped – which might give it at least an air of comedy. He agreed to have a go, and to come back on Friday with further versions. So by Friday we should be on our way with cast and poster. The set is almost designed. We go into action – well, into rehearsals – in eleven days' time. On Monday week.

11 May

Today we saw the two actors we'd transferred from Peter to Nick. The first, for whom I'd had high hopes, gave a perfectly accomplished reading, but there was something in him, a lack of warmth, that made his Nick seem an already beaten fellow, operating from the cunning of one who has had a very bad time throughout his school career and has learnt how to cringe and grin in order to win tolerance, if not respect. A craven Nick, in fact, while Nick has always seemed to me the reverse of craven – impertinent, deceitful, vulgar but always sure of affection.

---

* I mean here no reflection on the actor's private life, only a compliment to his professional understanding of the part.

† We offered him the part. He accepted on the spot. His agent didn't, etc. . . .

The other actor, whom I knew from a touring production of one of my plays, began by saying he was very bad in auditions (having proved quite the opposite the day before, when he'd read for Peter) then turned to me and said the only part he'd ever got through auditions was the one I'd offered him, and he wasn't quite sure what it was he'd done that had led me to give him the part. I said I'd given him the part because, out of the ten or so people who'd read for it, he struck me as by far and away the best. This surprised him, he said, as he was so bad at auditions. Harold then said something to the effect that he couldn't be *so bad* at auditions, could he, or we wouldn't have asked him back for another one after yesterday's, would we? The actor supposed, doubtfully, that we wouldn't. But he couldn't understand it, given how badly he'd read for Peter. Yes, well anyway, Harold said, let's come to the case in point – Nick. What did he think of Nick? Meaning, really, we'll have a few preliminary words about the part, and then on with the reading. What did he think of Nick, the actor repeated. Well, for one thing – and like a man methodically plaiting a noose with which he intends to hang himself, he told us what he thought about Nick, exposing Nick's insecurities, probing and then condemning Nick's morals, finding a soupçon of compassion for Nick's all-round unlikeability – all this with the confident air of a social worker analysing a particularly maladjusted case. Of course he wasn't confident at all. I think he'd merely hoped for a short intermission before taking the plunge into reading. The delay generated its own momentum, unfortunately backwards, further and further away from what he was there for. Harold became increasingly impatient, his questions, polite to begin with, got increasingly austere and consequently increasingly devastating; and the more devastating his questions became, the more desperately fluent the actor became in answering them, at one point correcting me in some observation I made in defence of poor old Nick. By the end, when the actor had finally closed the file on Nick and put him back on the shelf, a dead issue, Harold was convinced that he didn't want to direct him. We parted awkwardly, the actor having achieved what he'd set out to achieve, which was not to read at all. But he'd only achieved it in the end by having Harold not wanting him to read, either. A muddle of unfortunate feelings, responses, things taking the wrong turn. I blame myself really. I know the actor better than Harold does, and could sense therefore why he hurried so eagerly into a trap of his own making, and should have found some effective way of intervening. What interventions I managed fuelled him on to disaster. The upshot of it is that we still haven't got a Nick, which is a consolation all round, I suppose, especially with a whole nine days to go before the first rehearsal.

13 May

We looked at new versions of the poster. Instead of a desperate baby collapsing out of the typewriter on to the keyboard, the artist, encouraged to buoyancy and uplift, now offers us an exhilarated martyr surging out of the keyboard, skywards. He's still naked, still looks like a baby, a large, rugged baby. What is interesting, from our point of view, anyway, is that bits of the typewriter are flying about, from the strain of delivery. Hardly surprising, given what is being delivered. I wondered tentatively if we couldn't keep the exploding typewriter, but instead of the powerful rocket of a baby, have a pair of hands playing across the keyboard, very composed hands, in complete control, writing calmly, the type-writer exploding to the touch. Carlos took this up, did a quick sketch, and it looked OK. Perhaps that's the poster we'll end up with.*

15 May

Yesterday an urgent summons from Harold to report to the Lyric, where he was to meet an actor who would, he thought, make a per-fect Nick. Harold had worked with him before, and had admired him. The actor had also played Hamlet here and there (mainly in Scandinavia, I think) abroad. And he was a bit of a name. Why hadn't we thought of him before? He'd received the play last night, had read it during the early hours and phoned up first thing in the morning to say that he loved Nick, the best part in the play, he thought. Harold arranged for us to see him at five this evening.

---

* It was. The hands, though, were less composed than I'd imagined, looking more like claws, sinister. But the image was very striking.

Well, actually five thirty. I got the time wrong, but by a series of remarkable coincidences, to do with taxis arriving early for once, I arrived at five. I was sloping around the corner of the cafeteria with my coffee when I encountered Harold, who had just spotted our actor seated at a far table. He took me across to him. The actor was much as I had always imagined Nick. He had a lot of hair springing curlily from his scalp (still has, I imagine), his eyes bulged with innocence and wit, a neat little interrogative face and a thin, long frame – perfect, a perfect Nick, albeit with a Scots accent. But then why not a Scots Nick? We wanted him to do it, he wanted to do it, handshakes all round, the bargain sealed. Then he produced from his pocket a puckered envelope on which were written certain dates. It transpired that he'd also been engaged by the BBC to do a film in Norfolk. He assured us that this would be no problem. The dates on which he was scheduled to film allowed him to get back in good time for our rehearsals. The only difficulty was that one of the dates conflicted with our last preview. But again this was no problem, because he would see to it that the BBC got him back from Norfolk in time to appear on the stage. My heart, I must confess, began to sink. There was a kind of Scots cunning mixed into his general air of Scots ingenuousness that indicated that he was a little too much like Nick in life to be likely to appear as Nick on the stage. When he went on to say that if the BBC objected he would simply walk out on the film because he didn't care whether he worked for the BBC again, as after all what did the BBC have to offer but poor money, bad parts and long hours in rubbish, my heart sank further. This seemed exactly like the kind of thing a chap says when there's an agent waiting behind him to invalidate it an hour later. So I felt pretty gloomy about it though I shook him warmly by the hand and invited him to a drink, which he accepted. Time passed merrily enough until Harold and David Porter (casting director) offered to go up to Porter's office together and phone the actor's agent, whereupon the actor tossed what was left in his glass down his throat, and as Harold and Porter went up the upstairs to Porter's office, sped down the downstairs to the exit, calling out that he'd just remembered he had to collect his daughter, or anyway somebody's daughter, from school. Whereupon my heart sank well below the plumb-line. In fact, as Harold and Porter were unable to get through to the agent, the actor could have downed his drink at leisure. Harold, Porter and I stayed at the bar and had a few more celebration drinks. There was a general euphoria, induced in Harold and Porter by the assumption that, at the very last moment, we'd caught an ideal Nick; induced in me almost entirely by the drink.

The next day Harold phoned me at Queen Mary to tell me that the deal had fallen through. The actor had, in fact, signed a contract for the BBC for the whole of the film production, which went well into our rehearsal period, then beyond it into our preview period and our opening. None of his days was free.*

Six days before rehearsals I went up to Harold's to consider actors for Nick. It was too late to read anyone. We had to come up with somebody we all knew, or that some of us knew. David Porter and Robert Cogo-Fawcett were also in attendance. We went through name after name, touching tentatively on one whose work Harold knew very well, and I knew slightly, that we had considered at the very beginning for Stuart and for Martin, but not previously for Nick. This was Robert East. We went through the other names – I can't recall them now – and found ourselves reverting to Robert East. According to David Porter, Robert East was acting as company manager to a Ray Cooney Theatre of Comedy show at the Criterion, but there was a strong chance that he could get out of it in time to join us for rehearsals, if not on the first day, then very soon after. We tried to get hold of him on the telephone, but the line was engaged, and remained engaged until I left, and was still engaged when I got home and telephoned Harold. Beryl and I went up to the Chinese restaurant. When we got back there was a message from Ben (our son), saying that Robert East had received the play and was now reading it. My heart didn't actually rise at this. I went to bed wondering about Robert East's

---

* In spite of his behaviour, I bear him no grudge. I have borne a grudge against only two out of the hundred or so actors I have had dealings with; one of them because he did pratfalls and slow burns and double, even triple, takes in a part calling for the normal human responses ('But that's what I do. *That's* what they've come to see'); and the other, because he announced that he was leaving the production early (and therefore in the lurch) as he found it rather hot on stage, and couldn't stand the dreadful drip in his dressing room – I think he meant the one from the tap. I have made no effort to discover how many actors I have worked with bear a grudge against me, being unable to think of any reason that they should.

contract with Ray Cooney, whether he hadn't signed himself up for a year or two, for instance. The next morning, Harold phoned to say that Robert East wanted to do the part, and that he was available. He'd given up his job as company manager at the Criterion the previous Saturday because he was desperate to get back to acting, and had been waiting by the telephone for offers.

17 May

So that, at last, is that. Nicholas Le Prevost is playing Stuart. Ian Ogilvy is playing Martin. Clive Francis is playing Humphry. Simon Williams is playing Peter. Robert East is playing Nick. Nina Thomas is playing Marigold.* Harold is directing. The set has been designed by Eileen Diss, costumes will be designed by her friend, Liz Waller. The lighting man at the Lyric Theatre, whose name I will no doubt discover, will be doing the lighting, and the sound man at the Lyric Theatre will be doing the sound. The show is being produced by Peter James, Robert Cogo-Fawcett and David Porter of the Lyric Theatre. We began casting four months ago, and finished it today, four days before rehearsals begin. At least I hope we've finished it.

(We had. The four-day period between casting Bob East and beginning rehearsals was a period of deep tranquillity, disturbed only by flashes of intense panic, dread, etc., at the prospect of going into the production proper. I haven't covered the next five weeks day by day, but, as with the casting, have selected and condensed, reporting on incidents outside the rehearsal room as well as in it.

One of the things that struck me, when reading through this section of the transcripts, was not how much I recorded but, given its bulk, how much I managed to omit of the pleasure that the rehearsals gave. The reason for this, I suppose, is that my nature is of a worrying and fretful kind, and so each evening I came back and brooded aloud about what was worrying and fretting me,

---

* I have no record on the tape as to when we decided to offer Marigold officially to Nina Thomas, but it must have been weeks, if not months, earlier. We'd really cast her during her audition, which is why – along with all the hassles over the other casting – we saw so few Marigolds.

rather than describing what had given me satisfaction. The result is that I don't at any moment make clear my admiration for the actors and the director, although I feel pretty sure that those most concerned were fully aware of it at the time. I also fail to describe in general terms Harold's working method. But then his method, unclouded by theories and principles, amounts merely to the bringing of his concentration to every part of the play. In fact Harold demystified the whole directing process for me years ago. For example, previous directors had tended to keep me out of rehearsals while they were doing something called 'blocking' – 'No point your coming in yet, why not wait until I've finished the blocking?' and later, 'You might as well take a day or two off, I want to concentrate on re-blocking Act One.' And later Act Two. And sometimes, if I made a tentative reservation about where an actor was standing – or, indeed, a tentative reservation about almost anything on the stage – 'But if I change that, it'll mean re-blocking the *whole* scene.' I therefore assumed that 'blocking' was a mysterious, virtually ungraspable activity, at least to such lay-men as playwrights – until I at last saw Harold actually at it. Whereupon I immediately understood that 'blocking' is simply discovering where the actors should stand, when they should move, where they should sit, to the maximum dramatic effect while appearing natural. Apart from a few technicalities – for example, making sure that characters don't actually stand in front of each other (this is called 'masking') and can be seen from all parts of the theatre (this is called 'paying attention to the sight-lines') and don't 'upstage' each other, i.e. aren't so arranged on the stage that one actor engages the audience's attention when you actually want the other or both noticed – there is nothing to 'block-ing' except the usual application of common sense. When I initi-ally told Harold that I didn't really understand about 'blocking' he looked at me in bewilderment, and said: 'But that's the easiest part of the whole business. And you can always change it if it doesn't feel right.' Harold starts rehearsals by blocking rapidly right the way through the play, then goes back to the beginning, and works through the play again more slowly, examining the lines in relation to the moves as his understanding of a scene deepens, adjusting the moves accordingly. For example the first time around he might think a scene relaxed and playful, and so have the actors sitting in relaxed, if not playful, postures. Later, on uncovering various tensions in the scene, he might think it more effective to keep them on their feet. And so forth. There were various moments in our rehearsals when the blocking became of the utmost importance – one, which I've reported, when Harold unblocked and re-blocked a couple of scenes not only for immediate dramatic purposes, but to release the actors in a way that affected their total performances. But even this was a *practical* response to a growing sense that the actors had become slightly inhibited in their characters because inhibited physically, and not an example of specialised or privileged 'directorial insight'. In other words, anyone possessed of the requisite powers of concentration, instinctive sympathy with actors, and a natural dash of authority would have done the same, and can therefore direct a play.)

21 May

First day of rehearsals. I arrived at Turnham Green underground station – a long trip from Highgate – and walked along Chiswick High Road to the Ballet Rambert studios. Although I was nearly half an hour early, I saw Harold standing on the pavement in front of the Ballet Rambert, looking composed and powerful in black. We were the first to arrive apart from the stage management, who provided us with cups of coffee. Harold went upstairs to the rehearsal room to look at the model of the set. I sat in the green room attempting to look like Harold, composed and powerful, though in pink and blue, as the actors appeared in dribs and drabs. I took it upon myself to make introductions, thus bringing together with gestures and 'do-you-know-each-others?' Simon Williams and Ian Ogilvy, who had not only arrived together, but were old friends. I then attempted to introduce Liz Waller, the dress designer, to the stage management, then remembered that I still hadn't quite got the names of the stage management, so ended up introducing Liz Waller to herself. At about that point I gave up, hoping that somebody would start introducing me to somebody.

When all the actors had turned up, and we'd sat around for a bit drinking coffee and making meaningless conversation, Harold came down from the set, gave calm greetings, and led us back up to look at the model. It was extremely convincing. Models always are. We all muttered appreciation as Eileen showed us how the revolve worked, how bits of dressing and furniture could be moved off for the unrevolved set changes. We bent over it, crouching and gesticulating, stepping backwards for perspective and forwards for detail, but we all really knew that it was a formality – something to be gone through before getting to the reading which was the main, in fact the only, real business of the morning. It began when we'd all sat down at a long table, Harold rearranging people a little, so that the actors were together. I sat at the far end, my script on my lap, my pen in my fingers, as if I were myself 'Doc' Simon, already called in to add some one-liners and frisk up the text. I can't bear to look at the actors at read-throughs, partly because I'm convinced that my face is bright red from embarrassment.

Harold began by making a pronouncement about not wishing to make any pronouncements. Looking forward very much to the weeks of rehearsal ahead, exploring, discovering the text, feeling sure we would all enjoy it enormously, 'Simon, is there anything you'd like to say?' Redface, without looking up, shook his head and gobbled a few negatives. Pause. Then Redface gobbled, 'Looking forward to it very much.'

Harold went through the changes we'd made to the text. The only important one was to rename Hubert Parkin the offstage poet who accompanies Stuart through the play. It had occurred to me that as Parkin rhymes with Larkin and Hubert contains the same number of syllables as Philip, there might be imbeciles abroad who'd insist on confusing Hubert Parkin with Philip Larkin. I've always admired the sadness, wit and impeccable formality of Larkin's poetry, and as Parkin's life in the play is a long, sordid decline, I wouldn't want to give even imbeciles the opportunity for confusion. They'll doubtless make their own. I wonder what sort of poetry Parkin wrote, though. It would have to have *some* of the classical virtues of Larkin's to please Stuart. We spent some time in a parlour game, looking for a new name for Parkin, until somebody – I can't remember who, as I was still keeping my head lowered – suggested Stout. We all tested it. Stout, Hubert Stout. And accepted it. But none of the changes, not even that one, was really essential. Harold went through them only so that the actors could sit writing in and crossing out, to create the illusion that they were taking part in a routine process of which the read-through was merely the last mundane step.

But a read-through is never mundane. For my part, I find it almost impossible to listen consciously. Wherever I turn, however much I attempt to block my ears by thinking of pleasant matters like cricket and sex and the first glass of wine, or the later first Scotch, of the day, every word somehow gets through. The actors get through, too.

On the whole the actors were OK. Ian Ogilvy seems to have a sure-footed sense of the possibilities of Martin. Bob East was pretty bold with Nick, although I suspect he'd slightly over-prepared his reading, especially his last scene, in which he seemed to be dying hideously at the age of about ninety, instead of struggling for breath at the age of about thirty-eight. Simon Williams, clearly besieged by nerves, was a great deal less spontaneous and witty as Peter than he'd been in his audition. (Why wasn't he besieged by nerves then, too?) Nicholas Le Prevost's Stuart was certainly intelligent, certainly serious, but consistently dour and therefore dull, which was valuable as it showed the danger of the part. We'll have to avoid making him the play's 'meaningful' centre, and concentrate on keeping him as simply another (I hope, attractive and vivacious) character. Nina Thomas gave us a charming and individual Marigold. Her brief is to make up for the deficiencies in my writing, but I don't think we need tell her that. Clive Francis was vivid – he's never less than vivid – but turned Humphry into a posturing Cambridge queen, which seems to me not only wrong, but almost perfectly wrong. Humphry, as we eventually discover, is homosexual. But he is also always resolutely normal, the most down-to-earth character in the play. The scene in which his death is announced was ghastly, by the way, full of sickly reverence and low-toned melancholy, whereas I'd intended it to be, if not light, then at least matter-of-fact. But that was valuable too, as it reminded one of the obvious trap: of playing the play for laughs in the funny bits and seriously in the serious bits. We'll have to make sure that the funny and the serious are simply played naturally, leaving the audience to find out for themselves which is which. If the play is about anything, it's about the way things go on – 'old life itself' as Stuart says, just before his wife-to-be announces her abortion.

What worries me most, though, is me. My work. I found myself hating bits of the play quite a lot. For instance, a long stretch at the beginning of Act One, Scene Two, that seemed to me very lumpish, and an interminable patch in Act Two of lifeless exposition. There are also embarrassing lines scattered everywhere, some sounding facetious, and some brutal.

In fact, all in all, I was pretty depressed. Of course, post-coital depression is common to all read-throughs. The actors are convinced that the director and producer are already recasting; the playwright is convinced that as soon as the actors get home they'll be on the blower to their agents, demanding to be got out of this; the director is convinced that the playwright is blaming him for landing the play with a dud cast, while at the same time thinking that the actors are blaming him for landing them with a dud play. Of course, I may have got all this wrong. It's possible that every playwright swells with pride when he hears his play being read for the first time, that the actors in my own plays are dazed by their good fortune in having such plum parts, with such fine lines, in such a powerful, funny and moving piece, and that the director is gloating over his good fortune in having such a play, such a cast, to enhance his name with. The fact is, *I'm* always depressed after a read-through and certainly am so now.

We finished much earlier than Harold and I had expected. Does that mean the play is too short? Will we have to stretch it out with heavy pauses, long and complicated moves, numerous curtain calls? Today, at least, we solved the problem by stopping when we'd got to the end and going down the road to an Italian restaurant for lunch. Peter James, who'd strolled with us but didn't intend to stay for more than a quick drink, very sweetly ordered some champagne. I was the actual host, very lordly in my ordering, and felt distinctly shifty when the bill came and Peter James, who never quite got around to leaving, insisted on paying for all the other wine, too. It wasn't a particularly cheerful occasion, too much was drunk too quickly as a way of obliterating the memory of the read-through, and what conversation there was came from conscious attempts not to talk about what was most on everybody's mind. Yet the meal dragged itself on and on. It took over three hours to get back on the pavement, stomachs full of food we hadn't really enjoyed, heads swimming with wine we hadn't really wanted. Everything seeming, to me anyway, unreal and a little unpleasant. As if I'd banqueted my way through one depression into another.

Harold and I went to a coffee house in Holland Park and swapped our impressions. Harold was particularly disconcerted by Clive Francis's Cambridge queen, and determined to correct it immediately. I touched on the question of Nick Le Prevost's glumness, on my worries about the text. Encapsulated, the conversation would seem very brief, but of course we kept returning to the same points, or peering at dim but disconcerting memories through the haze of our indigestion.

We separated at about six, which left me with three hours to kill before meeting Beryl for dinner in the West End. She was coming on from a party at the college where she teaches. I thought of taking my depression off to a cinema, but found myself, willless, going home in the hope that I might catch her before she left. The tube was packed. Everybody seemed to get out at my station (Highgate) so I was jammed against the escalator rail going up. The only person on the escalator coming down was my wife. She came towards me, then went past me, completely unaware of my gesturings and callings out, intent on her own business. Rather alarming. And now I'm off to meet her for dinner, having spent most of the time since I got home dictating this into the machine.

22 May

Second day of rehearsal. We spent the morning discussing costumes. Liz Waller had brought along various magazines from the sixties, Ian Ogilvy an album full of photographs of himself and his friends from the early sixties to the end of the decade. I loathed the sixties while they were going on, and loathe them in retrospect. Whenever I come across photographs of myself taken then, I always assume that I was an anachronism, somebody whose spiritual home was in the fifties who had got born too late, or in the seventies, who had got born too early. My hair is short, I'm in cords, pullovers, big black shoes. Around me, invisible in the pictures, are the real sixties people, in flared jeans, beads, kaftans, mini-skirts, etc. So it was rather a shock to see from Ian Ogilvy's collection that the young actor of the time was really just a sprucer version of myself – hair shortish, pullovers, etc., though with something snappier on his feet, like suede. What surprised me most was the prevalence of ties, not only in Ian Ogilvy's album, but in Liz Waller's magazines.* Liz Waller tends to believe that people dress to a dominant trait in their character, which I suppose makes sense on the stage as it assists in instant recognition, but I am never entirely convinced. Lazy men can be fussy dressers, unhygienic men dress neatly. Furthermore, I believe that people's attitudes to their dress change considerably in the course of their lives. Some start off by being indifferent to what they wear, but pay more and more attention to their clothes as they get older. Others worry about the way they present themselves to the world when they're young, but as life closes in, take less trouble. Peter, for example, might be a bit of a peacock during the first scene when he wants to attract the young ladies. But in the scene before the Epilogue, when he is in his late thirties, and has to deal with two wives, lots of children, making do on a limited salary while desperately hacking out books he doesn't want to write that he knows nobody wants to read, he might give the impression of having dressed with indecent haste in the clothes nearest to hand. In fact, now I come to think of it, I'm not sure philandering and peacockery inevitably go together. A crumpled undergraduate could be just as obsessed with women, just as successful with them. The danger of dressing the actors to a dominant character trait is that we make them stereotypes. I suspect that none of the people in *The Common Pursuit* is interested in clothes except possibly Nick and Marigold. Anyway, who knows what immediate events, what subterranean history, makes people dress as they do on this date or that?

* In my day as an undergraduate (when the people in the play were also up), virtually everyone wore a tie, because we had to wear a gown for lectures, supervisions, going to hall, going into town in the evening. Wearing a gown meant wearing a tie. Of course, there were quite a few smartie-boots and fops who were prepared to change from their polo-necks to shirts when gown occasions came up, and I did, I suddenly remember, go in for polo-necks myself, out of which I didn't bother to change when going to town in the evenings, solving the problem posed by the gown–tie statute by not wearing a gown either. I was mortified at never being stopped by the proctor or his bulldogs (university policemen), who used to tour the streets looking for sartorial infringements. Evidently, I didn't look like a member of the university.

We talked about clothes all morning, Liz Waller seeing all the characters in terms of types and fashion, I arguing for unguessable-at haphazardness, Harold listening, commenting, reserving judgement. Then we had a brisk lunch, and began the rehearsal proper, not in the Ballet Rambert room, as we had all assumed, but on the stage at the Lyric, the Ballet Rambert having let out their rehearsal room to somebody else for the afternoon. Whether this was our muddle or theirs, I don't know. From tomorrow on we're back at the Ballet Rambert. But this afternoon, on the stage of the theatre in which we will finally present the play, we began our rehearsals. Harold worked his way through the first scene in Stuart's rooms in Cambridge, blocking the moves rapidly, and then got rather jammed in the long second scene, in Stuart's office in London, when it suddenly became clear that the furniture was badly positioned. One chair, set upstage, almost against the back wall, completely altered the focus. When Martin (Ian Ogilvy) sat in it, I was unable to look at anyone else. And yet Martin was meant to be shyly and diffidently on the outer fringes. Because of his position, he became majestically shy and diffident, all the other life in the room somehow sucked towards him. This accidental importance carried him through the whole scene, long after he'd got out of the chair, and found his proper place on the edge of the action. His questions, which were meant to be tentative and apologetic, seemed sophisticated ironies, his little disclaimers and gestures of discomfort signals of inner derision. In reaction, Nicholas Le Prevost's Stuart, already glum when he should have been cavalier, descended into a fatalistic melancholy, like a man who's discovered that he's about to lose not just a magazine but his wife, his pension and his dog as well, and what's more knows he deserves to. In fact, the whole scene was the wrong way around. What should have been down was soaring, and what should have been up was almost underground. And it all began when Ian Ogilvy sat in the chair. Which Harold then had removed, before giving a relevant little talk on the tone chaps like Stuart adopt when facing temporary disaster. Stuart, Harold said, would take for granted his friends' understanding of what the closing of the magazine meant to him, and share with them an enjoyment of the comic aspects of some of the circumstances. They'd have fun, in other words. And in fact I've noticed that when friends come around to talk about, for instance, their failed marriages or their messed-up children, anything short of the ultimate horrors, they do so with a great deal of irony, gaiety even. An evening devoted to the discussion of their misery turns out to have been quite a good one. Quite a jolly one. Usually. Sometimes it can be exceptionally boring, of course.

Well, Harold made his incisive and sensitive speech along the above lines, and started the scene again. Now that the chair had gone, and with Harold's words fresh in their minds, things got off on the right foot, which after a few minutes carried them smartly off in the wrong direction. Nick Le Prevost became glum again, Ian Ogilvy magisterial again. But this wasn't surprising, given the speed at which habits of thought and feeling develop, and at least the guidelines have been laid down. Harold let most of it pass, while Clive Francis (to whom he'd spoken privately before rehearsals) was already stripping away the Cambridge queen, and was on his way to a natural and pungent Humphry. Things went, if not swimmingly, then purposefully, until Harold and Bob East collided over the reading of a line. Over the reading of two words, actually. The two words were 'in fact'. I'd placed them at the beginning of a sentence. Bob East was placing them at the end of the previous sentence. So instead of saying, in answer to Martin's asking him how he came by a hangover, 'Drank too much. In fact, what's that stuff, slimy, thick and yellow?' he was saying, 'Drank too much, in fact. What's that stuff, slimy, thick and yellow?'* A small change, but acorn-like in the size of the argument it led to. Harold pointed out that where Bob was putting it, the 'in fact' was redundant. Bob East said, not really, he was using the 'in fact' to emphasise how stupid Martin's question was (after all, how does one get a hangover, except by drinking too much?) whereas if he put the 'in fact' where I'd written it, he would be seeming to be treating the question with a degree of courtesy. His way around he could get a bit of a sneer on it, you see, Harold. Ah no, said Harold. Nick understands perfectly well that the real meaning of Martin's question is, 'In what circumstances, at whose party, etc., did you get your hangover?' Nick, being Nick, is merely

---

* The answer is egg-nog. For the context of this exchange, see Appendix A, page 167.

pretending, very briefly, that he doesn't understand the question, for fun's sake. And then goes on, using the 'in fact' to slide him into the question about what made him drunk. The 'in fact' being not for emphasis, merely conversational oil. Bob East clung to his view, Harold explained again, Bob East redefined his position, I intervened with a powerfully pompous statement about the attention I gave to punctuation when writing my dialogue – *every* full stop, *every* dash, *every* comma. The increasingly strangulated discussion coming to an end only when Bob East rather grudgingly consented to say the 'in fact' where it in fact should be said.

At first I wondered whether this was one of those bouts of Indian wrestling between director and actor that frequently happen early in rehearsals, unusually protracted by Bob East's temperament on the one hand, and Harold's desperation for a cigarette on the other.* Certainly, not smoking has made Harold more tense than I've previously seen him in rehearsals. Normally he would simply have cut off the discussion, no, argument – well, it was somewhere between a discussion and an argument, having the formal good manners associated with the one but some of the atmosphere of the other (which is what I presumably meant when I called it strangulated) – and got on with the business to hand. But if he was being frustrated by his need for a cigarette, *and* frustrated by Bob East's tenacity over a detail of phrasing, he'd have had to keep a doubly strong hold over his impatience to avoid a doubly powerful explosion. Which he did, visibly. Although the sight of so much visible patience didn't unnerve Bob East. This surprised me until I realised much later that the discussion/argment wasn't over a detail at all, at least from Bob East's point of view. Given his line of reasoning, he must see Nick as someone who would instinctively sneer at Martin. Whereas Harold and I, given our line of reasoning, must (I know we do) see him as a high-spirited and likeable show-off. Certainly not a sneerer. Bob East's fight was for something fundamental to his understanding of the character of Nick, although I don't think he himself fully realised it at the time. Certainly I didn't, nor did Harold, but it explains

---

* Harold, who'd smoked about fifty cigarettes a day for the fifteen years I'd known him, had given up a few weeks before we began rehearsals. I should have mentioned this before. Sorry.

why, I suppose, we all sensed that something more crucial was at stake than the position of a comma and a full stop. I must remember to raise this with Harold tomorrow, the implication for the whole play of a sneering rather than a light-winged Nick.

To come back to Harold's struggle with smoking. I probably make things more difficult, being a chain-smoker. In previous rehearsals, we've chain-smoked together. This time, he chews away at his nicotine gum, with the smoke of my cigarettes leaking reminiscently up his nostrils, down into his lungs. On top of that he used to *use* his cigarettes in rehearsals, taking one deliberately out of the black box (Sobranies), putting it in his mouth, lighting it with a swift gesture, inhaling it deeply, as often as not walking a few paces away to take the cigarette out, study it, put it back in his mouth, inhale. It was a pantomime, an enactment of thought, he was making it clear to everyone that he was thinking, making it clear to himself that he had taken the time to think. Now, without a cigarette to resort to, he finds a lacuna between a question and its answer, which he can only fill with a baffled silence, which leads to further silence and further bafflement as the need to answer looms larger and larger, the people waiting for his answer no doubt seeming to do likewise. He hasn't yet found an alternative ritual to accompany thought, and I doubt if he'll find it in his chewing gum. You can't do much more with chewing gum than put it in your mouth and chew it. At least not without disgusting everybody.

One last thought. All the actors and our one actress are extremely attractive. People will enjoy looking at them. But can I take credit for that?

23 May

We are back at the Ballet Rambert, which is a relief. Yesterday, sitting in the stalls watching rehearsals going on, I suddenly realised how many days and days and further days of my life have now been spent sitting in the stalls of theatres in the dark, convinced that the sun is shining outside. Whether it is or not, there I am, with an ashtray full of cigarette stubs beside me, attempting to control my impatience and irritation at the slow progress we're making, while actually aware that my impatience and irritation are unjustified because there is usually enough time in which we can patiently and without irritation sort out the problems. When I was about to direct (my first experience of directing) one of my own plays, I asked Harold what to be most on the guard against, in myself. He thought for less than a second, then said: 'Your impatience.' When it came to it I found it much easier to be patient as a director running rehearsals than as a playwright attendant on them. It seemed to me quite obvious that the director and the actors have to find their own routes.* It's no good the playwright saying continuously, 'Well, actually what I meant here, heard here, saw here, was this. Now, you know, just cut the crap and get on with it.' But then of course I didn't have a nuisance of a playwright lurking at my shoulder, nagging away, which Harold has. Six straight weeks of *me* ahead, and *no smoking*. Poor Sod.

There's no point in making further excuses for my behaviour, so I might as well just cut the crap and get on with it. For instance, after yesterday, I simply can't understand why Ian Ogilvy is *still* displaying an irony that amounts to effrontery in Martin. I meant him to be ingenuous, eager, diffident, on *everybody*'s side really, but most of all on Stuart's. What he ends up getting (like Stuart's wife) he gets by burrowing away from within, and today (as yesterday) we had a Martin who is foraging cynically from without. We see him *at it*. Nicholas Le Prevost's Stuart is doing what Ian Ogilvy's Martin should be doing, offering ingenuousness and a glum (though I don't want that from Martin, either) stumbling sweetness. Clive Francis is now some distance from his Cambridge queen, though, being me, I keep suspecting that any moment the queen will make a comeback.

But it was Bob East that perplexed me. By which I mean, drove me crazy. It's true that Nick has a smoker's cough that begins as something of an affectation in the first scene, and gets worse throughout the play, until in the last scene (before the Epilogue) he actually has emphysema, but Bob coughed, and he coughed, and

---

* Two sudden memories should modify this boast. One, that during rehearsals I had a severe bout of flu, and then mysteriously damaged a nerve in my leg, which meant that for the next nine months I limped about with dropped toes. I've never been ill when present merely as the playwright. Two, that I adopted such a free and easy attitude to the text that at one point the actors ganged up and demanded that I show more respect for the playwright (i.e. myself).

Christ did he cough. My plays attract enough coughers in the audience. We don't need them on the stage too. I had a hideous vision of Bob East and the scattered coughers in the stalls (where they most like to sit, towards the front) going at it together, answering each other, developing each other's themes, capping each other in volume and meaning until the whole audience joined in, the dress circle, the circle, the gallery, led by Bob East in a mighty cough-along, the cathartic fulfilment of something latent in most evenings in the theatre. But even if we contain the effect, there are still technical problems caused by Bob East's coughing, particularly for the other actors, who risk having their lines drowned when speaking on cue, or may decide to meet the challenge by bellowing their lines above the cough, or, I suppose, hang about doing bits of business, therefore slowing down the action, etc., until he's finished his cough, then quickly squeezing in their lines before he starts another one. And finally, of course, in the delicate, and melancholy and quite amusing (I hope) scene in which Humphry's death is announced, by which stage Nick has got his emphysema, there'll be no chance for the audience to indulge in a little tender grieving, if at the same time they are watching another character in what appears to be his hectic death throes. So what was Bob East up to?

When Harold drove me to Holland Park after the rehearsal,* he asked me what I felt about Bob East's cough. I said it should be pared down, surely, to the bone, as a matter of fact, what had Bob been up to? 'Well,' Harold said, 'you wrote in quite a few coughs, you know. In the stage directions.' 'Yes, probably too many,' I agreed, 'and we certainly don't want them added to, do we?' So we agreed to eliminate any coughs written into the text, eliminate all Bob East's superfluous coughs, and start from scratch, finding out as we went along where the cough could be economically placed, with a proper reference to the context. 'The trouble is,' Harold said, 'he's obviously given a lot of thought to the coughs. Worked hard on them. They're not inappropriate, in realistic terms. He might want to cling on to them.' Harold finally decided he'd

---

* This became our evening ritual. First a drink in the pub, sometimes with members of the cast, sometimes just the two of us. Then the drive to Holland Park, where I either picked up a taxi to Highgate or if I felt up to it (i.e. no taxi available) got the tube home.

better discuss the matter with Bob East privately, over lunch, I to attend to give authorial consent to the cutting of coughs from the script. Neither of us is looking forward to it very much, given the long public tussle over his 'in fact' as opposed to our 'In fact' only yesterday. I told Harold I was also worried by a feeling that Bob East was isolating himself from the company. All the other actors stayed in the rehearsal room even when not actually working themselves, to observe the way in which the characters and the play is developing – or at least changing. Bob East stayed down-stairs all morning until summoned. I'd seen him there in the morning, when I'd had to make a series of panic-stricken tele-phone calls in an attempt to trace my son Ben, who'd failed, I'd been informed by his school just before I'd left home, to turn up to his first class at ten. I knew for a fact he'd left the house at eight, having bidden him farewell myself. As I'd dialled around London trying to track him down, entertaining the usual flood of parental images to do with tumbles in front of incoming tubes, fallings under buses, knives at Camden Town, etc., I'd been conscious of Bob East in the green room opposite, his head bent over the text, pencil in hand, and wondered – as I asked demented questions as to Ben's whereabouts* – why he wasn't upstairs with the others. I mentioned this to Harold, who said he also wished that Bob would join the company in a post-rehearsal drink, it wasn't good for company morale when an actor kept himself apart. I took this up, raising *en passant* my view that Bob East misunderstood something fundamental about the nature of Nick. By the time we'd finished we were both dreading the lunch.

Later Harold phoned to report that he'd gone through the text, and discovered that Bob East was coughing *only* where I'd speci-fied in my stage directions† and we could hardly blame him for that, could we, especially as we'd made such a big deal of his

---

* I finally got him at a friend's, where he'd decided on the way to school that that was where he'd prefer to spend his morning. Which allowed me to relax into a paternal tantrum. I pointed out that his school – tutorial college, actually – was very expensive, charging almost by the minute for teaching him, even when he wasn't there to be taught. I expect that during this Bob East was observing me.

† So *that's* what he was up to. For the powerful effect of my usually irrelevant stage directions see page 47.

slight deviation from the text only yesterday; that now he'd had time to think about it, Bob East was perfectly entitled to study his lines in the green room – every actor has his own way of working; and why should we insist that he has to have a drink with us when he lives such a long way from the rehearsal room, and has a wife and children to get back to, whose company he might actually find more congenial than ours. I see the point of every-thing Harold says, but I'm still worried about the lunch.

(What is recorded in the transcripts of our first conversation about Bob East doesn't do proper justice to its tone, which I remember quite clearly. In fact, what I really succeeded in doing was to convince us both that Bob East would fight, and to the death, to hold on to every single cough he'd so far coughed; that we wouldn't be taking him out to lunch but cornering him in a restaurant in order to strip him of his coughs, every one of them, by force if necessary. We'd have to back each other up, guard our rear, make it plain to him that not only was he not to cough except under strict supervision, he was also not to learn his lines in the green room but participate fully in rehearsals and, furthermore, we'd like an explanation as to why he wasn't joining in the post-rehearsal drink, along with the rest of the boys. And the girl. The transcripts go on to show, however, that the lunch was in fact an extremely pleasant affair, with Bob East agreeing that I'd written in too many coughs, and that it would be best if he were to find out where they should come in rehearsal. This must have taken about five minutes. The rest of the meal was apparently spent in discussing cricket, allowing me to transfer my paranoia to the England selectors, with, I expect, special reference to Peter May, for not picking Mike Gatting as captain, and so possibly ruining David Gower's career.

I realise in retrospect that Harold's brief and uncharacteristic collaboration in my original spasm of paranoia about Bob East came, not from his not smoking, or at least not *only* from his not smoking, but also, probably more centrally, from his long relation-ship with Bob East. He has always had a high regard for his acting. His name had been on our very first casting list. And then Harold directed one of Bob East's plays at the Hampstead Theatre Club, a play full of interest, I thought, which nevertheless – perhaps

I should really say therefore – most of the reviewers trampled over, wondering, as they've also done with my plays, why Harold wastes his time directing such stuff, etc. (The answer is, I suppose, that Harold likes directing, and such stuff is the stuff he likes to direct. Most people like doing things they do well. Also he gets paid for it, which I expect he also likes.) Harold also cast and directed him in a key role in the first production of *The Hothouse*, which Harold wrote at about the same time as *The Birthday Party*, decided to shelve, and recently rediscovered in a tea chest or a suitcase and did a few years ago at the Hampstead Theatre Club. On top of this, for many summers he had captained Bob East in the Gaieties Cricket Club, of which Harold was the president and founding member, Bob East the leading batsman and star all-rounder. And now here they were back again in yet another relationship, Harold directing Bob East in a new play by an old colleague. Such a history would inevitably contain a number of downs, a number of ups, the most dramatic of both probably coming during their cricket-playing days, cricket after all being life, and plays only art, or aspiring that way. After so many different and complicated connections, they were bound to be particularly sensitive to each other's feelings, and to their own about each other.

As for my own part in the Bob East incident, I should like to announce here that I don't normally behave like a paid police informer, or perhaps more accurately the school sneak, even in rehearsals at their most fraught. I see now, of course, that this really very minor episode marked a significant phase in the growth of my almost pathological relationship with the production, which was unlike my pathological relationship with previous productions only in the degree of its intensity, and the never quiescent sense that something had gone wrong somewhere, probably long before we'd gone into rehearsals. I think it's worth pointing out, though, while I'm still amazed by it, that all the above excerpts come from my recording on 23 May, after only three days of rehearsal, and that while I seemed to know something of what was going on in myself, I seemed, as subsequent events establish, unable to learn from it. My impatience, which at times over the following weeks blossomed into full-fledged lunacy, was unflagging, but clearly without much of a memory.)

24 May

I simply can't make out what Nina Thomas is up to. As soon as she enters a scene she stops and wonders aloud where she should move. Where an actor moves must depend, to some extent, on intention (and of course where other people happen to be, etc.) but the intention must be the character's. Not where the *actor* wants to go, but where the character, given his or her motives for entering the room, his or her relationship with the people in it, would naturally end up. Well, as a beginning, at least. But Nina Thomas is entering the room as Marigold, stopping, looking around, and saying, as Nina Thomas, 'Where should I go next? I feel I should sit down. Where do I make for? What is my plan here?' 'Plan.' She did this three times, not going anywhere, not sitting anywhere, just brooding about it at the door, halting the momentum of the rehearsal, also making it impossible to answer her questions. If she'd gone somewhere, as Marigold, one might have answered her, but as she'd stopped being Marigold, and refused to go anywhere as Nina, her question had no meaning.*

25 May

At the end of rehearsal, Harold and I arranged to meet the actors in the pub. We had to hang on for a while, to talk to the sound man (although he looked more like a boy, a boy with a beard) who had turned up unexpectedly. As there was nothing much to say at this stage about music, or sound effects (what sound effects?), we spent a pretty meaningless half an hour talking about having nothing yet to talk about, then hastened to the pub. It was empty. We toured around a few more pubs, looking for the actors, then returned to the original one, where they still weren't. This was perplexing. Pooter-like, I entertained the possibility that they'd deliberately suggested one pub, while actually going to another in order to enjoy a drink without the playwright and director spoiling it for them. Or (again Pooter-like) I'd simply misunderstood

---

* It probably had a meaning for Nina Thomas, who was probably indirectly asking a question about the other people in the room, or was anxious to discuss her attitude to them, or both. In other words, code for the usual message – help me – which was in due course decoded.

the directions, and had led Harold off to the wrong pub, and was now blaming the actors for not being in it. Anyway, we left the main bar for something called the Garden Bar, which turned out to be a concreted patio at the back of the building. Perfectly pleasant until the usual bloody awful music suddenly billowed out at us. We rose tetchily and found a wine bar further down the street. We sat down at a table and waited for the girl who was clearly meant to be serving drinks to serve us with a drink. She had her back to us, and was on the telephone, where she continued to be for the next ten minutes or so, sometimes talking urgently, as if to her lover, sometimes laughing intimately, as if to her lawyer (I'm trying to avoid stereotypes here), but completely ignoring the only two customers. As did the only other waitress, who came in and out carrying baskets of bread and bowls of potatoes. When the girl on the telephone finally hung up, she began a long conversation with the bread-and-potatoes girl, during which she picked up a pad, put it down again, picked up a pad, put it down again, picked up a pen, frequently beginning to back towards us, once even beginning a swivel that, if completed, would have brought us face to face at last. This series of movements, always interrupted by a further exchange with the bread-and-potatoes girl, at least suggested that the idea of service was lingering somewhere in her mind. Nearly twenty minutes must have elapsed before she got the pen and the pad in her hands, and came to our table, a mere second or so after Harold had risen to his feet, with a declamatory gesture and some words to the effect that he'd had enough of this, and taken himself to the door. Rising myself, I said that we'd been waiting an awfully long time for a drink, and she said (she was Australian), 'I was only on the 'telephone for a minute [a lie] and I couldn't help it.' (This was probably not so much a lie as a piece of irrelevant self-analysis.) Although I longed to continue our discussion, I was acutely aware of Harold, now out on the pavement and striding up and down past the windows. I tried to think of something crushing to finish her off with, failed, joined Harold outside. We both glared in at her through the window, then went off to Harold's car. Now the fact is we spent nearly twenty minutes in a wine bar, the only customers, with two waitresses in evidence, without getting a drink. That's not the point, of course – without *service*. No, that's not the point. The point is, was, without a drink. What was odd about it, though, is that we spent the whole of that time, except for the first two or three minutes when we talked about professional matters, watching closely, commenting on, and becoming increasingly incensed by the girl's behaviour. And I haven't the slightest idea, just a few hours later, of what she looked like.* Anyway, we drove back to Campden Hill Square, where we found Antonia, who had just returned from being honoured at a literary luncheon at Blackwell's. So we had our drink at last, several drinks as a matter of fact, and I described to Antonia (with pantomime) the effect Harold's not smoking had had on rehearsals so far. It was all very pleasant.

Saturday, 26 May

It's 1.15 in the morning. I am dictating this while of unsound mind. When I got home, Beryl told me she'd found a house that she'd liked the look of up in the village. (We've been planning to move, off and on, for the last ten years.) At nine o'clock we went up to look it over, having phoned the owner beforehand to ask if we might. It's a delightful house, seventeenth century, with a nice garden, but not quite enough rooms for our purposes. When we'd made the three mandatory inspections, one in hope, one to confirm it wouldn't quite work, one from courtesy, and had had a glass of wine and a gossip about military matters with the owner (he was a retired major), we'd been there well over an hour and it was time to go. Lucy, our fourteen-year-old daughter, had gone to the cinema with a friend from school; we didn't want her returning to an unaccountably empty house. The retired major, elderly with an unhealthy bald dome, led us to the hall, made a charming farewell speech, took out his key, with which he failed to unlock the door. He tried endlessly, it seemed, turning the key this way and that – failing to understand – didn't make sense – trouble was the windows were no good – double-glazed – wall around the garden about eight feet high – we could walk the gutter – jump – little dangerous – phone the police – really didn't understand. I

---

* I have a suspicion, though, that she was plump. I have a history of altercations with plump girls.

managed to control my mounting panic with the help of cooling-down looks from Beryl, although becoming convinced that the retired major was a madman who'd locked us in on purpose. I phoned home, to leave a message for Lucy (now due back) but also to make sure he hadn't cut the wires. Finally, when he did something precisely like the somethings he'd been doing all the time, the key turned, the door opened, and we hurried home, to find the house empty. This was all right for a quarter of an hour, was slightly less all right after half an hour. At twelve o'clock, just as it began to rain, I went up the hill to stand at the bus stop. At half past twelve, after a couple of buses had passed followed by no buses at all, I came home to find Lucy and friend sitting on the front step. They had been next door since a few minutes or so before we got back, we worked it out at, but as Lucy had forgotten her keys, they'd decided to watch television with our neighbours, confident that they'd hear our return, which was why Lucy hadn't bothered to slip a note through the letter box to let us know where she was. (I provide this information for the benefit of those who fret about details, motives, so forth.) Beryl and I had a brief discussion with Lucy (but not her friend) on the subject of thought-lessness, then I came in here to dictate this.

What disturbs me is not the little run of accidents that led to a spasm of parental terror, but the feeling that anything I embark on at the moment, even the simplest thing like looking at a house, is liable to go wrong. I suspect that my growing anxiety over Lucy somehow transmitted itself to the old major, who became there-fore more and more incompetent. After all, he presumably lets himself fluently in and out all the time, otherwise a good part of his day would be spent crouched at the keyhole.

28 May

Rehearsals began for me at about three this morning, when I started out of sleep with the conviction that Nick Le Prevost had a lisp, and was concealing it from us. I'd suppose this was the product of a dream if I weren't a straight-down-the-line literal dreamer. I don't dream in symbols, e.g. a mysterious dish of over-boiled carrots, I dream that I'm impotent. More importantly, I don't dream of children's parties, I dream that I'm in the middle of rehearsals, the actors getting their characters wrong as usual, Harold chewing gum and staring urgently at nothing, I shaking with impatience. So I took the dream about Nick Le Prevost's lisp quite seriously because I took it to mean that he had a lisp and was deceiving us about having it. I've got nothing against Nick Le Prevost having a lisp, but I do think the chap who plays Stuart shouldn't have a lisp. Or a club-foot or a hunchback. At least without giving me a chance to rewrite the text.

I spent the morning going through a draft of *The Rector's Daughter* with David Jones, attempting to keep my mind off Nicholas Le Prevost's lisping his lines and getting away with it by pretending that he was still working out their meaning. By the time I got to the rehearsal room, I had formed a plan to watch Nick Le Prevost's lips like a hawk, and the moment I saw or heard the lisp, to alert Harold to it. He could take it from there.

But Nicholas Le Prevost fell into such a natural, easy, amusing account of Stuart that not only did my preoccupation with the possibility of his having a lisp vanish, a great deal of my other worries about him vanished with it. He was steely, ironic and funny. When he was watching Martin, and then Humphry, his stillness made him the most impressive figure in the room. He's also beginning to find a lot of fun in lines that he'd previously made sound gloomy. What's more, no lisp.

On the other hand, Clive Francis was camp again. I suggested to Harold over lunch that, as Humphry's parents live in Exeter, we might encourage Clive to adopt a West Country accent, strong in the first scene and again in the Epilogue, but thinning out in the intervening scenes as he gets older. To root him in a background, in fact, and one, unlike Cambridge, with no tradition of queens. It seems to me difficult, though I've tried, to imagine a West Country queen. Though I suppose there are some, rolling about on tractors or running the Hardy museums.

During the afternoon, I made a few cuts and changes to the text, all of which pleased me, although I think I might just have overdone it. A terrible tendency of mine that Harold has to keep in check. Clive Francis rather wryly observed that the play was getting shorter and shorter. But there is nothing as irritating in a play as an unnecessary line, although no doubt many people will think almost every line in this play is unnecessary. But then,

I should do my best for *them*, too, shouldn't I, by giving them, if not none, then as few as possible?

What cheered me up most was listening again to the passage where Nick tells Stuart that the Arts Council is going to refuse a grant to his magazine on the grounds that it's elitist. I observed to Harold, on the way back in the car, that the same charge would probably be made about the play. He agreed cheerfully. So, in a spirit of *je-m'en-fou*ism (fuck-'em-allism), we drove elitely back to Holland Park in Harold's Mercedes to a glass of our usual tipple, champagne.

Monday, 28 May

Day six. And a bloody awful day it's been, too. It's Whit Monday and we appeared to be the only people in London working, at least in confined spaces, like offices. We laboured steadily through Act One, Scene Two. Almost every line in it seemed to be written dead by me, delivered buried by the actors. Furthermore, the Cambridge queen was back again, posturing and drawling away. When he made a comment about the quality of the wine in Stuart's room, he didn't even bother to glance at the bottles, thus making himself not only a peacock, but a fraud. The thing about intelligence, surely, is that it can't demonstrate itself in a vacuum, it requires an object both to animate it and to fix on. But then, now I come to think of it, Clive has just come from *The School for Scandal*, so perhaps his problem is that he still hasn't shaken himself free from Joseph Surface. Certainly his smirk when he tossed off perfectly simple lines as if they were French aphorisms belonged more to Surface, or Restoration Would-Wits, than to Humphry. Bob East's Nick was heavy-handed, by the way; Simon Williams was all charm and no rhythm; Nina Thomas, who a few days ago couldn't enter the room, is now either hovering at the door as if taking a curtain call, or racing in like a whippet. As these are all very good actors, the fault must be entirely mine. Either I've written a whole clutch of bad parts, or good parts that don't mesh. I don't know. But I do know the last moments of the scene don't work. They dribble away to nothing, to neither a situation in suspense, which is what I think I wanted, nor a situation concluded which would at least be something. The atmosphere at the Ballet

Rambert after we'd finished a run of the scene was one of defeat. The actors left with direly cheerful goodnights, see-you-tomorrow-loves, dears, darlings, sloping off into the evening as quickly as they could. We went to Harold's car, drove to a pub off Holland Park and discussed the problem fitfully, with intervals of remote and exasperated silence.

During rehearsal, my sensible impulse had been to leave Harold alone, and yet I'd kept rising to my feet, lumbering across the room, my finger half-raised interrogatively. There'd be a second between my proposal offered and my proposal considered, just a second's silence, during which Harold seemed to go through a physical transformation, his cheeks swelling, his jaw jutting, when I felt something quite different from either acceptance or rejection was about to take place. Then he'd discuss the proposal or point with a control that is more alarming, I think, than any actual outburst could be. Of course we've gone through this sort of thing together before although less perilously because he smoked, and one comes to take it as Pooter, or more likely his great descendant, A. J. Wentworth, might have said, 'in one's stride'. But we both acknowledged that it had been a miserable day, full of tensions and frustrations.

I wonder what there was about other professions that put me off them. Tonight I rather wish I'd been what my father was, a pathologist, especially as I feel I'm developing a cast of mind useful in the conducting of post-mortems; or as my mother was, a housewife, a breeder of children, a stately knockabout comedian who confined her most terrifying jokes to her family captives, pretending to me on an occasion when I brought her tea in bed – she always took an afternoon nap – that she was dead, lying half out of the bed, mouth open in a grimace, eyes fixed in vacancy. She didn't as much as twitch until I began to phone my father at his hospital. A few years later she announced firmly, with just the right hint of apology, to my younger brother who was about ten at the time that actually he was adopted. The best riposte to which, we worked out years later, would have been a cry of relief. I summon up these two shades not to comfort myself, but only to wish that their pooled genes had evolved me into a different line of work. God knows what I'll have to report tomorrow. I would tend to say that it can't get worse. Except that in my experience it can, and often does.

(Actually, it didn't. Harold talked to Clive Francis about adopting an accent, to give him a background and to avoid the generalised Cambridge queen. Between them, they settled on North Country. My own preference for West Country was partly because Clive had been North Country in the tour of *Quartermaine's Terms*. Nick Le Prevost, Bob East, Simon Williams and Nina Thomas all made, or at least so I felt, the right sort of progress over the next few days, although at this stage Ian Ogilvy still seemed to me to be contradicting the spirit of Martin by exposing the character's unconscious motives through his social manner. But much of my concern was with my own defects as playwright. I give a lengthy analysis of what I thought was weak about the ending of the first act, and what I did to change it, am pleased with the result, but go broodingly on.)

I've noticed that sometimes I've added a line because it seems like a good line, without sufficiently considering the effect it's going to have on lines further away. The other day, going through the proofs for the published text, I found myself writing into the speech in which Stuart compares himself to various noble animals in decline (a threatened lion, a tattered tiger) a concluding image of himself as a bankrupt rat. The next time the passage came up in rehearsal I stuck it in. It worked quite satisfyingly until I noticed this afternoon that the word 'bankrupt' turns up in two other places within a minute of dialogue. Then, at the beginning of Act Two, Martin says something about his secretary going into 'competition' with him as a publisher, and five or six lines later Martin refers to the 'competition' Nick is facing for his television job. These things are easy to sort out, but nevertheless make me feel a chump; and as if I had a tin ear when writing dialogue.

(There were also various things happening offstage, or behind the scenes, that Harold and I picked up accidentally as, for instance, when having a quick drink with the management.)

A row is going on between two of the actors about their respective billings. There is no problem about billing at the Lyric, where it is alphabetical, just as the pay is a flat rate all around. But if we move into the West End, i.e. into the free market, the billing and the

money become endlessly negotiable. Unfortunately, these negotiations actually take place when the original contracts are being
drawn up at the Lyric. Rather bizarre and a waste of time, though
I have no doubt the agents enjoy it. The intelligent moment to
begin West End negotiations would obviously be when and if we
have a West End theatre. The size of the theatre would dictate how
much the actors can be paid, and the likely run of the play and
the actors' desire to go on doing their parts would bring real
realism as opposed to agents' realism to the issue. The problem at
the moment is that one of the actors was signed up so late that
negotiations are still going on for West End money, billing, etc.,
even though he is now deep in rehearsals. He's probably entitled
to better billing than one or two of the other actors (particularly
one, he feels) whose billings have already been fixed. The odd
thing about all this is that it is *personal*, not an agent's disagreement at all. The actor in question is determined to get the number
two or three spot or whatever it is, the other actor determined not
to relinquish it. The argument between them is being conducted
entirely outside the rehearsal room. Inside, they are perfectly
friendly, and I gather that there are actually no ill feelings, merely
a genial determination on both sides to get their own way. I have
no idea how it will turn out and if we don't move to the West End
I will never know, I suppose, as at the Lyric, Simon Williams, for
instance, victim of the alphabetical system, remains at the bottom
of the poster, while Bob East, a beneficiary of it, remains at the top.
It doesn't matter where Nick Le Prevost and Ian Ogilvy are,
because they're somewhere in the middle where you don't read
names anyway.

30 May

A medium-sized confrontation between Harold and myself over
the end of Scene One. At the moment, Humphry sharply inter-
rupts a salacious conversation between Nick and Peter with a
demand for some music. Nick says to Peter, 'I wouldn't resist him
if I were you. He's got a rather powerful personality,' and puts a
record on the gramophone. This is exactly as written. The trouble
is that when I wrote it I visualised Humphry on the far side of
the room, Nick by the gramophone.* The present staging has

Humphry sitting close to the gramophone, with Nick and Peter some way from it. Thus Nick's crossing the room to put the record on makes him look as if he's turning himself into Humphry's handmaiden. A day or so ago, I proposed to Harold that either we change the dialogue to justify Nick's cross; or that we change the staging, getting Nick closer to the gramophone, Humphry further from it. I didn't mind which, although my inclination was to change the dialogue. Harold agreed. That, I thought, was that. Today, when Harold told the actors of the dialogue changes, really quite minor ones, they began to object. There are times when actors appear to have an anal retentiveness about any line, however inconsequential, that they are given in a play. Bob East (Nick) began to argue vehemently in defence of both his long cross and his lines, and Clive Francis (Humphry) joined in on the grounds, presumably, that he liked his sit and his lines. Harold began to see that there were arguments here that ought to be considered and discussed. I became increasingly impassioned, Harold increasingly resolute. At one point we were standing almost nose to nose, smiling grimly into each other's faces, insisting courteously on our own points of view. It ended with my saying that as far as I was concerned I had an extremely simple position on this one, I was convinced, *convinced* that we should change either the staging or the dialogue. And I was perfectly willing to change the dialogue. Harold said he would change the staging. Which he did. Humphry is now across on the other side of the room, Nick is close to the gramophone, and the whole scene is being played both as written and as I visualised it. But I now suspect that the dialogue is wrong in ways that won't be affected by the moves, and that it'll have to be changed anyway. I also suspect, from a rather cunning smile Harold gave me when he'd finished restaging, that he knows it too. But I think I'll leave that problem for a day or two. Or even a week or two.

1 June

The most dramatic moment came from Harold's wanting a line (at least for the purposes of rehearsal) that would make Martin's

* For the context of this exchange see Appendix B, page 167.

concern for Marigold and his feelings about the possibility of her having an abortion, explicit. As written, the scene goes as follows:

MARTIN The money was a gift to the magazine. You know how much I want it to survive.

STUART Yes I do. So do I. Want it to survive. But not as a subsidiary to something else, you see.

MARTIN Does that include Marigold and the baby? Sorry, sorry, none of my business, but – well, it'll break her heart –

The sound of footsteps, off, coming up the stairs.

HUMPHRY (*enters*) What's going on, this room reeks of passion, in the famous phrase. What have you two been up to?

Harold's point was that the line, 'it'll break her heart – ' is a dangling line, making it impossible for Martin to convey the real intensity of his concern for Marigold. I therefore suggested that Martin undangle his line, i.e. complete it, and that we then have a pause during which Martin and Stuart look at each other, a pause interrupted by Humphry's entrance. So what I proposed was that Martin simply say (what in fact he really means), 'It will break her heart if you don't let her have the child.' This gives to Martin a kind of moralising passion which is perhaps more than I had originally intended, but which I think is justified by Martin's state (that is, his love for Marigold). Ian Ogilvy tried the line out. Nina Thomas, who was sitting in her usual chair, doing the *Telegraph* crossword puzzle, jerked her head up when she heard it, and scampered* forward: 'I've only just heard that line. I've never heard that line before.' (Which was not surprising as the line had never been said before.) 'And I think it's the most repellent line I've ever heard. I don't understand what it's doing in the play.' There, facing her, was Harold (emphatically CND) who had asked for the line; Ian Ogilvy (very much a gentleman of the old school – Eton) for whom the line had been asked; Nick Le Prevost (far left and a declared feminist) to whom the line was being said; Clive Francis (of no known political opinion, but always a gallant)

---

* This is the word in the transcripts. It can't really be right (except possibly dramatically) as Nina is an elegant mover – not the scampering kind.

who had interrupted the line; and I (undecided between Liberal and SDP) who had provided the line. Five men who think themselves well disposed towards women vied with each other in putting Nina Thomas down. She finally withdrew, with little gesticulations of despair and distress. We proceeded with the rehearsal.

Everything was going well until we got to the next scene with Marigold, who announces this time (Act Two, Scene One) that she's pregnant. We quickly found ourselves in an intricate conversation with Nina Thomas, who began by asking what kind of state she should be in, what was the condition of the two men in the room – the very matter we had in fact been discussing before she made her entrance. So there was no progress. Actually, there was regress. I suppose there are two problems for Nina: one, that she is the only female actor in the company; two, that she comes on at the end of scenes, which means she has to sit for hours waiting her turn, and when she finally gets it, is quite naturally keen to make the most of it. Something like this also happens to Bob East, who is playing Nick, and to Simon Williams, who is playing Peter, both of whom interrupt scenes rather than originate and control them, and therefore feel a need, again quite naturally, to question and challenge. But whereas the discussions with Bob East and Simon Williams tend to move us forward, those with Nina sometimes tend to move animatedly nowhere, so that a decision about a line or a move seems, when it comes, like male bullying. I am sure Nina feels just as trapped in this ghastly web as we do.* At one point there was a dialogue between Nina and the rest of us about her entrance (yet again) which was really a dialogue about men and their inability to understand anything at all about women, and vice versa. The most interesting moment came when Ian Ogilvy tried to break the deadlock by offering to rearrange his text so that Nina would feel more 'comfortable' – her word, taken up by him – when she came in. In other words, he was offering to rewrite my play a fraction. At which point I claimed, no doubt incorrectly, that the lines seemed to me OK as they stood, thank you, Ian, etc. What touched me, or does now but didn't then, is

---

* One of the actors was rumoured to have said on the first day of rehearsal that things should go OK in this production as 'There are five men and only one woman.'

that a chap who on the surface has so little in common with the current feminist line should have countered the implicit feminist arguments with a gallantry that couldn't have affected those arguments in the slightest, but might well have been detrimental, though no doubt only slightly, to the play. Harold resolved the situation by changing the subject, and then going straight from the first scene to the play's Epilogue.

I was ashamed to notice how badly written the Epilogue is, and how clumsily it hammers its points home. I put it to Harold as we left – people scurried off at six o'clock – that I seemed to have botched it yet again. We discussed various possible rewrites without coming to any conclusions and then drifted to the pub where we found the whole company having a drink. Sitting there, looking haunted and charming, was Nina Thomas. I felt it crucial that I should engage her in conversation. I pondered deeply and then asked her what she thought of Viv Richards's innings in the third one-day match. There was a short pause, then Nina said, I think, something to the effect that she hadn't seen it. Simon Williams, or it might have been Ian Ogilvy, had, however, and took up the subject of Viv Richards with tremendous confidence and style for the next hour or so. The conversation then flowed around Nina Thomas, marooned, thanks to my social deftness, silent on her stool.

Harold and I drove back. He was going on to play bridge with Antonia and friends. I raised points – odd how these things surface – this surfaces, that surfaces, one notices, forgets, then remembers. He had things, I had things. We talked until he dropped me off at Holland Park where I had a meal by myself, worked through the Epilogue, came home exhausted.

4 June

Thirteenth day of rehearsals. An apt number, I think. It's been an unsatisfactory day. No, that's not right. An inconclusive day. Harold went back to the second scene of the first act, a very long scene, I think the longest in the play, and drove through it. I noticed his noticing my noticing that Marigold arrived to announce her abortion in much the same way as she'd done the last time.* Harold and I looked across the rehearsal room at each other, I don't know whose darkness meeting whose brightness, in a perfect glance of great politeness – but it was one or the other way round. We went through to the end of the scene. However, nothing radical was accomplished except that I became increasingly convinced that as we've added quite a few lines to Peter at the end of the act, a few of his earlier lines should be cut. He should get from the news about the magazine being saved to phoning up his latest fuck as quickly as possible. Anything in between is a kind of indulgence. However short the lines are, they're *longueur* lines. But I decided not to mention this to Harold until I've spent some time with the text.

5 June

When it comes down to it, today was simply one of those days I'd remember only because I'm making a record of it. Just another day in which I sat in my chair, chain-smoking and sometimes concentrating and sometimes failing to concentrate, turning towards my *Standard*, rising to my feet and molesting Harold with an enquiry or a proposed alteration. One of the things I have realised about rehearsals over the years is that the memory of individual days recedes very rapidly, blurring into one long day, without definition, except for little dramas here and there which I can never place in any sensible chronology when trying to remember them. On the other hand, it was probably one of those days in which the actors made progress, almost unnoticeably. Or regressed, unnoticed.

So, at 12.30 in the morning on 6 June, now Wednesday, I wish myself some sort of sleep. That's really all I crave. But I think this exhaustion grows, a developing exhaustion of spirit that actually, in the days before we open, transforms itself into a kind of (I wish

---

* In earlier rehearsals, we'd had a disagreement about the spirit in which Marigold enters after she has had the abortion. My view was that she would be chippier than usual as she'd want to conceal the fact of the abortion from Stuart and the other people in the room; Harold's view being that she would be unable to help showing something of the emotional and physical trauma of the abortion in the way she spoke, moved, etc. He finally came around to the chippier view when he realised that if the scene started on a sombre note, it really left itself nowhere to go and that there was also a danger that Marigold was (indirectly) letting the audience know that she'd had an abortion before we wanted them to know it.

I'd stop saying 'a kind of' and 'a sort of', by the way)* feverish animation. So there we are. I hope I remember to buy a new tape.

(Two days later we ran through the whole of Act One for the first time and therefore saw for the first time not snatches of performances, but what they amounted to in a whole stretch. This inevitably put one's previous reflections on the actors, the text, the direction into a different and larger perspective. I think it is true to say that the first complete run of an act is, for a playwright, a frightening prospect, taking its place somewhere between the read-through and the first run of the whole play.)

The beginning of the play was strangely drab and I began actually to fester with self-resentment, wondering whether I haven't written some of the dreariest dialogue I've ever heard on the stage. The exchanges between Martin and Stuart were very low key, boring *and* hurried. One of the reasons for this is that Ian Ogilvy has a tendency to push scenes along, perhaps because his last performance was in a farce. Secondly, it seems to me that Nick Le Prevost is still expressing certain passages of the play too seriously. He's an odd actor in that he suggests seriousness far better when he's being light and ironic than when he's being tortured and defeated.† It was glum in other words, the opening of Act One, Scene Two, and it wasn't helped by a slightly forced performance from Bob East, while Clive Francis seems to have invented for himself a rather strangely placed but invisible pocket just above his hip, into which he places his right hand. He then juts his right knee out. This makes him look like an Edwardian army officer, unrelaxed and posturing. But he's no longer posturing with his voice, and he's developing considerable charm, which can only be to the advantage of the production. On the other hand Nina Thomas was fine. Funny, individual and extremely touching. Overall, though, the problem that haunts me is to do with the dialogue. As always Harold and I had a talk about various things afterwards, a rather strange talk as he didn't want to go to the pub we've been using because he finds the wine undrinkable. So we sat in his car for

---

* I've edited most of them out, I hope.

† Not odd at all. Most people, whether actors or not, are more likely to get themselves taken seriously when not struggling to seem serious.

about half an hour, I smoking of course – chain-smoking – Harold not smoking. It struck me afterwards that it was the longest conversation we've ever had in which Harold had neither a glass nor a cigarette in his hand. But then I was partly distracted by his worry over the dullness of the exchanges between Martin and Stuart. He discussed it as if it were an acting problem. I couldn't bring myself to say what was most on my mind, that perhaps the real problem is that the passage is dully written. It was as if I'd got Martin to drop in on Stuart to ask him questions about his domestic life with the sole intention of providing the audience with information – information that they won't know they lack, and therefore won't particularly want. Could anything be more tedious in fact? Even Shakespeare tries to give a character a proper motive for launching into an interminable stretch of exposition, except in *The Tempest*, of course, when the only conceivable reason I can find for Prospero telling Miranda his life story is to expose himself as a ruthless old bore. And a bully too, as he seems to kick or cuff her fairly regularly to keep her awake and listening. The thought that I couldn't do better than Shakespeare depressed me.

On the way home, though, it struck me that a long time ago, when I wrote the play, I understood perfectly what Martin is up to in questioning Stuart. He's in love with Marigold. He really wants – *needs* – to know whether she and Stuart are still living together. Therefore, he's in Stuart's office on his *own* behalf, not the audience's. I suppose I'd forgotten this because there's been a greater gap between the writing of *The Common Pursuit* and its production than I'm used to, and so I've lost touch with the intention behind some scenes and lines. This excuse isn't good enough. I've merely been stupid. When I got in, I telephoned Harold and explained. He grasped the point immediately, and I'm pleased to say, blames himself for having missed it.

What this experience underlines is that dialogue with no proper intention behind it, however deft and witty it may sound out of context, is undramatic. This is probably one of the most pedantic and boring things I've ever uttered. Or what is worse, it probably isn't. Nevertheless, I need to keep remembering it. Especially as I have a distinct tendency – in *The Common Pursuit* anyway – to over-explanatoriness, as if I can't bear the characters not to report on every event in minute detail. This sometimes makes them sound like a gang of adulterers practising their alibis on each other. 'Why', one feels like asking, 'are you telling me all this? Come on, what have you *really* been up to?' All they're up to, of course, is expressing my literal-mindedness. With this literally in mind, I've spent the rest of the evening going through the text. I rewrote a passage between Stuart and Martin, the little scene in which they discuss whether Peter has gone to the Arts Council to try and get the magazine a grant, or whether he's really holed up in a hotel, having it off with a girl. The trouble with the writing here wasn't that it was over-literal, but that it was imprecise, thus making the two men appear incapable of marshalling simple thoughts coherently. Not too good, when they're meant to have razor-sharp intellects. I think I've got that right. At least it moves cleanly now. Then I settled down to a little cutting, all over the first act, a snip-snip here, a snip-snip there, a judicious and loving gardener, keeping the foliage in trim, is how I'd like to see myself, though Harold will probably see me as an old-fashioned barber, administering a short back-and-sides. I'll probably just show him the rewrite tomorrow, and indicate *possible* cuts, leaving it to him to listen in rehearsal and decide later.

8 June

I showed Harold the rewrite before he started the rehearsal, and he decided to put it in. Then he explained to Ian Ogilvy and Nicholas Le Prevost the real reason behind Martin's questioning of Stuart. Or at least tried to. He scarcely got beyond the first sentence before they were enthusiastically denouncing themselves for not having seen the point a long time ago.

Harold then assembled the whole company and talked about his feeling that nothing in this play should seem to be struggled for, that the characters were friends who had known each other for a long time, and that what therefore distinguished their relationship should be freedom and naturalness, except at very precisely observed moments. But what made those moments shocking was that they happened in a general atmosphere of tolerance, no, more than tolerance, of mutual acceptance. Therefore it was crucial that the actors should never feel physically at odds with a scene, and he'd become fairly sure, over the last few days, that he'd pushed them here and there into inhibiting positions. They had to *feel* free to move, even when they didn't want to. So he'd decided to start again from the top of the play, going through it scene by scene, opening it out, making it as fluid as possible.* He wanted to encourage them to occupy the rooms in their own particular way – especially in the first two scenes, when the characters were young and likely to roam about a room, sit wherever they felt inclined, lie on the floor in the middle of a conversation, etc. So the morning was spent with Harold re-blocking the play, or more accurately, with a collaborative re-blocking, Harold letting the actors move as they felt inclined, guiding them rather than directing them into positions. I thought it was invaluable, the scenes he got through becoming both more comfortable and more expansive, the rooms seeming to be inhabited at last by friends who had conversations rather than by actors who spoke lines to each other.

We lunched at the small Italian restaurant where we'd gone after the read-through. We both felt buoyant, as if his liberating the actors had liberated us, as well. Furthermore I was ravenous, having had an early breakfast. I studied the menu with the obsessiveness with which I normally study only my own scripts, and after considering *pollo* done this way, veal done that, scampi and even pasta, which I normally can't eat, finding it technically too complicated, selected a steak, chips, a green salad. Harold had chicken. We shared a bottle of wine. We gossiped and anecdoted and laughed our way through the meal, not once discussing the morning's rehearsal, nor the afternoon's to come. I mention this only because it was so clearly an interlude, badly needed by both of us, instinctively seized. There aren't many of them in rehearsals. At least not of my plays.

11 June

It's nearly midnight, the end of the eleventh day of rehearsal – can that be right? We seem to have been at it for much longer.† I got

---

* This is the episode I refer to when discussing blocking on pages 68–9.

† We had. In fact, it was the end of the fifteenth day. Although every working day was reported into the tape machine, I'd still managed to get the arithmetic wrong, mainly because I often forgot to give the date. But I didn't discover the mistake until much later. (See footnote on page 119.)

to rehearsals late, as I'd spent the morning on *The Rector's Daughter*, and was already tired when I arrived. I came in at a point that had been worrying me – when Stuart discovers that Martin (his best friend) has been having an affair with Marigold, and is responsible for her pregnancy, which she has just announced. Originally I'd written a long exchange between Stuart and Martin, but I got rid of it a week or so ago, though I left in Stuart's speech because Nick Le Prevost (Stuart) was keen on it. I have come increasingly to loathe this speech, full of passionate hatred for Martin, for Marigold, for the baby to come, mainly because Stuart seems to get to his feelings too quickly, too precisely, and too emphatically. In my experience it doesn't happen like that. In moments of crisis we never know quite what our feelings are, we fumble towards them, get them wrong, go off at tangents, possibly worry about our grammar. (A friend of mine told me that when he heard his father was dying, his first thought was, 'Bugger, that means I'll miss the football tonight.' He was deeply fond of his father, too, fonder even than of football.) Altogether, I felt it would be much more interesting if we were to leave Stuart floundering for his response, especially as Nick (Bob East), who has been entering on cue just as Stuart finishes his speech, would now have to enter just before Stuart can begin it, thus preventing him from making it at all. I suggested this to Harold. He agreed to try it. It seemed to work. And that was my only contribution to the day. I sat back, inert, while Harold went back to the beginning of the scene and worked through it again. Then he ran it.

(It was painful to come across, in the transcripts, the following description of what Harold ran, and I was of course tempted to censor it, not for what I say about the actors, but for what I reveal about myself. Nevertheless, it seems too central to the truth of the experience to omit. I have kept it in virtually as spoken. As no subsequent rehearsal had anything like this effect on me, I can only assume that I was either hallucinating when I saw it, or hallucinating later, when I reported it into the machine. I don't discount either possibility, but incline to the latter. I think possibly I had reached a point where fatigue, obsession, the dark premonitions that I've mentioned earlier, and probably alcohol, combined to produce a late-night poison that I discharged into the tape recorder, having nowhere else to discharge it. If I hadn't had to keep my diary going, I'd probably have had a few more drinks, dozed through some television and gone to bed, the memory, or rather the distorted memory, obliterated. I trust at least that that night the actors slept well, as I'm sure they deserved to. On the other hand, they may all have been sitting in their rooms at two in the morning, speaking into tape machines their views of the author's and the director's and each other's performances. Harold might have been at it too, for all I know. Anyway, this period was for me, I've discovered – thanks to this diary – almost the nadir. The nadir itself was to come very shortly.)

We moved into the theatre today, where we'll remain until we open. For the moment, of course, we're rehearsing on the set of a different play, *Black Ball Game*, which is currently in performance. This probably disorientated the cast. They've been working for two weeks in an extremely comfortable rehearsal room and now found themselves on stage, in the right space, with the right furniture, but in the wrong room. The setting of *Black Ball Game* is a conference hall in a tacky modern hotel. Also the stage, at least for *Black Ball Game*, has a slight rake. Either that or I was slightly drunk, or tired, or both. Anyway, the run of the scene seemed to me bizarre. For one thing, I had the distinct impression that the actors were either speeding downstage towards me, or labouring upstage away from me. When they came towards me they seemed, at the very last second, to be pulling up, braking in fact, their bodies inclining sharply forwards, then stiffening upright; then turning awkwardly around and clambering back up to the higher reaches of the room. I attribute this to the rake. If there was a rake. And, as I say, the actors seemed disorientated. Although this didn't explain everything about their performances.

Humphry, for instance. A lot of the time he was to be found absolutely centre stage. He stood with his back to the desk, absolutely dead centre, looking as if he were back in *The Rear Column*. In *The Rear Column*, the characters are meant to take up stage centre positions. In *The Common Pursuit*, the characters should always be slightly to the side of things, there is never quite a centre there. And yet there was Clive, where I was sure he'd never been before, absolutely and immobilely stage-centre throughout most of the scene. Until, that is, Simon Williams knocked him over. I always look forward to this moment, but for once it didn't work. There was a gap of about six inches between Simon Williams's fist and Clive Francis's jaw, though Clive Francis went down like a ninepin, whatever a ninepin is, whereupon one's eyes went straight to Ian Ogilvy, sitting at the far side of the room at the other desk, in fact lying prone over the desk, I think to suggest embarrassment at the fracas between Humphry and Peter, but of course looking as if he too had been felled by Humphry's blow, although in his case from a distance of about twenty feet.

Humphry went off, Peter went off, Stuart (alias Nick Le Prevost) trudged on, slowly, exhaustedly, leaning against the rake, if there was a rake, at an angle that suggested German Expressionist cinema. One of the melancholy madmen from *The Cabinet of Doctor Caligari*, for instance. His ensuing exchanges with Martin weren't helped by the fact that when he sat down in his tip-back chair, his face disappeared from view behind the desk, so one occasionally believed that Martin was quite alone in the room, either talking to himself or projecting his voice behind the desk. Enter Marigold, giving a double impersonation, now as a saint undergoing a minor martyrdom, now as a silent-movie comedienne, her eyes rolling, her mouth working, her words inaudible. After her, Bob East, snarling and laughing at his own jokes, not laughing because they've taken him by surprise, as people often are by their own jokes, but sneeringly, as if to make it clear that he'd heard his own jokes before, and still didn't find them funny.

After the run Harold and I went back to Campden Hill Square in the evening sunlight, and had a drink. I felt exhausted and depressed, but nevertheless sat analysing the run with Harold, who seemed to think it ropy and strained, but then the actors were tired after a long day, however lots of good things emerging, etc. I didn't have much to say, as I could tell that our experiences for once completely failed to coincide. I came home, had dinner, recorded this.

12 *June*

Most of today's work was spent on the Humphry death scene, and for most of the day the cast was lively. Harold had reminded them that they weren't there to mourn Humphry, but to deal with his funeral arrangements, and that this didn't preclude the jokiness of old friends gathered together. Section by section it went well, neither frivolous nor gloomy, all the characters to the point and relaxed with each other, and so, section by section, it seemed to be on its way to being touching, making no palpable claim on our emotions, etc. But when Harold ran the whole scene, it settled immediately into pathos. First Bob East, who had been saying, 'Hey, what about "Fear no more the heat of the sun?"' – the first line of the scene – in the spirit of one coming up with a bright suggestion for something that could be recited at the funeral, now said it with heavy melancholy, as if old Humphry's corpse were stretched there at his feet, and he was about to deliver the dirge itself, right over it. Which was what the whole scene then became, a dirge, not only making a palpable claim, but sending in the bailiffs too. When it finished Harold reminded them of what he'd reminded them of before the run, then set them to it once more. Bob East tried to get the scene off more lightly, but didn't quite succeed, Simon Williams picked it up a little, Ian Ogilvy pushed it along. We seemed to be on the right tracks, then Nick Le Prevost entered, knotted in gloom. Told of Humphry's death he'd previously asked, quite briskly, 'Was it suicide?' (After all, he *knows* all about Humphry's homosexuality and growing death-wish.) What he gave us this time was 'Was it – (*long pause*) – *suicide*?' and from there downhill all the way, right to the graveyard in fact. So. Having worked hard throughout the day in one direction, we nevertheless observed the cast, who had themselves worked hard and enthusiastically in the same direction, taking a completely opposite one when we did the run. Perhaps they're afraid of being thought irreverent, of being casual about the death of a friend. Or perhaps, quite practically, they haven't adjusted to the different time schemes. On stage Humphry has to go from live to dead in a matter of minutes; in life there would be a few days in between, time to think about the matter, discuss it over the telephone, etc., before meeting to work out the details for his funeral. I don't know.

After the rehearsal we all went to the bar. There was conversation, not very much and rather tense, about the day's work. Gradually everybody relaxed into a discussion about the armaments situation, the probabilities of a nuclear war within a decade or so, or even a month or two. It struck me that this was a far more serious matter than the murder of poor old Humphry, and yet we were pretty animated, anxious all of us to chip in with our little bits, our prognostications, snippets from reports we'd read in the papers, and in the middle of it I wished I could have videoed it, and played it back afterwards, saying: 'Look, this is how people really talk when they're talking about serious matters. How friends and colleagues do, anyway. So when it comes to Humphry . . .' Which, now I make the point, suggests to me that to some people there are more important things than the death of Humphry or even the death of the world, and that's how to get a scene in a play right. Which in turn leads me to reflect that that's precisely the point of the scene. All the characters are *talking* about Humphry's death, but are also *thinking* about various matters in their own lives. They're not ashamed of that, they acknowledge it in themselves and each other. Which leads me to the yet further reflection, which, being about life, 'old life itself' backed up by a quotation or two from Kant, I can't bear to impart. Too tired.

13 June

(The day when I believe I reached my nadir. The crucial section comes virtually verbatim. Towards the end of it some of my sentences became jumbled, but I think I've transcribed them accurately. I offer it up without excuse, having exhausted my stock excuses of nicotine poisoning, alcohol poisoning, fatigue, paranoia, premonitions. I trust, however, it has a clinical value.)

Eighteenth day of rehearsal. An unattractive day. A desperate day. A humiliating day. But let me be calm. Beginning at the beginning. We spent the morning running through Act One. Most of the things I didn't like seemed to me my fault. For instance, I thought that the end of Scene One went badly because I'd underwritten Peter, giving him only a few heavily signalling lines with which to establish his identity. Then the end of the scene, when Humphry puts a Wagner record on, was formal and plonking. The rest of the act had moments of intelligence and intensity, also moments of wit, until we got to the recently rewritten passage between Stuart and Martin, about whether Peter has gone to the Arts Council or is having it off with a girl. Nick Le Prevost forgot his new lines and he wasn't helped by a sudden banging overhead just as he came up to them, as if somebody was doing something radical either to the theatre or just outside it. Anyway, *something* made the whole rewritten passage seem very thin. Actually, what it really seemed was rewritten. I hope it was just the banging. I was relieved when we stopped for lunch, I wanted to get away from the banging, the rehearsal, the thought of rewriting rewrites, and when Harold went off to have lunch with Judy (our agent), I went off to the Italian restaurant, where I rewrote the rewrites. I felt awful.

We met again at just after two, plodded through the first scene. In fact that was as far as we were to go during the course of the afternoon. We considered passages at the very beginning of the scene, the middle of the scene and the end of the scene that weren't quite forceful or rich enough, or weren't quite explicit enough, etc. Then we partially incorporated my newly rewritten passage and stopped at six o'clock and went to the bar as usual. At least Clive Francis, Nick Le Prevost, Ian Ogilvy, Harold and myself did. After a time, Harold went off and talked to a plump girl* in a long dress who kept showing him things. I couldn't make out what they were doing as I was having quite an engaging conversation with Nick Le Prevost about films and politics, the usual kind of conversation that one has with Nick Le Prevost. Then Harold suddenly appeared before me and said, 'Simon, would you come over here?' So I plodded after him to this plump girl, who was looking down at some pictures. Harold said, 'The thing is about the programme. The fact is that we can't fit all the pictures – there is going to be photographs of all the actors and so forth, thing. And, one of the actors comes out badly, only once in a cluster of other actors, and he really ought to be in the pro-gramme on his own, too. So I just wondered whether we could cut you out of the photographs of rehearsals in the programme.

---

* Exactly. See footnote on page 86.

Do you mind if we cut you out and leave the rest in?' The rest being himself and the other actors. And I must say, the old gorge did its usual thing. It rose rapidly like a barometer in a fevered mouth, just shot up. I immediately thought how extraordinary that the one person to be cut out of the sequence of photographs to do with production was the author, who had been present at every day of rehearsals. But as I didn't really know this plump girl and felt that somehow pride, pride, pride was important, I got the old bile back down the old gorge and said, 'I don't care what the fuck you do, that's fine with me.' Harold said contentedly, 'I knew you wouldn't mind.'

But of course, from that moment on the whole matter began to ferment, the whole matter being, from my point of view, that the person who was responsible for the whole evening, i.e. the author, who had been present at every day of rehearsals, could simply be cut out of the pictures, so that present in the photographs of the rehearsal proceedings would be all the actors and, at various times in various photographs, the director, but under no circumstances the author, because an actor needed to appear twice. The actor appears twice, the author not at all. We had a very strained quarter of an hour in the bar after this, strain coming from Harold's sensing that I was angry about something, but having no clue as to what it was, and my feeling inhibited because we were surrounded by the actors. Robert Cogo-Fawcett, the director of the theatre, was also present. So it was difficult to say, 'Harold, look, the real problem is . . .' So I couldn't. We then went down to get a taxi that Harold had ordered – a minicab actually. In the minicab it was again impossible to be absolutely clear about my feelings because the minicab driver had no partition between himself and us. So that everything I would be saying to Harold I would be saying to the driver too. We discussed various aspects of the performances, and I suggested to him that one of our problems was that Nick, having recently done a very successful television series, was still acting to the camera rather than acting on stage. That he didn't really look at the people he was speaking to because he was in the habit of thinking that the camera would pick them up and they would subsequently be spliced into the sequence. This actually was a slightly tetchy conversation because Harold misunderstood me. When I said Nick, he thought I meant Nick the character, when I meant in fact Nick Le Prevost, the actor. So he was trying to make all this criticism correspond in some way to Bob East instead of Nick Le Prevost, and when we'd actually unravelled our misunderstanding, our being rather like two Mr Pooters in transit together, it was time for me to get out. I was seething all the way to Highgate, and when I got home, I phoned him up and put it to him that when it came to it, I really did object to being cut out of the photographs in the programme. It was actually, properly of the nursery.

He began being very calmly surprised by my objection and then, infected by my sense of grievance, became increasingly aggrieved himself. One of the things he said was, 'All I want to do is to get the play on. I don't give a damn whether I'm photographed in the programme or not,' and then went on to say that, anyway, he felt fairly strongly that the only photograph in which I appeared was one in which he was also present and he hated the shot of himself, so he didn't particularly want that to be published in the programme. And so it went, ending with his announcing that, under the circumstances, he thought the best thing was for him to get himself out of the programme altogether, kick out both of us. *Both* of us was his solution. Which I sort of vaguely conceded to at the time, but I think I don't when it comes to it.

As a matter of fact, this is vanity. Of course it is. I realise it is. But, on the other hand, I do actually feel very passionately that the play was written by me, I am the author, I have been present every day, and yet the only people who are going to appear in the programme are the actors and the director, with the author, the only begetter, not visible. If I were a member of the audience, I would say, but where is the author? What role did he have to play in all this? Didn't he come in to rehearsals? Why not? Actually if I were a member of the audience I wouldn't say anything. I probably wouldn't even note the author's absence. Harold said, 'But don't you see, I mean it's a matter of no consequence, it's only for the actors that it's important.' His boiling reasonableness against my mean-spiritedness made for a very unattractive, I think, telephone conversation, which ended virtually with our hanging up on each other. It's not a very satisfactory state of affairs because I do actually agree with him that the most important thing is to get the play on. Certainly that is the most important thing. I have, myself, no objections at all to getting the play on. I want it to get on. I also want it to get on at its very best. I also actually want to be acknowledged as the author which is what the whole fuss really comes down to. But instead, what seems to matter is that a particular actor should have two photographs of himself rather than the author allowed to exist at all. I don't know. I would like to say it's a matter of principle. I think in a way that it might actually be a matter of principle. I feel the kind of anger that generally comes to me when I'm quite sure that something is a matter of principle. But, on the other hand, I do have to acknowledge that finally it might just be a matter of vanity. Goodnight.*

So tomorrow I hope that I shall be talking in a very different tone. I actually do think it is all piffling, but crucial. It is like life. This is life. The awful thing about life is that it is so frequently a matter of egos on issues that are in themselves trivial. Anyway, that's all for tonight. Goodnight.

14 June

Nineteenth day of rehearsals. Nine p.m. The day began by my pondering the situation re the photograph and diagnosing more lucidly, in a morning condition and sober, my paranoia. I decided to phone Harold and say we should forget entirely any discussions about the programme, because we really had to get on. I felt like saying, let's not quarrel about *that* because there are far more important things to quarrel about, but I actually said that we had more important things to worry about, and went on to propose some additional dialogue in the first scene, which we discussed on the telephone. It was a fairly short conversation, as I had to get to the theatre to be interviewed by some fellow from *Time Out*. He arrived twenty minutes late, which was infuriating. With the rehearsals about to begin, with new dialogue to be given to the

---

* Many weeks later, after the opening, I explained coolly to Harold that the reason I'd become so frenzied over the photographs was that I wanted one for this diary. He saw my point at once, but a little later wondered why I'd become so panicked. 'After all, you could always get the photographer to develop some more from the negatives.' I conceded that that was true, but further explained – I forget precisely what. All I know is that there were a few brief moments when I felt that I'd salvaged my dignity.

actors, I was going to be stuck with *Time Out*. So I became very surly. In other words, last night's or this morning's paranoia was still there all right. When he was fifteen minutes late, I decided that I'd give him five more minutes and then just piss off, to hell with him. I was not simply merely angry at the inconvenience, but bridling that I'd been kept waiting, which I suppose again is my vanity. Really, you know, I think in the course of the production of a play, so many of the vices and the weaknesses, anyway the most unattractive aspects of one's character, are constantly being exposed. But I really did bridle. I felt offended that I should be kept waiting by a journalist from *Time Out*, though of course I told myself that I was offended because I should be busily concerning myself with the new dialogue at rehearsals. Anyway, he arrived, looking earnest and ascetic, with a kind of spoor of fringe magazine clinging to him, and I felt that I looked like a plump and pampered playwright, with a glass of white wine in front of me fairly early in the morning, and a cigarette to my lips already.* The PR lady brought me another glass of white wine as she introduced us, and to him of course brought an orange juice.

The conversation mostly centred on the question of my fashionableness and the nature of a well-made play. I said that many years ago I had read in the newspapers that I was a fashionable playwright, which I knew meant that from that moment on I had ceased to be fashionable, and would therefore have trouble continuing to be a playwright. I went on to defend the well-made play, along the lines that playwrights have an obligation to make their plays well in a way that a man who manufactures chairs or cars or sweets or writes sonnets or whatever has an obligation to do his work well. Anyone who does *anything* has an obligation to do it as well as possible, to make it as well as possible. I've never understood the sneer about the well-made play, and consider that although one might *fail* to make it well, one had an obligation at least always to *try*. We then discussed things like shape and harmony, etc. He was perfectly pleasant. He had a small recording device with him that I was very sure would fail to pick up almost everything I said. And indeed when he played it back what we mainly got was the clatter of tea cups and the occasional cough

---

* Actually, I'm not Jewish or American.

from the canteen, underneath which ran almost inaudibly a dis-
gruntled whisper, which I identified as my voice, and an agreeable
but slightly detached voice, much clearer than mine, which was
his. It was quite a decent interview as interviews go, and he
seemed actually to like my work. He said that he read *Butley*
regularly, every – it can't be, this must be some kind of fantasy of
mine that he said every month. I think he must have said every six
months. It will be very interesting to see what actually turns up in
Time Out.*

Anyway, that having been done, I cantered off to rehearsal just
managing to arrive as the new lines of dialogue for Peter were
being considered. There was tension between Harold and myself
for the first hour or so, as a consequence of the photographs-in-
the-programme business, but we eventually got back to our usual
routine. Then we did a run of Act Two. We weren't, by the way, in
the theatre – there was a matinee today – but in an unused bar,
above a peculiar pub called the Clarendon, an Edwardian mauso-
leum. Initially, I went into the pub itself by mistake. There were
three Irish drunks leaning against each other in a dark, cavernous
room, like something out of an O'Neill play. I moved out of there
pretty rapidly because I felt that, although the three drunks were
incapable of assaulting me, the barman looked up to it, and willing. I found my way around the corner and upstairs to the rehearsal. The room itself, though good for rehearsing, was surrounded
by several enormous bars which had obviously not been used for
decades. There were beer taps, obsolescent beer taps, high ceil-
ings, an air of dusty and sad majesty about the whole place.

We ran Act Two. I felt pretty good about it until we got to one
of the bits I'd most enjoyed writing, when Stuart describes (to
Martin) how Martina, his clumsy cat (given to him by Martin, of
course) attempted to jump from the kitchen counter to the fridge,
missed it and ricocheted off to the floor. It is a long speech, full of
details about Martina, the way she moves, speculations on her
character, etc. I found myself thinking, what the hell is this speech
doing here? It comes when the play is moving dramatically and
crisply (I hope) forward and suddenly there is this long, complic-

---

* Nothing turned up in *Time Out* – though the interview was announced in two
different issues, I believe.

ated aria, with the proper logical and emotional reasons for it simply not established.

We broke rehearsals off at about six, and Harold and I then spent twenty minutes trying to get a taxi. At Hammersmith, they've actually refined the art, the taxi drivers, of manoeuvering their way past you with their 'For Hire' signs up. They were swinging rapidly across to the other side of the road, bending their heads lower over their wheels. But we finally made it back to Campden Hill Square, where we looked at the last stages of the Test match, talked a bit about cricket, then went over to Harold's studio house, where we looked at the Martina speech. I made suggestions about cutting lines here and there, Harold suggested alternative and further cuts. Then I said, 'Frankly, I've now got terrible doubts about this whole section of the play anyway.' And he said, 'Yes, let's consider the value of the speech as a whole. It seems to hold up the action. Instead of fiddling around and cutting little bits here and little bits there,' he said, 'why don't we go the whole hog and find out what would happen if we cut it altogether?' My first response was one of shock, because, as I've said, I still remember my pleasure in the writing of the speech. Then I suddenly realised that nevertheless he was absolutely right. When we cut the whole speech, an enormous cut, we saw that it didn't create any real textual problems, just a few cuts in the next scene and some shifted dialogue. The whole section still made sense, which reinforced our feelings that the speech was irrelevant.

The next question was how to approach the actor (Nick Le Prevost) on this. We were both slightly apprehensive about breaking the news. In my experience, actors are loath to drop speeches and there is always something about a large cut that creates unease even in the actors who aren't involved. They start to wonder when their turn for the chop is coming up. Harold said he would make a short announcement to the effect that there would be a moratorium on cuts (unless of course we thought they were needed). I suggested he should phone Nick Le Prevost straight away. Harold said, no, on the whole he wanted tomorrow's run-through to be undisturbed by such dramas as cuts. We could cut on Saturday or get together and look at it again over the weekend and make sure we were sure about it before cutting it on Monday. On such occasions, Harold invariably counsels patience while I cannot bear to hear any speech in rehearsals or run-throughs after I've found it redundant.

15 June

Twentieth day of rehearsals. Harold phoned this morning at 9.30 to say that he had changed his mind. He thought that we should meet Nick Le Prevost, whose speech it was, and Ian Ogilvy, to whom the speech was addressed, at lunchtime, after he'd given the actors notes taken from yesterday's run-through of Act Two, but before the run-through of the whole play. The first real run-through. This was slightly complicating as I had deliberately planned a leisurely morning. I had to be interviewed by someone from the *Times Higher Educational Supplement*, and after that I'd anticipated a rather splendid and solitary lunch with a book, a steak and chips, and a bottle of wine at the restaurant down the road from the theatre, before going back for what is always the major ordeal, the third major ordeal. The first ordeal with a new play is the read-through. The second ordeal is the first run-through of the first act. The third, the run-through of the whole play. I thought that the more comatose I could be, the better it would be for my psyche, nerves, whatever. But Harold was determined to get the cut over with. He expected trouble, as indeed did I, and with every good reason, because, as I've said, my experience of actors when confronted with a large cut is one of anxiety and argument, a desperate determination to keep in this line, that line, 'What about that line? And this line always seemed to me the best line in the play,' and so forth until one actually finds oneself with almost the whole section back again, with perhaps a quarter of a line missing.* I said, OK, it seemed to me that under the circumstances I'd better cancel the lady from the *Times Higher Educational Supplement.* I didn't mention my feelings about having also to cancel my lunch.

I phoned up one of the directors of the Lyric Theatre, David Porter, at his home (I can never get anyone at the theatre itself

---

* My favourite: 'To tell you the truth, I only took the part because of this speech,' from an actress who had plenty of speeches. As she made them all sound, to my prejudiced ear, exactly the same, it didn't seem to me to matter much which she said and which she didn't – except, of course, where it affected the other actors.

before eleven in the morning), and said would he please ask the PR lady to cancel the interview with the lady from the *Times Higher Educational Supplement* because I had to be in rehearsal. I arrived at quarter to eleven, had coffee with Harold, proceeded to rehearsals. We were there for an hour when I suddenly thought that I had better make sure that the *Times Higher Educational Supplement* lady had been properly and courteously put off. I plodded down to the bar to discover one of the public relations girls looking rather fraught. The *Times Higher Educational Supplement* lady had turned up in spite of attempts to warn her off, and although she wasn't there at the moment – she had just gone off to the lavatory – she was upset because she hadn't been given any reason for the cancellation, apart from the fact that I didn't want to give the interview. I swelled up and burst out explosively just as the *Times Higher Educational Supplement* lady came back, forcing me to conjure on to my face a grin of welcome and apology. I explained that there had been a misunderstanding, but that it might be possible after all to do a brief interview. I scurried back to the rehearsal, told Harold I would have to give the interview after all, then scurried back again to the *Times Higher Educational Supplement* lady for the interview which was, as these things always are, amazingly tedious, enlivened only by losses of control on my part – when, for example, she informed me that a critic had pronounced the moral of my plays to be that education and intelligence were absolutely worthless, as they didn't help you to cope with the messiness of life, which led me into a harangue against the critic, on the grounds – I believe – that his own life (what I knew of it) was disordered beyond belief, as was his writing, in which there wasn't a shred of evidence to suggest that he had even a passing acquaintance with intelligence or education. I went on to say that it didn't seem to me the function of plays, mine or anyone else's, to help people cope with the messiness of life – my prime example here being Tolstoy, my point being that *writing Anna Karenina* didn't teach Tolstoy how to cope with anything, least of all himself. He was not only a mess himself, but the main messiness in the lives of quite a few others – i.e. his wife, his children, his friends. So did *she*, the *Times Higher Educational Supplement* lady, or rather the critic that she'd adduced, really think that *reading Anna Karenina* was going to reduce human messiness? Actually, I have an idea I spoke loudly as well as angrily, and that my frequent use of the words 'mess' and 'messiness' must have given the impression to coffee drinkers in the foyer that I was upbraiding the *THES* lady for her personal habits. For the rest, it was mainly routine question and answer (apart from another outburst, on the recent architectural barbarities of Cambridge). When we'd finished I scurried back to the theatre.*

Harold had just finished, and was organising lunch with Nick Le Prevost and Ian Ogilvy to disclose the news of the cut. I particularly dreaded Nick's response because, though he has been consistently intelligent and clear-minded and therefore very helpful about the text, he has also been resolute about lines that he doesn't think ought to go. And the Martina section is a very long one. We sat down at a table, ordered some wine, talked intensely on a number of subjects unrelated to our main concern – life, family life, art, some show that Ian Ogilvy had seen, the fact that Nick had the squitters and was constantly running to the lavatory, which I attributed to a chemical-free vegan's dinner he'd had the night before; that he attributed to a sandwich bar he'd visited when we were rehearsing at the Clarendon the day before. Finally Harold worked his way into a little speech about our moving towards clarification of the text – hadn't *quite* arrived there yet – this, he hoped, was to be the last major revision. 'Now.' He cleared his throat. Harold always clears his throat on such occasions. 'Now I'll turn you over to Simon, who will discuss the cut that we are all gathered here to discuss.' I said, 'Gentlemen, we are here to discuss an execution,' which I hoped was sufficiently facetious to pave the way to a warm and friendly conversation about killing off the cat, though really knowing that however warm and friendly the conversation might be, there were difficulties ahead. I was therefore slightly *bouleversé* to discover that the two actors not only accepted the cut, but welcomed it with rapacious eagerness.

My only objection to the passage was that it held up the dramatic drive of the scene. But it turned out that Nick Le Prevost hated the passage because he found it extremely difficult to do – it came, he asserted, in the wrong place. Whereupon Harold said,

* In fact the interview that came out in the *THES* is the only one I've ever given that accurately reported everything I said, and showed me a self I recognised (with the temper left out). A doff of the hat to the lady from the *THES*.

'Yes, it's whimsical, isn't it?' He went on to say that when he'd first read the play, he had had serious reservations about Martina and had hinted as much to me. If he had, I must say I'd forgotten it.* Then Ian Ogilvy said that he hated sitting through the speech because it had never seemed relevant, and he didn't know what expression he was meant to assume. It was really rather extraordinary. The two actors and the director competed with each other in slanging the speech that I had only been apprehensive about cutting for the actors' sake. Furthermore, their vocabulary was distinctly wounding – the word 'silly' crossed someone's lips at some point. So, far from having a tough battle to get the speech out, I was faced with an unflatteringly comprehensive victory.† I read out the few lines that were needed to make the cut work. They wrote them down and with the matter settled, we all had lunch. After which, we rehearsed the cut, then got ready for our first run-through.

Harold sat on the left of the stalls, I sat on the right, several rows behind him, feeling both sick and fatalistic. Did we or did we not have a play? If we did, what sort of play was it? A good one? A bad one? A run-of-the-mill one? The first act was OK, I thought. In fact, more than OK. What delighted me most was that all the work done on the text over the previous three weeks hadn't made the play worse, it had actually improved it. Harold was equally delighted. We agreed that the second act was bound to be a bit of a disaster, especially with the large Martina cut coming up, but settled down to it with almost complacent gloominess. But the second act was also OK. In fact, more than OK. So the whole play was OK, more than OK. Of course, not all the surplus fat has been cut off. There is lots more to be done. But, for me, the important thing is that the text is right, and once the text is right, other things begin to fall rapidly into place. Which means that the weeks of working in the dark, changing lines, making cuts, fretting about the performances, but all in bits and pieces, not really knowing what the effect would be when everything was seen in relation to

* Checking through the transcripts, I confess that Harold was telling the truth. He'd made the point at our first L'Epicure dinner in fact. (See page 15–16.)

† For the full (and in my view much maligned) Martina speech, see Appendix C, page 168.

everything else, hadn't been wasted. We'd been working our way towards finding the play, and now we'd got it.*

Everyone had a cup of tea, not saying much. Nobody ever seems to say much after a run-through. Harold gave a few notes, then ran out of steam. I think he was emotionally exhausted and also wanted to think about a number of things before commenting on them. We went upstairs to the canteen and had another cup of tea while waiting for the wig lady. Simon Williams, who has made so many happy contributions,† came over to the bar, to which we had now removed ourselves, and said that the chief pleasure of the run-through for the actors was that they had all found themselves *quite* liking the play again, after having gone off it for a long time. When I looked slightly surprised, Clive Francis said, 'Oh, don't take it as an insult. It's a compliment really. Because that's the truth. Let's speak the truth.' Which seemed to me more Humphry's voice than Clive's. On these occasions, I suspect I prefer Clive's to Humphry's, the truth being something I like to keep at bay until I'm ready to face up to it by myself, alone with a drink.

The wig lady eventually arrived, extremely late as a matter of fact, and held court at a table. On being asked whether she knew the play, she said, 'Oh, yes, of course I do.' On being asked whether she'd read it, she admitted that she hadn't. 'At least, not all the way through.' But somebody had obviously given her its gist because she talked confidently about its time span, then did some measurements of Bob East's head, Bob East being nominated for a wig, then did some more on Nina Thomas's head, Nina requiring virtually a wig per scene.

Harold and I drove back to Notting Hill Gate, talking of various things, some good, some that needed attention, in the production. What we both felt, as we admitted to each other, was that whatever the public future of the play might be, we were on our way

---

* Actually we hadn't. When casting for the American production I found myself rewriting the whole play – not for any American audience, but because I was dissatisfied with it.

† Two others I still remember: one when he said, 'I think I can help the dialogue out here a bit if I do –', accompanied by a gesture, presumably intended to support the dialogue by distracting attention from it; the other when he said, 'I think I can take the curse off this scene if I do –' I can't remember again what he did to take the curse off the scene, or whether he succeeded.

to realising our own understanding of it. It was a nice little journey. We stopped to look at a house in Addison Road where Joe Losey had once shot a film. A strange house of Victorian lavatorial architecture, with lots of green and purple glazing outside, of the kind that you expect to find inside. I got off at Notting Hill Gate and came home, had dinner with Beryl, and dictated this. I still feel pretty good, though knowing that tomorrow I will probably be back to my usual desperation. I hope to God it will be desperation and not despair. But then tomorrow is Saturday. There will be a brief rehearsal in the morning (the first time on a Saturday), and then I will take myself off to Lord's. So everything should be all right. At least tomorrow.

(From now on rehearsals took on a different tempo. With a week to go before previews,* Harold called a run-through every day, not all of them as gratifying as the first one. Indeed, the very next one, on the following Monday, I describe as seeming to take place 'under water, muffled, blurred, frantic and drowning', but only, I think, because our expectations had been raised and we (I, anyway) became impatient if progress, *visible* progress, wasn't being made from day to day. I continued to do work on the script, at one point, about two days before we opened, presenting Harold, whom I'd tracked down to a restaurant where he was lunching with Judy, with a newly rewritten scene that I wanted him to incorporate that afternoon. He folded my pages (I had only the one copy) and slipped them into his briefcase, commenting that we should wait and see, his own view being that it would probably work as well, but no better, than the scene I'd been trying to replace it with, which the actors had now been rehearsing for nearly five weeks. The scene as it was only embarrassed me, he said, because I knew it was coming. But an audience, happening on it for the first time, might be surprised, even – which was what we wanted – shocked. Then there was a tussle with Clive Francis. He became remote for a day or two, evidently pondering something,

---

* It was the day after the first run-through, Saturday, that I discovered I'd mislaid a week in memory (see footnote on page 101), having gone back at the end of a week and started it again numerically. I've always had a good sense of watch time, a lousy one of calendar time, which presumably means something, i.e. living for the minute, not for the future?

then put to Harold that he felt that the North Country accent he'd adopted to get away from the Cambridge queen had served its purpose, he'd now like to abandon it. I suppose he disliked the idea of continuing to employ what had after all been a ruse, now that he was in command of the real Humphry. I sympathised with him, though I'd become fond of the accent, and Harold, who'd also become fond of it, encouraged him to stay with it on the grounds that it had long since ceased to be a ruse, had been integrated into the part, was a fascinating reminder of Humphry's background. But the general movement I believed at the time (and still believe) was forward, the actors increasingly at ease, the text increasingly refined, Harold in full control – although not always of me: I conclude one entry halfway through the week with the hope that 'Beryl will drug my food, or even knock me out with a hammer, anything for the sake of a rest from myself. And for her sake too. And the children's. And Harold's. And Hazel's.')*

19 June

Yet another exhausting day, perhaps the most exhausting so far because of the heat. The air conditioning isn't on in the theatre although, perversely it seems to me, they've taken the roof off, or anyway somehow opened it, so that there is a constant whistling of wind. But what wind? No discernible wind down below, just its whistle to disturb the actors, but no change in temperature to cool them. Just whistle and heat. This isn't flaming June, but sultry, resentful, punitive June.

We began in the morning with a dress display, all the actors turn-ing up in their costumes, vanishing to change them, reappearing. There was one moment when Stuart and Peter both stood on stage, shoulder to shoulder, in ties of similar design; one blue with a red stripe down it; the other red with a white stripe down it. The effect was to make them look like members, brothers and members, of the Artillery Club, or old boys of a minor public school. Apart from such details, Liz has done well, as far as one can judge when a parade of clothes is bound to be an intrusion, an intrusion nevertheless crucial to the success of the play. The only reward for meticulous

* Hazel is my dog. See page 10.

attention to costumes is that they *aren't* noticed by the audience.

Then the music. We listened to Bach, specified for the beginning, and to Wagner, specified at other points in the play. The choice of Bach was fairly simple, but with the Wagner we found ourselves listening several times to a passage from *Parsifal*. It would have been apropos, if I hadn't used *Parsifal* in a previous play of mine, *Otherwise Engaged*. In the afternoon we did a run-through. The Bach we'd chosen, when amplified, killed the opening dialogue, making Stuart and Marigold seem as if they were miming their emotions, as in a silent movie, but without benefit of subtitles.

After rehearsals we went to the multi-storey car park to collect Harold's car. He was saying, 'I don't know if you've noticed one thing about my approach to the actors . . .' Then he stopped. He stared with intelligent vacancy at a completely empty spot in the lot and said, 'Oh my God!' After checking a couple of levels above us and the level below us, we went down to the car park gates where Harold reported that his car had been stolen. I was interested in the contrast between my response, which was merely one of irritation at not getting to the tube station as quickly as I'd hoped, and his. Because I don't drive, I have no interest in cars at all. I see them merely as taxis that people who drive have to keep in the garage, as opposed to taxis that fail to come when people who don't drive phone them up. But Harold's Mercedes is some seventeen, I think it is, years old.* In fact the same car that he had shown me shortly after its delivery the first time I met him. It had meant absolutely nothing at all to me then. Simply a gleaming and expensive-looking car of no particular denomination, that he was clearly very proud of. But between its purchase and its theft, it has become an antique or vintage car, to be even more cherished. All I've vaguely noticed, although I've been driven in it many times, is that it has a rather elegant, wooden dashboard, and smells of leather. So I had to make an imaginative leap to grasp what Harold must have felt about his car – much as I felt about my fountain pen (which I loved for seventeen years), I supposed, when burglars stole it from my desk about six months ago. I made a puny effort at such a leap, then left him dealing with the

* See page 38.

prospect of the police, and got a taxi – it took hours to draw one to me – and came home, where, after dinner, Beryl pointed out my stars (Patrick Walker in the *Standard*. I'm a Libran): 'Sometimes it is necessary to be cruel to be kind, especially if you now instinctively feel you are spending too much time trying to get *someone else* to get to grips with a particular problem.' I'm sure he's right, but which particular 'someone else' does he mean?

20 June

The day began with Harold phoning to ask me if I was going to the Dramatists' Guild dinner on 6 July. Well, it actually began with Harold phoning and getting Beryl. Before handing him over, she asked him about the car. He skated over that with an intimation that everything had turned out all right, and requested in a deep and husky voice to be passed over to me as quickly as possible, implying that there was serious business to talk about. The serious business was whether I was going to the Dramatists' Guild dinner on 6 July. I said I was, then of course asked about the car. He said, 'Yes, well – uh – very odd thing. Rather embarrassing actually is that – well – the fact of the matter is – well, it is slightly embarrassing –' he made a sound somewhere between a cough and a laugh – 'I didn't park it in the car park at all. I actually parked it on the road. In fact I was walking away with the chap at the gate to report the theft to the police. I suddenly smote my forehead because I suddenly remembered that I'd actually parked it in the street. And there the car was. I saw it there actually.' So that was that.

The afternoon period of rehearsal was particularly difficult, at least for me. We seemed to go through an interminable stretch when either the moves seemed to expose the dialogue (do I mean by this, didn't sufficiently obscure its inadequacies?) or the dialogue seemed to expose the moves (by which I suppose I mean, sometimes made them seem irrelevant or over-precise). I was at my fussiest, quite unable to prevent myself interrupting with suggestion after suggestion, and so stretching and stretching Harold's patience. Every time I got up to make a point, I would be conscious of Harold's fingers rapping on the stage. (He stood in the front row of the stalls; I sat beside him.) It must have been exasperating for him to feel that a scene had been properly dealt with, and then the clatter of the seat going back as I stood up, stammering slightly. I know that he knows that I always assume a stammer before trying to wriggle my way into a point which he knows also, knowing me very well, I am determined to make.

The day was partly redeemed at the bar after rehearsals. Simon Williams (of course) said that he was doing a charity show fairly soon, and that he did think on the whole that, as actors weren't paid for charity shows, they really should be allowed to choose their own material. After all, he said, when you're paid, you expect to do any crap, making a kind of gesture towards me, as the author of the crap he was currently being paid to do.

21 June

Twenty-fourth day of rehearsal. Always so difficult to get the day into perspective. In fact, about the only thing I really remember, apart from waiting interminably at Harold's for a taxi that never arrived, is the bizarre fracas over the cold beef. Why? Anyway, what happened was this. Before going back to the Clarendon to rehearse (there was a matinee in the theatre) we had our lunch in the Lyric self-service restaurant. Harold, who has a particular passion for the beef there – as indeed have I, because it's very good – was told very sweetly, but quite firmly, by the girl behind the counter that he couldn't have any beef because 'the staff', she said, 'isn't allowed to have beef'. Harold said, 'What!' She said, 'The staff isn't allowed to have beef, I'm afraid, the staff isn't allowed.' 'What do you mean?' Harold said. 'Well, it's just that the staff isn't allowed to have beef.' Whereupon Harold became extremely angry and demanded further explanation, e.g. 'What do you mean? What are you talking about?' etc., until everyone in the queue had become very attentive. When he'd finished, the girl behind the counter said, 'You see, it means if – um – you have the beef, you'll have to pay the *proper* price for it.' Whereupon Harold, when he had emerged from his state of shock, said that he 'would *indeed* pay, he would *indeed* pay' the proper price for the cold beef and, on paying the full price, was allowed to pass with his platter piled, less high than I suspect he would have liked, with cold beef. There was an altercation, which I slightly missed as I was behind him in the queue to do with some girl with a foreign accent reprimanding him for something.

Anyway, we sat down at the table. Various people passed by, functionaries of the theatre. Harold called one or two of them over to register a complaint about the incident, his point being that it was acutely embarrassing to be treated as if he were one of the winos that hang out just below us in Hammersmith. Come in off the streets, so to speak, in the hope of a cheap, or even free, platter of cold beef. While this was going on the actors came in, and see-ing us engaged in a series of important-looking conferences, began to settle down at tables with glasses of wine, coffee, etc. Harold, noticing this and suddenly realising that we were on our way to being late for rehearsals, broke off and said, 'I think we should go over immediately, don't you, to set the example?' So forth we went to the Clarendon, Harold leading the way, Nick Le Prevost and I trudging behind him, the other actors fanning out behind us, down Hammersmith Broadway, through the traffic and the dreary heat of this summer, up the stairs of the old Clarendon, into the rehearsal room, where it was at least cool.

I suppose I thought the run-through was OK but I'm not sure I can tell any more.

22 June

The twenty-fifth day of rehearsal. I'll try not to preface it with 'Another exhausting day.' We were back in the Clarendon with a run-through at 10.30, which I contrived to miss because what with this and that – a late dinner and a few drinks when I got home – I was so tired from the previous day, tired and sluggish, that I actually felt unable to propel myself towards my duty.

I got there in time to have lunch with Harold, who said that it had been very much a ten-thirty-in-the-morning kind of run-through; there was a great deal of struggling, over-compensation, etc. There was also a problem with Nick Le Prevost in that, having got rid of all the gloom, he had begun to get a trifle cute. I began to argue that I would rather cute than gloomy, then remembered that, as I hadn't seen the run-through, I was hardly in a position to debate the matter. It was a very long lunch break because the actors needed time to recuperate. Nick Le Prevost ordered a bottle of wine for everyone, and then found nobody prepared to drink it with him because it was warm. He clearly drank a bit too much himself, and then drank a little too much of a small bottle or two he ordered for himself subsequently.* He became a bit strange. On the way to the Clarendon, he was extremely impassioned on the question of the reselection process for Labour MPs, who, he said, were now more representative of the people that had elected them. Well, I said, they were certainly representative of the views of the minority that could be bothered to turn out for constituency meetings, but not necessarily of the thousands of people who had far better things to do with their lives than attend them. He took this up very vigorously, and then launched into a hectic sermon about my apparent unwillingness to do anything to change the world, a flaw of mine that he clearly took quite personally. By the time we got to rehearsal, he had become almost belligerent. Nevertheless, the rehearsal proceeded amicably until Marigold's outburst in Act One† – the moment when she turns on Humphry and says, 'You don't always know everything.' Harold said that he thought that there was something wrong with the way in which the other characters reacted to this; they took it too comfortably. Whereupon Nick stood up and said he wanted to dispute the way the scene had been directed. He thought it was wrong. Harold said, yes, that's precisely why he wanted to look at the scene again, because it was wrong. But Nick, unaware that they were in perfect harmony, went on building up his case. In no time at all, he was making a speech about sexual politics, his specific point being, I think, that everybody's reaction to Marigold's outburst was patronising, as if they (therefore we, the play, the director and the production) were saying, 'There, there, little girl. We all know women are prone to work themselves up.' As a matter of fact, I suspect Nick put his finger on the problem. The trouble was that he was more interested in continuing the debate, even though there was nobody really to continue it with, than with getting on with the scene. Harold, handling him with a potent combination of severity and diplomacy, said we would return to that particular scene tomorrow.

* This, I hope I need hardly say, was not only a rare occurrence, it was unique.

† For this line in context, see Appendix D, page 168.

But this is certainly the most gruelling of my experiences in the theatre, not because it's more tense, but because the tension seems to have been going on much longer. Anyway, on this self-pitying note, I end, reminding myself that tomorrow, instead of doing half a day's rehearsal, which is what I had hoped, and then spending the rest of the afternoon at Lord's, we are going to do a full day. So I'll probably be able to get only an hour or so in at cricket afterwards. Not at Lord's in fact. The Oval.

Saturday, 23 June

Twenty-sixth day of rehearsal, I believe. And, my God, how deeply sick I've become of this diary, but, having gone so far, I suppose I'll have to go on to the end.* I haven't really anything to report of great interest today. We were due to begin rehearsal at 11.15 back in the theatre. I arrived rather late because the taxi chose to swoop with great rapidity to Notting Hill Gate, and then take a number of rather eccentric detours around to the Lyric Theatre. At the end, I ran up the stairs to the auditorium, my heart pounding, to find that the little bit that I had particularly wanted to see, which was the exchange in Act One, Scene Two, between Martin and Stuart about Marigold's pregnancy, had already been worked on, and that the actors were sitting around waiting for the next bit of rehearsal. This didn't take place for another fifteen minutes because the other actors had been given the wrong call. Odd how valuable fifteen minutes of rehearsal seems to be when it isn't being used. When they turned up, we proceeded to implement a few notes, look at various passages, particularly the passage we'd had to abandon yesterday because of Nick's bout of disputatiousness.

I had suggested a slight addition so that after Marigold's outburst to Humphry – 'You don't know everything. You don't always know everything' – she could then retract slightly, saying, 'Sorry.' Nina tried it. Harold suggested that she make the 'sorry' harder, more a dismissive 'sorry' than a request for forgiveness. He went on, trying to explain what he meant about the difference in tone to Nina, who sat staring at him like a bewildered puppy, com-

---

* I reminded myself frequently that Simon Callow had reported himself – in his admirable book, *Being an Actor* (published by Methuen) – unable to continue his diary of rehearsals after the tenth day. This helped to keep me going.

pletely silently, without responding. He explained again, she continued to look at him like a bewildered puppy, until he ran out of explanation and stood gazing at her – like a bewildered dog confronted by a bewildered puppy. Finally he said, 'Well, what do you think?' and she said, 'Well, I think we'd do better without the "sorry" if it's going to involve all that.' Her timing must have been brilliant. Anyway, there was a lot of laughter.

The first act was very sprightly, so much so that I began to notice actors' characteristics: Simon Williams has a habit, for example, of sniffing between speeches; Nick's hands make various courtly, expostulatory gestures, which I think are quite redundant. Ian Ogilvy also sniffs. So there's a lot of sniffing going on and a lot of unnecessary gesturing. But the fact that I was able to notice it was, I thought, a fairly good sign, or so it seemed to me at the interval, when I had to heave myself upstairs, carrying a chair, with an Antipodean-sounding photographer from *Time Out*, for a photograph to accompany the other day's interview. I was actually so tired and so busy thinking of sniffs and gestures, that I didn't give myself fully to the experience of being photographed. I sat in a kind of blankness, initially, and then found myself being commanded to lie on the floor with a typewriter beside me, amidst the wreckage of a table and spilled paper as a complement, I suppose, to the poster. I then went downstairs and had lunch with the rest of the company.

The whole cast was at the table, and a fairly jolly, perhaps too jolly, half an hour was spent before we went back to run Act Two, which therefore got off to a rather ropy start.

28 June

This evening Harold started on the lighting, which at this stage is an interminable process. All the actors had gone. There were just the stagehands on the set to give an indication of the effect the lighting would have. I kept Harold company until one of the PR girls came in and asked me if I'd do an interview for a BBC arts programme which should also be reviewing the play. I'm not at all keen. There is nothing more likely to make you look an absolute dolt and duck of a fellow than to give an interview in which you are encouraged to talk enthusiastically about your work, only to be followed by a review putting you emphatically in your place. Especially if the reviewer is someone I've come across once or twice, and is the author of quite a few unproduced plays. Of course much better writers than me can fail to get their plays produced, but given the way of the world I'd rather be reviewed by a green-grocer or even a professional critic than by an unproduced play-wright, whose main thought during the evening is likely to be, 'Why him and not me?' Of course I may be maligning the chap in question. In fact, I hope I am. He may have several plays in the pipeline to the West End at the moment, or he may come to the theatre in the spirit of one anxious to salute a fellow vineyard-labourer who's had better luck than he's had . . .

I offered these ruminations to Harold, pointing out that we couldn't stop the review by either Raban or Raven (by this time I was against either of them) but that I could at least avoid the fall-guy interview, was in fact inclined to do so, what did he think? He said 'I think you're quite right. Especially the way *you* do inter-views.' This seems to me a bit hard, as the only thing I've ever believed wrong in my interviews is the interviewer. For example the chap from the *Daily Telegraph*, many years ago, who began, 'Well, Mr Gray, or may I call you Simon, is this going to be another of your disasters?' I told Harold rather coldly that I'd continue to think about it. Which reminds me that tomorrow I'm having lunch With Michael Owen of the *Standard*. At least that'll be an interview without a review. Altogether, tomorrow will be a long day. At two there is a technical rehearsal with the lighting, the doors, entrances, exits being worked through. It will probably go on until midnight. For me, it'll be an unspeakably boring day. There is never any point in my being present at technical rehearsals, but I can never bear to stay away from them, convinced as I am that there will be lots of little things, important little things, to notice. And of course it's followed by the dress rehearsal, which is followed by the first preview – the first performance before an audience. So how can I possibly keep away? But what on earth is the real point of going?

Saturday, 30 June

Running four days behind on the diary, having been too involved in the previews and too exhausted when they'd finished, to make it to the tape recorder at night. I'll do my best to recall events as they happened, from the dress rehearsal through to last night's (Saturday's) preview.

Tuesday

Had lunch with Michael Owen of the *Standard*. A convivial man who seems to know a lot about my plays, and the sheer nobility of my life. There were two revealing incidents, however. We were talking about football, which he loves, and had got on to Liverpool's European Cup Final. Both our minds went blank. We couldn't remember who Liverpool had beaten and where they had beaten them, except that it had been on the opponents' ground. Michael Owen suddenly remembered. 'Roma,' he said. 'Liverpool beat Roma,' lifting his glass with rather charming insolence to the Italian waiter who had just come to our table. When the interview came out yesterday (Friday), this was reported as follows: 'He [that's me] raised a glass in an Italian restaurant to Liverpool's recent triumph in the European Cup and tried to remember which team they had beaten in the final. "Roma," said the Italian waiter icily, and turned on his heel.'

We also had a conversation about the Leavis/Snow controversy in which I quoted Snow's 'We die alone' and Leavis's rejoinder, 'Yes, but we also live alone.' In the interview both these observations are attributed to me, not so much out of context as in no context at all. 'We die alone and we live alone,' I suddenly and meaninglessly pronounce. Thus presenting myself, I think, as an impoverished but self-important philosopher. He also attributes to me two daughters, an error that my son, Ben, has taken badly, speculating on whether it constituted grounds for a libel action; which my daughter Lucy took badly.

After lunch, I went to the technical rehearsal, which didn't finish until midnight. All I remember about it was my relief at seeing the revolve work smoothly.

Wednesday

On Wednesday we had the dress rehearsal, about which again I remember little except that we seemed to be in reasonable shape. Our main worry was Nick Le Prevost's voice, which didn't carry properly, even in the empty theatre. Also he was tending to withdraw from lines. I suspect that after so much work in front of the television cameras it will take him time to find a natural vocal level in the theatre. The last thing we want, though, is any projecting from the actors. I suspect Nick is too canny for that. Anyway, Harold and I decided to keep calm about it for the moment.*

Thursday

The first preview. Inevitably it was a difficult day to get through. There was a dress rehearsal in the afternoon (Nick's voice was OK) after which Harold gave his notes. The actors seemed fairly confident, some of them positively eager to get before an audience, and Harold is always supremely good at controlling the atmosphere, presenting an image of benevolent reassurance, though I sometimes wish he wouldn't wear his customary black for these occasions. I try to take my cue from him, not speaking unless I'm sure I'll be able to stop my voice from quavering, going in for little jokes and amusing asides, but of course, for most of the time, I'm sick with terror – at least until about an hour before the curtain goes up, when I become almost preternaturally calm, with a gallows fatalism on which not even whisky has an effect. Harold gives no

---

* We probably both had in mind the first preview of another play of mine, when someone (connected with the management? a member of the audience? an usherette? – we never found out who) smuggled a complaint through to the cast during the interval about their audibility, or rather lack of it. Most of the actors, knowing the hazards of playing before an audience in the theatre for the first time, which includes not yet having discovered the right vocal level for that particular theatre, took it in their stride, either making slight adjustments or deciding to ignore the complaint until the problem could be considered next day, with the director. But one of the actresses, inexperienced, and convinced that the note had an entirely personal application, looked and sounded from that time forth like a participant in a speech-training experiment, walking stiffly around the stage, delivering her lines with a ghastly precision, not so much throwing her voice out at the audience, as throwing each word out, as if it were an egg that had to be caught, unbroken, in the stalls. However hard Harold worked to relax her every afternoon in rehearsals, the terror gripped her all over again every night. I don't think she ever succeeded in giving a natural performance. I learnt two things from that experience. Never let anyone get a note to actors during intervals of first previews (or any other previews or performances, come to that), using any weapons that come to hand to stop them. And never panic over inaudibility – deal with it in a casually matter-of-fact manner in rehearsal, with some such phrase as, 'And, oh by the way, there might be a *slight* problem about whether you're actually being heard . . .'

indication of strain at all, although an alert observer might notice that his Adam's apple becomes restless, and that he seems to walk more upright than ever, sometimes even inclining slightly backwards. The truth is that both of us, I believe, felt quite proud of what we'd put on the stage, but had no idea what an audience would make of it. Over the weeks of rehearsals, lines and situations cease being funny or sad in themselves, first reactions to scenes are long forgotten.*

I was sitting at the very end, right, of the first row of the dress circle. Harold was sitting at the very end, left, of the same row. Beryl and Antonia were down in the stalls. It was a full house, and it went OK for a first preview – more than OK. The first act had dead areas in it caused by, or I hope caused by, the audience not properly hearing Nick Le Prevost (which also meant of course they couldn't always make proper sense of what the other actors said when replying to him). But I reminded myself of everything Harold and I had reminded ourselves of about vocal problems, etc., and also took into account that the character of Stuart is in some ways a reticent one, and furthermore that for Nick there is the extra problem of having just come from prolonged television work, and in other words I wanted to kill him actually. I was convinced that he was reducing the value of the evening by about fifty per cent. But the curtain fell to decent applause, and Harold, running around the back of the circle to the exit before anyone else could move and I nipping out just ahead of him as I was right by the exit – it occurred to me subsequently that anyone in the audience seeing us would probably have thought that he was chasing me – made it to a little room on the side, which we'd marked as our hideout, where there was wine and Scotch, waiting for us, and where we were joined by our wives. Gravely, over drinks, we

---

* During the early rehearsals of *Otherwise Engaged* Alan Bates and Nigel Hawthorne were physically incapable of getting past a moment when Nigel Hawthorne, playing a minor-public-school teacher, had to step forward and announce aggressively, 'I am the latent pederast.' Both Alan and Nigel doubled up with laughter again and again. Weeks later, when the same moment arrived before an audience, they were bewildered by its reacting exactly as they once had done. Within a few nights they'd not only come to expect the response, but had incorporated it smoothly into their performances, and might even, if they had been less puritanical performers, have found themselves milking it by prolonging it a little.

anatomised the way it was going so far, with sedate references to the question of Nick's voice. We got back just before the curtain went up.

The second act seemed to go OK too, I thought, with Nick vocally fuller, the whole company gaining in command, and everything unravelling at the right tempo. There was laughter, sometimes scattered, sometimes collective – the line about Nick's offstage media rival ('Nappies' Harrop) leaving his television programme to become theatre critic on the *Sunday Times* where 'they seem to be impressed by his lack of qualifications' brought the house down. But I have to admit that I wasn't as touched by Humphry's death as I have been through virtually every run-through and dress rehearsal. Perhaps the first act wasn't sufficiently light and flowing for the darknesses of the second act to gather. We lurched, I felt, from mood to mood. But the audience was lively and interested, and there was a nice, full-blooded response at the end. I didn't notice anybody leaving before it, anyway.

We went back to the little room after the curtain, Harold and I again doing our Tom and Jerry to the exit. The mood in the room was pretty good, high-spirited, a general sense of confidence – the play obviously works, is there to be liked or disliked on its own terms – although with work to be done. What I really mean by this is that if we are going to be hated it won't be for having failed to realise what we wanted to realise. It would be genuine (or fraudulent) hatred for the thing itself. In fact, there was a muted air of celebration, much assisted by Beryl's and Antonia's pleasure in the evening. After the theatre cleared, we went to the bar to see the actors. I think their spirits had begun to rise after the first tentative few minutes, when they'd begun to take in that the audience was laughing, thus establishing at the very least that the audience was listening. Laughs are a perpetual trap for actors. I hold primly to the view that any of my plays could be played without getting a single laugh, and still keep the audience's attention. But then I don't have to go up on stage and do it, do I? And I'm not sure that I'd like to sit through the experience in the audience, either.

Among the people in the business hanging about and having a drink was an actor of about sixty with whom I'd worked a few years ago. Good actor. Very good actor. He came up to me, puffing on his pipe and looking extremely wise, wisely worried was what he looked, and gave me a note about Nick's inaudibility, especially in the first act. He was forthwith replaced by another actor of about the same age, also extremely good and with whom I'd also worked, who gave me a note about Nick Le Prevost's inaudibility, especially in the first act. So these two sterling old pros confirmed what every member of the audience knew, that Nick Le Prevost had been from time to time inaudible, especially in the first act.

We stayed with the actors for a while, then went on to dinner at a restaurant near Hammersmith called the Trattoo. I was slightly drunk, as is usual at that time of night under these circumstances. Under most circumstances, in fact. I expect Harold was too. The alcohol that had made no impression on us up to and during, and even immediately after the preview (although we were adding to it all the time, in the interval and then in the room afterwards, and then at the bar) suddenly broke through the dam of terrified propriety and sluiced through all parts of the system. Or something like that. We went from feeling and seeming stone-cold sober to being and behaving drunkishly, only a few minutes after sitting down at the table to a fresh bottle of wine. Neither Beryl nor Antonia was the slightest bit affected – by drink, I mean; they were probably affected by us – because (a) they're by nature more abstemious, and (b) are more sensible and grown-up and (c) for all their wifely devotion and sympathy, hadn't quite had the day we'd had, although I don't mean (c) to cancel out the tribute intended in (a) and (b).

I settled into a long compulsive whine about this and that, an actor here, a move there, a weakness in the text, what about the lighting in Act Two, Scene Two, and the music at the beginning and the end sort of stuff, until I noticed that Harold had gone absolutely still. Rigid. He looked either very ill or very furious, I couldn't make out which. Or was it both? I asked him what the matter was, had I said something? Certainly no one else had said anything because I hadn't given them a chance. He said, 'Nothing,' grimly. 'Really?' I said, and proceeded to put that right with a denunciation of Harold for his glumness, and more than that, for his smouldering glumness, then loped off for a pee. When I got back he was delivering a series of pronouncements to Beryl and Antonia like a fighting general in the last stages of battle fatigue, dealing with two lady journalists down from the Hilton, then sat silently for a moment, then said he wasn't feeling too well, and had better go. He then left. Antonia, lingering only to mention that actually he'd woken that morning feeling rather ropy, followed. I turned my attention to my wife, with whom I was clearly still on speaking terms. At least *I* went on speaking. Analysing, worrying, complaining . . .

Friday

Hungover but back to work at the Lyric. Harold and I began 'by apologising to each other. He attributed his condition to dyspepsia consequent on too much white wine. I've observed that quite a few people, amongst them myself, consider that white wine is an alternative to alcohol, which is probably a mistake.* For one thing, I'm certain it does far more damage to one's stomach than, for instance, Scotch does. The trouble with Scotch, on the other hand, is that it makes you drunker quicker, and it also makes you, or me anyway, a great deal more volatile emotionally. By which I mean ill-tempered and unpleasant. When we'd done blaming our drinks for ruining our wives' evening out, we went on to consider a number of textual changes, small ones that had arisen where we'd felt the audience was failing to follow the story. We decided that clarifications were necessary all over the place, in fact, then discussed how to approach Nick Le Prevost on the problem of his voice, deciding finally to tell him that there were places where he wasn't being heard, and then specifying them. We had various other notes, Harold's recorded on page after page of the small Asprey's pad he uses, mine swimming about somewhere between memory and unconsciousness, to be groped for. Then we went to rehearsal, Harold opening with a small speech summarising how he thought the evening had gone, then going on to the notes, and then running little passages where the text needed pointing, moves needed correcting, etc.

At lunchtime I had to give a brief interview for a television programme. The interviewer was a great friend of my younger

---

* Best exemplified by a young but well-known journalist. After, even by his own standards, a very heavy night, he was asked by his hostess what he wanted for breakfast. 'Oh, God,' he said, 'I'd better not have anything to drink. Just a glass of white wine, please.'

brother, Piers. She has always struck me as an alert and intelligent young woman, but her questions, probably perfectly reasonable, really, seemed, at least when put to me on the set of *The Common Pursuit,* with a camera aimed at my large, not to say sumptuous nose, like a parody of all the worst questions I've ever been asked since journalists started asking me questions. There was, for example, a version of 'What does it feel like to work with Harold Pinter?' and a version of 'What gives you the idea for a play?', along with more specific probings – 'Don't you think people might find your preoccupation with five Cambridge friends incestuous?' With the first preview only some hours behind me, I still managed a more than passable imitation of La Fontaine's frog competing with the bull, swelling with fury and self-righteousness until finally bursting out with a statement to the effect that no one of any sense wanted to hear playwrights, or any other writers, talking about their work. The work was *there,* wasn't it? What could the author say that would change it by a jot? Or a tittle? The producer, roaming about behind the camera, raised his hand when I'd got to the end of this ill-natured bombast, declaring that here at last was something he could use. God knows how I'll turn out.*

After this, lunch with Harold, Harold not drinking, my keeping him company with a glass of wine or two, then back to rehearsals, on to a second interview.

This was for the BBC arts programme to precede the review by the unproduced playwright. I was under the impression that I'd refused to do it, but one of the PR girls appeared, flustered, to say that the producer had arrived, and was waiting for me. I can't remember what he looked like, though I retain a vague impression of spectacles, a small, clean young face, a tie, and a recording device, which he tucked away on the promised dot. He had the great advantage of not having seen the play, and seemed healthily unfamiliar with my work. Most of his questions were of a general nature, and I didn't mind the interview nearly as much as the lunchtime caper.† On into the preview, after a brief exchange at the bar with Harold, still not drinking. Again, a good house, assisted by a vocally clear Nick Le Prevost. In fact, he was fully there, audibly

* I didn't turn out, apparently. They cut the interview.

† I didn't hear the programme, so have no idea how or even if I came out.

with us, if sometimes only just. He dropped very few words, though he swallowed occasionally (this was the first time I'd really taken in the swallow) in the middle of a sentence or trapped himself in a slightly clogged rhythm, as if he were compulsively choking the words back, but these were moments apart, and he had great presence and style. I thought that the evening worked as a whole, probably for all kinds of accidental reasons – a second preview with the adrenalin still flowing from the first, along with the confidence engendered by the first having been reasonably successful. In fact it seemed to me an *almost* perfect account of the play, which is the most one can ever hope for. I was genuinely moved (as I hadn't been the night before) by the Humphry death scene, perhaps because this time the first act was fluent, the dramatic rhythms easing into each other, rather than alternating with each other. All in all I was quite pleased with myself, grateful to Harold, grateful to the cast.

Coming into the bar some way behind Harold, I passed a table at which a famous Noël Coward-type actress was sitting with a coterie of admiring johnnies that looked as if they were out of those pages in the *Daily Mail,* or wrote them even, one of whom was asking her, 'Well, tell us honestly, darling, what did you think of it? Did you enjoy it?' To which darling replied, 'Yes, I did.' (Little pause, little *moue.*) '*Quite.*' I reflected, as I unbunched my fist, that firstly this was a free country, secondly that she didn't know I could overhear her, and thirdly – and thirdly, I entertained people at the bar with my imitation of her, which was all the more effective, I believe, for the differences between our faces, hers being long and fine, mine being round and on the coarse side. I got the inflection on the '*Quite*' rather well and the pause before it, though I'm not too sure about the *moue.*

Harold and I stuck about a bit, talking to the actors, not drinking too much – he rather less than me, as he had nothing at all – then he went off to meet Antonia at the Trattoo (why?) and I had a quick dinner by myself down the road, during which I drank water and therefore returned home, to my surprise, extremely sober. Rather a wasted effort, in a way, as Beryl had gone to Guildford with Judy to see the touring production of *Butley* and she didn't get back until two in the morning, when I was in bed, deeply asleep in what no doubt looked like my usual hoggish coma. But really I'd had a calm and happy evening. We'd given a satisfying evening in the theatre, possibly even value for money. Anyway nobody, in my hearing, asked for theirs back.

Saturday

We met the company at two o'clock, to clean up entrances and exits, make a few minor adjustments to the text, etc. The two audiences had taught us a great deal, and as the actors were now completely at ease with their lines and their moves, they could make adjustments quickly. I am always deeply impressed by actors' memories, even more so by their ability to cancel memories. Moves and lines that, after six weeks of rehearsal, run-throughs and now performances, would have (I'd have thought) become habits were altered within seconds.*

We decided to leave the actors alone for the matinee, letting them play the play in the knowledge that they wouldn't receive a single note on it afterwards. I went for a walk in Holland Park, trying to look like a chap to whom sunlight and fresh air were a part of his daily routine, rather than a profound shock to his nervous system. The excitement of a production is a drug, and I'd become a junkie weeks before. Really I wanted to be back there in the dark, watching, thinking, getting exasperated; not rambling unsteadily among the Holland Park children and parents and nannies and squirrels and such. I dallied beside the pens, forcing myself to admire the peacocks, who at least had the grace to look entirely artificial, until the pubs were open and I could sit over a drink, smoke, jiggle my leg impatiently in a congenially foul atmosphere. I managed to hold out there until shortly before the evening curtain went up, met up with Harold in the bar of the theatre, went in.

The house was packed. It was very much a Saturday night audience, vastly less appreciative† than the previous night's, and

---

* A few hours before we opened *Butley* to the London press, I cut a substantial exchange, which involved Harold's finding new positions for the actors – and they'd been playing those lines, doing those moves, for three weeks out of town. But in the performance that night the exchange went so effortlessly that I couldn't remember quite where the cut had come. This has taught me never to believe a director who says it would upset the actors to make late changes.

† And were therefore either vastly more or vastly less discriminating, depending on your point of view.

the cast dealt with them as they (I hope) deserved, coarsely. There really wasn't much to be learnt from it. I sat there stoically, as did Harold. After a brief visitation to the bar, a few words with the actors, we went off to dinner, raised points about the acting, the text, in a desultory fashion. Then I went home by taxi (dropping Harold at his car *en route*) to an almost unendurably patient wife, and to bed.

Sunday

I've spent this morning struggling to recall the events from the first preview on until last night. Obviously there are blanknesses, but I believe I've recorded all I care to remember, and a bit over. I'll try from tomorrow, the last preview, to keep a daily account. There are only a few more days of the diary to go, anyway, thank God. It's a beautiful day. I'm now toddling off to the Oval to watch cricket.

Monday, 2 July

During the weekend Harold telephoned Nick Le Prevost, Clive Francis and Ian Ogilvy, and arranged to meet them in the theatre cafeteria for private talks about aspects of their performances that had grown apace since the first preview that he wanted to eliminate before the first night. When I arrived he was just moving from Nick's table to Clive's, or from Clive's to Ian's, or from Ian's to Nick's, I can't remember from which to which, but he was passing in black from one to another like a salesman from Exit. I stood at the bar, trying to look as if all my interest was in the drink (white wine) in my hand. Then we went into the theatre for notes from Saturday's performance.

The effect of Harold's consultations and notes was evident in the show. Really rather a good performance, a distinct advance on Saturday night's, though probably lacking the *fresh* confidence of Friday's. In fact it was a consolidation, just the right sort of performance to give before an opening. I wish we'd had more of them, before the opening, to give. After the show we dallied with the actors at the bar, had dinner together, compared observations, went to our respective homes. I came into my study, Beryl asleep, the children asleep, to dictate this. Tomorrow is the first night, so

I shall probably sleep well. I always do, before first nights. From which I deduce that I'll sleep my deepest the night before I'm hanged. I think this is what's called withdrawal.

Tuesday, 3 July

Woke realising that I had done nothing about first night cards and presents. I hustled over to Notting Hill Gate and spent the morning controlling my panic by looking around the shops, until I found one that specialised in Victoriana. I chose some original Victorian greetings cards, all of them yellow with age but charming (I hope) and delicately coloured. In retrospect, I don't really know whether these make appropriate presents. If not perhaps they will suffice as *mementos mori*. I then spent a considerable time at W. H. Smith's unravelling a conspiracy to prevent me from buying the right-sized envelopes. Had lunch in an Italian restaurant where I wrote on the cards, thus destroying their value, and went to the theatre for the rehearsal, which had been called for 2.30. Harold went through his notes, changed some of the blocking on the first scene, then ran Act One, Scene Two, so far the most treacherous scene in the play. I watched it alone from the upper circle, cigarettes going as usual, doing my best to concentrate on what was immediately before me rather than on what was to come. It seemed to me, though, that it had taken on a great deal of authority, Nick Le Prevost flourishing in it. Usually one rehearses before the official first night in order to give the actors specific things to think about, in other words to help their nervousness. And one's own, come to that. On this occasion, the work was, I think, valuable in itself.

Afterwards, Harold and I went back to Campden Hill Square. We wanted to watch the end of the Test match, but it finished virtually as Harold turned the set on. We missed Greenidge's magnificent 200 and whatever it was not out, catching merely a glimpse of the back of his head and his upraised bat as he entered the pavilion. Harold went up to have a bath and change, I lay on the sofa. I had come kitted out for the occasion. Dark suit, black shoes, and a dark blue tie (in my shoulder bag). I wish I had some of the bravura of the old-time playwrights. Carnations, walking stick, cigarette holders, tails, etc., or conversely, that I could start

an entirely new trend, although I don't know what it would be.*
Antonia appeared with Orlando, her seventeen-year-old son.
They'd spent the afternoon at Lord's. Orlando, being a great fan
of Greenidge, demonstrated some of the highlights of his innings.
Antonia went up to change, Harold returned in his black suit,
sombre and spruce, and watched attentively as Orlando demonstrated the Greenidge highlights again. When Antonia came back,
we had a glass of champagne. No, *they* had a glass of champagne
each, I had a couple of Scotches.

At 6.15 we set forth in the car that Harold had hired for the
evening. The show, being a press night, began at seven o'clock.
The traffic was appalling, a road somewhere having been blocked
off, no doubt to assist the flow. We arrived at quarter to seven,
later than we would have liked under the circumstances. The
foyer was full of various first-night types. Critics, accident collec-
tors, friends and relatives of the participants, unidentified groups
who might actually have been there because they wanted to see
the play, although anyone who really wants to see a play would
do better to come on almost any other night. Beryl arrived a few
minutes after us having also been held up by the traffic. She and
I have shared this grisly experience so often that I've come to feel,
if not reassurance, then a reassuring sense of alliance, the second
I catch her face coming towards me in the crowd.† The four of us
went to the little room, had a quick drink or two, went into the
theatre. Harold and Antonia sat together at one end of the dress
circle, I sat at the other. Beryl, who finds my first-night under-the-
breath comments and frustrated gestures distracting rather than
educative, sat by herself in the stalls. The lights managed to go
down, the curtain managed to go up, the music managed to be at
the right level, and I settled into the irascible stoicism that is my

---

* Perhaps garments that harmonise with a pair of six-shooters buckled around
the waist, a knife in the belt.

† She was snowed up in Devon for the three days before the first night of *The Rear
Column*. The *Daily Express* offered to helicopter her to London, but she made it to
Axminster station on a tractor (though she didn't drive it herself) and arrived at
the Queen's Theatre about ten minutes before the curtain went up. Michael
Codron, seeing her enter the foyer, said: 'Ah, now I know everything's going to be
all right.' Actually it wasn't, as the critics hated the play, but I didn't and still don't
really blame Beryl for that.

normal condition at any performance of my plays, especially on first nights.

The first act was the best it has ever been. It had authority, the consequence really of Nick Le Prevost's authority, and also seemed to have a lot of wit and charm, much helped by Ian Ogilvy, at his most relaxed and sympathetic; furthermore (and more to the point) getting a decent response at the curtain. We spent the interval in our little room, where we were joined by the theatre administrator, Robert Cogo-Fawcett, and several of the theatre's guests, who inhibited conversation by (a) being introduced, and then (b) saying nothing. The silence, broken only by elliptical sentences and the sound of drinks being poured, became quite tacky, although Beryl, Judy and Antonia announced, at various points, that if was all going really rather well.*

As at the first run-through, the second act should therefore have been a disaster. As at the first run-through, it wasn't. It went rather better than the first act, in fact. The scene that for me has become the litmus test of the evening, reporting retrospectively on the first act and the first part of the second act – the Humphry death scene – was really touching. The reason for this must be, of course, the affection aroused by Clive's Humphry. What Clive gives us is a man deeply rooted, full of wit, and yet somehow poignant. The only tricky patch came in the Epilogue, when something went marginally wrong between Nick Le Prevost and Bob East. Some lines were either dropped or fluffed, I couldn't make out which. But, generally, every single member of the cast came through superbly, the production flowed smoothly, remarkably smoothly given the limited number of previews; in other words, the play was there, as a person or a building or a geranium

---

* Better than the first-night interval in San Francisco but a few short months ago, when I was followed into the private room by one of those perpetually middle-aged American ladies, jaunty on high heels, bold under a blue rinse, crying, 'At least we get a drink!', jostling the director and myself away from the table to make sure that she, and her rather large party of friends, did, immediately. Our attempts to escape into a further room where drinks were also on display were blocked by that rare creature, a churlish Californian (most Californians are sunny to the point of imbecility) who informed us we weren't welcome in there because it was available only to people properly connected to the theatre. So we had to go back into the first room, having now made ourselves interlopers there, too.

or a toad can be said to be there, emphatically itself, to be liked or disliked on its own terms. Not to mince matters, from the playwright's point of view an extremely good night. Not least because the audience at the final curtain suggested that they thought so too. Anyway again nobody asked for their money back, at least in my hearing. More importantly, nobody asked for their evening back, at least in my hearing.

We went to our little room to wait until the critics, their partners and the other first-night perverts* had cleared off, and then went on to the party the theatre was giving in the circle bar. It was an unexpectedly lavish affair, with wine, spirits, sandwiches and celebrities all milling about. A PR job, in other words. Everybody seemed perfectly relaxed. Everyone but me, that is. I was depressed. No doubt post-coitally so, as I always am on first nights, my eyes going glazed, my movements wooden, my voice leaden with hopelessness.† But this time I couldn't understand it quite, as there was nothing specific to be depressed about, given how things had actually concluded only a short while before. But I *was* depressed. Perhaps it was just my usual paranoia about critics. I was already convinced from past experience that on the whole they wouldn't like the play and it was certainly in this spirit that I responded to Peter James, the artistic director of the theatre, who approached me full of confidence and congratulations. Almost simultaneously (I subsequently discovered) Beryl was dealing in the same manner with the theatre administrator, Robert Cogo-Fawcett, who, like Peter James, jubilantly refused to believe that the Lyric had anything but a hit on its hands.

In spite of my Cassandra self and my wife Cassandra, the party went swimmingly, the general buzz of success uncheckable by either of us. There was an odd moment when Ian Hamilton, the editor of the magazine on which the magazine in the play is based, met Nick Le Prevost, playing the part based on Ian Hamilton. Nick, about seven or eight years younger than Ian, looked as Ian looked seven or eight years ago; both their wives – Ahdaf, Ian's wife; Aviva, Nick Le Prevost's wife – are pregnant to almost,

---

* I've left this in because, though no doubt unfair about first-night audiences, it's true to my feelings about them at the time.

† This is not, in fact, how I behave post-coitally.

I should think, the same week, and both have teenage sons by their first wives. There they stood, the four of them, talking.

Around the walls of the bar was an exhibition of Clive Francis's cartoons, which were also for sale. They were of cricketers (a splendid Ian Botham),* tennis players, actors and actresses, a few old stars (Bette Davis). There was also, side by side, one of Harold and one of myself, the only two, as far as I could see, so far unsold. The one of Harold is actually anachronistic, as he's holding a cigarette, but otherwise catches him accurately in a mood of ferocious geniality. The one of me I frankly consider Clive's only failure, as he appears to have given me a rug (my hair is thick, and my own), a pair of bloated cheeks, and has the tip of my tongue, or it could be an extra layer of underlip, protruding lasciviously. I noticed that nobody lingered before this study.† At first I assumed because they didn't recognise me. Then I realised I was named on a placard beneath it. So perhaps they couldn't place either the face or the name.

I don't remember any specific conversations at the party, apart from the long one with Peter James in which I already appeared to be gloating over my bad reviews, and a number of short and gratifying ones with friends. But I enjoyed, cynically, a mite, the spectacle of our son, Ben, moving with aplomb among the actors, paying out compliments as he knocked back the drinks and sandwiches. The affair came to an end when a cake in the form of a typewriter was brought out. I was ushered forward to assist in the ceremony by one of the PR girls, but modesty held me back a fatal trifle. One of the Friends of the Theatre, a severe, schoolmasterly looking woman, interposed herself between me and the cake, clearly under the impression that I was a close relative to the wino Harold had been taken for in the cold beef incident. By the time the misunderstanding had been sorted out, Harold had sliced the cake open, to the pop of flashbulbs from the Hammersmith newspapers, the theatre's PR people, and further Friends of the Theatre. I gathered that the woman who held me back had herself furn-

* This now hangs in my study, next to Clive's study of Clive Lloyd (the West Indies cricket captain).

† Clive subsequently gave this to me. I still don't think he looks like me, though sometimes suspect that I am beginning to look like him.

ished, perhaps even cooked, the cake. Presumably she'd believed I intended to devour her masterpiece, or in some way demolish it, before it could be photographed for posterity to wonder at. While slivers of the cake were being passed around, Harold, Antonia, Beryl and I went off to dinner at Thompson's, the only restaurant I know that can contain in one sitting everybody in London I wish to avoid. This evening it was a good place to be. We've had so many of these first-night dinners, just the four of us, and while they are, in a sense, interludes, the work finished and behind us, the question of reviews and the future of the production still to be faced, they always seem to me the real climax of the experience. Afterwards we went back to Campden Hill Square, for a last glass or two of champagne, and then Beryl and I came home to what, all in all, I consider to be one of the most hair-raising moments of our life together. Our answering machine signalled that we had a solitary message. What we got when I wound it back and played it was a baby crying, crying as if it were being tortured. I immediately thought of Lucy, who is fourteen, being reduced to gibbering terror by some psychopathic brute who'd kidnapped her.* Ben returned, I played him the tape, his face went white. Beryl said that before I phoned the police, the obvious next move, she'd better call her sister, Jennifer, in Exeter. Which she did. Between them they worked out the explanation. All that had happened was that Jennifer's baby who had held the receiver while Jennifer dialled, had suddenly started crying in the way that babies do. Jennifer had taken the receiver from her to speak into it, and hearing the machine and having nothing particular to say, had hung up, not realising that the baby (Alice) had left a memorable message.

And so to bed, and a deep sleep. One of the better things about getting older is that one gets more callused. I no longer dread the trek down the stairs to the morning papers and the reviews until after I've woken up.

Wednesday, 4 July

Woke up, took the long trek down the stairs to the papers, dreading the reviews. Nothing in *The Times* or the *Mail* yet. Billington's

* Lucy was in Paris at the time, on a school outing – a fact we forgot in the stress of the moment.

line in the *Guardian* is that it's 'a good and intelligent play' but not 'a great one', which he finds a pity as apparently I have the capacity to handle 'large themes' (whatever they are). My major problem, apparently, is that I lack 'magnanimity of spirit and largeness of vision', as is evidenced by 'a running gag' about a theatre critic and poet 'we could all put a name to'. Later Harold phoned to report on the *Financial Times* review which gives a robust and even seemingly enthusiastic account of the play, going so far as to compliment me on my writing, then draws indirect attention to 'Nappies' Harrop, and concludes: 'I can't say I enjoyed any of it very much.' There's an agreeable, if low-key, review by Milton Shulman in the *Standard*. A friend phoned to report on the unproduced playwright's review. He'd spotted him hastening from the theatre into a taxi, and guessed from the eager expression on his face what he was going to do. Apparently in doing it he got the location of the play and bits of the plot wrong. As I didn't hear it, I can't comment. Harold phoned again to say that there was a very favourable review in the *Telegraph*. I think this must be the first favourable review I've ever received in the *Telegraph*. What's going on here anyway? So far the production and the actors have come out of the reviews well. Harold clung to the belief that the Sundays would do us justice. We agreed to meet at the theatre and to do our best to raise the morale of the actors.

Shortly after, a friend rang to report that she'd got a friend who works on *The Times* to read out its review, which would be appearing tomorrow. It was unpleasant, she said, and again made a reference to 'Nappies' Harrop.

Met Harold at the bar of the Lyric just before six. Bumped into Robert Cogo-Fawcett, Peter James and David Porter. Robert Cogo-Fawcett said he was surprised that none of the investors had yet tried to withdraw their money, 'in spite of the reviews'. Three of them had called, however, to ask whether the play had any future, and if so where? I said, 'But of the reviews published so far, we've had one very good (*Daily Telegraph*), one good (*Standard*), one favourable if equivocal (*Guardian*), and only one bad (*Financial Times*), and the unproduced playwright who surely doesn't count.' I didn't mention *The Times*, my line being that we'd done better than I'd expected, at least so far. He said, 'Yes, I know. But they're not what *we* expected. We expected raves.' 'But Beryl warned you,'

I began, 'And I warned Peter James . . .' At which point Harold, who'd caught fag-ends of the conversation and therefore its general drift, said grimly that it was time we went in to speak to the actors, to raise their morale. As it turned out, the actors' morale didn't need raising until after we'd done our best to raise it. They thought that the critical reception had been rather encouraging, couldn't quite see why we were so worried, lots of plays transferred, did well in the West End on far less, mild euphoria should surely be the order of the day. 'Yes,' we said. 'But –'

5 July

The *Times* review is apparently as unpleasant as it was reported to be. I haven't actually seen it, nor has Harold, as it failed to appear in our copies of the newspaper, mine in N6, and his in W8. The only person who appears to have read it is the friend who got the friend to read it out yesterday. She lives in SW6. She says it's so badly printed as to be almost unreadable. The reviewer responsible wasn't Irving Wardle. A pity, I can't help feeling, as at least I could have got him on the blower, for one of our ding-dongs.

6 July

No reviews, no news.

Saturday, 7 July

We were reviewed on *Critics' Forum*. I didn't hear it, but gather that it was generally unfavourable.

Nevertheless I spent a fairly pleasant day at home, walking up and down our strip of a garden with the shamble of a lifer patrolling his cell. ('Those lime-tree bowers my prison' came to mind, though, of course, we haven't got any lime trees.) In the evening, before going up to the Chinese restaurant, I set the video to record a television programme on which a Cambridge professor of English was to talk about the poems of Bob Dylan, and then to review my play.*

---

* I've only met the professor a few times (years ago), but liked him for his vivacity. He was described by a TV critic – reviewing the programme on which he reviewed my play – as 'dazzling', for which I think I may take some credit.

Beryl and I sauntered contentedly around Highgate in the summer twilight, took our Chinese repast (among other delicacies, seaweed without the grated sea-slug), sauntered home in the darkness. As soon as I got in I made for the video, began to wind back, fast-forward, etc., then noticed a message on our answering machine. A friend to report on the Cambridge professor of English. He'd loved the Bob Dylan concert, hated *The Common Pursuit*, being particularly incensed at the jokes about Cambridge dons being unfaithful, getting themselves murdered, etc., though he conceded that the audience – 'the people', as he apparently called them – enjoyed it. I decided under the circumstances not to watch the programme, winding the tape back and setting it on play/record to cover the Cambridge professor. I'd no idea of what I'd recorded over him until Ben came in, a few minutes ago, in fact, and said, 'Ah, I'd hoped you were recording that film that Harold wrote, what's it, *The Servant*. He acts in it too, doesn't he? D'you mind if I watch it?' It's an ill wind.

I've just given Beryl stern instructions that, should she be awake before me, she is on no account to look at the Sunday reviews, but to plop the arts sections – we take the *Sunday Times* and the *Observer* – into a drawer in my desk; but please to leave out the news and particularly (with the McEnroe–Connors final coming up, and all the cricket currently going on) the sports pages. Actually, I invariably wake first, so take these instructions to be to myself rather than to Beryl.

Sunday, 8 July

Slept like a log, woke at ten. Beryl was already in the kitchen, the papers minus the arts pages waiting for me, along with the coffee. About an hour later Harold phoned, making it clear, in a few terse sentences, what he thought of the *Sunday Times* and the *Observer*. The *Sunday Times* reviewer was brief, hostile and referred to the 'Nappies' Harrop joke, identifying its butt as his predecessor, who is currently campaigning for the Chair of Poetry at Oxford.* The *Observer* piece was longer, equally hostile, but so perplexingly

---

* This is, as I'm sure everybody knows, an elective professorship for which candidates are obliged to solicit votes from members of the university. The ex-*Sunday Times* theatre reviewer polled well and ran a good second, I believe.

written, Harold said, that it was difficult to make out what his objection was. The *Sunday Telegraph* began by saying that *The Common Pursuit* was the wittiest play in London, but went on to hint that it lacked substance. All in all, he (Harold) felt so enraged that he'd decided that he wouldn't after all go and watch his club, the Gaieties, playing cricket, but would stay at home and regain control of himself. I think he found my tone – I was aiming at insouciance, but suspect I hit facetiousness – rather irritating, until I explained that it was somewhat like Hamlet's madness, 'north-by-north-west', feigned to prevent me from going mad. Also, I said, I'd had my breakdown when the reviews of *The Rear Column* came out, and couldn't afford another. At the moment it was only veneer, but I hoped to thicken it into a carapace, then reminded him of the buccaneering contempt he'd displayed when dealing with the first reviews of *Betrayal.* He said he understood, but begged leave to continue fulminating. I graciously gave it to him, and we agreed to meet on Monday, probably.

Several friends phoned during the day to register their outrage, thus giving me the opportunity to practise my flippancy. Now there are only the weeklies to get through, and this part of the experience of *The Common Pursuit* will be over.* What worries me immediately is the effect the reviews might have on the management (Peter James, Cogo-Fawcett and Porter) who were so shell-shocked on Tuesday. It occurs to me now that Harold and I would have better spent our time rallying them, rather than the cast, making sure that they get on with the business of looking for a West End theatre to transfer to. What worries me in the long term

---

* Not quite true. On Monday the *Mail*, which we'd all forgotten about, published what I can only call a rave. Of the weeklies, *Time Out* was very good, *Punch* was a mixture of praise and reservations, but was a bit of what's known in genetics as a sport, raising the 'Nappies' Harrop joke in order to relish it. The *TLS* had a review by the editor, complaining of weak characterisation and ponderous ironies, but on the whole was favourable, concluding with the suggestion that T. S. Eliot and F. R. Leavis, those well-known admirers of weak characterisation and ponderous ironies, would have approved. The *Spectator*, by the man who compared *One for the Road* with *King Lear*, was unfavourable, saying that my reputation was a mystery. People always thought they quite liked my plays until they remembered that they didn't really. I don't know of any others, but suppose that *City Limits*, *What's On*, *Vogue*, *Tatler*, the *Harringay Gazette*, the *New Statesman*, the *Jewish Chronicle et al.* carried reviews.

is that there has always been something wrong with this production. I'm not talking about what's on the stage, but its career as a production, its future in another theatre. Of course every production has its own life, seeming to become an organism quite independent from the many people who contribute to it, and this particular organism seems to me to have been poisoned at the start, with all the initial muddle over Michael Codron, UBA, etc., and I strongly doubt that it will survive. Oh, this is probably rubbish. I'm merely going on in this vein because I'm rather enjoying sitting here, at about midnight, drawing on a cigarette, sipping a whisky, ruminating like some old campaigner.

Monday, 9 July

Harold and I met at the Lyric bar before the performance, to do a repeat job on the actors, who again needed no rallying, having regained their spirits after our last attempt. Not surprisingly, as they'd all had excellent reviews in the Sundays, except for one critic who referred disparagingly to Ian Ogilvy, Simon Williams and Bob East as 'ageing boulevard actors'. This amused rather than irritated Simon Williams and Ian Ogilvy, but left Bob East incredulous, as well he might, as no equally talented actor with his sort of looks has had less opportunity to get on the boulevard stage. The extremely cheerful atmosphere was only lowered now and then by the appearance of Cogo-Fawcett or Porter (Peter James having gone back to Israel), who were both adopting the stance of men struggling gamely but ineffectually against an unsolicited social disease. The actors went off to get ready for performance, Harold left to play bridge, I hung about with a drink, wanting to leave but drawn inevitably to the performance. I didn't actually want to see it, but also I didn't want to spend the rest of the evening wishing I had. In the end, I went in, reminding myself that after all I hadn't seen the show since the opening night.

As it turned out, I wish I had spent the evening wishing I had been there. The problem, I suppose, was that the actors, after a day off but still not having played the play often enough to be completely at ease in it, were remembering effects and therefore exaggerating them. The performance lacked spontaneity, and furthermore I had the impression that their reception on other nights had led them to take the audience's enjoyment for granted.

None of this was surprising, but I couldn't help being depressed at the interval; and further depressed when I returned to my seat and noticed, just as the lights went down, the distinguished grey head and noble profile of Michael Codron. He was sitting halfway down my aisle. The second act was no better.

In the bar after the show, I tried to have a quick word with all the actors. This was difficult, impossible actually, because they were surrounded by friends, the clusters lapping into each other to make up what was in effect something of a party. After a time, I gave up, joined the celebrations, came home.

Tuesday, 10 July

Phoned Harold and gave him my views of the performance. We agreed to go in and have a look at it together on Thursday.* Then Michael Codron rang. He addressed me in a tone of gloomy compassion, telling me he didn't really want to discuss on the telephone what he'd seen on the stage, but he did say that he found it an extraordinary experience, attending a play of mine that he hadn't produced himself, feeling both a part of it but excluded from it. We agreed to have lunch soon.† I said I was sorry he hadn't seen it at its best. Usual stuff.

Wednesday, 11 July

Went to the theatre in the afternoon, to attend a publicity session. Was slightly surprised to observe on entering that neither the *Telegraph* nor the *Mail* review had been blown up and displayed, nor were there any quotes anywhere to be seen. Mentioned this when I was in the office, was assured it was being attended to. Our plan was to put a large display ad in the *Guardian* and *The Times*, alternating favourable quotes with unfavourable ones. It was both fun and quite gruelling, but what emerged, to everybody's surprise – Porter, Cogo-Fawcett and two ladies from the PR office in attendance – was how many favourable, or favourable-seeming,

---

* We did. The show was in excellent shape.

† This lunch did in due course take place; was extremely pleasant; and concluded with Michael's offering to produce my next play – if I write it, and he likes it.

quotations could be picked out of even unfavourable reviews. In fact, there is rather more going for us than we'd supposed. Porter and Cogo-Fawcett became quite animated, both showing a gift for juxtaposing abuse or downright nonsense with praise, so that the final version, which we reached late in the afternoon, reads like something from *Alice Through the Looking-Glass*, anyway will, I hope, read amusingly in the *Guardian* and *The Times*, where space has been booked, though for tomorrow week, when we'll be half-way through our run. I asked why we were appearing so late, and as nobody seemed to know, suggested that we try for an earlier date. Agreed unanimously.* After the meeting, I hurried off to see the touring production of *Butley*, which arrived at Dartford last Monday, the producer wanting to bring it into the West End for a short season. The auditorium was vast and empty apart from a few OAPs who were sitting with heads bowed, reading their pro-grammes presumably, or asleep or dead. The stage was very wide, very deep, as if designed for ice-skating exhibitions, and the actors, whose previous stop had been Guildford, which has a very com-pact stage, hadn't quite adjusted their performances. The few leisurely steps they were in the habit of taking to cross the room were now inadequate in this large space. They were virtually hav-ing to sprint to get to their usual positions, so inevitably they were speaking quickly as well, far too quickly. It was quite ghastly, in fact, the actors whizzing about, rattling off their lines as if con-trolled by a video fast-forward, the finger controlling the button belonging to someone who hated the play.

Of course, I was in no condition to judge the production, which I also suspect was in no condition to be judged. I tried to leave at the interval, but was intercepted at the doors – the theatre is a hideous edifice, by the way, wound about by ribbons of concrete leading to motorways, flyovers, vacant lots, etc., and, thank God, the railway station – by a rather farouche young man, unshaven, the bottom of his shirt hanging loosely around grubby trousers, whom I took to be a stray tramp, seeking succour, but was in fact the company manager.* He bought me a drink at the bar, and accompanied me back into the stalls for the second act. I stayed for

* I don't know if an earlier date was tried for. The ads appeared when scheduled, three weeks after we'd opened, three weeks before we were due to close.

ten minutes, slipped out, struggled across a pedestrian rampart to the station, waited nearly half an hour for a train, came home, dictated this. I don't feel quite up to appreciating the irony, that a travel-ruined production of an old play of mine that I don't believe anyone really wants in the West End may be going there, while a strong production of my new play that I believe quite a few people actually do want, may not.

The next few days were concerned with the Lyric's attempts to transfer the show to a West End theatre. I don't, of course, understand the business complications of transferring a play from a theatre where it is set for a limited run to a commercial theatre where it will run for as long as the management can keep it going at a profit. I gathered, though, during the course of conversations with Peter James, Robert Cogo-Fawcett and David Porter that it would cost about £45,000 to move the set from Hammersmith to Shaftesbury Avenue, and do a proper publicity campaign. This money would be provided by the shortly to become celebrated Lyric shareholders, who of course would have to be paid back before the play could run into profit. The choice of theatre is therefore clearly very important. If a play transfers to a big theatre, and does excellent business, it will run into profit quickly. If to a small theatre and does excellent business, then obviously it will take longer. If to a small theatre and does only good-to-average business, it might never run into profit at all, while to a big theatre doing good-to-average business, it might *eventually* run into profit, etc. In London, shows that seem bound to make a loss (i.e. flops) generally close in about six weeks, which, compared to Broadway, is a lingering death.[†]

---

* When I came across him on subsequent occasions, in London, he was always immaculately turned out in a dinner jacket. So either he was just showing the effects of a long and exhausting tour in a rather personal manner, or I was hallucinating him, too.

† My first Broadway play closed after three performances (see 'Flops and Other Fragments' on page 173 for a description of this), and I've heard of one that closed at the first interval, and of others that closed during previews. An actor friend of mine, an exceptionally handsome man with golden hair, shaved his head especially for a part on Broadway, and learned the morning after the first night that the play had already closed, just a few minutes too late to prevent his wife and children, who were coming over for the second performance, from boarding Concorde.

But back to the Lyric and our attempts to find a theatre to transfer to. There was talk of the Albery, the Fortune, the Phoenix, the Comedy, Wyndhams, the Mermaid, the Vaudeville. All, except the Fortune, turned out to be either hopeless commercial propositions, or to pass through swift reversals of circumstance in favour of the play in occupation. At Wyndhams and the Vaudeville, for instance, *Passion Play* and *Benefactors*, both rumoured to be about to come off, suddenly started to improve at the box office, as did *The Little Shop of Horrors* at the Comedy. The proprietors of the Albery, on the other hand, turned the theatre over to a consortium that intended to do plays of its own; while the Mermaid was deemed by the Lyric management to be too far from the centre of London to be of any use except for plays doing a limited season, and we'd already done ours at the Lyric; and the poor old Phoenix seemed to have become, over the last few years, the sort of theatre where plays looked as if they were on a squat, waiting to be forcibly ejected, rather than settling in for a run. Finally, although the Phoenix* and the Mermaid bobbed up until the last gasp, the only convincing possibility was the Fortune, the management of which were keen to have us, and on which Harold, Eileen Diss and I were more than keen, believing that its size – it seats about 450 – and the close relationship between the stage and the auditorium would perfectly suit the intimacies of *The Common Pursuit*.

Moreover, its stage could accommodate our revolve, if only just. We went to the Lyric, to talk to the management. The management hoped we'd come to a fairly swift decision, as there was another play they were interested in bringing in. The other play was, inevitably, the touring production of *Butley*. We reported to the Lyric our view that the Fortune would be right for *The Common Pursuit*, and heard back from the Lyric management that their only worry was that the Fortune, seating so few people, would have to play almost to capacity, not only every night of the week, but on the two matinees, to keep us just above profit. The point being that unlike, say, the Albery, they hadn't the seats to recoup

---

* The outside of the Phoenix has been refurbished since, and now looks both smart and welcoming. It is currently housing a Dario Fo farce and, I hear and hope, is doing very well.

on good nights what they might lose on bad. Nevertheless, negotiations were going ahead. Something might be worked out.

I tried to concentrate on other matters in my life, looking for
calm at cricket matches, and playing my annual game with Harold
Pinter's XI against the *Guardian*. It was an experience I don't care
to reflect on, even three months later. We batted first, and I was out
second ball, prodding myopically forward to an off-spinner that
briefly visited the top of my bat on its way to second slip. The only
reason I failed to drop a couple of catches when fielding was that
I was running in the wrong direction when they fell. In the last
two overs the *Guardian* needed about 18, I think it was, to win.
One of their early batsmen, on 60 or so, hit the ball straight at me.
The ball, like a savage rat, aimed itself at my throat, then kidneys,
then ankles, before scudding viciously under my falling body to
the boundary. When the batsman took guard again, he turned his
face, crafty under its cap, towards me, singling me out as the fielder
who was going to win the game for him, and hit another four right
past me, then another one under me. The remaining runs were
taken comfortably, and although I was responsible for only two of
them, I think I can claim to have lost the match single-handedly.
The following day, Monday, I spent keeping a low profile, dealing
rather briskly with Harold who phoned to ask how I felt about
the match.*

The next day I went to have lunch with an old friend, Tony
Gould, who is the literary editor of *New Society*. We met at his
office, where there was a message from Beryl relaying a message
from the Lyric Theatre, Peter James having at last returned from
Israel, that there was going to be a meeting at Harold's studio at
5.15 to discuss the future of the play, with special reference to the
possibility of a transfer to the Fortune. I phoned the Lyric to say
I'd got the message. Tony and I had a leisurely lunch, after which
I sauntered about doing a bit of book buying, before picking up
a taxi that got entangled in traffic jam after traffic jam, the driver
seeming to have a nose for them or a yearning for them, seeking

---

* I now recall that Harold, at slip, had dropped this same batsman when he'd
scored about 16 or so, the ball bursting through his hands on to his chest, bouncing
off his chest back through his hands, on to the grass. That was when the match was
lost, I now believe. (NB For an apologia for my chequered cricket career, see Part 4
of this book.)

them out by detours, etc., so that I actually arrived ten minutes late.

Harold greeted me at his door with a look of utter astonishment, and asked me where I'd been. I said I'd been involved in the traffic, why, what are you worried about? He said, 'Oh, I thought – I just thought – that you hadn't actually – you didn't know where you were meant to be.' 'But didn't the Lyric lot pass on the message that I'd got the message about where I was meant to be?' He said, 'Yes, yes, I got the message, they passed it on when they got here, they're upstairs now, as a matter of fact. It's just that you're late.' He wasn't irritable or accusing, merely wondering, slightly confused, as if my presence was in a way as much a mystery as my absence had been. I was also confused. We stood quite a time on the doorstep, revolving the question of messages, presences, absences, lateness, a surreal conversation, in fact, with metaphysical overtones. I think the truth was that neither of us really wanted to go upstairs and talk to Cogo-Fawcett, Peter James and David Porter. Finally he led me upstairs, to his sitting room, and there indeed were a whey-faced David Porter, unable to meet my eyes; a glum, inward-looking Robert Cogo-Fawcett, unable to meet my eyes; and an extremely tanned, just-back-from-Israel Peter James, unable to meet my eyes.

They had called the meeting urgently, Peter James explained, because they were going to go straight on from it to meet the shareholders of their production company, and wanted a little chat with us so that they could present the shareholders with our feelings. We talked for about an hour, or mainly Peter James did, during which David Porter contributed half a sentence but got whiter, and Cogo-Fawcett kept taking out of his pocket little bits of paper on which scraps of numbers appeared to have been written down and was occasionally invited to contribute some of these numbers to what wasn't so much a dialogue as a monologue from Peter James, who talked on and on in a soft, worried, compassionate fashion, there in his sandals, his grey hair falling to his shoulders, his decent, honourable, gentle face registering sorrowful emotions about nothing specific, something nebulous. Neither Harold nor I, while it was going on, could quite make out what his sorrowful emotions were about. And David Porter, as I've said, increasingly whey-faced, unable to contribute anything except the half-sentence I can't remember. It can't have been a relevant half-sentence, because I don't think it redirected Peter James's flow by as much as a pause. Then they left, Peter James saying he was glad we'd had 'this little natter' as it gave him something to put to the shareholders, especially the chairman of the shareholders. They looked, as they trooped out of the room, like an illustration out of the updated Bible. The three wise men, perhaps ducking out of a situation and on to the pavement.

'Who are these shareholders?' I asked Harold. 'They never said they had to consult with shareholders before.'

'No,' said Harold. 'They didn't.'

'And the chairman. What chairman?'

'I don't know.'

'Did you notice David Porter's face?'

'White.'

'Yes.'

'And he didn't say anything. What was he doing here?'

'I don't know. Perhaps they have a pact to do things like this together.'

'Yes.'

We discussed it for a time, both of us by now perfectly aware of what we'd been told, in spite of our not being told anything, and then I phoned Judy and reported our suspicions. She said, with Boadicean grandeur, that she would go immediately to the Lyric and try to be present at the meeting. If she failed she would confront the triumvirate, and the chairman of the shareholders if necessary, when they came out. I said I thought that was terrific. Harold took over the phone and said he thought it was terrific. While Judy charioted through the streets from Paddington to Hammersmith, he and I sipped a few more glasses of champagne, talking to no purpose about the perfidy of the human race, and of theatre producers in particular. Then I went to meet Beryl and Lucy, back from school for a few days, in an Italian restaurant in Highgate, and bored them – Lucy anyway – with an account of the meeting, doing imitations (my Cogo-Fawcett consulting his scraps of paper was reasonably well received) and paraphrases, and we went home.

There were two messages on the machine, both from Judy. In the first she said that she'd got to the Lyric just as Peter James,

Cogo-Fawcett and Porter were coming out of the meeting. They reported that the chairman of the shareholders, and the other shareholders present, hadn't responded with much enthusiasm to the idea of the Fortune. They wanted the Queen's, the Globe, the Albery, anywhere central on Shaftesbury Avenue. But she would talk more in the morning. In her second message she said she was sorry about the first message, as the news was worse than she'd implied. In reality there was not the slightest chance that we would be going to the Fortune. We would speak in the morning.

My transcripts record that we spoke in the morning. Indeed over the next few days there were interminable conversations between Harold, Judy, myself and Peter James; or Harold, Judy, myself and Cogo-Fawcett; Harold, Judy, myself and David Porter; Harold and myself; Judy and myself; and no doubt Harold and Judy; but clearly the question of the Fortune was closed.

One morning, rancorous with disappointment, I went to Chelmsford, where Essex was playing Middlesex (I think it was), determined on tranqullity. With Gooch going strong on 36, I found myself haring towards a suddenly spotted public telephone to take Peter James through the matter yet again. Why, I put to him, with all the vivacity of a man discovering the question for the first time, had he insisted that the Lyric become sole producers of the play, cutting out such potential producers as Michael Codron, DBA, etc., without mentioning that the Lyric production company was itself owned by invisible but omnipotent shareholders? He didn't know.

On another occasion, in the bar at the Lyric, I put it to Cogo-Fawcett that he, Peter James and David Porter had already decided, before consulting the chairman of the shareholders, not to accept the Fortune's offer. He admitted that they had. I then hinted that therefore the meeting at Harold's had been a bit of a charade. He supposed it was. But really they just wanted to break the news as painlessly as possible, he explained, by indicating what might happen before actually making it happen.

However much we grilled and expostulated, we could never get an answer to our main question – viz., why it would be such a financial risk to go to the Fortune. Given the revolve, we virtually had a one-set play; there were only six actors, the costumes would all be provided, surely we were cheap enough – if not, how could *any* play that wasn't performed solo ever make it to the Fortune? The deal they were offered, they kept stonewalling, just wouldn't work. And there were mutterings, so casually muttered that we scarcely noticed them, about some of the actors being a trifle expensive. This led me to recall one of Peter James's humble asides (I think it was addressed to his sandals) at the meeting at Harold's. 'Don't forget,' he'd said, 'that we're completely inexperienced in this sort of thing. Moving plays to the West End ourselves, I mean. We still don't know much about it.'

This was probably the nub of the matter. A month after *The Common Pursuit* had closed I learnt from a West End producer that a transfer to a theatre as small as the Fortune had been out of the question from before we'd begun rehearsals. Apparently the Lyric had committed itself, and whatever West End theatre it might move the play into, to paying three of our actors the kind of money normally only paid to one. 'The actors' agents ran rings around the Lyric,'* he ended, with a compassionate smile. I can't say his explanation cheered me up. I'd hoped for something more arcane, the kind of mistake that not just anybody could make. Our consolation, I suppose – Harold's, the cast's, mine – must be that *The Common Pursuit* provided Peter James, Robert Cogo-Fawcett, David Porter, their shareholders and the chairman of their shareholders, with invaluable experience.

But this explanation was, as I say, offered only recently. Back there in late July, after negotiations with the Fortune had finally spluttered out, two other theatres tantalisingly displayed themselves as possibly available. One was actually in Shaftesbury Avenue. True, it had just moved in a thriller, but everyone, including the theatre owner, knew it was a bummer. The theatre owner claimed that if the reviews were as bad as he considered they ought to be, he would give notice to the show to quit immediately, and we could move *The Common Pursuit* in within six weeks. Would that suit us? It would, even if it meant a playwright waiting ghoulishly for a fellow playwright's catastrophe, actors waiting to replace fellow actors, a director picking up a fee or royalties a fellow

---

* In running rings around the Lyric, the agents had probably also run rings around their own clients, all of whom might have been happy to appear in the West End for substantially less than had been negotiated for them, given the chance.

director was going to go without. (*That's* show business.) In fact, the reviews were almost as bad as predicted, but the producer, whom nobody had thought fit to consult, ruined everything by declaring that he had no intention of taking the thriller off, whatever the theatre owner's attitude. He would feed money into the box office, if necessary, to keep takings above the level at which the theatre owner had the right to close it.* The other theatre was down the road and around a corner or two from Shaftesbury Avenue. Its final excuse for rejecting us was that it wanted to be a permanent house for musical comedies. A musical comedy went in there, stayed a few weeks, came off. Its posters still don't quite cover the posters of the show that preceded it, or of the show that preceded the one that preceded that. The theatre, currently vacant, its recent and sorry past littering its facade, looks like some desolate image from *The Third Man*.

Given our preoccupation with finding a theatre it's odd that, as far as I can make out from the transcripts, I never got around to discussing with myself, late at night into the tape recorder, the kind of business we did over our six weeks at the Lyric. I can't believe I didn't take an acute interest in it. I do remember, though, that every time I went in myself during the run it seemed to be at least three-quarters full, once or twice completely full. Checking over her files and receipts, Judy Daish reckons we played to an average 60 per cent or more, which she also reckons was pretty good, at least in a particularly hot August with most London theatregoers out of London, and American tourists not familiar with Hammersmith, let alone the Lyric, Hammersmith, and given the management's whimsical policy on publicity – i.e. none until it was too late. I also remember that at the fateful pre-shareholders' meeting in Harold's studio, I assumed from the management's attitude that we must have been doing badly. Peter James, however, explained that actually we were doing well. At least better than most new plays at the Lyric, and certainly better than any previously put on there at that time of year. However his, and I suppose Cogo-Fawcett's and Porter's, personal standards were rather high, their touchstone being Michael Frayn's farce, *Noises Off*, which had played to 100 per cent capacity before

* It's still running as I write this.

moving to the West End. The next new play at the Lyric, *Tramway Road* by Ronald Harwood, which had better and longer reviews than mine, at least in the influential Sundays, is currently doing somewhere between 10 and 15 per cent, at a more propitious time of year, but on the other hand deals with English expatriates in South Africa, which may not be a crowd-pulling theme. The play immediately before *The Common Pursuit* – *Black Ball Game* – played to between 15 and 20 per cent, I believe. Presumably the Lyric's long-range scheme is to wait for another *Noises Off*, and transfer it. If their shareholders allow them to, of course.

Anyway, by the time Harold went off *en famille* to Portugal for his annual holiday, and I went off *en famille* to Italy, it had become clear that *The Common Pursuit* was to have no future, at least immediately, in London. There was nothing to look forward to on our return but its demise at Hammersmith. When I got back from rolling off rocks into the sea, eating, drinking, playing poker, etc., I phoned Harold, who'd got back from doing much the same. We agreed to bring our joint adventure at Hammersmith to as graceful a conclusion as possible by taking the cast out to dinner at the Trattoo (why?) after the last performance, and to invite the actors to invite a loved one as a companion. With Beryl and Antonia, there would be sixteen in all.

(NB The following account is a combination of transcript and memory. The transcript being coherent at the beginning, but falling into passages of gibberish or measured nonsense, had to be structured by memory which is no doubt faulty in details. But what I've stitched from the one and the other is roughly what happened as I remember it, I think.)

Saturday, 11 August

Went to the Fortune, saw a preview of *Butley*, the matinee.* Whipped around with a few notes, then scurried across London to the

---

* I had had to take the production over, the director having committed himself to directing something else before he knew *Butley* was going to the West End. It lingered at the Fortune for a briefer season than the brief season originally intended. It was an event almost without meaning, except (for me) in its contribution to the history of *The Common Pursuit*.

Lyric, arriving half a minute before curtain up to see, as I ran up the stairs, Peter James and David Porter at the bar. Peter James followed me up the stairs, and went into the stalls, I think. I went to my regular seat at the end of the front row of the dress circle. As I sat down somebody coughed behind me. A recognisable cough. Harold, smiling, holidayed, in black for last supper.

It was a good performance that would have been better if it hadn't been the last. The actors pushed slightly, trying to wring every nuance out of every line, every silence. We heard later that it had been going very well so naturally, with no more opportunities to come, the actors wanted to go a stage further, which is always one stage too far. Or so I felt.

During the interval we went, not to our old room, but to the bar where Peter James had laid on a bottle of champagne. I managed not to overhear the kind of comments I'm usually destined to overhear by adopting the simple tactic of talking and laughing very loudly myself. Thus, I suppose, presenting the image of the boastful playwright bent on hogging the interval too, and so didn't notice David Porter until we were all clearing back into the auditorium, still standing at the bar in much the same position as he'd been in at the beginning of the first act, a poignant image of solitude and exclusion, his tankard of ale in his hand. The same image greeted me when I came back down the stairs, the first out as always, Harold chasing me as always, at the end of the second act, although of course I couldn't tell whether it was the same tankard with the same ale in it. I was about to go solicitously over to him when Harold took me by the arm and led us back into the auditorium, on to the stage, where the stage management was holding a farewell party.

It's a true comment on the egoism and obsessiveness of my relationship with this production (with *any* production) that so far in my account I haven't as much as glanced in the direction of our ASM, Tana. From the first day of rehearsal right through to the last performance, she was devoted in her duties, discreet and efficient, a provider of comfort, coffee, tea, lost lines, necessary smiles and photocopies on photocopies of altered text. She had given up smoking at about the same time as Harold, and chewed nicotine gum almost it seemed, in rhythm with him. She also jogged, bicycled and did sponsored walks. I mention all this only to prove that I was actually aware of her outside her function, and I was very glad of the opportunity to raise a glass (full, inevitably, of wine she'd provided) in tribute. It was a nice party, the only intruders being a few friends, all of whom either liked the play or were happy to pretend that they did, and it was made specially pleasurable for me when David Porter put in a late appearance, relaxed and jovial, so putting an end to my anxious speculations about the personal griefs that might have kept him at the bar, away from the last performance of the play he'd co-produced and helped to cast.

The evening should have ended there, with our going our separate ways in our own little groups, the company breaking up for the last time. But life, 'old life itself', of which I'm so fond when I encounter it on the stage or the page, but less so when it turns up in its usual dishevelled fashion in old life itself, was waiting for us at the Trattoo (where else?) in the small private room, with a round table large enough to accommodate all sixteen of us. The virtues of a round table for dining purposes are known to everyone. No quarrel need be confined to an area at the top, or the bottom, or the middle, as in a long table. By simply swivelling your head in the course of delivering a sentence you can see the face of everyone you're insulting with it almost simultaneously. In short you can get from tranquillity to complete uproar with a single ill-judged remark. Or well-judged one, depending on your intentions and mood.

I'd like to draw a veil over the dinner at the Trattoo, with the observation that never, in my experience, has a round table proved its value as did this one. But that won't quite do. The round table provided only the opportunity and the means; the motives lay elsewhere, in Harold and myself, quite indistinct to each of us, I believe, the result of months of tension, hard work, exhaustion, culminating in dashed hopes. In the cast, whose experience had been shorter, but just as intense – more so, at times. In the waiters, with their – I can't speak for the waiters, except to say that I blame them too, if not above all, for everything that happened. It's just that I haven't worked out any conceivable motive on their part, and indeed they showed, when the dinner approached its climax, an unseemly sense of panic, running in and out of the room as if we were members of a family from Palermo refusing to be calmed even when informed that we were merely celebrating *The Common Pursuit*. I don't know what they made of this, but I do know I've never been treated with so little ceremony by Italian waiters, not one of whom sang into my face when I left, or offered to help me into my coat.

Not that there was any actually physical violence at the dinner, merely threats of it, and those merely implied, as when Harold jounced an ashtray in the palm of his hand when replying to my suggestion, delivered with some vocal power and the flourishing of a steak knife, that he was an imbecile. Or when Actor A (unnamed because he can't really have meant it), glimpsing an opportunity for political suasion, made a grave speech on the difference between bad bombs and good bombs, bad ones being the ones that fail to go off and kill people, good ones being the ones that go off and kill the right people, i.e. those who disagree with him, which on a quick count meant almost everybody in the room. Or when Actor B (unnamed because he can't really have meant it) proclaimed – but I'm getting ahead of myself.

At the beginning there was no hint that anything lay before us except a somewhat lacklustre dinner, our real farewells having been taken, as I've already mentioned, at the stage management's party back at the theatre. The only perturbation came from the realisation that the restaurant had opened many bottles of red wine, and spread them across the table, while there was no evidence at all of white wine, which everybody really wanted. White wine turned up in due course, if rather less speedily than required, and everyone fell to talking, rather listlessly perhaps, to those next to them. I don't believe a major dangerous exchange took place until after an hour or so, though I can't be sure of this as I fell into a light coma for a time. I was aroused by hearing Actor B exclaim that if a son of his had done a thing like that, he'd have broken every bone in his body and smashed out his teeth. He was talking, from the other side of the round table, to Beryl, who was sitting next to me. Thinking for a moment that this was his response to one of her affectionate descriptions of a boyish mischief our son Ben had got up to, I shook myself into battle position. But it wasn't so, he was in fact expressing his feelings about the three public schoolboys, from Stowe, I think it was, who had planted a dummy bomb in some nearby hall that the widow of the late Airey Neave, himself actually blown up by a bomb, was going to visit. I took the view that however disgraceful the boys' behaviour might have been, paternal bone-breaking and teeth-smashing weren't really the answer to their problem.

The conversation got rowdier, spreading around the table like the proverbial wildfire, until Harold, who had fallen into a coma of his own, reared into consciousness. His opening intervention was equally based on a misunderstanding: to wit, that Beryl and I were actually toasting the behaviour of the three boys (I wonder if it would have given them satisfaction to know that their dummy bomb, laid somewhere in the environs of Stowe School, actually went off weeks later in a fashionable restaurant in West London) and it was through a sequence of misunderstandings, as neither would allow the other more than a half-sentence in explanation, Actor A's sermon on the difference between morally good and morally bad bombs; further rousing descriptions from Actor B as to what he'd like to do to a son of his, etc.; some gruesomely inappropriate common sense from Beryl; some grossly redundant attempts at calm and clarification from Antonia – that we reached our climax and someone had to reassure the waiters, streaming in and out of the room aghast, that all this was merely in celebration of *The Common Pursuit.* They didn't of course realise that this was the title of a play.

The row subsided as quickly, as mysteriously, as it had arisen. There were two or three minutes of silence, during which Harold put down the ashtray and I wafted the echoes of my insults out of the room with lazy gestures, as if they were so many stray wasps. Then Harold made a speech about the experience of the production, I made a speech about the experience of the production, Harold paid the bill, and left,* and in due course, in bewildered pairs, loved one with loved one, the rest of us left. And that, I suppose, was the end, the ceremonial end, anyway, of the adventure of *The Common Pursuit.*

But life, 'old life itself', going through one of its shapelier phases, hadn't quite finished with us. A few days later, *Butley,* the play with which Harold and I had begun our association, opened at the Fortune, the theatre which we had once hoped would house

---

* I eventually paid my share, I'm anxious to report.

The Common Pursuit. And a day or so after that, returning from Judy's office in a taxi at about six in the evening, I found myself wheeling around just off Holland Park and running parallel with Harold, who was walking across the street, carrying a copy of the *Standard* in his hand. I think, in the course of our fifteen years' association, that this is the only time I have come across him accidentally. I whistled through the window several times. He didn't hear me. My taxi slewed around and went up towards Highgate. He walked steadily on towards Campden Hill Square. We each maintained a dignified silence for a few days, until I sent him a note, he made a telephone call, both suggesting lunch. We had it in a restaurant situated in Holland Park itself, overlooking the nannies, parents and children among whom I'd stumbled one afternoon between a preview matinee and the evening preview. It was sunny now as then, this being one of those summers that turn up from time to time, though mainly in literature or in memories of childhood.

The lunch got off to an inauspicious start, with my waiting downstairs in the bar for him, while he waited upstairs at our table for me. I sorted that out by reminding myself of Harold's punctuality, and going upstairs to check. There he was, in black, framed against the large, sunny window, and there was I, bag swinging from my shoulder, a glass of half-drunk champagne in my hand. Both of us, I suppose, at our most characteristic, so how, under the circumstances, could the lunch not be like all the lunches we've had down the years? We agreed that at the Trattoo the demons that had pestered *The Common Pursuit* from the start had finally taken a brief but full possession of us, and then dropped the matter in favour of the things we cared to remember, of which there turned out to be quite a few, though not many of them, I now realise, reported into my tapes. Perhaps the problem with keeping a diary, and the reason I'll never keep another, is that one records only the things one would prefer to forget. At least if one has a temperament like mine.

Appendixes

Appendix A

NICK (*enters, coughing slightly, looks around*) Where's Stuart then?

MARTIN He said to wait, they'd be right back.

NICK They – oh, of course, Marigold. Well, isn't there any coffee on the go or anything? I've got a hangover.

MARTIN Really? How did you get it?

NICK Drank too much. In fact, look, what's that stuff, slimy, thick and yellow?

HUMPHRY That covers a large number of revolting substances.

MARTIN Oh, it must be advocaat, mustn't it? You know. Egg-nog.

NICK That explains it. I'm allergic to eggs. Probably allergic to nogs too. If they're what they sound like. It was that bloody girl from Girton – Muriel what's-it?

MARTIN Hoftstadt?

NICK Yes, she produced it. I was perfectly all right until then.

Appendix B

HUMPHRY Can we have some music instead? (*Little pause.*) If we're going to wait, could we at least do something worthwhile.

NICK I advise you not to resist him. He has a powerful personality. (*He goes to the gramophone.*) What would you like to hear?

HUMPHRY Wagner would probably be the most inappropriate. So let's have him.

NICK I don't know if Stuart goes in for Wagner. (*Hunting.*) Or anything musical, really. Except for reverie and romance. Ah, here's some. (*He puts the record on the gramophone.*) Mainly snatches from the great tunes, from the look of it. I hope it'll do. (*He sits down.*)

Wagner fills the room. Nick lights a cigarette and coughs. Humphry
listens. Martin assumes a listening posture. Peter listens idly,
smiling pleasantly. They remain in that position as the set revolves
off, the music still playing, while Stuart's office revolves on, Stuart
at the desk, for Scene Two.

Appendix C

Martin has just attempted to persuade Stuart not to resign from
his publishing firm. One of the inducements he offers is that Stuart
will edit Humphry's long-awaited book on Wagner, and suggests
that Stuart should go up to Cambridge to talk to Humphry about it.

STUART Of course I'll talk to him. And there's nothing I'd rather
read than a book by Humphry on Wagner. Almost. But I won't
edit it. I have *got* to quit, Martin. You see, the real thing is –
well, last night, just before you and Marigold got back from
the concert, I was sitting in the kitchen drinking coffee and
watching Martina strutting about on the counter. Then she
did one of her things. You know, squatted on her haunches,
arched her neck, stretched her legs. Went into a kind of trance
of concentration. Aimed herself at the top of the fridge. And
missed of course. No, she didn't. She caught the corner and
ricocheted off, to the floor. And then she strutted away. Looking
pleased with herself. And instead of finding her funny and
endearing, I found myself thinking that either she was a freak –
because a clumsy cat's a contradiction in terms, isn't it? Or
she's a pervert. Because she *prefers* getting to the floor by way
of a ricochet off the fridge. And I actually found myself
loathing her as a – a – oh, obviously as a symbol of my – my –
Anyway, I went from loathing Martina to loathing it. My life
I mean. And so back to first causes, and remembering that
I only came in with you – well, you know why. To have
children. Comfortably. You see. At your expense. I now realise.
And there's quite a lot wrong with that on any terms, but
especially if there aren't any children. To justify it. Partially.

Appendix D

STUART Actually, let's face it, or let me face it, at last. It's
probably the right decision. The fact is that the magazine

doesn't really matter, to anyone except me. As Nick pointed out. (*Little laugh.*) To do him credit.

MARIGOLD Yes, it does. It matters to lots of people. Hubert Stout* among them. Or he wouldn't have given you his six new poems, would he?

STUART He only gave them to me because I gave him that bloody party, which was finally what bankrupted us, as Martin has always refrained from pointing out, although he came close a little while ago. Anyway, the Stouts will get themselves published somewhere far more public, and for real money, instead of promises of it.

MARIGOLD But you're not seriously talking of giving up! Not now! You can't. He can't, can he?

STUART Oh, yes I can.

MARIGOLD But – but it's not fair. (*She gives a little laugh.*) It's actually not fair.

STUART Being fair has nothing to do with it. The printers want their money, and why shouldn't they have it, they've worked for it? The landlord wants his rent, and why shouldn't he have it, he owns the place? I can't pay the telephone bill, the electricity bill, I can't even pay for the issues of the magazine I fail to bring out. If fair means anything it's not fair on them. And above all it's not fair on you. It probably never has been. But certainly not now. Come on, Humpty. Let's hear the truth.

HUMPHRY But you've just spoken it. Almost. Even if you get the grant doubled you'll be having a version of this conversation a baby or two from now.

STUART Yes, well, trust Humpty to go the unpalatable stage further. But he's right. In the end it won't survive.

MARTIN It will. If you come in with me –

MARIGOLD You don't know everything! You don't always know everything! (*To Humphry.*)

Humphry looks at her, makes to speak, doesn't.

I – can I – look, do you mind if I – well I want to talk to our editor, the literary gent, you see. Sorry. (*Little laugh.*)

---

* In the published text Hubert Stout appears as Hubert Parkin, but I have kept the name we changed to in rehearsals to avoid confusion.

2

Further Experiences in
An Unnatural Pursuit

Flops and Other Fragments

There was a party at Sardi's to celebrate the opening of my first play on Broadway. The producer, whose only venture into the theatre this was to be, sat sobbing at the end of a long table in an upstairs room that had emptied with the arrival of the *New York Times* review (epoch of Clive Barnes).

GRAY Oh, come on now, no need to cry now. Only a play! (*Little pause.*) Old chap?
PRODUCER Only a play? When I invested all my wife's money in it? And I haven't told her yet?

Early the following morning, my wife and I stole with our luggage through the hotel lobby, to avoid the manager who had given us cheap rates, a high standard of service and mysteriously obsequious smiles because, as we'd also learnt at the Sardi's party, he too had invested money in us.

Back in New York some months later, with a new piece. Standing in a bar next to the theatre during the interval of the second preview, my third large whisky smouldering in my mitt. A friendly figure hovers beside me, orders himself a drink.

FRIENDLY (*after a pause, turns*) Saw the same guy's last. That was crap too.
GRAY (*shakes his head gloomily*) State of Broadway.
FRIENDLY Somebody ought to give him the bum's rush. Got enough crap of our own. Don't need his.
GRAY Yeah.

This piece first appeared in Ronald Harwood (ed.), *A Night at the Theatre*, London, Methuen, 1982.

A smooth theatrical production, though, interrupted only by life itself. Our youngest actor mugged twice in his dressing room during the first week of performance. One of the understudies raped in a car park during rehearsals. Our leading lady held at knife-point for two hours behind the theatre. Flying home after a week of previews, I phoned from the airport.

STAGE MANAGER Hello.
GRAY Hello. Simon here.
STAGE MANAGER Oh, hi, Simon, what can I do for you?
GRAY Just wondering how it went this evening.
STAGE MANAGER The first act went pretty well, I thought.
GRAY Good. (*Pause.*) And the second act?
STAGE MANAGER There wasn't a second act.
GRAY Oh. (*Pause.*) Any particular reason?
STAGE MANAGER The company went to see *Hello Dolly.*
GRAY Instead of doing the second act, you mean?
STAGE MANAGER Right.
GRAY Oh. (*After a pause.*) Any particular reason?
STAGE MANAGER Somebody reported a bomb in the theatre.
GRAY Oh. (*Attempts lightness.*) Which?
STAGE MANAGER (*laughs politely*) Ours.

On my third visit to Broadway, all went well apart from the discovery of the wardrobe mistress's body in the wardrobe an hour before curtain up on the first night. Natural causes, however, which in New York, opening doors on to inexplicable mysteries, are more alarming than the run-of-the-mill foul play.

In Berlin the German translation of my first play was almost a complete triumph. At curtain call the cast received a prolonged ovation. The director, one of the Grand Old Men of the European theatre, was summoned to the stage, and cheers sounded; which continued as he beckoned me up to join him. Two usherettes led me through the wings, and out, centre stage. I tipped myself forward, shyly.

GRAY (*after several bows*) Why are they booing?
GRAND OLD MAN It's normal, you see.
GRAY (*bows again, to increased boos*) Well, who exactly are they booing?

GRAND OLD MAN You.

GRAY I see.

GRAND OLD MAN You must take another bow, please.

GRAY Why?

GRAND OLD MAN Because it is bad manners if you do not.

GRAY But if they're booing me . . .

GRAND OLD MAN (*irritably*) It's quite normal.

In Rome the theatre burnt down a month before we went into rehearsal for my fifth play. Or so the Italian translators claimed.

One of my plays had its premiere at the Charleston Festival (twin to the Spoletto Festival) while the wardrobe-lady-dead-in-the-wardrobe play was still running on Broadway. I made Charleston headlines with 'Gray Hits Town' which I took to be a set-up for reverse headlines when we opened a few days later. The humidity was such that every morning, in my air-conditioned hotel room, my clothes were soaking before I put them on. Either humidity or the usual terror. Unusual terror, actually, as I kept receiving messages, delivered by hand to reception, from a member of the cast, a swarthy and muscular youth who, in the course of the play, was called upon to garden-shear an old man to death in a fit of pique. His messages, scrawled on scraps of what looked like lavatory paper, were rambling but unmistakable threats against my person, brought on by my interference at rehearsals. One evening I returned to find waiting for me at reception the messenger himself. I fell instinctively into my favourite defensive posture, the academic stoop, which I at once realised made me resemble his nightly victim. Readjusting myself perhaps excessively upwards, I strutted the two of us to my room, and woofed him disdainfully into a chair.

GRAY So. What's the problem?

YOUTH You're killing me.

GRAY Ah. How so?

YOUTH The way you keep trying to make me hold back. I got something special to give the audience. Something special. You got to let me give it.

GRAY (*reverting to academic*) Well, you see, what I feel is, you see, is that this is a shy inhibited boy, the part I wrote, who can scarcely talk to other people, as I mark clearly in the text, I feel you'll agree, or even look at them except humbly and gauchely.

YOUTH Jeez!

GRAY But you, you see, you come bounding on stage, you see, and furthermore, I know I've mentioned this at rehearsals, forgive me if I'm labouring, woof woof, and you stand there ogling the audience, if you follow, and doing that odd business with your eyebrows I've mentioned, woof woof, and bellowing and leaping about, sometimes you give the impression woof woof that you're about to do a cartwheel or sing or take out a guitar and strum it. (*Pause.*) Woof.

YOUTH OK. (*Pause.*) Right. (*Pause.*) OK. (*Slides his hand into jacket pocket, where Gray suddenly observes a lumpish object, clearly lethal.*)

GRAY Now. Woof. Now – (*Calculating: too small to be garden shears themselves. Knife? Pistol? Dusters? Clublet?*) Why not a drink? (*Moves smoothly to telephone, picks it up suavely, trembling.*) Call down for (*Help! But calm, keep calm!*) Scotch for myself, d'you fancy anything?

YOUTH Got one. (*Takes can of Charleston beer out of jacket pocket, rips it open.*)

GRAY Woof. Send up Scotch please or some such. Woof woof. Now?

YOUTH The tradition I work in, you see. Commedia dell'arte. That's where I am. Commedia dell'arte.

Settles powerfully forward in chair, expatiates on commedia dell' arte, his talent for it, my suppression of it, while supping down Charleston beer, until –

Telephone rings.

NEW YORK Just to confirm, Simon, that you're coming to the Tony awards next week, Simon right?

GRAY Hadn't thought to, actually.

NEW YORK Now look, you got to come, Simon.

GRAY Why?

NEW YORK You've been nominated!

GRAY Yes, I know. But I'm not going to win. That play about people dying nobly of cancer is going to win. So there doesn't seem much point in coming all the way to New York, and being locked in a large room, and being shown on television for a few seconds watching somebody else winning instead of me if you follow – (*To Commedia dell'Arte.*) Excuse me.

NEW YORK (*passionately*) Who says cancer is going to win, Simon? Who says you're not going to win, Simon?

GRAY Well, everybody. Including me.

NEW YORK Well, I'm not allowed to say who's won and who hasn't, but what I want to tell you, Simon, is this, Simon, that there are a lot of people in this town who think you're going to win, and are rooting for you to win and are going to be very, very surprised if you don't win, Simon.

GRAY Well, I still think – (*To Commedia dell'Arte.*) I'm *very* sorry –

On the day of the Tony awards I left Charleston, where the commedia dell'arte youth had stolen all the notices – he was welcome to mine, as they weren't up to much – and flew to Washington, *en route* to New York. Or London. My tussle was even shorter than Robert Frost's in the snowy woods. I watched part of the awards programme on television at the airport, and noted that the noble-death-by-cancer winner expressed profound surprise at his success. So perhaps he'd been rooting for me too.

A small, plump, engagingly camp American who once wrote campaign speeches for a famous but no-hope Republican candidate moved to London with a dream: to produce a play at the Haymarket Theatre, London. A play of mine, small, domestic and mildly troubled, was put in his way. Stopping only to pick it up, and certainly not finding time to read it, he raced with it towards his dream. And lo! lo! it came to pass that he stood at the famous doors, in white tie and tails, and welcomed in the elderly fashionables and the usual gang of critics, etc. About three weeks later he phoned me.

PRODUCER What do you think went wrong?

GRAY Oh. Play too small? I suppose. Or theatre too large. (*Pause for thought.*) Both, probably.

PRODUCER Yes. Well, you did your best.

GRAY Thank you.

PRODUCER Thank you.

GRAY Not at all.

PRODUCER (*after a pause*) And we did it at the Haymarket.
GRAY Absolutely. That's where we did it!
PRODUCER Thank you.
GRAY No. Thank *you.*
PRODUCER (*whinnies; pause*) Be in touch.

He hasn't been. Although I've heard that he's back on the American election trail, campaigning for another loser.

My first and still my favourite flop was at the Aldwych, about twelve or thirteen years ago. Rehearsals went well, as they're wont to do in the real flops. There was a great deal of easy, after-rehearsals talk about the transfer, its venue and date and even, reaching ahead to the end of the first run, about replacements. Wood was, of course, touched, and other superstitions honoured, but nothing, it was felt all round, was likely to go wrong. Four weeks of work, and there wasn't a single fragment of the play – and each fragment was being meticulously polished up and polished up – that didn't seem exactly funny, exactly sad. What conclusion could be drawn from this, other than that when the fragments were aligned, the whole would be exactly right? Perhaps the truth is that at that stage we – the two producers, the director, the cast and I – had quite different versions of the play which none of the fragments, still invitingly open-ended, could contradict. It was a tribute to the camaraderie of the company that we listened to each other's versions in a spirit of friendly, though sometimes impatient, disagreement.

So it remained until the first real run-through, which took place in Sadler's Wells, at about six in the evening, some twelve or thirteen years ago.

Few buildings are as desolate as an unused theatre, which seems to exude all the cold shadows of its past failures. One of the producers turned up, previously a chain-smoker and now a gum-chewer, and isolated himself in an aisle seat to the front of the stalls. I remember peering towards him when the lights went down but before the stage was lit, and noting that, with his face rising attentively out of the collar of his overcoat, and with his jaw flickering, he looked like some strange reptile, a lizard of the dark; and then looking around at the rest, scattered at intervals in the ghastliness – gargoyles, undertakers, murderers from Victorian novels – a brotherhood from Hieronymus Bosch.

Some three and a half hours later, again frailly human in the lights of the pub around the corner, we tried to speak of what we'd seen – all those fragments, still with their polish on, but resting inertly next to each other. Continuity, which was to give us our whole at last, had in fact emptied the fragments of all their possibilities. Four and a half weeks of rehearsals had provided us with seven or eight little corpses of seven or eight little plays. Such an entertainment had at least found, in that theatre's ambience, its appropriate audience.

Desperation set in at once, and our voices were calm with it. Most of our sentences began with, 'No, all it needs is . . .' or 'What we've got to do really, is just a matter of . . .' though I also have the impression that the word 'life' figured significantly; as in, for instance, 'No, what we've got to do really is just a matter of giving it life.' 'That's right, you're quite right, a bit of life is all it needs.' Well, we were right. Does any corpse need more?

In the following run-throughs in London, then between audiences in Brighton, we worked for life. Our attempts took various forms, and were ingenious. The director thought out new moves and assisted the cast into new readings. I rewrote incessantly, adding scenes here and cutting monologues there. We changed the ending, sometimes twice in a single conversation, and of course and almost by the way, we continued to polish up and polish up. Ultimately, because nothing pays off like hard work and a willingness to adapt, we were rewarded. We established connections, we achieved coherence. Our little plays joined themselves into one whole play. Our little corpses swelled and joined into one big corpse.

About halfway through the Brighton run we had an illumination. Our key phrase became suddenly to do with the need to salvage the 'real text' – although I think we suspected that none of us any longer knew what this was. We had made so many alterations, insertions, revisions of alterations, and addenda to insertions that probably the authoritative script was buried deep in the collective unconsciousness. Still, we must feel our way back to the 'life' of the 'original'. But each struggle with our now immaculate corpse simply produced increasingly complicated arrangements to its limbs – fresh ways, in fact, of laying it out. Which eventually gave rise to yet another proposition (for what could be manipulated could also, in a sense, be said to 'work') – that though we had to pursue our quest for its life, we nevertheless mustn't lose what we had already got. So we watched the audience fall as if palsied before our piece, and laboured in whispers to reconcile our two quite opposite intentions – to preserve our articulating corpse, which at least kept people in their seats; and to recover that forgotten impulse that might actually make them sit up. Once again, but with a proper reverence for the dead, I rewrote; again the cast relearnt; and again the director redirected; and again our corpse walked, corpse-like.

Midway through our second week at Brighton I sat in the foyer of one of the grand hotels, half an hour or so before curtain-up, and wondered, as I nursed my fourth refill, whether I could make it to the theatre. A new guest arrived, a smart, plump, on-the-town sort of johnnie. As he signed in he spotted the small poster on the desk advertising the play.

GUEST Ah, that looks good. Think I'll pop in on that.
RECEPTIONIST (*applying right thumb and forefinger to nose,
    squeezing it, while jabbing left thumb down brusquely*)
GRAY (*decides he can make it to the theatre after all*)

At the interval a wizened and effete novelist from a bygone age, famous for his vivacity, introduces himself into the familiar cluster of demoralised author, despondent director and hopelessly brave producer. He makes to speak frankly of what he's so far seen, is cut off by a swift introduction to myself. Upon whom he fixes a gaze of malevolent compassion, and proceeds to speak of his cats and his garden and other wholesome topics until the bell releases us back to our torment.

It was an odd thing about the play, that though the audience clearly loathed it, and though Brighton is celebrated for the sound of up-tilting seats at almost every stage of every performance of any play ever performed there, nobody actually walked out on us, or even left us at the interval. Nor did they cough, shift irritably or applaud at the end, though there was always a rather eerie rustling when the curtain dropped as of spectral hands or autumn leaves. Perhaps we sapped their will, or they felt that having looked in by mistake on a corpse, they were obliged to keep the vigil with us.

A director friend of the director was summoned to Brighton to save us. He came straight from the station to the theatre, and afterwards, over a fish dinner, told us that all we needed, really, was a bit of life. Yes, ah yes. And a lot – lots and lots and lots – of colour. Ah. Ah-hah! Yes! And you also need – don't you? – more movement? With his fresh eye and unshattered morale, we saw through the haze of our fatigue a small light dimple. Work began on the set the next day. It was halved in size and coloured up until it began to look like the interior for a naughty postcard. The cast were given some new moves, which they were asked to execute on the run; and some new lines, which they were asked to deliver on the run, but which were actually only a down payment on a whole new folio of rewritten scenes I provided over the next few days, also to be performed on the run.

The transformation from Brighton to London was miraculous even to those of us who had worked the miracle. Our Lazarus hadn't come back from the dead, of course, but with his cheeks freshly waxed and rouged, with his false nose and funny trousers, he was up and about his newly half-sized grave, up and about and on the run. Galvanised himself, he succeeded at last in galvanising our audiences. Groans of irritability, early and resonant departures, angry complaints at the front of house, full-throated comment at the interval – he conjured up all the recognisable components of a swiftly recognised flop. We allowed him a limited run at the public before performing the last rites and piling the earth on top of him. But he managed to keep rearing up, vivid in an endless sequence of obituaries. The dailies were followed by the weeklies, the weeklies by the monthlies. The chappie in the *Daily Mail*, a scourge of our times, based on it, in a full-length feature, his whole case for bringing booing back to the theatre. Should I be around some night when the graves give up their dead, I know which corpse, capering festively, funny trousers flapping and false nose pointing, will head straight towards me.

A few months ago the telephone rang.

WEST END Ah, Simon? Just to make sure you'd be coming to the theatre awards next week.

GRAY Well, Eddie, I hadn't really _

WEST END But you're up for four. Best actor, best actress, best
director and best playwright.

GRAY Really?

WEST END So you've got to come. Haven't you?

GRAY Why?

WEST END Because of all your nominations.

GRAY Yes, but as we're not going to win – that play about the
deaf-and-dumb girl is going to win. So there doesn't seem
much, well – in coming all the way into town, and being locked
into the Café Royal, watching somebody else winning instead
of me, if you follow.

WEST END (*suavely*) Simon. Let me just say this. Nobody knows
who's going to win.

GRAY I do.

WEST END *Nobody* knows. But – if you won't come – let me put
it this way – who do you want to pick up your award for you?

We went, my wife and I, and watched the actor and actress pick
up the awards for themselves, as well as for the author, expressing
on each occasion, in prolonged passages of deaf and dumb, their
delight and surprise. So . . .

So. I can claim after fifteen years in the theatre that I've learnt
only that I've learnt as little from my few correct decisions as from
my many mistakes. In that respect too, it has been a second home.

Confessions of a TV Playwright

I became a writer of television plays entirely by accident, before I was in possession of a set or thought of television as anything other than a magic machine that transmitted cricket and football matches into the living rooms of friends; who were thus victim to unexpected visits during, and to deft cultural jokes between, important internationals. I didn't know – wouldn't have been caught dead knowing – who Honor Blackman was; had never in my life clapped eyes on a ballroom dancer, at least in action; and wouldn't have believed that people actually wrote plays *for* television. Now, a mere two and a half years later, I can usually identify by name the second villain in *The Avengers*, feel that my judgement ought to carry weight in the ballroom competitions, and have once or twice been overheard saying a soft goodnight back at the closing-down announcer. I am an addict. The only respect in which I haven't changed is in my ignorance about the nature of television plays, although this ignorance is now a complex and active state.

The first play I did was an adaptation of a short story I had had published in *Voices*. The BBC offered to buy the rights, and my agent was anxious to sell them, but there was never, in the early stages of negotiations, any intention on either side that I should do the adaptation myself. But when the script editor revealed in a slip of the tongue that the rights were worth less than the work of adaptation, I became both thoughtful and bold. I told my agent that I was sure I would soon 'pick it up', my agent presumably told the BBC that I had already picked it up, who courteously but presumably with qualifications agreed that I might at least be allowed

This article first appeared in *The Times Literary Supplement* on 19 September 1968.

to try to pick it up. For the next few days I worked at visualising the story in television terms. When on the bus or in the bath I would project it on to an imaginary screen; I went to the public library and scrutinised a book with a title like *Writing for Television;* and I struggled to realise a weak recollection of having once seen a television script, while struggling to forget that I had had to put it away from a dizziness induced by phrases like 'boom-in', 'angle right cam', 'angle left cam', and 'tracking shot'. I still have no idea whether these words actually exist in the television vocabulary, but I became frighteningly convinced that they or something like them did, and that it was the merest part of my function to know when they should be employed. I didn't, of course, know what a television camera looked like, but another recollection of certain films suggested that it was sat on by an expert in headphones who drove it backwards and forwards, sideways and in circles, in accordance with this crucial code. So my visualisations became now feeble, now frenzied, and my library pursuit of knowledge became more eccentric (to the point, actually, of reading Gilbert Harding's autobiography; for his was a name I did know), and in other words I did everything that I thought might assist me write the script except arrange to watch a short play on television. I suspect that in those two weeks I did as much genuine research as I had ever done while a registered PhD student, and to approximately the same effect. In the end there was nothing for it but to sit down at the typewriter and begin.

It took me about four hours to produce the script (it was a half-hour play); for my approach, when the chips were down, was simple to the point of imbecility. I eliminated all the prose between the dialogue – of which there was, thankfully, a great deal – and then replaced the prose with terse but masterful instructions. So instead of describing the way in which a character entered a room, I wrote:

JOHN (*Opens the door, comes into the room, walks towards the sofa. Stops. Turns. Sits down on the chair.*) Good God are we really . . . etc., etc.

Occasionally and experimentally, as for instance when I couldn't think of anything to go in parenthesis, I wrote in 'close-up', or 'hold camera', or 'track significantly'. When I had done this, I typed the whole out again and, with the confidence of a man who is in possession of thirty neat pages, had them delivered to the BBC. The script editor telephoned the next day to say that everything was fine, although there *was* a problem.

The problem was that the play was to be done 'live'; by which was meant that the play was not to be taped or filmed; which in its turn meant that I would have to think again about continuity; which finally and specifically meant that a man who is in the bath in one scene cannot be expected to appear fully clad and halfway through a cigarette in the next (which I in fact had expected of him) and vice versa (which I had also expected of him). *So*, the script editor said, if I could just think of ways around this problem. I thought of them immediately, for I was not afraid to draw on all the resources that I assumed were at the disposal of so technologically complex an organisation as the BBC, only to hear, in amazement bordering on contempt, that these vaunted experts could manage very little in the way of expertise after all.

'You mean you *can't* superimpose water on an actually empty bath in which a nude man is sitting (who have you got for the part, by the way, have you toyed with Gielgud?), *but* cutting off his head so that Gielgud's head *looks as if* it's on the top of his neck – a perfectly simple trick shot I should have thought, actually (what about Olivier?).' At the end of the conversation it was agreed that I would rearrange the scenes; a matter, I was comfortably told, of only a few hours' work.

It was a matter of only a few minutes' work. I moved another scene in between the bath scene and the dressed-with-a-half-smoked-cigarette scene, thus allowing Gielgud or Olivier a full 75 seconds to change into a suit and get into his fag; and I retyped two other pages that had become grubby in transit, and I sent it in again, and it was accepted as the final version. I had written a play for television.

I had never before attended rehearsals for anything, although (again) I had seen enough films to know what authors looked like when they did so. I took my posture from Henry Fonda – an authorial hunch, a humane smile, an air of inner grace. I paused, for a second, before the door behind which the first reading was to take place, checked a minor lesion of confidence, then stilt-walked inside. A number of instantly familiar faces turned towards me, smiled courteously, turned away from me. I found an empty chair and, with flaming cheeks and lowered head, tried to become deaf to my own dialogue. I don't believe that, in the six or seven rehearsals I attended after this, I exchanged more than a few phrases with any of the actors, who were unfailingly but mutely polite, as if there were water between us. The director, on the other hand, warm and loquacious, contrived to use effusion as a means of evasion. I was thus kept isolated, by two contrasting types of charm. It wasn't until I had experienced the same thing in longer plays that I came to realise why this happens. The writer, until he becomes hardened, is acutely embarrassed at hearing his lines said aloud by people who are publicly stuck with them; the actors are acutely embarrassed at possessing voices, faces, even personalities, that they suspect are deeply at odds with the lines they have to say, which they also suspect they haven't understood anyway; the director is hysterically alert to any whiff of conspiracy between the author and the actors. He knows (quite falsely) that the overriding ambition of any author is to direct his own work, and that, foiled in this, his next immediate ambition is to direct the director by taking over the actors. But during rehearsals for that first small play of mine I had only the desire (too modestly held even to pass as an ambition) to be allowed to mingle with actors I had admired in the cinema, and perhaps to pick up pieces of praise from here and there. To have a small part, in fact, in the whole magic process.

Oddly enough I made more real contact with the actors on the night of transmission than I did on the occasions when there was no immediate strain. I was escorted down to the dressing rooms by the script editor, instructed in the etiquette of well-wishing (hugs and kisses for the ladies; powerful hand-clasps and confident smiles for the men) and in each room I found, not an egomaniacal star eagerly awaiting the moment when he or she could hog the cameras, but a diffident, sympathetic and extremely nervous person who would have given a great deal to be somewhere else, about to do something else. Up to this moment I had myself been unimaginatively confident (after all, *they* were professionals, even if I wasn't) but before so much bravely contained panic it was impossible to be anything but sick with fear. I was shown around the set, which had cost some £6,000 to construct, and which seemed an extraordinary chaos. The studio itself was a muddle of trailing cables, abandoned cameras, and meaningless (to me) steel constructions that rose, with sinister imprecision, to a roof so high that it was almost out of sight. Here and there a cool fellow in jeans loitered, negligently. Dumped arbitrarily, or so it appeared, in all this vastness was the set; a clutter of fake rooms, fake offices and fake corridors, the totally fake and yet hideously extravagant realisation of those peremptory phrases – 'Goes down a corridor, enters office, proceeds through it to bar' – that I had thrown so casually down on paper. The original story, from which all this had blossomed, had taken a day and a half to write. The television script a few hours. The scene changes a few minutes. My total expense could not have been more than sixpence and the story anyway had never seemed more than a trifling exercise between important literary adventures. And here were the consequences of that cool frivolity. Six thousand pounds of debris, six terrified actors, and a host of ace (judging by that negligence) technicians. I could see only two possible conclusions. Either denunciations from press barons and money chancellors, or universal recognition for a genius whose throwaway jokes, even, had to be brought to the attention of the widest possible public, no expenses spared.

I trudged beside the script editor, up to a little glass box with a television set and two armchairs inside it. This room gave on to a window-lined corridor from which I could take in a descending panorama – by way of the director and his assistants in a kind of science-fiction control room immediately beneath – down to the floor of the hangar below. I had, under the pressure of reality, abandoned my Henry Fonda imitation in favour of a country-bumpkin-in-the-big-city bewilderment – a role that on the whole better suits my *fils du peuple* face. I made incomprehensible conversation with the script editor and kept my eyes off the clock.

What started at ten precisely was both agonising and amazing. By walking a few feet out into the corridor my gaze could rest, first on the director, who sat at the centre of a large desk, with subsidiary directors beside her and a row of television screens, all giving off different pictures, in front of her; then I could shift my gaze down to the muddle of the studio – over the cables, the struts, the blank spaces that surrounded the set; then across to the set itself. There, with cameras aimed at them, the actors were at last at work, live. They bobbed out of balsa-wood doors to re-appear in balsa-wood corridors; they whipped around untelevised corners to saunter smoothly into roofless bedrooms; they stood frozen with tension before relaxing into abrupt expressions, emit-ting easy bursts of laughter that were followed by swift sprints to seemingly arbitrary spots where they froze again, into perhaps postures of rage. I remember particularly the leading actor, sen-sual in a bath, replete, smiling; then out of the bath, behind a camera, thrashing himself into shirt, trousers, tie, jacket, and a half-smoked cigarette that was passed smoothly to him by a lady in a smock with a script under her arm.

On the other hand, by returning to the glass box, I could watch a polished little piece (I refer only to its visual appearance) in which men and women moved up and down the halls of a modern office block or in and out of the boudoirs of Hampstead Garden Suburb. I could watch this and marvel. Yes, marvel at my own mastery.

When it was all over, at 10.30 precisely, the script editor led me down to the dressing rooms again. This time I needed no instruc-tions. Intoxicated, I embraced the men, shook the ladies warmly by the hands, preened among the experts, who still loitered negli-gently, and modestly allowed myself to be escorted up to the BBC bar and bought drinks. I deserved them, for had I not peered into the abyss, and seen not simply order, but an order composed of brilliant and witty surfaces, conjured out of it? I rode home in a BBC taxi, my self-esteem burgeoning naturally out of the mor-row's headlines. As I glanced out of the windows into the London night, I knew what the nation was talking about. The morrow's papers, which dealt in idiot detail with some Cabinet crisis or foreign war, failed nevertheless to mention my play. I was never mentioned at all in the press, to my knowledge; which was vast, as I was still scanning the television columns ten days later.

But if fame was still deep in the bushes, its scent had reached my nostrils. I made my first move down the trail by hiring a set from a shop in Kilburn, and my second, more important move, when I telephoned the script editor with an idea for a new piece, one that would last for a memorable length of time. The script editor, who had just been transferred to the *Wednesday Play* series, listened attentively, jotted down some details, and telephoned a few days later to say that I could go ahead. Before I had even begun to think properly about the project, I was in receipt of the first half of the fee. It was then, on my way to the bank, that I knew finally that I had jumped from having written a television play to becoming a television playwright. There was nothing in the experience that has not been repeated, with varying degrees of intensity, on every subsequent occasion – the sensation of confidence, a temporary impersonation of the wealthy man, followed by a vertiginous descent into a depression that was marked by a compulsion to telephone the script editor, my new agent, the publishers of my novels. But what distinguished it radically from the previous experience was simply that I did not have thirty pages of dialogue with adaptable passages of prose to start from. I had only the memory of a scrappily written and hastily read account of a murder committed in the 1930s, and the knowledge that this time the result was to be taped. The first draft amounted to about a hundred pages, which seemed to me just right. The script editor, however, explained that by this reckoning my first draft would run to a few minutes under two hours. Could not the normal limits of the *Wednesday Play* be expanded somewhat? I reckoned back at him, to accommodate every pause and pan that I was prepared to burn at the stake for. They could not. A *Wednesday Play* was one and a quarter hours long. Mine was to be a *Wednesday Play*. It was to be one and a quarter hours long. Furthermore, there was no stake to burn at. Only the chance that the play wouldn't be done, the second half of the fee wouldn't be paid, and fame would continue to lurk free in the bushes.

I sent in the second draft, which amounted to some seventy pages, confident that *now* everything was just right. This time it was the director, calling in person at my flat, who explained what was wrong. The problem amounted to a curious legacy from the half-hour live play. Whereas in that piece I had allowed the scenes to follow on in the manner of the original short story, with no worries about the consequent difficulties for the cast, I now made absolutely sure that none of my characters ended a scene without being able to step naturally into the next one, or, if that were impossible, had at least a five-minute break in which to slip out of an overcoat. The result made for a chronological coherence that in no way compensated for the disordered dramatic logic that puzzled everyone who read it. Each scene went on for too long, very little seemed to happen in it, and yet there lay behind it some curious atmosphere, really, of purpose.

There was a tentative suggestion from the director that perhaps I had not thought about the visual freedom of television, a suggestion I indignantly repudiated. But in the course of the ensuing apology and counter-apology I suddenly found myself in possession of two crucial facts. One: in a taped play one could jump from here to there, from now to then, because the production could be stopped and started at will (not quite true, as it happens; there are prescribed major breaks and even prescribed minor breaks; but true enough to make all the difference between live and taped). And two: that one was permitted eight minutes of film that could be incorporated into the tape during performance. I approached the third draft with a sense of freedom that could well have culminated in disaster, but the methods I had already and mistakenly confined myself to held the play in a secure grip. I could change and cut, let things happen as they dramatically ought to happen, without being able to distort the basic structure. And so I completed the third and final draft.

Again my relationships with the actors failed to develop until the play had been performed, and again the director manoeuvred charmingly around me, and again I felt as if I were present as either the poor relation or the bailiff. But this time I did have at least the wit to watch what everybody was doing. At first sight they were merely rehearsing in a large, draughty hall owned, I think, by one of those military groups that people like the Duke of Norfolk are constantly appealing to the nation to keep alive. Photographs of uniformed men, massed together and staring hopelessly, hung about the walls between insignia, paintings of cannon, and handwritten directions to the lavatories and snack bar. The wooden floor was marked at intervals by chalk lines on which the props or their substitutes were placed, and here, oblivious to the cold and to the sad, unused spaces around them, the actors were acting with passion and intelligence, and the director was directing them with passion and intelligence and something more. Crouching over a chart with squares and numbers on it, or crouching a few feet away from the actors, boxing off his vision of them from now one angle, now another; pouncing forwards or leaning sideways, he was clearly practising at once the most secret and the most significant part of his craft. What he was doing, as I found out at the post-performance party, was calculating possible shots for the television screen; being, in fact, the camera.

While I, taking up an inconspicuous position at a convenient distance from the actors, was being a theatre spectator. It never for an instant occurred to me that the whole of what I was seeing was in bulk much more (and in significance much less) than what would finally be taped. This seems to me a crucial point, not only against myself in my naivety but about writing for television in general. The audience of a television play has no choice at all, far less even than a cinema audience has. For the fact that the television screen is very much smaller than the cinema screen means not that the effects are merely smaller, but that they are totally different. All through those rehearsals I behaved like a man in the front stalls, with a view of the stage or screen that was certainly comprehensive but could be made selective. Sometimes, as at a film or a play, I watched one actor's face, sometimes another's; sometimes I focused on a detail – the accidental movement of hands or feet. And it became apparent to me, when I read the script again the other day, that I had written out of the same misconception.

I *saw* the characters in their physical completeness, embracing each other or standing away from each other, and assumed, in my quite potent ignorance, that this would be how the final audience would see them. But of course on the television screen there is room only for either a diminutive version of everything or a larger version of something. It is the director's responsibility (and ultimately the writer's also) to ensure that what fills the screen is what is dramatically most necessary. Which is precisely television's strength, for the continuous act of concentration and exclusion amounts to a positive discipline. A television play, in fact, is not a play done on television. Nor is it a film for the small screen. It has its own laws. And this is after all another way of saying that the medium has created a form, flexible and generous when explored imaginatively, inhibiting and even destructive when accepted grudgingly.

When I sit down to a television play now, I do so in a very different spirit from when effecting that first casual adaptation.

I know that I am involved in a different mode of realisation, one in which the exchange of dialogue is more likely to be the starting point than the conclusion. But at the same time – as I confessed at the beginning – I know nothing about the real nature of television plays, what it is, for example, that distinguishes the writing of a good one from the writing of a bad one. That secret is as inaccessible as the secret of writing good films, good novels and good stage plays; as inaccessible as the secret behind all art. A familiarity with the possibilities of the medium makes the beginning merely a beginning, just the same. And although the bushes still rustle, and my nostrils still twitch to the scent, there are many days when I would gladly exchange all my experience for that time of innocence, when ballroom dancers danced in a million homes, but did not dance for me.

I should like to make it clear that I do not hold myself responsible for any inaccuracies in this account of my early experiences as a television playwright. I have merely been as faithful as possible to what I now think it probably seemed like.

3

Culture and Environment

The Pursuit of F. R. Leavis

One of my abiding memories of Cambridge is of a walk I took, one brilliant winter morning, with my current research supervisor. He was a celebrated literary critic, both the author of a number of distinguished books and a well-known reviewer in the Sunday papers. He was also an influential figure in English Faculty politics. He had an easy, anecdotal manner, always treating me with consideration, never bullying me for work, and on our infrequent meetings I found myself liking him a great deal.

As we passed along the Backs he raised for the first time in our relationship Leavis's name. What did I think of Leavis? I tried to tell him, beginning with the effect on me of *The Great Tradition* and *The Common Pursuit*, going on to discuss the influence of his seminars and lectures on my intellectual development – my supervisor listened with his usual inattentive courtesy. 'Yes,' he said fretfully, when I'd nearly got into my stride, 'I do wish he'd hurry up and die.'

His impatience may of course have been with my labouring literalness. After all, I was threatening to answer in detail a question that was probably intended, in the Cambridge manner, to answer itself. Even so, I'd clearly goaded him into a literalness of his own. He hated Leavis, as did many of his Faculty colleagues. Frequently there was a personal history to account for the hatred. For instance, I was subsequently told that my research supervisor had begun as a great admirer of Leavis, had once gone around to visit him with his just published book on a subject Leavis had also written about, had slipped it shyly on to the Leavis dining table,

This review of Denys Thompson (ed.), *The Leavises: Recollections and Impressions*, published by Cambridge University Press, first appeared in the *Sunday Times* on 21 October 1984.

and had had it returned the following day with a covering note from Leavis saying that he could only assume its author had left it there by an oversight, as it could be of no conceivable interest either to his wife or to himself.

During my decade or so at Cambridge I heard many such stories, some of them no doubt apocryphal, but there is evidence in Denys Thompson's collection of *in memoriam* essays to suggest that rather too many of them were true. Leavis wounded his colleagues (though never his students, as is universally acknowledged) where people least like to be wounded, in their vanity. The pain must have been worse for those who'd previously thought that they were his natural allies.

I suppose that in some respect his sense of his own integrity was rather like Coriolanus' sense of his own honour, as dangerous when flattered as when abused. The most poignant epitaph in a collection full of epitaphs comes from Leavis's old collaborator, D. W. Harding. 'I am left,' he writes, 'half wishing he had been different enough not to have had to endure, and to cause, so much unhappiness.' But as Harding recognises in his next sentence, Leavis *couldn't* have been different, if he was to do the work he set out to do. This double note sounds through many of the essays in the book.

Another note that sounds, sometimes faintly and sometimes distinctly, is that it was not really Leavis, but his wife, who was the cause of all the trouble. It was she who snuffled out unintended offence, unsuspecting traitors, blameless enemies, and obliged Leavis – desperate to preserve marital harmony – to wage the public battles and to continue the private acrimony. In this reading Leavis becomes a grimly active variation on the henpecked husband, bullied by his wife's sense of grievance (amounting almost to paranoia) into an aggression quite foreign to his nature – his innate courtesy and charm are reported in essay after essay.

My own limited experience would seem to confirm this view of Queenie. She struck me as formidable and discomforting. In her company Leavis frequently seemed to fall into a kind of wry trance, his eyes flickering with what I took to be an ironically simulated vacancy between his wife – who would usually be enthusiastically demolishing the reputation of a colleague, or an ex-friend or a famous writer – and myself, who would be nodding hypocritical agreements, anxious only to leave. I took what I was sure was his side, of course, and felt a disagreeable pleasure when, after Leavis's death, stories began to leak out that Queenie was claiming that Leavis plagiarised her work. It seemed in character – at least in the character I'd attributed to her.

But several of the essays also mention that when Queenie married Leavis she was promptly and permanently disowned by her Jewish family, in whose love she had always felt secure. After such a profoundly scarring experience she might well have been on the look-out for betrayal from every quarter, even – perhaps especially – from those who came closest to her or to her husband. It was her way of protecting them both, perhaps.

And there are glimpses in the book of a spirit very different from the one I'd seen – the excellent cook overwhelmingly hospitable, the busy housekeeper warmly interested in children (though she seems to have frightened some of them or their parents, with her educational intensity), and towards the end (in a touching essay by Nora Crook), a kind and companionable sort of aunt to a young mother bewildered by Cambridge life. So some of the virtues that survived that traumatic maiming were, ironically, the recognisably Jewish ones. One can never speak confidently of marriages, but hers and Leavis's was an exceptionally long one that perhaps – that one hopes – had at its centre a sustaining love.

Almost all the essays in Denys Thompson's book offer moving little insights into either Queenie or Leavis, or their relationship, and almost all of them capture some elements of Leavis's genius as a teacher, or pay proper tribute to Queenie's gifts as a scholar. I'm deeply grateful for them. Leavis is the only great man I have met, so I suppose it's not surprising that the sentences that have already begun to haunt me come from Michael Tanner's description of Leavis dying:

> he was sunk in unapproachable and terrifying gloom. I can't imagine seeing anyone look so desperate. All he said was 'I'm not feeling chirpy.' Not long after he became completely quiet and docile, and spent nearly all the time in bed dozing. I would go round and see him occasionally; he seemed to like to have someone sit with him and Mrs Leavis did all the time. His death was a relief.

My Cambridge

When I was three I was evacuated to Montreal with my slightly older brother, to live out the war with our grandparents, then in their late sixties. Our grandfather was a businessman who spent the weeks in Toronto and only the weekends at home. My grandmother, an alcoholic, was mainly confined to a large, musty room at the back of what remains in memory a large, dark house. Occasionally she emerged, smelling strongly of peppermints. There was also an aunt, in her early forties, who had long before resigned herself to looking after our grandmother – her only child, so to speak. It was an unhappy household. My father told me, many years later, that his father remained passionately in love with his mother, who had never loved him. Thus, his weekly absences; thus also, perhaps, her addiction to drink; and our aunt's servitude. Whatever their feelings about each other, their interdependence was so complete that when my grandmother died – some twenty years ago – my grandfather and my aunt followed within a few months. The causes of their deaths were medically different, of course, but in reality they had long since come to form one organism.

However these three actually viewed their responsibilities to the two children that war had thrust upon them, they quickly simplified them into catering arrangements. They fed us with all the foods that were to remain unobtainable in England for another decade. They made sure we had clothes, clean sheets and were well shod. They made sure we went to bed at night and got up in the mornings. But they never played with us and only rarely

This piece is taken from a collection of reminiscences entitled *My Cambridge*, introduced by Ronald Hayman, London, Robson Books, 1977.

spoke to us. In other words, they treated us as members of the family.

As soon as we were old enough, we were sent to a local school where, after an introductory month during which we were beaten up when we arrived in the morning, beaten up in the first break, beaten up at lunchtime, beaten up in the second break, and beaten up on the way home, we were accepted into one of the gangs, and joined in beating up less adaptable children. After school and in the holidays we hung about street corners, or went down to the drugstore for sodas and Cokes, beat up the sons of the two French Canadian families in the street, and three Jewish brothers, one of whom was called Harvey. We read and exchanged comics and smoked fairly heavily. By my eighth birthday I was on ten cigarettes a day. Our grandparents gave us pocket money, but not enough for our style of life, so we stole more from them, or from the parents of other members of the gang. I also practised on my own a form of begging. I would write on an envelope an address in England I'd copied from one of the letters that arrived for my grandparents, take up a position by a post office, and cry. On being asked what was the matter, I would explain that I'd lost the stamp money for my letter to Mummy and Daddy, and so would collect in the course of a session anything up to two dollars. I only stopped when a middle-aged plain-clothes policeman told me that if he hadn't been on his way home, he'd have taken me down to the station. He said that from then on he would have me watched by other men in plain clothes. There are moments in my life now when I believe he still does.

We had left England with the moppet hairstyles, the piping accents, the submissive feelings and no doubt manner, of the nanny-trained, middle-class infant. We were returned to it with crewcuts, harsh North American accents and (in my case – I can't speak for my brother, a lawyer) criminal habits. In our grand-parents' house there had been several photographs of our father, their son, whom we failed to recognise from our own past. I don't recall any photographs of our mother. We were therefore as horrified by the powerfully built man and the tall, vivid woman who claimed us from the ship at Southampton as they were by their two overfed sons, with their cropped heads, jug ears, and cunning eyes. We were far too old to be the children of such young parents, and they, who had no doubt often dreamt of clutching again the mere children who had left them, were ashamed of us. I don't recall the trip from Southampton to Hayling Island, where my father had become a GP before the war, and where he had now settled again to become a pathologist, but I do recall our bath, that first night. We were put in together, and our mother washed us. She had us nude and defenceless, but we were no babies of hers. At least, not yet. This was known on both sides.

Our re-education began at once. Our mother gave us elocution lessons (the key words were 'water', 'tomatoes' and 'laugh') and we were sent to the only girls' school on the Island. I suppose that if our mother was to achieve that hold on her two sons that is the inalienable right of middle-class Englishwomen, she had at short order to induce the correct sexual confusions. Two years there were followed by three at a boys' boarding school in Portsmouth, which were followed by two at a prep school in London, where we'd moved after the Portsmouth contribution and at which I was alternately fondled and caned by an extremely possessive pederast; which were followed by five at a famous public school – Westminster for me, St Paul's for my brother – as day boys. At eight and nine we had been acceptable, indeed dominant, members of a Montreal street gang. At thirteen and fourteen we appeared to be acceptable, indeed dominant – because we were both good at sports – members of our years at our respective London public schools. At seventeen my brother had decided on Sandhurst and a career in the British army; at sixteen I had settled for Oxford and the intellectual life. I remained, however, something of a thief (at fifteen I'd been almost expelled for a sustained fraud on the London underground, which had led to an appearance in juvenile court) and a total liar. I was determined never to fuse my life at school with my life at home, and so told lies in each about the other, and told lies in each about everything else as well. I can't explain, of course, what it was I was protecting, but the habit of fluent evasion (my lies not being simple denials of actuality, but complicated alternatives to it) marked me out at school as a clear scholarship candidate.

The intellectuals at Westminster in my time had been comprehensively prepared in Latin, Greek, English and English manners. My Latin and Greek were feeble, my English essays designed to conceal that I'd only partially read, if at all, in the subject on which I was writing authoritatively, and my English manners, being acquired by observation and imitation, could be rapidly adjusted to circumstances. My little peroration at the juvenile court hearing elicited more than one appreciative nod, for instance, just as my General Paper essays in the History Sixth were acknowledged as models of that cultivated but not disturbing originality that wins scholarships.

While in the History Sixth I had a passionate friendship, which never became quite an affair, with a more clever and daring boy who was frequently and romantically ill (he died at Oxford in his early twenties) and I dramatically renounced all games and corps, in order to devote myself more fully to an intellectual life that was all the more shapely in form and epigrammatic in expression for being barren of content. I really did know *almost* nothing, which was exactly enough to spread through the Oxford scholarship papers. If my performances were confidence tricks, then my expensive schooling had given me the confidence to pull them off. I had infiltrated Westminster, in the decreasing though continuing expectation of being found out. Through Westminster I would infiltrate Oxford. It was all quite easy.

Unfortunately my expensive education had drained my father's finances. Just as I was poised to slide out of Westminster and up into Christ Church, the means test, the hospital politics that evolved out of the National Health Service, and a new set of taxes, compelled him to emigrate back to Canada. My distress at having to sacrifice my heritage was alleviated by the realisation that I would at least be escaping National Service. I had long suspected that nothing in my nature or education had prepared me properly for that.

Nobody who came across me during my four years in Halifax, Nova Scotia, would have had reason to believe that this was, for me, a return visit. There was anti-Semitism in Halifax, and a general dislike of French Canadians, but there were no street gangs that, for safety's sake, I needed to join. It was a coastal town, clean of air, with vast beaches and a pervasively moral atmosphere. Along the main street there were almost as many churches as there were banks. I allowed my hair to hang to the nape of my neck – in my first week a policeman stopped traffic in order to wonder aloud at its length – and my Westminster drawl contrasted pleasingly, to my ears anyway, with the nasal Scotian twang. The irony of a chap destined for the Oxford quads actually finding himself on the Dalhousie campus was one that I further enjoyed by bringing it pointedly to the attention of the natives. I sauntered about the college (which now houses the largest collection of Rudyard Kipling in the world) with the poems of T. S. Eliot in one pocket and a pencil and a pad of verses in the other. I saw myself as a boulevardier fallen among provincials, and discovered only after I'd left that I'd been seen in my turn as the campus pansy. My career as a student was a succession of triumphs. I was treated by Anglophile professors and associate professors and assistant professors of English with reverence. Quite a few of them were New Zealanders; others were underqualified Englishmen, or mere Canadians even; too nervous of being seen through themselves to dare to see through me. My essays were passed about the department, and sometimes on into other departments. Once a professor (or assistant, or associate) of Economics searched me out in the library, where I held court by isolating myself in a far corner, to congratulate me on a slimy pastiche of James, borrowed from an equally slimy but more skilful pastiche by Beerbohm. In seminars I could force abdications with a phrase. Fellow students scribbled my rehearsed throwaways into their course notebooks. Those teachers in whose eyes I caught any glimpse of the sardonic, I boycotted for fastidious reasons that helped guarantee my reputation while satisfactorily undermining theirs.

I also made two close friends, one the son of a rabbi, the other of the principal of a Baptist theological college, with whom I read Shakespeare, Plato, Aristotle, Kant, Heidegger, Sartre, Camus, and one or two medium-to-light weights; with whom I went to Westerns and gangster films, discussed life and sex (we took them to be synonymous), and to whom I showed my poems and various novels; in collaboration with whom I founded a literary magazine in which we published my more major works and anonymously, for fillers, some of my minor ones; and from whom, therefore, I received whatever in Halifax, Nova Scotia, I did receive of an education.

I also had one or two experiences with girls – those who were of an intellectual bent themselves, and therefore thought there was some cachet in cuddling the campus pansy (who also, by the way, had a weight problem, owing to a secret addiction to candy bars, hamburgers and Coca-Cola); but on the whole kept sex down to those conversations about life, or firmly back in the head from which I frequently expressed it into socks and handkerchiefs, in the usual manner of adolescents, which I no longer was. The campus pansy/intellectual was in one or two respects, perhaps, a mite regressive, though in fact heterosexual enough for two – the penalty, I now see, of insisting on remaining an English public schoolboy (which, you must remember, I'd never properly been).

But otherwise I grew, and not only fat. I'd started my career at Dalhousie by presenting myself as an English boulevardier. I concluded it as a citizen of all civilisation, known as France. As soon as I'd taken my degree (a most distinguished one romantically marred only by a couple of failures in compulsory courses that demanded, along with application, knowledge), I departed for Clermont-Ferrand to teach as an 'assistant' in its *Collège-Technique.* I was going there to be, not just a Frenchman, but (from the Anglo-Saxon point of view) a thoroughgoing frog, which would entail losing some inches in height, changing the colour of my eyes, wearing a beret, stinking of garlic, despising the English (this I'd managed in advance), acquiring a mistress a decade older than myself and, if necessary, picking up some of the language. By the end of my first week I realised, as I sat in a café puffing Gauloises and sipping marcs with the five or six other outcast English students who infested the educational institutions of that magnificently provincial city, that I was already on the right lines. But during my year I didn't advance much beyond that first circle, except into several official *vins d'honneur*, from one of which, through an excess of wine, I failed only by inches to make it out of the door over which I vomited, and thus had the honour of hearing myself described by one of the thoroughgoing frogs at the back of the room as a *sale cochon anglais.*

At Clermont-Ferrand I became close friends with the English *lecteur* at the university, a man of twenty-six who had been doing the French circuit since coming down from Downing three years before. He introduced me to the novels of D. H. Lawrence and the critical writings of some Cambridge don called Leavis, about whom I'd once read an article in the *New Statesman*, I think it was, by

J. B. Priestley, it must have been, and of whom I therefore also had the measure (as, by the way, I had of J. B. Priestley, having read a Leavis or Leavisite reply the following week). I spent the next two months on the bed reading Lawrence, and then Leavis on Lawrence, and then Leavis on George Eliot, Henry James and Conrad (the Great Novels course had included *Adam Bede*, so I'd got the measure of her; and *Lord Jim*, so I'd got the measure of him; and *The Ambassadors*, the victim of my plagiarised pastiche, so I'd got the measure of him), and then I read George Eliot, and then Henry James, and then Conrad; and then Leavis on all of them, all over again. My real introduction to English literature was thus made in a bedsitter in Clermont-Ferrand, with five years of an English public school education, and three years of a Canadian university already behind me. And my introduction had come through an accidental encounter with a teacher whose writings showed me I still hadn't learnt to read. It became a matter of great importance to get to Cambridge as quickly as possible, for Cambridge – in English studies at least – was evidently Leavis.

I wasn't in Cambridge long before I discovered that Leavis was hated by many members of the Faculty who, if they didn't as a whole take literature seriously, took seriously any of their colleagues who did. Not that Leavis was yet as isolated as he was to become. He still had his Fellowship at Downing, still gave his weekly seminars and lectures, and had a self-appointed coterie of Downing graduates and a girl or two who had fallen in with Downing graduates. It must be admitted, however, that these chaps and their girls weren't, except when viewed from a distance, much fun. They spoke in almost inaudible voices (the girls didn't speak at all) and were masters of what I can only describe as moralising *longueurs* – i.e. sustained passages of silence, which were boring even though one knew that adverse judgements on oneself were being formed in and expressed through them. Febrile personalities (such as mine) could be panicked into hysterical utterance, by which they stood further condemned. In my first year as an undergraduate I bumped into one of the Leavisites in a pub. (But what was *he* doing there? Unless waiting for someone like me.) He was a chunky fellow, broad of shoulder with a broken nose and the characteristic mumble of profound seriousness. He greeted my greeting with a small movement of the mouth, which inevitably impelled me into an extravagant dilation on some film or other I'd seen that week – it might even have been that day; there were long periods of my life when I went to the cinema twice a day; one week, by a judicious use of taxis, I got it up to three times. When I'd come to my throbbing conclusion, he regarded me for an hour or two with an expression of pondering or ponderous humility, muttered 'I see' and departed. I later heard, as one always did hear these things in Cambridge, that he'd finally forced me, in some pub or other he'd caught me in, to expose myself as a 'brute'. A brute. The campus pansy had found his balls, at last.

The only time the Leavis circle – in which, by the way, I never saw Leavis himself – came to life was when it was debating such matters as whether it was the cleaning woman, or Dr Q. D. Leavis, or Leavis himself who'd hung up the washing that had been observed flapping from the garden line shortly after breakfast, but which had been taken down (by whom?) some time before lunch. Inaudible or even silent on so many topics, they were dreadful gossips – in the double sense – on any aspect of the Leavises' domestic arrangements. They were, not to mince words, a pretty grisly gang; but time, thank God, has wreaked its usual shapely havoc. I've heard reports of one who, famous for his scathing silences from which he fired questions so remorselessly personal that they can only have been intended to elicit angry stammers from men and tears from women, or both from both; who shrouded his own movements in such mystery but to such seemingly sinister purpose that his was the face I always conjured up when asked to imagine the traditional knock on the door, at three in the morning, in Kafka and other police states; who seemed so totally without warmth, or even intellectual sympathy, or any but the vilest curiosity – I've heard reports that he has long since sunk cosily into a provincial nook, where, a gentle but bonhomous homosexual, he dispenses hospitality and kindly advice to all who need it; and doubtless to quite a few who don't.

I myself started at Cambridge as a postgraduate. I concocted in Clermont-Ferrand, with my Downing friend's help, a specious outline for proposed research on Henry James, which was accepted by whatever board was responsible for those matters; then, having gained my entrée, insinuated myself back to under-graduate status – I was anyway only twenty – and settled down at Trinity to my two years (my three at Dalhousie being assessed by Cambridge as worth one of Cambridge) of life and literature. Of life through literature.

Those two years, of the in fact eight I spent altogether in Cambridge, ended in the usual unnatural fashion with the Tripos examination. In preparation for it I had only one supervisor, who did me no harm and almost certainly meant me none. We walked in the Fellows' Garden in good weather, or sipped coffee in his college rooms in bad, and we gossiped of this or that great writer, soothingly. He was intellectually versatile, with a grasp of different disciplines – law, philosophy, modern languages, classics, even mathematics – and also an elaborate traditionalist. When I once turned up for a supervision without a gown, he sent me back – a matter of a mile or two – to get it; and on another occasion, when I confessed I was desperate for a cigarette, he pointed out to me that I was having a supervision, and was therefore obliged to wear a gown; and that undergraduates were not allowed to smoke while wearing gowns; then resolved the problem by informing me that he was about to leave the room, and that as long as he was out of the room the supervision was not taking place; and that therefore as long as I took my gown off, and kept it off while he was out of the room, I could smoke my cigarette. He may, of course, have been something of a comedian as well as a traditionalist.*

The only lectures and seminars I went to were those given by Leavis. This was not because I was unduly discriminating, but because in the gap between being a child and having children I found it difficult (having little reason) to get up before lunch; on top of which we weren't allowed to smoke in lectures, a prohibition less disabling to my career as a student than it is now to my career as a lecturer.

As for Leavis's teaching – well, whatever I learnt from it, I carefully refrained from summoning forth during the examinations, for which I trained myself up on the side, so to speak, of my interest in literature and in which I employed the techniques

* He also, by cunningly indirect routes, taught me more than I had the grace to acknowledge when I wrote this piece.

I'd acquired at Westminster, in the History Sixth, with the Oxford General Paper in view. I suppose that my predictable success (I'd predicted it, anyway) was an agreeable late return to my father for the money he'd invested in my public school education, but I mustn't completely disclaim my own contribution – that part of my nature which had combined smoothly with circumstances to make me, from an early age, an accomplished liar. I wrote all my papers with a fraudulent fluency that could have taken in only those who were bound by their own educations to honour a fluent fraud – at least to honour him more highly than any churlish Leavisite whose sense of the texts depended on close and therefore uncertain readings. The rewards were considerable. A first-class degree, and the pleasure of knowing that if I hadn't got the measure of Leavis himself, I'd got the rest of the Faculty dead right.

My moral and social education (they were, in important respects, synonymous) proceeded along the same lines as my intellectual one, to this extent at least: that in public I was a fraud, of ever-increasing fluency. I had polished opinions on novels, poems, plays, films and all pieces of music, including those I hadn't read, seen or heard (I am almost tone deaf). These opinions, however phrased – and the phrasing was all – could be reduced to one uncomplicated formulation: *overrated*. Everything was overrated. Except by me, of course. I went of an evening to the rooms of friends in their colleges, and drank whisky, and curling my voice as a way of curling my lip, delivered my opinion for two hours or so. Then, with the air of a man with more stimulating assignations to keep, I made my exit on a valedictory sneer, then slunk anonymously through the dark streets to the cinema where I sat completely rapt before films that nobody, including their writers, their directors, or the rest of the audience, would ever overrate, or rate at all. After the film, I would go to the rooms of friends in their colleges, with an air of having kept some stimulating assignations, and join in a poker game that often lasted until two or three in the morning. We played for sums we couldn't quite afford, and so frequently ended up, all our cultivated urbanity corroded by whisky and fatigue, in squalid squabblings over our winnings and losings. I remember that one night a man who had lost hand after hand to the tune of ten pounds or so, collected two shillings and sixpence on a straight flush. I drew no conclusion from this, or indeed from any other event in my nightly life, which in retrospect seems to have been one long night, although the routine must quite frequently have been broken by circumstances, if never by inclination. After the poker game, my mouth burnt out with cigarettes, my head aching with whisky, and my stomach dipping from both, I went to bed. At least I suppose I did. I have little recollection of the period between the last dead hand and the first cup of tea in the morning.

Being a sort of alien, with a distastefully complicated background, I wasn't offered rooms in college. I lived in a boarding house with a couple of aspirant politicians from Ghana or Tanzania; an extremely old mathematical historian of twenty-six or seven who was engaged on a work so comprehensive and detailed that he couldn't see his way to begin the actual writing of it for another decade, at least; and a straight up-and-down sort of open-faced chap who was doing one of those fringe courses set up by the Colonial Department a year or so before the Department was wound up, along with a large part of our national history and influence, for ever. We were, in other words, and in our different ways, all aliens. As was our landlord, an extravagant Pole who dressed and spoke as if he ran a tenement in the Bronx. His wife, however, was a sweetly plump, soft-spoken little Englishwoman whom one from time to time suspected of spooning rat poison into the sugar bowl. She served the breakfasts we all ate together, uncommunicatingly; and she made the beds we never shared; and she made sure the water was hot only between 7 and 7.13 in the evenings, as it was her boast that her lodgers could have baths as often as they liked – which, under the circumstances, wasn't anything like as often as they needed them. I have no inclination to go into the room now, small and dreadful as it was, having had to go into it when it was my home, with such despairing regularity, twenty years ago.

My daily life, those long stretches of it that weren't spent with my supervisor or at the Leavis seminars, or lying in bed with a hangover, passed in a kind of blank fretfulness. I did some reading, of course, in my calculatingly selective way, dully, with a pencil to hand for the notes that would (and did) recall it all in the week before the Tripos, but many of my afternoons drifted by in the cinema, or as I tramped and tramped the Cambridge streets. I went to Boots a great deal, passing aimlessly between the counters, or mulling listlessly through the books in its subscription library, turning the pages of the identically spined and coloured volumes in its Western, Thriller and Romance sections, following fragments of the different stories until they cohered into one dully lunatic, unconcludable epic. Sometimes I went to Lyons, and sat over a cup of tea, reading the *Standard* and the Cambridge *Daily News*. Once I stood in the Market Place, in the rain, for about an hour, unable to decide where to go until I became so wet I had (thank God) no choice but to return to my room and sit shaking before my meter-operated gas fire. It seems now, in recounting it, like a kind of madness, and perhaps it was. I have no idea what my soul was up to, although its sporadic yearnings were not unlike the continuous, unassuaged yearnings of my body. Perhaps I was just waiting, getting through the hours until my first public appearance and the first airing of my single opinion.

I was saved by the vacations, part of which were spent back in Halifax, Nova Scotia. In the summer I swam in its great cold harbours, and worked with undistracted if cynical clarity for the Tripos. The winters were bitterly cold, and yet I could trudge the almost snowbound streets with a dizzying sense of purpose and even a future, as if Cambridge had been only a long dull dream from which I had awakened at last.

To which I inevitably returned. But as the Tripos loomed nearer, so did my concentration achieve a focus. I still put in my opinionated public appearances, still played poker, went to the cinema, and did my Boots–Lyons circuit, but for shorter periods, and always with a redeeming sense of something that had to be got back to. In the last weeks of my second year, in the general atmosphere of examination terror, I came to terms with Cambridge for a brief spell at last, positively enjoying even its beauty, which I seemed to see for the first time as I walked to the examination hall in the bright morning, and away from it in the soft afternoon. When the examinations were over, I lay on the Backs in the sun and celebrated my imminent triumph, while simultaneously swearing that when I left Cambridge in a few weeks it would be for ever, and that I'd never open another book; except from interest, disinterestedly.

Next year, lodged as a fraudulent research student (I'd resubmitted my Henry James piece) I organised, in a magazine I edited with a friend, an examination of the examinations. We debated whether the questions they contained could successfully provoke anything but fluency and fraudulence. It's a tradition of English life that though we might sometimes be compelled to bite the hand that feeds us, we never bark at it in public places. Among elderly Faculty members we were dismissed as 'bounders' (the word was actually used), while in the *Cambridge Review*, edited by younger Faculty members whose primary qualifications we had denigrated, we were described as 'psychopathic hoodlums' which my co-editor, a mild-mannered man of disinterested intelligence who'd anyway read History, could well have been; and which I, in spite of my most secret inclinations, had so far found myself unable to be. The *Listener* took up the matter of examinations, as did the *TLS*; and found against us, as did the *TLS*. I should like to claim that from then on my life as a research student was made insupportable by vindictive dons of all ages, but it wasn't so. I was allowed to stay on, and on; and long after I could stand it, on. I had early been alerted to the fact that by changing my research subject every year, I could jostle back to the beginning all over again. When I finally managed to leave, eight years after arriving as a first-year research student, I was still in my first year of research, which I still hadn't begun.

But of the six years that followed my degree I remember little more than the little I've already recorded. Often, when I lie sleepless at night, I need to invoke certain scenes from my past (a late cut executed in the middle of my fifteenth summer, say; or a coolly taken goal, lifted with the toe over the heads of the backs and into the left-hand corner of the net – that, in my great Junior Colts season) in order not to be invaded by those many other scenes I wish absolutely to revoke. But of the new or ancient shames that bring me out of bed and downstairs for tea, cigarettes and monotonously unconvincing justifications, none belongs to or points back to my Cambridge years – not even my undergraduate ones. This eerie infertility may be the result of my having written two novels about being in Cambridge while I was still there, so that I'd seen the experience not only published but in part remaindered before being completed. Or it may simply be that those eight years contained nothing of any consequence, except in their inconsequential passing. From the brightest perspective eight years can be judged as no time at all, especially if one doesn't remember noticing them going by; and could therefore be described as a period of unruffled calm, or happiness perhaps.

But here are some facts. Having begun by not being offered rooms in college in my two years as an undergraduate, in all subsequent years, as I became more deeply habituated to the seedy bedsitters from which I could conduct my furtively independent existence, I declined them. In my last years, and from a panicky sense that loneliness had become an unendurable addiction, I moved into a cold little warren of rooms above a coffee shop which I shared with two other outcasts, one of whom, a Classical research student from King's, was a friend with whom I could eat, for instance, a Christmas dinner of sardines on bread. One winter it was so cold that we wore overcoats in the sitting room, and I had to take two blankets to my favourite cinema – at which, on midweek evenings, I was the only patron. Back in my first bedsitter I used to be kept awake by two young men from Trinity, I think, who quarrelled shrilly beneath my window. One of them committed suicide by tying his head into a plastic bag. The other then went down, or was sent down, or possibly simply followed suit. There was a man from Sidney with alopecia, three tufts of hair growing from a thin blotched head, whom I saw on the streets regularly every year except my last when, instead of dreading the sudden sight of him, I found myself eagerly looking out for him. There was another man, from Trinity again I think, an asthmatic whom prescribed drugs transformed in a matter of months from youthful slenderness to bloat decadence. He also took his life. There was a small, elderly Scots tramp who ran about the town shadow-boxing (like so many of the rest of us) until one term I realised that he too had gone. There were May Balls, to which I always seemed to go in the company of girls who'd waited until the last minute to be invited by other men, with whom they nevertheless succeeded in meeting up after about the third dance of the ball itself, and on my ticket so to speak, and danced my dances with them before allowing themselves to be led off by them (while still morally on my ticket, so to speak), just before dawn, to somewhere that was far beyond the reach of my glaring eyes and acquiescent smile. There were quite nice afternoons on the river with friends, but far better ones alone in the cinema. I drank more and more as the terms succeeded each other with less and less definition. After taking my own degree, I supervised undergraduates. I wrote two novels and began a third, which I concluded after I'd got away, at last, to London. And yes, of course, the bells. The bells rang incessantly, tolling my terms in, pealing to my departures, from which they tolled me back again. The winter light always seemed to dim by three in the afternoon, just as the crocuses on the Backs invariably came up earlier that year. Those are some facts. But even recording them doesn't help me to remember them, except thinly.

I have an abiding impression, though, that something was continuously, undiagnosably unpleasant all the time I was there – apart, that is, from myself. An impression that becomes vivid on those occasions (as few as I can make them) when I go back. There is the moment, as the London train slides along the interminable Cambridge platform, when my stomach lurches, and I violently wish I were visiting somewhere else I used to live; or even better, somewhere I've never lived at all.

4

Real Life

My Place in Cricket History

I didn't see my first cricket match until I was nearly ten. My brother and I had been evacuated to Canada during the war, and our Montreal leisure activities had consisted of smoking, pilfering, comic-reading and general thuggery. The only outdoor sport we knew was a kind of street baseball, played for money and frequently – especially in its later, violent stages – without a ball.

When we got back to England, we were unprepared for any aspect of English life, particularly cricket. But our mother, who had sent off a pair of Christopher Robins and got back a couple of Bowery boys, was determined to rehabilitate us, and at speed. She worked unremittingly on our accents and our table manners, and furthermore she knew – her father had been something of a cricketer and a devoted cricket-watcher – the part that cricket played in the formation of the English male psyche.

So one afternoon on that first summer of our return, when our hair had had a chance to grow out, and our ears had resumed a less grotesque relationship with the sides of our skulls, she took us to Lord's. She prepared for this ritualistically, with a packed lunch of bread and marge, three eggs set aside from the rations, and a thermos of tea (to which we'd only just been introduced, and which we hated).

Our immediate impression of the game of cricket can best be expressed in one image. There, on a large stretch of grass, an elderly 'chappie' in white clothes was imbecilically lolloping a red ball at another, much younger chappie in white clothes, who, stooping imbecilically over a large bat, paddled the red ball either straight back to the elderly chappie or to one of the other white-clad chappies who stood imbecilically about. In fact, it took us

This article first appeared in *Wisden Cricket Monthly*, October 1979.

something less than two minutes to realise that, like most things English, cricket was boring and preposterous.

Also, like most things English – except the women – it was unmanly. We spent the afternoon improvising some rather more virile games of our own, pausing occasionally to observe our mother who – adhering poignantly to her education plan – clapped or called out 'Good shot, sir!' and 'Well played, sir!' in the manner, I suppose, of our maternal grandfather. I've often wondered since what match was in progress. Perhaps Middlesex were playing Gloucester – Goddard being the elderly ball-lolloper. The chappie with the paddle might even have been Compton, though I doubt this. When I next saw Middlesex play, Compton was at the crease, and it was love at first sight.

Of course my attitude to the game has changed a trifle since then. I won't go into my own triumphs as a batsman – not even to linger over a perfectly executed late cut in my fifteenth year that I still evoke when I want to remind myself that life isn't all dross; nor how, in the next season, I swept an ex-England spinner for four when opening for my school. I'll merely record that my development took a classically English line (and bound to, after such an alien beginning) from cavalier smiting and reasonable scores, through coaching and the close study of manuals to creasebound inhibition, declining scores, and a premature retirement.

I play an occasional game now, but I read about cricket and watch it incessantly, and in wangling myself membership of the MCC I've already gone further than my maternal grandfather. In fact, my one contribution to the highest reaches of the game came on my first afternoon in the Lord's pavilion, when, demonstrating to some old stray with watering eyes and the usual veins on his nose how Doug Walters *ought* to be playing the cover drive in English conditions, I stepped back and trod on Doug Walters's toe just as he was clattering his way through the Long Room to the crease, after lunch. He was out almost immediately, having been going, before lunch, threateningly well for about the only time in the series.

I doubt, though, whether my mother, who would have been out of tune with so much in the modern game, would have been proud of me. But then, as we all now know, ritual can blind us to realities, especially in cricket. I suddenly recall that my mother had forgotten to boil the eggs on the evening before that afternoon, thirty-four years ago.

Memories of Lopez

I'd been batting with my usual fluency against the faster bowlers, including the fifteen-year-old who was already reputed to be the fastest bowler in the school, and had rattled up an easy twenty or so runs. The fastest bowler in the school, who I think was called Kemp, and who I know was exceptionally tall and thin, with a long, fearsome and gangly run-up, took himself off after I'd scored three successive fours by simply playing the ball gently and almost, but not quite, straight back at him. I felt pretty good. In those days, until a few minutes later that day, I always felt pretty good when I was batting; and was generally able to attribute my downfall, when I gave the matter any thought, to an act of negligence, unconstrained violence, or to a ball that somehow and unaccountably got through. I was always completely in, in fact, until the moment when I was suddenly out, and that was that. But then the bowlers I always faced simply bowled as fast and as straight as they could, Kemp-like.

So Kemp, who was also the captain, replaced himself with a chap I'd vaguely seen around the school and had heard was something of a bowler, but apart from reputation and a certain foreignness of appearance, was not in the slightest worrying to a boy who'd never been worried at the crease. His name was Lopez (Lopez!) and at fifteen he was slightly balding, and he was sallow. I looked forward to his first ball.

I spent quite a time looking forward to it, because it was quite a time coming. Not that he had much of a run-up, Lopez. There was a short amble from behind the umpire, a stutter of feet as his left elbow came up, and all the time in the world to watch his right arm

This piece first appeared in Michael Meyer (ed.), *Summer Days: Writers on Cricket*, London, Eyre Methuen, 1981.

come over. And then more time as the ball rolled gently through the air, and fell within easy reach of my bat, somewhere just outside the line of my off-stump. As I'd located it so early, I myself had lots of time to gather myself up before scampering powerfully out to smash it where I would. My bat curved through the air, there was a scuffling and a shuffling from behind the stumps, and if the wicket-keeper hadn't made as much of a hash of it as I had, he could have stumped me three times over.

I decided I'd better watch Lopez's next more carefully. This time I took in that actually he was coming from the wrong side of the umpire – i.e. bowling around the wicket – and this piece of information, which I hadn't bothered to register when he'd bowled his first ball, lodged like a piece of grit in my mind all through the ball's flight, and indeed long after it had passed my bat and was being tossed from fielder to fielder back to Lopez. I pondered the implications as he appeared yet again, raised his elbow, stuttered his feet, brought his right arm over, etc.; then turned his back, not even bothering to watch as I picked myself up out of the tangle I'd made of myself just inside the crease.

Nothing like this, I must repeat, had ever happened to me before. I can understand now, having first watched and then listened to Jim Laker on television, that Lopez was a precociously expert bowler of off-spin, with no doubt a master plan for each over and a separate policy for each ball, along with a shrewd insight into the psychology of each incoming batsman, even if he'd never seen him before, and by the time he bowled his fourth ball I had at least grasped that his action was so casual only because it was so accomplished. But the real devastation, of which Lopez was only the efficient cause, was the result of my seeing myself suddenly and for the first time in a different light. It was as if my feet had swollen, my pads grown almost to my chin, and my bat become both so heavy that I could scarcely lift it and too small to make contact with a ball that strayed wilfully in and out of my line of vision, without seeming at any moment to hurry itself. I survived to the end of the over, ran my partner out in the next over, and was out – I can't remember the details, but I have a clear impression – presumably a moral one – that I was lbw, caught, bowled, stumped, and made to hit wicket all at once – off the first ball of Lopez's next. For the first time ever, I welcomed my end.

I went to the boundary, some distance away from where the Junior Colts had dumped the pads and the scorer, and watched a chap of no known class – he'd only been picked twice for the team that term – attempt to cope with Lopez. He did somewhat better than I, eventually perishing nobly in the covers off a stroke that at least looked like a stroke. Some of the later batsmen, including one of the tailenders, actually knocked Lopez about a bit. But then they probably had no idea what they were up against.

Those seven balls from Lopez marked a change in my life. From then on I never faced a halfway decent slow bowler with anything like composure. The ball ceased to be something I hit, and became a revolving tangle of contradictory opportunities – play forward; play back; get to the pitch; smother; *hit him off his length!*; use your pads; get your pads out of the way – that were invariably not taken or taken simultaneously, and either way left me stretched in some ignominious posture astraddle the crease. I think it is true to say that post-Lopez, though I continued to love cricket, I never enjoyed playing it again.

Nevertheless, by application – I took to wearing a cap, the peak of which I jerked before the bowler began his run-up – I managed to make it in due course to the school's First XI, as an opening bat. I survived there for a while because I could still usually see off the fast bowlers, but it was eventually noticed by the captain and the sports master that my departure invariably followed the first bowling change. 'It's a matter of your feet, Gray old chap,' the sports master explained quite sympathetically, as he pinned up the Second XI list, with my name on it. He was quite wrong. My feet were perfectly nimble. It was my mind that it was a matter of.

My slide into the Second XI was the first stage of my slide out of cricket altogether. Having been defeated by thought (my own, or Lopez's) at the wicket, I began to take it up in the classroom, and was thus able to claim that the demands made on me by essays on existentialism, *The Republic*, the French Revolution, and such, made it impossible for me to fritter my afternoons away on a cricket field. I withdrew into the library, emerging only on the occasional golden afternoon as a supercilious spectator who had outgrown even memories of the game, and I made sure always to take a book (Kafka, perhaps) with me, to help me make a telling image on a distant boundary.

Some years later, after periods in Canada and in France, I became, by a process too subterranean for me to be able to mark its stages, a cricket addict again – but only as a spectator, naturally. I spent almost as many hours as I do now watching or listening to the Test matches. Any game in a park, even between squabbling children, would bring me to a long halt, and I read the newspapers mainly for the county scores. I also had opinions, strong ones, on Test selection, and must have composed at least 500 unsent telegrams to the selectors, all of them abusive. My interests became known to my students – I was supervising at Cambridge – and one of them invited me to a knockabout at the College nets. I refused, of course, with just the right amount of flirtatious shyness, until properly persuaded; and one evening proceeded, in the manner of a chap bent on humouring his juniors, to an evening session.

It was as if I went straight back to a time before Lopez and other disappointments had touched my life; or rather as if I'd really spent those seemingly drab years somewhere where I'd discovered a far more skilful cricketing self. I had, for one thing, mastered a curious but effective top spin, holding the ball in a grip that must have come from imagination or pre-natal memory, and by flicking my wrist and twisting my fingers at the arm's arc, at different points of the arm's varying arc, I became my own kind of Lopez to the best batsmen in the College's Third or was it Fourth XI? Furthermore, within minutes of my starting to bat a small group had gathered around my net to note my off-drive (and its follow-through), my on-drive (a stroke I'd found unplayable during my immature prime) and my wristy little turn to leg. At the end of the session I was invited to play in next week's game. Flushed with success, or the folly that frequently follows it, I accepted.

I was put on to bowl first change, the two opening batsmen proving efficient and stubborn accumulators, though not actually dangerous – at least, until confronted with my flickering wrist, twisting fingers and my arm's varying arc. The captain, in whom a spirit of scientific curiosity, or perhaps mere good manners, at that stage prevailed, kept me on for three overs in all, and so was as responsible as I was for changing the course of the game. In one of my resting overs I also managed to drop a catch; a slightly more difficult one than the catch I dropped almost immediately after I was taken off.

My batting was worse because it lasted longer. I played immaculately down the line of the fastish, fastish-medium, and mediumish, so tapping the ball straight back to the bowler, or in the direction of fielders it just lacked the power to reach; or in the case of the slow bowlers either missed the ball completely in my innate style, or had it skid off the bat's base to slips, third bounce. This little swine of an innings – or lengthy swine of a little innings – was complicated by my complete inability to judge a run, which meant that I remained moribund in my crease while my partner, every time he hit the ball, spurted yelping a few yards from his, only to be checked by my imperiously raised hand, and dignified instructions to no, go back. I eventually adopted a bit of a limp, to explain the inexplicable, and tried to deafen my ears to the perturbations from around the pavilion, and the increasingly hysterical gestures from a captain now no longer scientific or polite. I decided to settle for an honourable draw. As long as the next eight men could hold up the other end, I could hold up mine. But the man currently at the other end summoned me to a mid-wicket conference, in which he laid out certain facts hitherto (so I still believe) kept from me. This was a limited-over match, in the new-fangled mode. There was either victory or defeat, with nothing except a tie in between. 'But a cricket game,' I attempted to philosophise, 'that couldn't end in a draw was scarcely a game of cricket. For one thing –' 'Look,' he said, 'you've either got to run or to get out.' With my concentration thus disturbed, I was bowled a mere four overs later, which even so wasn't quite soon enough to prevent our having to concede the game through a series of suicidal run-outs and scything blows that were taken both adeptly and fumblingly on the boundary, with two wickets still standing.

This game, played some seventeen years ago, and some fourteen years after the Lopez match, ended my career as a practising cricketer. I draw no conclusions from either game, or even from both taken in relation to each other, except to affirm that for me, I now realise, cricket has been too much life itself ever to serve as a metaphor for it. Just as Lopez's off-spins altered my development at school, so did that last innings lead, and not too indirectly, to a bizarre outburst at a Cambridge literary party that blighted several delicately forming (in the Cambridge manner) friendships and love affairs. I have a fairly recurrent daydream, though, in which I replay my last innings with a full swing of the bat, in the cavalier spirit that was my own true self, I know, before Lopez robbed me of it; and another in which Lopez himself, still balding, sallow and fifteen years old, appears from behind the umpire, around the wicket, and I dance down to cover-drive him off his length – a dream that I can revive almost at will, even though I've long known that Lopez died by his own hand shortly after leaving school, a victim of depression and, I suppose, circumstance.

HOW'S THAT FOR TELLING 'EM, FAT LADY?

A Short Life in the American Theatre

For Judy Daish

'Hey, Joe, Let's Don't Pull the Plug on This One – Yet!'

Thursday, 12 December 1985

Sitting in my study, my dog Hazel under my desk, talking into this machine as a way, really, of confirming that I'm back home. I arrived in London, disconcertingly, at the same hour as I left Los Angeles. The flight was OK, comfortable in fact, and champagny, though I didn't really enjoy tottering out of the airport with a couple of meals and quite a lot of alcohol inside me, with most of the day still to get through. Actually I feel inert. Irritable and inert. Not perhaps the best state in which to begin a diary. I must remember to record all the dates accurately.*

I was in Los Angeles for the casting of a play of mine, *The Common Pursuit*, which is being done at the Matrix Theatre. The Matrix is a 'waiver' theatre, i.e. its auditorium is so small (it seats 99) that Equity waives all its rules on professional rates of pay, and everybody works for nothing. The actors do it because it gives them a chance to appear in the kind of parts they don't get offered on television – or because they're out of work anyway, and would rather work for no money than not work for no money. I suppose the director and the designers do it for the same sorts of reason. I'm doing it because I'll go anywhere, and do anything, to have an unproduced play produced – although, as a matter of fact, *The Common Pursuit* has been produced twice before. Once in London, at the Lyric Theatre, Hammersmith, directed by Harold Pinter, where it almost but not quite moved to the West End; and once at the Long Wharf Theatre, New Haven, where it almost but not

---

* I didn't, actually heading one report '31 April', a day that doesn't even exist. All the dates have therefore to be taken as approximate.

quite moved to Off-Broadway. So the Matrix is my chance to get it on the move again in the States – possibly all the way to New York. I did a lot of work on the script for the New Haven production, and I've done a lot more since for the Matrix – in fact, I spent a lot of the ten days I've just come back from rewriting sections that I'd substantially rewritten just before going. By the time we finish I hope I'll have got the script absolutely right. Well, as absolutely right as possible.

The casting itself turned out to be the usual exhausting process, only more so. Casting is *always* more exhausting in the States, and casting at the Matrix turned out to be more exhausting than anywhere else in the States, in my experience anyway, partly because a lot of the actors were involved in television series and so their schedules caused problems, and partly because Kristoffer Tabori, the director, and Joe Stern, the producer, were meticulously courteous with the actors. I'm all in favour of that, but sometimes they passed beyond courtesy into what seemed to me very like perversity, if not actual perversion – actors who were seen to be wrong for their parts within two minutes being kept long past their scheduled ten minutes, as if spinning out their ordeal (and ours) made it up to them for their being no-hopers. One chap came in for the part of Nick, who is meant to be a bright young Cambridge-educated middle-class English type on the make, and offered a boisterously anti-Semitic version of an East End Jew, complete with lisp and even a touch of a drool. Tabori and Stern kept him at it, not for the courteous ten minutes, not for an inexplicable twenty minutes, but for forty minutes – lisping, slobbering, whining, wheedling, wringing his hands. Furthermore he *looked* completely wrong, being short and bald, with a beard. (Actually, now I come to think of it, the chap who got the part – Bart Braddleman – is short, balding, with a bit of a beard and is apparently a Sephardic Jew. But he got everything else right. Or seemed to at the time.)

Every casting session ran two or three hours over. We weren't altogether helped by our casting lady, who would sometimes forget to notify us of cancellations, and then of substitutions, so that I would write down my impressions beside the wrong name, which would lead to endless muddles afterwards. 'No good,' I'd say of the actor I took to be – let's call him Sprinkleman. 'For one thing he's far too old. For another he obviously can't do English.' 'Too old!' Kris Tabori or Joe Stern would exclaim. 'He's twenty-six. And what do you mean, he can't do English, he *is* English!' 'English! He's from the Bronx, from the sound of him. And at least forty.' And so it went, until the casting lady would suddenly remember that the one I'd got down on my list as Sprinkleman had in fact been replaced by Yorricks, or whatever, hadn't she mentioned it, sorry. Of course Joe Stern and Kristoffer Tabori, being familiar with most of the actors around Los Angeles, could spot on sight the difference between a Yorricks and a Sprinkleman, and knew exactly who they were talking about. The result was that for long stretches of utterly worthless conversation I must have given the impression that I wasn't only highly unobservant, but positively out to lunch.

The casting lady also had a penchant for actors – particularly actresses – with whom English seemed to be a second, if not a third language. There was a Polish girl, for instance, who was kept for a quarter of an hour. But that may not have been their fault because she had trouble first understanding, and then pronouncing her lines, so it may well have taken her fifteen minutes to get through her short scene as a bright, Cambridge-educated, middle-class English girl. In fact the part of Marigold for which she was auditioning – the only female part – went to the director's wife, Judy Geeson. This decision was preceded by some pretty heavy private conversations between Joe Stern and myself. The reason I was against casting Judy Geeson wasn't because I didn't think she was right, or a good actress, but because I'm going to be around from the second week of rehearsals on, and I want to be able to discuss the actors' progress frankly and fearlessly. I mean, I can't imagine myself saying to Tabori, 'Look, what the hell is your wife up to in the first scene?' sort of stuff. And I also want to be his closest confidant and ally. Unlikely if his bed companion and breakfast mate is in the production too. In the end I gave in without ever confronting Tabori directly on the issue, deciding that it was better not to have as my director a chap whose judgement I'd questioned in the worst possible way, by overruling him on the casting of his wife. No doubt she'll be very good. She certainly seemed to be at the read-through we had the night before I left. In fact, she seemed to be the only one of our cast who knew what she was doing.

So what with all the casting hassles, and the intensive bursts of rewriting, I really feel I've been away for months, not a mere ten days. But I've enjoyed telling my family about Los Angeles – not the working part of it, but the place itself, and especially about the little cottage lent to me by Tabori's sister-in-law. I painted pictures at once vivid and lyrical of orange trees, humming-birds and so forth, until I detected from the slightly sickened expressions on the faces of wife, son and daughter that what I was bringing before their eyes wasn't unlike some sugary sequence from the Walt Disneys of my childhood. They probably half expected me to burst into song, or imitate the cute American chatter of the red squirrels.

I shall miss the cottage – Tabori's sister-in-law has rented it out to some Japanese, and Joe Stern seemed uncertain about where precisely I'm going to live when I go back the week after next. He assured me, though, that I wasn't to worry, he knew of a house, a little house, a *nice* little house, just up from the Taboris, and if that falls through and all else fails, I can always stay at the Magic Hotel, gesturing out of his car window (we were on our way to the airport) at a large, institutional-looking building, quite evidently remote from anything in the way of bars, restaurants, and even shops. 'That'll be all right,' he said, 'because it's cheap.' I said, with a heavily warning inflexion, that I hoped it wouldn't come to that, and reminded him that I didn't drive. He said, 'No, no, don't worry, we'll find you something. A nice little house . . .' I must remember to keep Joe on the job when he phones. I've no intention of ending up in the Magic.

Beryl has just come into the study to remind me that we have to be off in an hour to Queen Mary College, for a ceremony in which I'm being made a Fellow.* She said that I looked *louche*, jet-lagged, ill-tempered. I said that that was how I'd looked every day of the twenty years I'd taught there – the effect of an hour on the tube followed by a walk down the Mile End Road – they might be confused if I appeared in a different guise, might not even recognise me. 'Anyway,' I said, in genuine bewilderment, 'why

---

* I'd had a rather stationary career at Queen Mary's, starting as a mere lecturer, and ending up, twenty teaching years later, as a mere lecturer. I was disqualified from promotion on the grounds that I never wrote anything – or at least anything useful, like a critical work.

am I doing it?' She explained that I was 'doing it' to prove to scep-
tics, among whom she numbered herself, that I had a generous,
not to say magnanimous spirit. 'But why to them, why there?
Can't I prove it to someone else somewhere else later in life?' But
Beryl, who always tends to treat my most urgently practical questions as if they were merely rhetorical, advised me to shave, and
to shampoo my hair. I'll compromise. Shave one cheek and shampoo some of my hair. I'll leave out the bits that are sticking up at
the back.

Sunday, 15 December

Back in my study, Hazel for some reason on the sofa, staring at
me with her usual compassionate unintelligence. Joe Stern has just
phoned with two pieces of news. The first, infinitely complicated,
to do with some airline ticket deal he's made with Stephen Hollis
in Dallas – I'm going straight on to Dallas from Los Angeles to co-
direct an old play of mine, *Dog Days*, at the New Arts Theatre.
Stephen, who is the artistic director and an old friend, is going to
co-direct with me. Joe saw an opportunity here to save money by
getting the Dallas lot to pay my fare to Los Angeles. In return he'll
pay my fare from Los Angeles to New York and back when I have
to pop over there for a few days for the *Dog Days* casting. I can see
how this benefits Joe, but not quite how it benefits Stephen and
the New Arts, although I have some idea that the New Arts has
some sponsorship thing going with British Caledonian, which, if
I understood it, would probably explain everything. Anyway,
there was Joe on the phone going into all the details of flight
schedules and doing sums aloud – at one point he seemed to be
forbidding me to go to New York on a Sunday because the ticket
cost 800 dollars more than on any other day of the week – can this
be right? – when I cut through with a question on the subject I
really wanted to hear about. The rehearsals of *The Common Pursuit*, how were they going? 'Well,' Joe said, 'the main thing is that
Bart Braddleman' [*the Sephardic Jewish chap playing Nick*] 'has
walked out.' On the grounds apparently that he couldn't do it,
didn't know what was wanted, couldn't understand what the play
was about, and had been offered another job. So Ted Larkins, an
English actor who had looked in auditions as if he ought to be a

good Nick, but had given a cute, laid-back rendering, has stepped in in his place.* 'Oh,' I said, 'I see,' thinking that this might possibly be a change for the better, and deciding not to get too despondent. 'Well, how are things going apart from that?' Joe said he really didn't know, there wasn't much to report on yet because, he said – making the old heart dip, lurch, sway and jump about – they'd only been at it a week and they'd spent it breaking the play down. 'Breaking it down – what do you mean?' 'Well, you know,' Joe said, 'sitting around the table and analysing it. Scene by scene.' Analysing it. Around a table. For a week. I had thought that that kind of rehearsal had gone out some time in the sixties or so. But there it was again, at the Matrix Theatre, in Los Angeles. I tried not to sound too appalled, but did inevitably say something to the effect that you can really only find out about a play by doing it – straight from the start – moving it, getting the actors to move, say the lines and discover it, the play, in practice. Sitting around tables and analysing is for academics, etc. 'Yeah, well – ' Joe said, 'I dunno. Anyway, that's what they've been doing.' We then exchanged Christmas salutations, looked forward to seeing each other in a few days, hung up. I felt dispirited. And irritated with myself, as I'd forgotten to ask Joe whether he'd found my little house, nice little house yet.

Monday, 23 December

Had lunch with Judy Daish, my agent, after a bout of Christmas shopping. Remarked that I'd heard nothing further from the Matrix, things must be going badly.

Tuesday, 24 December, Christmas Eve

One of those link-up telephone calls from Los Angeles, Joe at the theatre connecting with Kris Tabori at his home, connecting with me in Highgate, Hazel at my feet. They were calling to tell me that four days previously – *four days* – John Delancey (Stuart) had come to Joe and said he couldn't play the part, was completely at a loss with it, could he bow out? At the same time Joe and Kris Tabori had come to the conclusion that Clancy Brown – the chap who

---

* For reasons that will become apparent, I have changed this actor's name.

was playing Humphry – couldn't play the part, and should be asked to bow out. Their solution, therefore, was that Clancy Brown should leave the production; that John Delancey, who insisted that he'd always wanted to play the part anyway, should take over Humphry; that Kris Tabori should bow out as director and take over the part of Stuart; and that a new director, a chap called Sam Weisman, should be brought in. I received this news, one, two, three, rap, rap, rap, on my chin, just like that. Dazed. When I finally managed to speak, I asked why they'd waited four days before they'd let me in on the facts. 'Oh well, you know,' said Joe, 'we didn't want to ruin your Christmas.' 'We wanted to wait,' Tabori said, 'until we'd got it all sorted out.' 'It should work out fine,' Joe said, 'except it'll mean a delay in rehearsals.'

I said that I could see that it might work out. Going by the read-through John Delancey would almost certainly make a better Humphry than a Stuart, and Kris Tabori, being the right age, and with the right acting pedigree (as I'd gathered), would probably be a good Stuart, but why, I wondered, bring in a new director, wouldn't it be better to let me direct it, as I knew the play better than anyone else; had been through two previous productions? 'Well, no,' Joe said. He had a special thing against writers directing their own work. It never panned out. And the man they'd brought in, Sam Weisman, loved the play, had wanted to direct it himself from the moment he'd finished reading the first (Lyric, Hammersmith) script, had directed Harold Pinter's *Betrayal* with great success the season before, was an old colleague/friend and an associate director of the Matrix. He would do a good job.

Before I could pursue my own claim to direct, Joe shifted the subject – Kris Tabori dropping off the line – to my flight to New York to cast *Dog Days*, explaining that as we were now running late in Los Angeles it would be better if I went to New York later. The juggling with dates confused me – anything to do with dates always does – but I was pretty sure that Stephen Hollis would be fed up at being postponed yet again. I asked him if, under the circumstances, he would break the news to Stephen. He said of course he would, what's his number? I found this rather odd. As he's spoken to Stephen quite a few times, he presumably has the number. Nevertheless, I found Stephen's number, and gave it to him, adding that if Stephen had left for England for Christmas,

the theatre in Dallas would be able to give him his number here –
I myself didn't have it, as Stephen had just sold his London flat,
and would therefore be staying with friends, relatives, whatever.
Joe said OK, he'd phone the theatre, try and catch him there, if he
didn't, would get his London number, phone him here. We closed
down on fond wishes for Christmas, etc., looking forward to seeing each other in the New Year, etc., although I felt my throat
constrict as I uttered my share. After all, I'd spent ten days in Los
Angeles specifically to help cast the play, and now here we were,
with a new director, a new leading man, a new Humphry, a new
Nick – what had been the point of my going? And to have waited
four days before telling me. And what about the little house – he
didn't mention it. I must remember to ask Judy to tell Joe that the
Magic Hotel is out of the question.

Friday, 27 December

Talked to Stephen Hollis, who got in a few days ago from Dallas.
Actually getting in touch with him was an irritating and expensive business. As I didn't know where he was staying, I had to do
what I told Joe to do, i.e. phone the New Arts in Dallas in order to
get his telephone number here in London. After we'd arranged a
meeting to go through the text of *Dog Days* I asked him whether
he'd heard from Joe Stern about the date changes. He said he
hadn't. I phoned up Joe to ask him why he hadn't yet been in
touch with Stephen. He replied that he'd phoned Stephen in
Dallas, but Stephen wasn't there, he'd gone to London. 'But Joe,'
I said, 'I told you that Stephen would probably be coming to
London, didn't they give you his number here?' He said they
didn't have his number. 'Didn't have his number?' I said. 'But Joe,
they've just given it to me.' There was a pause. Then he said, 'Yeah,
well I phoned just after he left so I suppose what they meant was
that they didn't have his number while he was in transit.' As 'in
transit' could only mean while Stephen was in the air, it certainly
did seem unlikely that they would have a number for him. I
allowed a heavy silence to reign for a moment or two, the implication of which he must have grasped, because he burst into what
seemed to me characteristically American bombast. I say American
because I've heard its like only from Americans and it always

includes phrases like 'I've been busting my ass off', with lots of
references to money. What it specifically amounted to was that
he'd been 'busting his ass off' to put this show together, in which
he had so far invested 35,000 dollars, and yet here I was phoning
up to be querulous about his treatment of Stephen Hollis, *so what
the hell was going on around here?* Actually it was difficult to follow
any clear argument because it wasn't so much speech as a series
of angry barks down the telephone which were not quite directed
at me. I allowed yet another silence to reign. He then said, 'I've
been thinking of pulling the plug on this show.' That was his
phrase, 'pulling the plug on this show'. And went on to imply that
it was only his grace and generosity that had prevented him from
'pulling the plug' on the show already. As I too began to feel that
it would perhaps be advisable to 'pull the plug' on the show, I
allowed another silence, a dignified one, I trusted, unlike the previous two which I had intended to be recriminatory. He abruptly
reversed tack, apologised for being 'so snappish', and asked me to
give him Stephen's telephone number, which I did. He then told
me that Sam Weisman was going to be in London in a few days'
time and would make contact with me, and that, by the way, he'd
fixed up a really nice little house, I'd love it.

   We parted, under the circumstances, on fairly amicable terms.
Actually it's a recurring feature of my relationship with Joe Stern
that almost all our telephone calls contain passages of hostility and,
on my side, acute suspicion, none of which is present when we are
in each other's company. The telephone seems to bring out the
worst in both of us, perhaps because we both depend a great deal
on our gestures and expressions to explain our language. Joe in the
flesh is one of the most engaging people I've ever met. He's in his
mid-forties, and bears an astonishing resemblance to some kind of
soft animal, rodent-like but affectionate. He has a pack of straw-
coloured hair on his head. In fact, now I come to think of it, he looks
like Walter Matthau, always on the move, jerking in and out of
rooms, talking a great deal and with great intensity, with a kind of
curious Californian-Jewish wit, I suppose it is, although actually he
is much more like my idea of a New York Jew – cynical, guileless
and funny at the same time.* I don't think I've ever met a man who

* He was actually brought up in the neighbourhood of the Matrix, the synagogue
which he attended as a child being only a few hundred yards or so down the road.

comments on the different angles of the life in front of him so incessantly – whatever he sees prompts a joke, an observation. He seems
not to listen completely when you speak, picking up half-phrases
of what you've said and translating them into arias of his own,
usually arias of reminiscence, going right back to his childhood.

One of his specialities is a kind of verbal practical joke springing a series of unrelated questions at you, talking solemnly back
to you in your own accent, then switching mid-stream to a Bronx
accent, or plunging without preamble into a passage of Pinter, for
instance – one of his favourites is Max's speech about horses from
The Homecoming: 'Horses! Don't talk to me about horses!' – somehow tangling it into the conversation to surreal and heady effect.
So much extravagant, free-flowing fun can leave him curiously
vulnerable to counter-attack, though. On my last evening in Los
Angeles he took me out to dinner – an event he clearly wanted to
be very special. As we approached the majestic and expensive
restaurant he said, 'Well, I hope you're going to like this place.' I
said, very emphatically, 'I *know* I'm going to.' He said, 'How do
you know?' I said, 'Because I was here last night.' He looked absolutely appalled. He said, 'What? Oh come on, you were here last
night? Oh Jesus, I wanted this to be new – oh Christ, you were here
last night?' I had to explain that this was merely a little joke. I was
attempting here a little joke. He looked astonished that he'd had
played on him the kind of joke he likes to play on other people,
and kept referring to it for the rest of the evening. 'So it was a joke,
eh? A joke. Well, what about that?'

Monday, 30 December

Sam Weisman is in London, and phoned to arrange lunch. I suggested Peter Mario's, an Italian restaurant in the Chinese section
of Soho – the same restaurant, I now realise, where I first met his
predecessor, Kristoffer Tabori.* Perhaps not a wise choice, as it

His wife, by the way, runs a synagogue. A peculiar kind of job – at least it had
never really occurred to me before that there is a profession, as opposed to a
vocation, of running a synagogue, though I admit that I don't quite know what
running a synagogue entails, practically.

* For years I went there several times a week. I not only had my own table but an
understanding with the management that whenever I came through the door the

hadn't worked out too well with Tabori, at least to begin with. But then Tabori's appearance in London had been surrounded by mystery. On several occasions he'd phoned from Los Angeles to announce his arrival, naming the day, and then a few days after the day named would phone up to name a further day, on which he also failed to turn up, until at last, after a couple of further postponements, he phoned up on a hitherto unnamed day from London itself, to announce that he was here. I had a funny feeling about Peter Mario's even as I suggested it, especially when he wouldn't let me give him directions. He said he knew his way around London, and anyway had a terrific street guide, which he loved using. He turned up about an hour late, having got lost. Probably not altogether his fault. I've lived in London most of my life and still get lost, even without the help of a street guide, but being kept waiting always puts me in a rage, which turns into a kind of simmering headache when I have to suppress it.

He's actually got a very personable appearance and manner, large brown eyes, wide, ingenuous smiles, very fluent – rather like a young academic in his first job. Also he talked very well about the play. In the end we parted on the best of terms, though I remember being made uneasy by his habit of addressing me as 'sir', not, I hoped, to draw attention to our age difference, or even (which I wouldn't have minded) to a difference in our professional status – I a battle-hardened campaigner of many productions, he a boy soldier who'd not yet had the sniff of blood (his own) in his nostrils – but rather as if it were some kind of nickname I'd picked up without being aware of it. Not quite 'sir' as when one calls a dog 'sir' in 'Get down, sir!' for instance, but certainly more intimate than hierarchical – which is a kind of contradiction, really. The odd thing is I can't recall whether he's called me 'sir' since. Joe has, once or twice, but with him the intention is simply ironic. 'And how are you today, sir?' sort of stuff. I very much hope Sam Weisman doesn't call me 'sir'. Even ironically. Especially on a first meeting.

As I was recording this I suddenly noticed that I had two cigarettes going. Two. One between my fingers, newly lit. The other in

piped music would be turned off. It closed while I was in Los Angeles on my second trip and the premises converted into yet another (surely unwanted and certainly unneeded) Chinese restaurant.

the ashtray, half smoked, damp on the underside, staining yellow near the top, a long trail of ash dangling from it. I've really *got* to give up. On the first day of January I'm going to make a serious attempt. It's probably madness to try with so much tension going on, but then there are always likely to be tensions going on either professionally or on the home front – rows with my children, and worries about Hazel's health. She is now very blind and very deaf, though she is still capable of sniffing the air, twitching her head alertly about, and rushing dramatically to the front door to bark at it with spirited aggression, usually when there is no one there, thus showing that even though her senses may be on the decline, all her instincts are still in some sort of working order. Our walks in the woods are being conducted in a more colourful manner than usual because in this cold weather she has to wear a strange woollen garment that Beryl has manufactured out of an old sweater. For Hazel this amounts to clothing and I think she feels that she has taken a step up the evolutionary ladder. A clothed dog is some-where on the way towards being a human being, a status which, for some indecipherable reason, she dearly considers worth gaining.

Anyway, to come back to the other subject. I am going to try to give up smoking on the first of January. I remember that Harold gave up during the first production of *The Common Pursuit* at the Lyric, Hammersmith, and was much helped by a nicotine chewing gum called Nicorettes. So on Saturday I moseyed up to the chemist for some Nicorettes, to be informed that I could only get them on prescription. On prescription. I asked the reason. The chemist wasn't quite sure, but he thought it might be because nicotine chewing gum could be addictive. I said, 'It can't surely be any more addictive than cigarettes?' No, he said, certainly not more addictive than cigarettes. I asked whether it was harmful in any way and he said, no, not that he knew of, certainly nothing like as harmful as cigarette-smoking. He added that Nicorettes were also very expensive, almost as expensive as cigarettes in fact.

When I got home, I phoned up my doctor at her group practice. As she wasn't there I said to the receptionist, 'Well, perhaps one of the other doctors can help me. I'm giving up smoking in the New Year, and I need a prescription for nicotine chewing gum.' To which she replied, 'No, there's nobody here who can help you on the telephone. You'll have to make an appointment and come in.'

'Come in?' 'That's right,' she said. 'We can't give out prescriptions on the telephone.' This receptionist was Scots, and sounded as if she were in her mid-seventies, though she was probably only twenty-five – but she had that sort of prissy, Edinburgh accent, every vowel and consonant a salute to morality and education. 'So you'll have to come in.' 'But,' I said, 'I don't want sleeping pills, or heroin. Simply nicotine gum, to help me –' 'I'm sorry, there's nothing I can do. You have to come in and see a doctor if you want a prescription for your nicotine gum. Because it's a pre-scription. We can't just let you have one on your say-so over the telephone, you know.' Recognising that a Scot is a Scot (I'm half one myself) I hung up. Then, remembering that my doctor is, in fact, perfectly normal, pleasant and helpful (Welsh), I wrote her a letter explaining that I was buggered if I was going to sit about for hours in a germ- and baby-filled waiting room just to get a prescription for nicotine chewing gum that I was going to have to pay heavily for into the bargain. I enclosed a stamped, addressed envelope. At least I hope I did. My preliminary manoeuvres to give up smoking have resulted in the kind of irritation that usually leads to my stepping up my smoking.

Tuesday, 31 December

Had the lunch with Sam Weisman. He was on time, which got us off to a good start. He's in his late thirties, possibly early forties, with rather startling blue eyes – no, not startlingly blue, startling *and* blue, as if magnified unnaturally.* He has an intelligent Jewish face, thinning ginger hair swept back, a goat-like beard, and best of all, a direct, uncomplicated manner. We spent the first hour fencing – i.e. not talking about the subject we'd come to talk about. He'd just read *An Unnatural Pursuit*,† and asked questions about casting in London. He could scarcely believe, he said, that Harold Pinter and I had encountered the same sort of problems that he and other stage directors had encountered in Los Angeles. He'd imagined actors over here would queue up, if not actually lie

---

* I discovered in Los Angeles that he wears contact lenses. Perhaps they magnify the eyes as well as the vision.

† My diary of the London production of *The Common Pursuit* [*see above*].

down on their stomachs, for the opportunity of appearing in stuff written by me, directed by Harold. I greedily accepted my share of the compliment while also accepting that this was so much fol-de-rol, and muttering something dark about the independent-spiritedness of our lads and lasses, along with the high quality of our television drama, which offered lots of very good parts for reasonable amounts of money, finally nudged the discussion on to the Matrix, and all its recent turmoil – the director taking over as the leading man, the leading man taking over the part of Humphry, the chap playing Humphry leaving, the chap playing Nick being replaced, and not least, his own emergence as the new director. He allowed me to air all my doubts and worries while calmly assuring me that all could still be saved. We parted on the understanding that we would meet up again in Los Angeles in a few days' time. Greatly relieved, I phoned my New York agent, Phyllis Wender, to say that I wasn't going to exercise my own option to 'pull the plug out' on the production, though I was entitled to do so, having director approval as well as casting app-roval. 'Well, no, as a matter of fact you haven't, Simon,' she inter-rupted me. 'As the contract was drawn up after you'd approved Kristoffer Tabori as the director, there seemed no need to put anything in about director approval.' So it was a good thing I'd approved of Sam Weisman, as there was nothing I could have done about it if I hadn't. That's how things stand, then, on Tues-day morning, half past midnight. I leave for Los Angeles on Satur-day, midday, and on Sunday, back in Los Angeles, I'll have to sit through a read-through of the new text, with the new, or rather revised, cast.

Wednesday, 1 January 1986

Evening   Beryl, her sister Jennifer, Jennifer's two-year-old daugh-ter Alice, and I saw the New Year in with glasses of champagne, after watching a film on television called *The Black Stallion*, about a boy's relationship with a horse, which would, I think, have been a fine film if its last section hadn't been devoted to establishing that boy and horse were American-style winners, i.e. won lots of money in races. Pity, because the first two-thirds had been touchingly about their growing trust and mutual dependence. There was consequently something obscene in seeing the boy turning himself into a successful little jockey, and this fine animal becoming a successful commercial proposition, both looking proud of it. Still, it was a more wholesome experience than we'd have had if we'd ventured out to a party. Nowadays the sights of London, even on the least festive nights, resemble sketches by Hogarth.

Our son, Ben, on the other hand, did go to a party, to which he hadn't been invited. He and his friends had made up a list during the day of five or six parties, to not one of which they'd been invited, but to which they somehow assumed (correctly, as it turned out) they'd be welcome. How news of these parties reached them is quite incomprehensible to me – a kind of town-crier, or town-whisperer, system seemed to be at work. The party they selected, after much consideration, had about forty people at it, apparently, all of them also uninvited. The hosts were two young television producers, both of them small and bearded, who presented each uninvited guest with a bottle of champagne on arrival. This wasn't their night's ration, but a sort of door-prize, as apparently there were bottles of wine and spirits scattered every-where. Most of the guests were in their late teens; the two hosts were in their mid-thirties, but neither Ben nor his friends could tell me much more about them, not having much inclination to meet them, let alone talk to them. 'But what was it *like*?' I cried, finally, in bewilderment. 'It was all right,' he said. Perhaps he attends such affairs all the time – certainly I only learned about this one because I happened to ask him how he'd spent his New Year's Eve. Lucy also went to a party, a disappointingly mundane one, as it was given by somebody she knew. All they did was dance, drink, smoke, and whatever else people of sixteen do with each other these days.

Stephen came around at about ten, to read *Dog Days* with me. He brought a camera with him. Beryl was slightly surprised to discover him in various of our rooms, taking snapshots of book-shelves, fireplaces, cluttered desks, for the benefit of the Dallas set designer, who wanted views of the inside of a downmarket North London residence, of the kind in which you'd expect to find an under-achieving, would-be-philandering literary type, and his adulterous, deceitful and moralising wife. I said rather frostily that I believed Beryl and I were a cut above the two characters in my play, both socially and morally, turned him around on the stairs as he was making his way up them to our bedroom, camera at the ready, and ushered him into my study where we sat down to our reading of *Dog Days*.

I found myself loathing it. Absolutely loathing it. After the brief opening scene I could scarcely bring myself to speak the lines, they seemed so smart and predictable – as if I'd once written down a number of jokes, and then filled in the feed lines a few years later. Nothing sounded spontaneous, nothing simply happened – everything worked for, then crunchingly arrived at. I therefore disliked the chap who'd written it some fifteen years ago, and by the end of the second act could scarcely believe that in six weeks' time I'd be going to Dallas, to add my name to this little horror as co-director, as well as sole author. I tried to share these doubts with Stephen, who brushed them robustly aside, saying he was delighted with what we'd discovered, looking forward to his part in the production immensely. Perhaps he sees it as his duty to unmask me publicly in western America.

We talked for a short while about casting, bandying names about, until I suddenly remembered Ian McShane, an English actor who'd worked successfully at the Matrix a few years back, and who more years back had appeared in a couple of Harold's plays. I phoned Harold, who spoke highly of him, and then phoned Joe Stern – McShane now lives in Los Angeles and has become a friend of Joe's – to get his telephone number. What of course Stephen and I had forgotten was the eight-hour time difference between London and Los Angeles. I got Joe at a quarter to five in the afternoon our time, at a quarter to nine in the morning his time, on New Year's Day. I realised this immediately from the confusions of his voice when responding to my New Year's greetings. I went on to give him an enthusiastic account of my lunch with Sam Weisman, and oh, by the way, I interrupted myself, do you by any chance have a telephone number for Ian McShane? Whereupon Joe, who until then had sounded drowsily touched by my concern, became galvanised. 'What,' he asked, 'what do you want Ian's number for?' Oh, merely thinking of him for *Dog Days* in Dallas, I explained. '*Dog Days* in Dallas, well, you know. I just want to assure you that there's no possibility – no *way* – that Ian will be interested in doing *Dog Days* in Dallas. For one thing Ian has lots of commitments, for another he's going over to London where his wife's going to star in a big, big show,* for a third thing he'll want to stay on in England while his new television series is released there, and anyway why should he want to go to Dallas, he's a much-sought-after actor, no *way* will he go to Dallas, why should he want to go to Dallas, who'd want to go to Dallas?'

I tried out one of my pauses, indicating through it that I at least was somebody who, while not perhaps *wanting* to go to Dallas, was nevertheless obliged by circumstances (shortage of funds) to go there. He met the pause with a pause of his own, then said, 'You know, I'm just trying to save you wasting your time.' 'Well,' I said, deciding to shelve examining with Joe the question of his proprietorial, not to say positively possessive concern for Ian McShane, 'he can make up his own mind, I suppose. I mean, he won't object to being *asked* if he'd like to go to Dallas, will he? Do you have his number?' Joe abandoned the phone for two or three minutes, then came back with a number that I took to be Ian McShane's, though I got no answer when I tried it.† I thought it wiser not to ask after the little house, whether he was sure it *was* a nice little one, and had he had a video installed yet, etc. (I'd asked both Judy Daish and Phyllis to remind him of my need for a video), feeling that I'd already done enough damage to his first morning of 1986, so again wishing him Happy New Year, see you soon, hung up.

Friday, 3 January

It is eleven at night. I leave for Los Angeles tomorrow, the plane departing at midday. Nothing much has happened since the attempt to communicate with McShane the day before yesterday, apart from a conversation on the telephone with Harold, on the subject of my giving up smoking. I wanted to know how he'd

* Big, big, *big* show called *Chess*, though as I haven't seen it, I have no idea what part his wife played, or perhaps still plays.

† Nor did Stephen when he tried it regularly over the next few weeks. But Joe was dead right. I met Ian McShane in Los Angeles, during *The Common Pursuit* rehearsals, and he made it clear, though with great charm, that no way would he consider going to Dallas.

negotiated the nicotine chewing gum – the Nicorettes – stage of his withdrawal, how he'd got from cigarettes to nicotine gum, and from nicotine gum to no nicotine at all. He asked, rather strangely, I thought, 'What do you want to know for?' 'Well,' I said, 'I might one day contemplate giving up smoking and I just wondered about some of the details.' He said, 'But what do you want to give up smoking for? I mean, what are you talking about, I'm sure you don't want to give up smoking.' Well, I said, I did. Everyone wanted to give up smoking, didn't they? I mean everyone who was fool enough to smoke wanted to give up smoking. He said, 'Yes, but I mean you don't want to give up smoking, it's not really – I mean, you've got a few years of smoking left in you.' I said, but what about health and so forth? And he said, 'Oh well, yes, I mean it's not really – I don't think you should worry about giving up smoking.' I asked him how old he'd been when he gave up smoking. He said, 'Fifty-three. And that's – really, I mean the thing is that you should – perhaps you should hang on until you're that sort of age before you give up smoking.'*

* I am now fifty-one.

Flexing the Life-Muscles

Saturday, 4 January 1986

Here I am, back in Los Angeles at 7 p.m. their time, having two hours earlier, at one in the morning my time, checked in to the Magic Hotel. But it's not at all as I remember it when Joe pointed it out to me from his car. For one thing it isn't cut off, being in easy walking distance of the Grauman's Chinese Theatre end of Hollywood Boulevard, and therefore close to lots of bars, restaurants, shops and cinemas. For another it isn't at all institutional, either architecturally or in atmosphere, consisting of a series of studio flats on three floors. Each of the upper two flats possesses its own balcony, which faces over a kind of courtyard, in the middle of which there is a rather engaging little swimming pool surrounded by a mysterious grass substitute, Astroturf I suppose, which also covers the floor of my balcony. I find the whole effect oddly pleasing, even at three in the morning my time, and am looking forward to sussing out the bar, trying out the restaurant – I haven't located them yet.*

In fact the whole day has turned out to be rather pleasing, in spite of beginning badly by my waking abruptly at seven, summoning a phantom Joe to my bedside and having a row with him on the question of my being booked into the Magic, news of which I'd received through Judy Daish the evening before. These ghastly, schizophrenic outbursts – or inbursts I suppose they are really – must be essential to the workings of my psychic system, but I do wish they'd occasionally take a different tone, loving and tender remonstrances, for instance, with a dash of eroticism thrown in.

---

* They weren't there, to be sussed out, tried out, located. The only hotel I've ever been in that couldn't furnish you with a drink or a sandwich at any time of the day.

But if I could manage that, I hope I wouldn't be wasting any of it, but especially the eroticism, on the phantom of Joe Stern. Things cleared up once I was out of bed, on the move, in the grip of my usual pre-flight panic, but all went smoothly for once,* recrimination-free farewells with my family being followed by a step into a waiting taxi that took me to a punctual train to Gatwick, where I was advised at the check-in counter that I'd been upgraded from 'Super Club', which is neither, to First Class – my natural flying environment, to which I was reintroduced by way of a glass of champagne *before* take-off, when I most need it.

I drank and ate well but not extravagantly, read, dozed, dreamed, read, ignoring the in-flight film (*Pale Rider*, starring and directed by Clint Eastwood – a sacrilegious rip-off of *Shane* – I'd seen and hated it in London) and was only disturbed at finding myself, a couple of hours before we were due to land, engaged in another frenzied conversation with the phantom of Joe Stern on the subject of the Magic Hotel. I sucked down a large whisky, to prepare myself for the usual American customs and immigration ordeal. As I always make a point of travelling light, just an overnight bag that I take on the plane with me, I was pretty fast through to immigration – and through immigration pretty fast too, as the pleasantly smiling young official turned out to be sympathetic to my plight – my plight being, apparently, that I was an indigent Englishman trying to pass himself off as a playwright of some consequence. He asked me whether I'd got a return ticket, and when I made a gesture towards my pocket, held up his hand as if he didn't want to be embarrassed by the pantomime of searching I was about to go through before announcing its loss. 'No,' he said, 'just *tell* me whether you have it, let's leave it at that, eh?' I said, 'But I do have it, actually,' though at that second not visibly, as my hand was in the wrong pocket. He said, 'OK.' There was a brief pause, the two of us staring at each other, then he said rather ominously, 'Look after yourself.' The customs officer, a Spanishy-looking middle-aged woman, was disconcerted both by the small-ness of my bag and then by the discovery that it was only half full, especially when I told her I'd be staying for six weeks or so, but she decided against a body search.

---

* It usually does, for once.

Kristoffer Tabori and Judy Geeson were waiting for me along with their dog Digby, actually a female, who seemed quite pleased to see me, and made no attempt to go for my shoes. On my previous visit she'd taken a positively lascivious interest in my shoes, particularly my-left one, which she would seize between her jaws and try to pull off my foot. The Taboris also have two cats, Flora and Asia. On the first night of my first visit to Los Angeles I had entertained Flora, a black and white cat, on my bed – I'd lured her in with a bowl of milk which had been consumed by Digby who'd bowled in ahead of her, then clamped her jaws around Flora's head, and dragged her around the room. Flora clearly resented this but submitted to it passively – wisely too, as it was probably the best tactic to employ to avoid having her head bitten off. That was the only night Flora spent with me. I think she thought I'd lost respect for her, like a Victorian maiden that had been ravished. Yet she continued to haunt my house, frequently spending the night staring reproachfully in through the glass door.

I never saw Asia, her sister, who had vanished a few days before I arrived, but the Taboris assumed that she'd been abducted and consumed by a coyote – if one gets up early enough one can apparently see packs of coyotes swarming steadily up and down the complacent-looking, suburban streets, rather as office workers swarm towards the tube in London, I suppose. If ever a puppy, a cat, or a baby goes missing around here, its absence is generally attributed to the coyotes, which may be a plausible explanation, though I've noticed that even in London babies, cats, dogs vanish, and we don't generally attribute this to packs of squirrels or foxes, nor even to packs of office workers. The Taboris' other pet is a parakeet who had just been released from quarantine when I was here the last time. Her name is Ben, owing to initial confusion over her sex, and she's now seventeen with a life expectancy of ninety. But apart from that – that as she is likely to outlive one by several decades at least, she now and then induced intimations of mortality – I found her a quite enchanting creature, extremely affectionate, and with considerable dignity. Digby, for example, would stand staring into her cage for hours – I mean *really* for hours, just stood staring through the cage bars at her, while she hopped about pecking at grain, or stared back past her, as if Digby were a particularly uninteresting piece of furniture. When she came out of her cage she would flap ponderously around the room before alighting on a Tabori shoulder, where she would sort of purr with her beak, a cluck, cluck, purring sound, of sheer happiness.

When at last she chose to land on me, she gripped my finger with her claw, not a grip for security, but out of affection also, then ran her beak up and down my cheek – although I have to admit that the moment she first came at me was rather terrifying, as she aimed herself straight at my face before sort of collapsing on to my shoulder, though she then set about calming me down with her beak-nuzzling and beak-clucking and claw-gripping. Digby, of course, who had pursued her across to me, stood staring indignantly up at her, then pursued her back to the cage. But I don't believe it would have made any difference if Ben had chosen to make the journey on foot. Her will was evidently much stronger than Digby's, and will is what counts between animals, as between most humans. Anyway, I've never been so entranced by a bird. Never even saw the point of birds as pets before – and actually, because of the methods employed in catching, crating and shipping them, I don't think I could allow myself to have one. But if there are any knocking about, already caught, crated and shipped, then I wouldn't mind doing some sort of deal with it. It could share my study with me as far as I'm concerned. Although I expect Hazel would have some objections.

I asked the Taboris after Flora (fine but still shy), Asia (still missing, presumed dead), and Ben (radiantly happy) as they drove me to a supermarket, then on here to the Magic. They are due back in a few minutes to take me to a nearby restaurant, where we are to have dinner with Joe and Pepe Stern, Sam Weisman and possibly Sam Weisman's wife. Half past three in the morning my time, and I'm standing with my feet on my turf-clad balcony at half past seven in the evening Los Angeles time, waiting to go out to dinner. But as we have a read-through of the play tomorrow morning, it's all quite sensible – my plan being to stay awake until around 11 p.m. (Los Angeles time, naturally) in the hope of getting a decent night's sleep.

Before I sign off, I should say something about my other, larger plan – to stop smoking. I've brought with me an enormous load of Nicorettes, enough to see me through at least four weeks. I chewed quite a few pieces during the flight. The trouble was that I also smoked. There was a foul moment when I realised that I had a box of Nicorettes on one knee, and on the other, or just beside it, in the adjoining seat, a packet of cigarettes and my lighter, and that between my lips I had dangling a cigarette, while between my jaws a piece of nicotine gum, as if in some way the latter cancelled out the effect of the former. Altogether during the flight I must have worked my way through half-a-dozen pieces of gum, without my smoking being in the slightest affected. Which means, of course, that I managed to take far more nicotine into my system than I'd normally have done. Very depressing. I suppose I can claim that the boredom and tension attendant on a comparatively long flight* aren't conducive to a chap's giving up smoking, but then tomorrow I've got to endure the boredom and tension of a read-through, and after that weeks of boring and tense rehearsals, so when in Los Angeles am I likely to give up smoking? I'm desperate to try but when it comes to it suspect I haven't the will, the resilience, the sense of long-term preservation, to give up for twenty minutes, let alone for the rest of my life. All I can say now, with any confidence, is that I don't want to end up with my lungs rotting from cigarettes, while my stomach rots from the gum I'm chewing in order to give up cigarettes. Goodnight. The Taboris have just phoned to say they're waiting for me in the lobby. Goodnight.

Later that night   Yes, well, it's twenty past ten in Los Angeles. Or is it? No, it's ten to eleven in Los Angeles. Ten to seven in the morning in London. I've just come back from dinner. Sam Weisman was unable to turn up for some reason (though none was offered) so there were just the five of us. The evening got off to a distinctly ropy start, at least for me. I'd hardly settled into the back seat of the Taboris' car when Judy Geeson informed me that she had some bad news – I was forbidden to smoke in rehearsals. My hackles, what I have of them – and I suspect I've got rather a lot – rose immediately, while Judy Geeson's hackles, what she has of them – and I suppose I can assume the usual human amount –

* Given my previous description of the flight as pleasing, there seems to be a contradiction here, but only of a kind that is routine in this sort of self-justification, I think.

remained infuriatingly dormant. I spoke powerfully from the back, she turned her head slightly sideways to speak gently from the front, while Kristoffer Tabori dropped out of the arena through the simple expedient of concentrating on the steering wheel, the gears, the traffic lights, the signals – behaving, in fact, like a learner driver on his first public outing. According to Judy the chief stirrer up of strife is John Delancey, the actor who started as Stuart and is now playing Humphry. He finds cigarette smoke offensive, Judy explained to me, and when Kristoffer Tabori was the director had organised a 'petition' (she actually used the word) requesting/demanding that nobody – including Tabori, a strictly amateur smoker – should be allowed to puff smoke around the rehearsal room.

I can't remember the details of my counter-attack, but I know I touched on cars (I have a suspicion I called them motor vehicles) as a source of pollution and ill health ('I'll stop smoking in rehearsals if everybody else promises not to drive to rehearsal' – hah!) and then went on to question the propriety of actors (didn't, I hope, use the phrase 'mere actors') daring to dictate to the only author and begetter, without whom none of them, not *one* of them, would be at the Matrix at all (ignoring the possibility that they might be somewhere more glamorous, doing something far more lucrative) and concluded with a threat to the effect that if I couldn't smoke in rehearsals, then I wouldn't be coming to them, would in fact be shortly on a plane to London. She responded to this, as indeed to everything else I said, with deft sweetness, like a nurse explaining away the pain of an operation the patient suspects has been bungled, until I found myself on the verge of demanding that we skip this dinner altogether, let's drive straight on to the airport and the next plane home, at about which point we arrived at the restaurant, where Joe and Pepe were waiting for us.

The restaurant was Joe Allen's, and the dinner turned out to be pleasant. It was good to see Joe Stern in the flesh, rather than as a fantasy antagonist in one of my schizophrenic hand-to-hands. Most of the time we spent discussing old films, very old films, going back to the late forties and early fifties, summoning from the past, probably even from the tomb, such figures as Charles McGraw (superb in the superb *The Narrow Margin*) and a strange German director/producer called Hauss, whose films we'd both seen but the stories of which we only half remembered. All was well, in fact, in spite of Joe's requesting me early on, I think just after the starters had been put in front of us, not to smoke while people were eating – I chose to take this as a knowing little joke on the rehearsal smoking ban and, grinding out my cigarette, lit up another one immediately.

Now here I am back in my sitting room at the Magic, on the balcony, talking into this machine while I square up to the fact that my smoking or not smoking may turn out to be the main story of my time in Los Angeles – which may turn out to be a briefer time than was expected. Revolving also the irony that though I'm desperate to give up smoking, I won't allow myself to be forced into giving it up. Does this mean that I won't, or that I can't? Or that pride, vanity and self-indulgence come before a concern for my own health and the well-being of others? Yes. From where I stand, by the way, I can see across the pool into the studio opposite mine. When I arrived three or so hours ago there was a most elegant black chap lying on the sofa with his feet on a stool, surveying himself in a mirror beside the television set. Now the television is on, he is still in almost exactly the same position, but has at his side a beautiful black girl, whose arms are around him. They are both watching television, but should they shift their eyes a few inches to the mirror, they'll be able to see how they're getting on in terms of ageing. In his case the minutes have already turned into unreclaimable hours, for both of them the day is almost done. Yet they look happy. Happy and comfortable with each other. Behind me in my sitting room as I watch and talk there is Antony Hopkins on the radio playing bits of music from this Mozart, that Bach, his Radio 3 programme incorporated into a Los Angeles musical programme, I assume. So there we have it. Two beautiful black people enfolded, watching television in the studio opposite, here in Los Angeles, while on the radio Antony Hopkins dealing out Bach and Mozart, also in Los Angeles, I standing watching, listening, talking into this machine.

Sunday, 5 January

Joe picked me up at the Magic at twenty past nine, and we arrived at the Matrix ten minutes later, the read-through being scheduled for ten o'clock. The Matrix is a very inconspicuous-looking theatre from the outside, almost like a shoe shop it seems to me, but inside it's very charming. You go through a wide lobby, past Joe's office, down a passage that leads to an auditorium, which seats its ninety-nine people very comfortably, much more comfortably than most theatres of this size do. The stage is immensely wide, but in proportion very shallow. When I last saw it it had a set on it for a play with which Joe Stern wasn't involved as producer – he had merely rented his theatre to an independent company, a rather strange company actually as it was formed by a one-time Miss America who had married a chap who wanted to be a playwright, and had written a drag farce–thriller.

I left Joe and Sam Weisman discussing various technical matters, to do with the set, went into Joe's office and sat smoking, waiting for the actors to arrive. They came in in little dribbles, here a pair, there a single, looking like well-dressed convicts. No – not like convicts, like children delivered for their first day of school. The only one who seemed to be at all pleased at finding himself in the theatre was our Humphry, John Delancey, whose intelligent and sympathetic face, not at all the face of the leader of an anti-smoking lobby, by the way, radiated contentment with his lot. Anyway, in the rest came – Wayne Alexander (Martin) smiling furtively, Judy Geeson (Marigold) and Kris Tabori (Stuart) walking close to each other but rather formally, Christopher Neame (Peter) flashing by with an odd saluting gesture, Ted Larkins (Nick) pale and unshaven, as if on the flit, then John Delancey (Humphry) – all of them passing the open door of Joe's office, in which I sat, crying out my 'hellos' and 'good mornings' and 'good to see yous', my mind not so much on them or the play, but on my smoking and the problems raised by it.

Just before ten I went back into the auditorium. The actors were sitting around a table on the stage. I carefully selected a last-row corner seat, from which, as it turned out, I could see only the backs of three of the actors who mainly blocked out the fronts of the three actors sitting opposite them, but at least it was a seat in which I could smoke without fear of a rational complaint. I had my nicotine gum in the adjoining seat.

Absolutely nothing was made of my smoking at all. John Delancey, the one who is meant to have the strong objections, occasionally rolled his eyes towards me, but simply out of curiosity, to see how I was responding, or so I deduced from his looks, which were invariably accompanied by genial and handsome smiles. Sam Weisman, the other chap who, according to Judy Geeson, is worried about smoke, seemed quite oblivious, sitting below me to my left, concentrating on the read-through. It's true that Judy Geeson occasionally looked in my direction. Brief glances. Enigmatic, I thought. Could have been about anything. Or about nothing.

After the read-through Sam Weisman said, 'Thank you, great, terrific,' Joe said, 'Great, thank you, terrific,' I said, 'Thank you everybody, many, many thanks,' then Sam and I went next door to the Café Melrose, where, over lunch, I put to him various worries I now had about the text, made a few changes in his presence, then when he left to re-address himself to Joe and then the actors, stayed on to make a few further changes. I went back to Joe's office, showed the changes to Sam. He incorporated them into his script and then came with me into the theatre and read them out to the actors, who wrote them down very carefully, sometimes asking for the changes to be read out again. Joe came in, and we began the main business of the day, a run-through.*

A lot of the blocking was both clumsy and fussy, placing actors in static clumps in which they were nevertheless irrelevantly busy, i.e. eating, drinking, shuffling papers, adjusting their positions on chairs, etc., all of which I hated. On the other hand the actors had a reasonable sense of their characters, and the first act had a good thrust to it, better perhaps than had been managed (given the different texts) in either London or at the Long Wharf. But it was clear that still further work needs to be done to the play itself. Every scene needs more economy; and in several scenes the dramatic emphasis is wrong. I hope this is only a matter of a few judicious cuts. I dread the thought of having to do any serious rewriting.

After the run Sam Weisman, Joe and I repeated our 'greats', 'terrifics' and 'thank yous', I still in my corner, puffing away, before Sam Weisman went back to the top of the play, and began to work slowly through the first act. After about an hour or so he stopped,

---

* In a run-through the actors try to perform their parts, on their feet and on the move; as opposed to a read-through, with which we'd started proceedings, when the actors, seated, simply read through their parts.

and talked generally to the actors about their problems, concentrating specifically on the word 'pain', noting the presence of 'pain' in the text, the lack of it in the actors' account of the text. 'We gotta find the pain. *You* gotta find the pain,' he said, several times. I didn't really know what he meant by 'pain', unless, of course, he assumes that as all life contains pain it becomes axiomatic (if tautological) to assert that any character in a play has in some way to communicate it. I don't know. What depresses me is that the actors seemed to think that there was some profound value in the word, in fact behaved as if they were expecting it and would have been disappointed not to have it fired at them – they nodded, blinked, swayed their heads, painfully confessing their failure to come through with the pain. Sam concluded on a wave of resonant statements and interrogatives, actually the same statement and interrogative, frequently repeated – 'Ya know. I'm talking about the pain. Know what I mean? Ya know. The pain. Know what I mean? Hear what I'm saying?' – and then all the actors eventually departed (including Judy Geeson) except for Kristoffer Tabori, who wanted to pursue with Sam Weisman the idea of the pain in his part as Stuart.

It was missing somewhere, he couldn't find it, especially in the first act, after he discovers Marigold is pregnant, and then again when he discovers that she's had an abortion – where in the gaps between these discoveries should he locate the 'pain', how express the 'pain', where is the 'pain' that runs through this man's life, *is* this man's life? By this time I'd come to hate the word, thinking that it's best applied to specifics, like a throbbing tooth, a headache, an extra-strong spasm of guilt over this or that betrayal, unpaid bill, unreturned phone call, etc., but not wishing to push into the discussion in a too bluntly Anglo-Saxon style – especially as Sam Weisman was responding to Tabori's re-employment of the word with sage paragraphs, energetically delivered – I inserted myself shyly between them and begged them both to remember that yes indeed, I said suavely, there is 'pain' knocking about in life, and of course we must be aware of its presence in the play, but we mustn't forget, must we, that in the first act the characters are young people, who feel sure that when they make a decision, the decision sorts life out. But of course what we discover, don't we, as we go on is that the definitive decisions tend not to be definitive.

Life, 'old life itself'* won't allow them to be. I went on for some time in this vein, sounding, I suspect, rather like an elderly vicar ruminating aloud to the local literary society on the moral themes in *Middlemarch*, but my intention was to get as much mist as possible around the idea that Tabori and the other actors should go looking for the 'pain' in their parts – I knew what kind of production *that* could lead to.

Sam Weisman, who's clearly attended a few postgraduate seminars somewhere or other,[†] came surging straight out of the mist with another dangerous monologue to do not only with 'pain' but with 'life-muscles' – a term with which I'm already familiar through conversations with Joe Stern.[‡] I must try to find out which of them induces this vocabulary in the other. Anyway what he actually said to Tabori, who with his friendly youthful manner and large bespectacled brown eyes, resembled an exceptionally eager student, was that we all have this 'muscle', this 'life-muscle', that some of us allow to go undeveloped, so that when a crisis comes, and we need the power of our 'life-muscle', we find not only that it's become useless, but that it's a hindrance, even. I must say that while I quite enjoy the idea of a life-muscle, I find it disconcerting when offered to an actor making enquiries about his part. All I care about is the kind of discussion that leads to a result on the stage, and I don't really see how talk of finding the 'pain' through the discovery of the life-muscle can lead to anything on the stage – except posturing and meaningful pauses. But I may be wrong. Perhaps this is the way you have to talk to actors in Los Angeles, perhaps they're conditioned to it, and would feel deprived without it.

Anyway, I did my best to get some mist swirling again, with further prattle about encouraging the audience to understand and *enjoy*, a word I kept hitting, *enjoy* the ironies of my piece by

---

* A phrase that Stuart used at the end of Act One in the London version of *The Common Pursuit*. I cut the phrase when rewriting the play for the Matrix, and it never found its way back into the text.

† Yale, I subsequently discovered.

‡ Joe Stern also liked to talk about the need for actors 'to go to that place they don't want to go to' – I could never make out where that was, but then I'm not an actor.

encouraging the actors to understand and *enjoy* the ironies of their dramatic circumstances, through the language in which they speak about them. I mean, I said, one of the *pleasures* of the play, surely, is that it slightly offends our moral expectations: we want people, ourselves included, to be punished for our vices, rewarded for our virtues, whereas there were times in *The Common Pursuit* when it seemed to be working the other way round – on and on I went, smilingly aiming their attention towards cheerfulness, jolliness, upness, hinting that the darker strands of the play would express themselves more fully in a bright atmosphere – until Tabori took himself off, his head I hoped full of mist rather than muscles. Sam Weisman then talked briefly, and I'm glad to report practically, of what he'd noticed in specific performances, and I got Joe to drive me back here.

It's a quarter to seven, I have a malt whisky in my hand, another already sluicing warmly through my system, and I feel, in spite of my dismay at Sam's monologues (I'm clutching the back of a chair in my kitchen, in the hope that it's made of wood – it looks and feels like wood) that in the end this production is going to turn out OK. I have an intuition that it will, in fact, just as I had an intuition from the beginning that the London production would in some way go wrong. In a minute I shall saunter down to Hollywood Boulevard, choose a restaurant for my dinner, then have an early night. I quite enjoy the pleasures, or are they vices? – yes, they're vices – of solitude. I shall pick out a restaurant, and have a leisurely meal with a book. With a bad book. Sidney Sheldon. I've got a Sidney Sheldon in my bag for just this sort of situation.

Oh, by the way – I'd forgotten. I phoned Joe before recording this to give him a heavily edited version of my views on the production so far. He said at one point, 'I don't mind being rejected as long as I'm not dismissed' – which had what I take to be a Hollywood ring to it. I was about to reply that I wasn't sure I had a preference, but decided not to pursue it. And now here I am, out on my balcony, my tape recorder still in my hand, on an evening that's nippy and humid simultaneously, with a sort of pervasive muckiness in the air, which is, I suppose, the famous Los Angeles smog. From the room next to mine there comes a confused blaring of tempestuous music and gunfire, as if the radio and television were both on together. Every room in the hotel is somehow public.

In the ones opposite me, on the other side of the pool, I can see flashes of this and that through the thin curtains – a man sitting at a table, eating rapidly as he writes on to a legal pad; a coloured woman of about twenty-five with a child; a laid table. I don't know whether this highly visible privacy is characteristic of Los Angeles, or simply a charming accident in the design of the Magic Hotel. Anyway off I shamble with Sidney Sheldon to find a restaurant. Goodnight.

I still haven't left. I'm back on the balcony holding in my hand a curious kind of muzzle it looks like, anyway a plastic construction with a strap and a patch of white cloth – actually it looks like a cricket box,* though I would think that it's meant to cover the mouth and nose. I found it hanging on the back of the bathroom door when I went in a few minutes ago (after I'd last spoken) to have a pee. It could of course be some kind of disguise given out free to guests who want to do a spot of mugging, but it's more likely to be something to do with the smog, a filter, I assume. But it's been quite smoggy all day, and I didn't see anyone wearing any kind of muzzle on the streets around the Matrix. I must find out more about it. I must find out what this is for. If it *is* a filter, I can take it into rehearsals, and clamp it over the mouth and nostrils of anyone who complains about my smoking.†

Monday, 6 January

It's eight twenty on a nippy, fog-bound Los Angeles evening. I'm reporting this in a state of some exhaustion, as I have been at the theatre since half past ten this morning. The day got off to a bizarre start. While I was waiting in the Magic lobby for Chris Neame to pick me up and take me to rehearsals, I suddenly realised that I couldn't go on expecting people at the Matrix to give me lifts. I went to the man at the desk, a sort of remotely sunny, always smiling guy with a beard, about thirty, I suppose, perhaps younger. I said, 'Look, can you give me a number for

---

* A cricket box is a white plastic construction that looks like a muzzle, though its function is to protect the testicles of batsmen in the game of cricket.

† It was, in fact, a muzzle for protection against the smog, or so John Delancey informed me. I never, in my weeks in Los Angeles, saw anyone wearing one, though.

when I need a cab?' The smile remained on his face but it was an uneasy smile. He said, 'What? What do you want?' I said, 'A number for a cab.' He said, 'Well, I dunno, I dunno. You want a number?' I said, 'Yes, that's right. I want a number for a cab. So I can phone up for one.' He said, 'You mean you wanna phone up and *talk*?' I said, 'Yes, well, to get one around actually.' 'Get one around?' he said. 'Get one around?' I said, 'Yes, you know, get a cab around when I need one.' 'Well,' he said, 'there's only one and it sort of – you've seen it, it lives on the premises.' I said, 'What?' He kept on smiling through all this, smiling, but he also looked extremely worried, if not slightly frightened.

He obviously found me menacing in some way – not surprisingly as it turned out that he thought I wanted a number for a cat. Cat. In fact he thought the telephone number I was actually after was of the cat that hangs about in the hotel, a very charming cat that sits at the edge of the pool in the morning, and whom I met on my first evening – in fact, he was in my room, as if waiting to receive me. Unfortunately the Taboris, who came up with me, brought Digby along. Digby, of course, growled at the cat, who responded with a cuff to Digby's eyebrows, making them bleed and sending her yelping about the room, actually dancing back at one stage, her front paws in the air, while the cat, maintaining its dignity, walked slowly and thoughtfully out of my room, out of my life, to all intents and purposes. I'd dearly love to get him or her back, especially at night, when I feel the need for some living company, but even I hadn't thought of making contact by telephone. But how am I going to manage in a society in which people are mad enough to assume that you're mad enough to believe that all you have to do, when you want a cat, is phone one up and ask it around? Call-cats, like call-girls, I suppose.

Even the elementary and necessary things here are complicated by this sunny, almost radiant, incomprehension. Actually not *always* sunny, almost radiant, now I come to think of it. There was that odd experience I had the last time I was here when Joe and Pepe Stern took us out to dinner at a very expensive ranch-like restaurant. The waiter asked me if I wanted a salad. I said, yes, just a lettuce salad, please. Something odd happened to his face. He said, 'What do yer mean?' I said, 'Just a lettuce.' He said, 'What's that?' I said, 'A lettuce, you know, a lettuce. I only want a lettuce. Nothing else but a lettuce.' He said, 'Well, I dunno what yer mean. What yer talking about?' His voice got tougher and tougher, as if at any moment he was going to take me out to a nearby alley at gunpoint. Fortunately Judy Geeson explained what I meant by a lettuce, putting the proper name to it. Apparently in California they have all varieties of lettuce, which means you can't have just a lettuce. It's got to be a something lettuce. And furthermore I don't think they actually use the word 'lettuce' at all. They call it a something salad. But I don't believe this semantic confusion really explains the increasingly infuriating effect my use of the word 'lettuce' had on the waiter, who was, I remember, tall and rather distinguished in a Latin way, exactly like a *consigliere* in *The Godfather*. But I should keep him in mind whenever I fall too easily into the habit of assuming that incomprehension here is at least benevolent.

I went to the theatre resolving not to smoke, resolving not to interfere too much in rehearsals. I wasn't successful on either count, though I did manage to chew gum for an hour without smoking which I suppose has to rank – how pathetic – as an achievement. But I didn't go for more than ten minutes without interfering. It would have been quite a good morning, all in all, if I hadn't been rather disconcerted by something Ted Larkins told me over lunch. I'd invited him to discuss his accent with him. He's been assuming a chirpy Cockney one, which I think quite inappropriate for Nick. But before I could get on to the subject he blurted out that he was finding things very difficult because after he'd only been working for four days – called in without warning to replace Bart Braddleman – Joe Stern had driven out to his house after rehearsals and suggested that he should leave the production because, he said, he didn't think that Ted could do it. He couldn't see the 'pain', he said, in the man. The 'pain', the 'reality' and the 'pain' in the guy. And he also apparently wondered aloud to Ted Larkins whether Ted Larkins could act. He had the feeling that perhaps Ted Larkins couldn't act. 'Couldn't *even* act' apparently was the phrase he used. So there was that to be dealt with.*

We spent the first part of the afternoon going through Act One, Scene One, which seemed occasionally to take off, but more often

---

* There is no record of how I dealt with it.

to sink into a kind of dull posturing. Proceedings weren't helped by John Delancey, who may well be (I suspect is) talented, interesting and intelligent, but nevertheless seems to feel a need to articulate every passing thought and stray doubt about every line and intention and motive in the scene, thus constantly holding us up. I was further irritated by the way that the previous director (Kristoffer Tabori) had filled it with a lot of unnecessary activity: for instance, constant recourse to the coffee pot. I always hate the coffee/tea syndrome in plays – that is, when one feels that a director has stuck a beverage on stage for the characters to help themselves to, in order to create a bustle and urgency quite unrelated to the text. Thus the chap playing Peter (Chris Neame) entered the room carrying not only his gown and some books and papers (as specified in the text) but also a sandwich, and made straight for the coffee pot, so that within seconds of his arrival we had him munching a sandwich, gulping down coffee, getting out of his gown, messing about with his books, all this while talking to various other characters on stage. American actors have a fixation about food, it seems to me, as if they can't act unless they're eating.* Anyway, there he was, munching on this *enormous* American sandwich – all sandwiches in America are enormous; in Los Angeles they seem to be twice as enormous as the sandwiches in New York – saying his lines and getting out of his gown and putting books and papers down.

Joe was standing at the back of the theatre watching, but went off just before I had the coffee pot taken away, then the mugs taken away, and finally the sandwich taken away. When he came back, he was appalled to see that all the business had been surgically removed, saying, 'But we needed all that to energise the scene.' I said, in what I concede was a rather pompous manner, that if the scene didn't 'energise' itself through the characters and the events, then no amount of coffee-making, coffee-pouring and sandwich-munching would compensate. 'Yeah, yeah,' he said, he understood my point, but at the same time we didn't want this to be a play about people just sitting down and talking to each other, then

---

* Though I'd forgotten that Chris Neame is English, I still hold to my position about American actors and eating. Note any American play, television series or serial, whatever. Perhaps they feel it adds a dash of realism, or perhaps the actors simply happen to be hungry when the scenes are being shot.

standing up and talking to each other, then sitting down and talking to each other. I said, 'Joe, if the scenes don't carry because the conversation isn't interesting, then we should perhaps forget it.'* Because, I said, the drama of the play comes through people talking to each other. That's all they do. Talk. There's no getting away from it. He looked baffled, made one of his short, metaphysical speeches about the purpose of movement, the 'muscle' of energy, withdrew.

After rehearsals Kris Tabori, Joe Stern and I went to a bar. A chap with a moustache, in a peculiar white chamois top and chamois trousers, kept turning up to ask if we were being served with a drink, and when informed that we weren't, bustled off to arrange it, then returned to ask if we'd been served, bustled off to arrange it – it took about half an hour for the drinks to arrive, delivered by a very elegant young faggot with a plump moustache, a thick mane of hair and extravagantly good manners, who kept enjoining us to have a good evening,† enjoy our drinks now, you're very welcome, kind of stuff, that constituted a serious interruption to a story Tabori was trying to tell about an elderly West Coast actor with whom we were all three acquainted, whose main assets on stage were a deep, trembling voice, a strangely trembling body – offstage he spoke and moved quite normally – and a racking cough, which he probably couldn't help, as he chain-smoked, but which he didn't try to suppress either.

According to Tabori this actor once appeared in a Shakespeare production – I forget of which play – directed by a young man, also from the West Coast, who refused to give him, or indeed any of the other actors, any notes whatsoever. Furthermore, the young director remained very guarded about what the set was going to look like, where the furniture (if any) was going to be placed, even where the exits and entrances were to be. At last, impatient with so much secrecy, the elderly actor demanded to be given a note, any note, on his work so far. The director led him off to a quiet corner of the rehearsal room, whispered to him briefly. The elderly

---

* I.e. 'pull the plug out'.

† On my previous visit a young and attractive actress and I had been instructed by a waiter to 'have a good night'. Various retorts had sprung into my mind, but luckily not to my lips, as the response to them might well have been a fork through the throat delivered by the young lady or the waiter, or possibly both.

actor looked at him, then repaired to the green room, where he was found stumping up and down in a fury, bellowing in his onstage trembling voice, *'Be more real!* He won't even let me know where the fucking doors are, but he tells me to *be more real!'* Now this story, interrupted as I say by the faggoty waiter who'd taken half an hour to get us our drinks and then kept molesting us with his sunny but imbecile courtesies, seems to me to bring into focus sinister elements both professional and social in Los Angeles life. But would it do any good if I went around shouting, *'Be more real!'* Would it, in the end, even get a cat up to my room?

Tuesday, 7 January

Yes, well, I'm extremely cold actually. It's one in the morning and there is a curious icy mist around Los Angeles which makes me feel as cold as I would feel in London in January – having spent a very hot day indeed. Every time I went out of the theatre I felt heavy, almost inert with the heat. And then suddenly it goes from that to this.

Anyway, to report on my day. I didn't have to be in the theatre until eleven so I loitered about in my flat for a time, and then sat on the balcony, staring down at other geriatrics who were in short trousers or swimming suits, sitting around the pool, reading magazines. I thought of going down to join them but decided against it – I think mainly because I suddenly remembered the last time I'd sat by a swimming pool, just before Christmas when staying at the Tabori cottage. I'd have felt pretty good in my deckchair, a glass of champagne and my cigarettes to hand, if I hadn't been so aware of my stomach, pale, bloated and even slightly wrinkled. I'd thought: so here I am, undeniably middle-aged, sitting effetely by a swimming pool in Los Angeles like a gangster boss in a movie – all I need is a terminal visit from Clint Eastwood. So within minutes I was back in the cottage – dressed, still smoking and sipping at the champagne, but at least out of sight. But nobody this morning, around the Magic pool, seemed to be expecting a visit from Clint Eastwood. Most of them seemed quite pleased to be where they were, whatever the condition of their stomachs. One very old chap, wearing sort of Hawaiian shorts and a blue peaked cap, was reading a book with a Victorian – no, Edwardian, more like – binding. It had a kind of Rider Haggard look to it. Every so often he'd put the book down and smile. And why not, down there in the sun with his Rider Haggard, or whatever?

The thing I remember most vividly about the day's work is what happened to Ted Larkins. He made some real progress in the morning, suddenly seeming to flower into a richly comic, whirling motor of a Nick; but in the afternoon, at the run-through, went to pieces almost at once – as soon, in fact, as he saw the producer, Joe Stern, sitting in a seat in the middle of the stalls, staring intently at him. The theatre is so small and there was the director, Sam Weisman, sitting at the front; there I was, sitting at the back because I was smoking; and there, with his peculiar straw-coloured hair and Walter Matthau muzzly face, was the producer, Joe Stern, staring at him. So he completely disintegrated. It was most extraordinary. Everything that had been done during the morning, everything that had been both precise and emphatic, vanished and he became your chirpy little Cockney sparrow all over again. I yearned for the director to call an end to the proceedings and say: let's all go and have a drink and talk about something quite different.

Afterwards Sam Weisman made various observations, some to the point and some of them in his psychologising American fashion about the nature of the characters, the nature of acting, where you have to be as an actor, reaching into yourself and finding yourself and then finding that the self you've found isn't the self you need because you've got to go on and make that self into the character self. So forth. Odd, because he also slipped in quite a lot of useful information about what the actors should understand this or that line to mean, how they should work towards this or that moment in a scene. But really, whether being useful or useless, he couldn't touch publicly on the main point, the dominating point, which was Ted Larkins's performance. (I wish to God Ted Larkins would shave before rehearsals, by the way. He always contrives to appear with a heavy shadow, which makes him look as if he's on the skids.) What he did say to Ted Larkins, not touching at all on his acting, either in general terms or in detail, was that perhaps he should wear some heavy boots to rehearsal, to root him in the part. Ted Larkins said he didn't have any heavy boots, only ordinary shoes or trainers. Well, Sam

Weisman said, he was sure heavy boots would be a help. They stared at each other in intense vacancy for a moment, then Sam Weisman turned back to, or forward to, life-muscles, I suppose, while I continued to wonder why Sam Weisman thought a heavy-booted Ted Larkins would help Ted Larkins to create a fleet-footed (physically, as well as mentally) Nick. A heavy-booted *and* five-o'clock-shadowed Ted Larkins would place Nick among the down-and-outs on a Camden Town tube platform, bumming pennies and cigarettes – anyway certainly not (as Nick ends up) in a television studio, running an intellectual chat show.

After rehearsals Ted Larkins drew me aside to say what I already knew – that the moment he'd seen the producer who'd wondered to his face whether he could *even* act sitting staring at him from the stalls, he'd lost every shred of the confidence he'd picked up during the morning. I tried to find some sympathetic words, while (I have to admit) feeling that if he went to pieces before the producer, how would he cope before an audience, then watched him go off, depressed, some way behind the other actors. I was about to leave myself when Joe stopped me, there, in the auditorium, saying he'd like a word, got a minute, Simon? I said yes, I supposed I had a minute, and down we sat, with Sam Weisman sitting to the side, like a referee, while Joe quizzed me on the text – the meaning of a line here, the value of a scene there. It went on, this interrogation, for two hours – *two hours* – in spite of my attempts to explain that I was still thinking about the text, didn't want to discuss it until I'd had the chance to consider each part in relation to the whole, some few run-throughs on from now. But Joe, who relishes discussion and debate, the offstage drama of the theatre, went on remorselessly, saying, 'Simon, one question. *One* question. Just one *question*,' actually raising a finger to indicate the figure 'one' for his one question. He must have raised about a hundred 'one' questions in the course of the two hours, his finger raised in front of his Walter Matthau face with its bushy straw hair on top. Up would go the finger, up would come the question until finally, exhausted and fairly angry, I said I'd had enough, see him tomorrow. During all this Sam Weisman was mostly mute, though I discovered that Kristoffer Tabori had some-how found his way back into the auditorium, and was listening in from a seat further along, to the side, in the shadows.

I got Tabori to drive me to a restaurant called Musso and Frank's, on Hollywood Boulevard and fairly close to the Magic. I sat at the counter and had a lobster salad, trying not to stare too hard at the guy next to me – he was about seventy, corpulent, with newspapers piled in front of him and meals seeming to come in at him from all quarters, beginning with a number of hors d'oeuvres and followed by a large platter of swordfish, and then some other main dishes. There was something about his devotion to his food and his newspapers that I found, after the tumult and rigours of the Matrix, rather comforting. After dinner I slouched into the first available cinema and found myself watching a film called *The Jewel of the Nile*. I fell asleep a quarter of the way through, woke up just before about halfway through, to discover that nothing had improved on the screen, and left. Came home. Am about to go to bed. And that's really all I've got to say – oh, except that I don't think I'm going to make it to Dallas for the New Arts production of *Dog Days*. For one thing, I've become too involved in what's going on at the Matrix. For another, I'm already so tired that I don't believe I can even make it to New York for the casting. For a third, I don't really want to direct *Dog Days* anyway. It's such a boring and repellent little play that I'd rather not be associated with it.

Thursday, 9 January

It's nine thirty in the morning, and I'm pacing about my living room in the Magic, trying to recall the events of the last two days. It's hard to concentrate, though, as it's very hot – the sun striking blindingly through the windows, and out on the balcony there's no breeze at all. One of my preoccupations – my many preoccupations – is with my clothes. For some peculiar reason I packed for New York, where I'm going to spend only four days (if I go there at all) and forgot to pack for Los Angeles, where I'm going to be for at least another month, or for Dallas which is also hot, where I'm going to be for at least two weeks. So here I am in the heat, with three pairs of unusable heavy trousers, and the pair of medium-weight cords that I arrived in and am still wearing. I'll have to go out and buy some light trousers later this morning. If I've got the energy.

But let me try and remember the events of the last two days. The reason I've missed out on the reports is that I've been too depressed by what has been going on, and failing to go on, in the rehearsal room that I couldn't bear the prospect of hearing myself recapitulate it. I have a suspicion, though, that the source of the problem has been myself, my impatience. I have twice been where this production has to get to, while the actors and the director are still groping to discover the proper direction, which – it's axiomatic – they must do to some extent on their own, otherwise it'll be a false journey to a false destination. Yes, I know all that. But sometimes the routes they're taking are so obviously wrong, so obviously leading nowhere, that I sit in a kind of seething frustration that leaks around the rehearsal room, making the actors jittery, and unsettling Sam Weisman, who therefore – anxious to maintain his own dominance – finds it difficult to refer to me. I still haven't made up my mind whether Sam Weisman is any good as a director, but I frequently wish he weren't, so that I could elbow him out of the way* and get on with the job myself – in which case I would, of course, uncover all the patience I lack now.

Anyway, there we are, or were, rather, the day before yesterday – my sitting in the back corner of the stalls, resenting every wrong move and stress of the actors, the actors aware of it. And resenting every wrong direction, and even sometimes half-right direction of the director, the director aware of it. And resenting myself for neither interfering vigorously, to a positive purpose, nor keeping still and affable, biding my time. As a consequence I left the Matrix at the end of a long day feeling foul, had myself dropped off at Musso and Frank's again for what I intended to be a consoling dinner. I can't remember whether I've described this restaurant properly yet, but it's large, two large rooms with upholstered leather seats in booths for four and six. The atmosphere is rather like that of an English club or a certain style of Republican (or so I imagine) New York restaurant. I'd got hold of a *Guardian* and a London *Times* from the news-stand opposite the restaurant, and was looking forward to settling into one of the booths to read them over half a bottle of wine and scallops – looking forward to

* I seem, at this stage, not to have noticed that Sam Weisman had a couple of elbows in good working order of his own.

absenting myself from the angers of the rehearsal, in fact. But I wasn't allowed a booth – though most of them were empty – this grey-faced and rather sinister maître d' conducting me instead to one of the swivel stools at the counter, where the light is too dim to read comfortably by. It's very American, or so it seems to me, to refuse to allow you to sit where you want to sit because there's some code that has to be enforced, even when it's irrelevant. Anyway, the irritation of being compelled to swivel away at the counter lingered in spite of the perfectly decent mussels and wine, and was intensified on my leaving when I discovered that they'd locked the front door, which meant that I had to go out through the back, through the parking lot, and around to the street. I remember walking back, composing grave letters to Musso and Frank, both of whom I visualised as thickset, middle-aged Italians smoking cigars and wearing rings, with a pride in their jointly owned establishment and therefore worthy and sympathetic recipients of my communications. I reported my admiration for their food, for the ambience they'd created, etc., and then went on to say, regretfully but with subdued passion, that it was a pity therefore that in the end I'd found my evening not only uncomfortable, but positively uncivilised. And *furthermore* –! It is extraordinary, this aspect of myself that is bad enough at home but becomes far worse when I'm abroad and on my own – presumably because I haven't a wife or friends to help turn it into comedy. So I seethed away, behaving within myself as if I'd been debagged by Musso and Frank rather than merely inconvenienced by their minions in a very minor way.

Anyway, back to the Magic, where the foul state induced by my day at the Matrix and the foul state induced by my evening at Musso and Frank's blurred into a further, undefined foul state, the figures jumbled together, Musso, Frank, the actors, Sam Weisman, Joe Stern all seeming to be part of a lunatic world, vicious caricatures – I mean not only viciously caricatured but also caricatures in themselves vicious. I paced about smoking and drinking Scotch, thinking I ought to be recording the day's events, unable to do so.

The next day (yesterday) I woke feeling as if I'd been poisoned. Rehearsals didn't 't begin until four thirty, a lousy hour for me as I can never think energetically in the late afternoon. Also it meant we wouldn't finish, given the normal eight-hour stretch, until midnight. I spent the first part of the morning on the telephone to Beryl. I keep trying to cut down on these appallingly expensive calls, but on the other hand I think they're emotionally necessary – for her, I hope, as well as for me. Afterwards I went for a walk, steaming along Hollywood Boulevard in my medium cords and a heavy shirt, with the intention of buying some appropriate togs. I went into a likely-looking shop where two moustachioed gays, bandido-moustachioed gays, one of them wearing a sombrero, refused to take their eyes off me for a second. I became extremely self-conscious, going about fingering material but really feeling as if I were, or anyway appeared to be, touching up the garments sexually. I turned and left abruptly, trouserless,* but did manage to find a shop that sold Silk Cut. I bought a carton, and was steaming my way irritably back towards the Magic – the street up to it was for once quite crowded – when a chap I've seen hanging about in the Matrix office, a kind of assistant to Joe Stern I think he is, passed me in a car, shouting out of the window as he did so that he'd be back in forty-five minutes. I thought, why should he be back in forty-five minutes? Back *where* in forty-five minutes? Did he mean back in my hotel in forty-five minutes? If so, why? I couldn't remember any arrangements to meet Chip Estees† anywhere, at any time – and then recalled that one of my campaigns here has been to get a video installed, so that I can watch films late at night, when I'm too tired to do anything, including watch films on a video. I further recalled that there'd been some talk of the video arriving after lunch (yesterday). So perhaps Chip was on his way to collect it, passing me on the street by coincidence at about two o'clock. This all turned out to be correct, except that Chip didn't come back in forty-five minutes, at a quarter to three, he came back at five to four, five minutes before I was due at rehearsals. I had to stand about smiling pleasantly, fulminating within, while he figured out how to install the video. He read the instructions aloud slowly and carefully, put plugs into sockets,

---

* Apart from the pair I had on, that is.

† Actually his name may have been Chuck Johnson, or Chip Johnson, or Chuck Estees. As I no longer have a copy of the Matrix programme I can't be sure which permutation is the correct one. I have settled for calling him Chip Estees.

extracted them, reversed them, so forth, until he finally declared that he'd done it, it should work now. I hadn't got a tape to test it with, so I have no idea, really, whether it will work or not. All I know is that it's sitting there bathed in sunlight, winking at me as its flashing clock tells off the minutes of my life.

Chip drove me to the theatre, which therefore meant that I had to make conversation with him. He's a nice man, very handsome, very polite, but a trifle literal in that American way, tending to unravel your little jokes and asides before your very eyes, so to speak, and to give you information that you've asked for only out of courtesy, without expectation of response. In other words, talking to him made my ill temper worse. And arriving late at the theatre, with the actors and the director hanging about waiting for me, made it worse still. I sat down where I'd been sitting the day before, a few seats away from Sam Weisman, who said, 'Oh, one thing. Could you do me a favour? Could you sit at the back so I don't get your cigarette smoke? My voice was really very bad last night.' I twitched immediately, then said that I would indeed sit at the back. I would INDEED sit at the back, I would INDEED. Actually I sat at the back of the back, nostrils flaring, eyes narrowed, psyche smouldering, and watched the scene.

Every word the director and the actors said struck me as being wrong. Quite simply wrong. I tried to remind myself of everything I'd said to myself yesterday and everything I'd said on the phone to Beryl about being patient and letting them explore the characters and find their own way, but finally found myself up on my feet and emphatically, not to say melodramatically, stubbing out my cigarette and slipping out. Not slipping out really, because I had to plod right past the director's table, and then go up the aisle and past the office. Joe was on the phone – he's always on the phone – looking extremely serious, so probably he was talking to his bookie.* I gestured that I'd like to speak to him when he was free. He followed me next door to the Café Melrose – which, by the way, is run by Japanesy looking people, who don't look thoroughly Japanese – where I put my problems to him.

---

* Joe is an almost professional gambler. For years he supported his family – and presumably the Matrix – from what he won from bets on football and baseball matches, and in regular poker games.

I said that I thought my main difficulty was that I was not having what I was used to having with my directors, a discussion after the day's work over a drink. Sam Weisman has got a very young child, possibly even a baby, and a wife with a flourishing acting career, and therefore dashes off immediately after rehearsals, presumably to take domestic charge. Perhaps he even wants to see his baby. Or his wife. Or both. While I understand his situation, or think I do, I said to Joe, it does mean that Joe and I never meet in the valuable – because relaxed – period after rehearsals, to exchange notes (I meant, of course, for Sam to get *my* notes), which is why, I explained, I find myself intervening so often during the rehearsals themselves. As I think I've said before, every time I talk to Joe on the phone, especially long distance, I suspect him of bluffing and even of lying, but the moment I'm with him in the flesh I'm convinced that he's a decent and honourable man whose company, furthermore, I find myself enjoying. So we talked very amicably, he saying that he'd got wind of the fact that I was manifesting my impatience because one of the actors, Chris Neame – it would be Chris Neame, somehow, English and late of the Royal Shakespeare Company – had said that when I sat in the front row, next to the director, he found my face too present, my personality too overpowering, my feet too large, my cigarette smoke too effusive – in short, I put him off his stroke and stride. I had to concede to Joe that there was a certain wheedling and pathetic justice in what Neame had said – otherwise I myself wouldn't have felt so strongly that I'd been having a negative effect. We talked it out, Joe agreeing that the solution was for him to ask Sam Weisman to organise either the rehearsals or his domestic life in such a way that we always spent time by ourselves at the end of the day.*

I went back with Joe to the theatre. He sidestepped into his office and the telephone, I went on into the auditorium – it was now about six in the evening, I suppose – and I suddenly found it quite easy to intervene. The rehearsal took off, Sam Weisman and I developing for the first time a true spirit of collaboration,

---

* We never did – at least not until we were in previews. But I don't know, as I never asked, whether this was because Joe didn't pass on the message, or did and Sam Weisman refused.

talking across the stalls but quite openly and effortlessly about each problem as we saw it arise. How this happened I don't really know, although I assume a good part of it had to do with Joe – he'd found some way of releasing me from my tensions, perhaps, and had sent me back less fraught, and therefore less destructive. Anyway, the rehearsal positively flowed along, I becoming for the first time spontaneous instead of deliberate and measured, Sam Weisman receptive, quick to pick up my points and anxious to share the development of his own. I came back to the Magic feeling quite cheerful, indeed rather self-approving at the way in which I'd managed to deal with my irascibility and impatience, though inwardly acknowledging that it was really the conversation with Joe that had turned me around. I slept well, had a good breakfast, and here I am now, on my balcony in the sun, finishing off this account before setting forth to buy myself a corkscrew and a bottle of champagne – I wouldn't mind a glass or two of champagne before I go into rehearsals, which begin at midday. This evening Mr and Mrs Sam Weisman are taking me out to a show, I don't remember which one. Tomorrow I'm going to dinner with Roddy McDowall, an English actor long domiciled in Hollywood, who began his career as a child star, and is more recently famous for his remarkable impersonation, when incarcerated in an ape's body and head, of an educated ape.* I met him some years back, just after he'd played the lead in *Otherwise Engaged* in Florida. I've very much liked him on the few occasions we've met, so for once I feel OK. Perhaps Hollywood will come to suit me, even if I don't come to suit Hollywood.

Friday, 10 January

This morning I decided to try out my video machine. I have been feeling uneasy about it as Chip Estees seemed to me to sink the plugs into the sockets in a rather arbitrary fashion. I went down to a shop called 'The Wherehouse' – a very hot walk in this hot weather – to hire some tapes. The Wherehouse, which had been recommended to me after a lot of thought by the sunny at the desk, turned out to be an amazing building, dwarfing a shopping

---

* In *Planet of the Apes* and various sequels.

arcade that looked as if it had been built as an afterthought to the car park opposite. The ground floor was devoted to 'hardware' and tapes for sale, the upstairs floor to an enormous video library. This library was without air-conditioning and therefore very hot. I sweated copiously in my thickish trousers as I went about trying to make my selection – I was after decent thrillers. Even indecent thrillers. The heat, and a large, centrally placed television screen, from which came loud and random excerpts from pop videos or violent films, induced a headache that made my progress both lethargic and unpleasant, but I finally got together three films that looked promising from their covers – men with guns, girls screaming, that sort of thing – and took them to the counter where I had to go through a wearisome American business – numerous dockets and receipts produced and signed, my American Express card checked out.

When she appeared to have finished ('she' being a medium-sized black girl with acne – I noticed the acne as our relationship quickly developed into one of implacable hostility – she also had a rather shapeless body), she said, 'Now could I have some identification please, sir?' I said, 'What sort of identification?' She said, 'Yer driver's licence, please, sir,' I explained that as I didn't drive I didn't have a licence. You could have cut her incredulity with a – I don't know what you could have cut it with, but it hung there thickly between us, her incredulity, and not just her incredulity, her suspicion. Suspicious incredulity, presumably from encountering for the first time in her life a middle-aged man whose toes weren't actually sticking out of his shoes who claimed he couldn't drive. I suppose she worked out that I'd been banned for drunken driving or whatever, and was trying to save face. Anyway she said, well, she was very sorry – 'Very sorry, sir, but you may not have the tapes without identification.' I said but surely my credit cards were identification enough. So it went. I got hotter and hotter – suppurating with heat – and angrier and angrier, but still managed to *explain* to her in what I thought was a reasonably poised manner why her request was preposterous, as I could apparently *buy* the tapes on a credit card without showing identification, just as I could buy meals in restaurants without showing identification, etc. She kept saying, 'It's to protect you, sir, it's to protect you.' I kept insisting that I was prepared to be unprotected in this matter.

Eventually she called over some young jerk with a sort of seventeen-year-old moustache wisping across his upper lip, who said that it was a house rule and then called over somebody else who then, unbelievably, went and got somebody else. So I actually ended up with five, I think it was, people from The Wherehouse, all of them explaining to me that (a) it was against company policy to accept credit cards for television rentals without identification, and (b) that they themselves didn't actually understand why this policy existed. Occasionally the girl, the acned black girl with whom I'd begun the negotiation, would interject that I didn't drive. 'You see, he doesn't *drive.*' I could see *their* suspicion growing. In the end I felt rather as if I were surrounded by policemen, who at any moment were going to handcuff me and drag me down to the station for attempting the use of a credit card without being able to drive. I began in fact to find something very suspicious myself in my not being able to drive. In the end I went out shouting what I hoped was dignified English abuse, without fully raising my voice, and at least avoided having my shoulder bag searched by the heavily armed guard at the door.

On the pavement I spotted a grimy-looking liquor store further up the arcade, slogged my way towards it, bought some bottles of white wine and champagne – enough of each to fill four carrier bags and strain my arms – then slogged up the hill in the heat, averting my face from the heavy traffic fumes. As I neared the Magic – a mere hundred or so yards from it, in fact – I had the consolation of trudging damply past a liquor store which advertised a delivery service, thus rendering every aspect of my little shopping expedition gratifyingly pointless.

I'm glad to report that from there everything got worse. It was a truly dreadful day in the theatre. No doubt some good work was done here and there, but everything was coloured, and in a sense nullified, by Ted Larkins's rapid decline as Nick. He went from merely going to pieces – which he'd managed when trying to perform in front of Joe – to a self-sacrificial passivity. His voice had also developed a rhythm, a feeble rhythm but a rhythm nevertheless, in time to which I could have nodded my head. I suppose he'd surrendered, demoralised by his previous débâcle, and was now dutifully offering himself up to the axe – I don't know. All I know is that he can't possibly have believed that what he was doing bore any relation to the dynamically mischievous Nick that the scenes needed and that he'd once or twice come close to giving us. Sam Weisman seemed incapable of effecting any change, speaking an occasional jerky sentence that for once, mercifully I suppose, didn't carry him on into a muscle-mono-logue. He just ran through the scenes again and again, almost as if hypnotised by his own helplessness, or by the limping rhythms of Ted Larkins's delivery, perhaps.

In the end, in despair, I left the auditorium, went out on to the pavement, where I saw Joe standing a few yards away, almost on the corner.* . He asked me how it was going. I said, 'Dreadful.' He said, 'What's the problem, Larkins?' And I said, 'Yes, problem.' He sort of raised his eyebrows. I raised my eyebrows back, then heard myself saying, 'Any chance we can replace him?' I don't believe I've ever said those words before in all my time in the theatre, though of course I've heard others say them, once or twice. 'Yes, but who with?' Joe replied, 'That's the problem.' I found myself – speaking and thinking at the same moment – saying, 'Nathan Lane, the guy who played Nick at the Long Wharf. He was brilliant. Wonderful actor.' I went on to explain that I knew Nathan was free because Caroline Lagerfelt,[†] just back from New York, had phoned yesterday to say hello, pass on greetings from mutual friends, among them Nathan Lane, whose Broadway show, a musical version of *The Wind in the Willows* (Nathan play-ing Mr Toad) had closed after three days. Why don't you think of Nathan for *Dog Days* in Dallas, Caroline had said *en passant* – a suggestion I'd found intriguing, because although Nathan is not exactly right for *Dog Days*, his talent makes him right for almost

---

* It didn't occur to me at the time to wonder what he was doing there, but I do remember that he was neither coming nor going, just standing. I now find some-thing odd in the image of Joe, who doesn't smoke and is always so active, just standing on the corner of the street.

† I first met Caroline Lagerfelt when she was cast as the wife in *Otherwise Engaged* on Broadway. Since then we've done five plays together. Though her first language is Swedish, she speaks both American and English (she went to school in England) with outrageous ease and naturalness. In fact she's a kind of linguistic schizo-phrenic, able to switch from soft southern counties English to savage New York in the course of a sentence. She lives in New York, but pops over to Los Angeles from time to time to work in television.

any part, including the ones he's not exactly right for. I'd decided to pass his name on to Stephen Hollis, and see him when and if I went to New York – all this to explain why his name was already in my mind, and sprang so quickly from my lips, there out on the pavement with Joe. Joe said, 'Well, would he come out?' I said I thought so – Caroline had mentioned that if nothing interesting were offered to him soon, he was going to come to Los Angeles and check out television possibilities. Anyway, I said, 'We can always ask him. I know he loves the part.' Then I also remembered that Nathan and Ted Larkins were friends. Almost the first thing Ted Larkins had said when I'd met him on my return to the Matrix was that Nathan sent his love. I found this rather disconcerting – after all it's likely to make for less awful feelings all round if the chap one is replacing is unknown to the chap one is replacing him with. Nevertheless, I said I'd ask Nathan in confidence whether he would be interested in coming to the Matrix, where we could offer him the chance of working hard in an uncongenial atmosphere for no reward. Unless you count doing a disservice to a friend as a reward.

The conversation with Joe depressed me, not only because of and on behalf of Larkins, but also because of the hardness that had surfaced in me so unexpectedly, in such a matter-of-fact fashion. I wished – still wish – that the idea of replacing Ted Larkins hadn't come from me. I wished – still wish – that the idea of replacing him with Nathan Lane hadn't come from me. I suppose I'm glad that both ideas came from somewhere, but behind the obvious moral embarrassment lurks a sense that we haven't done as well by Ted Larkins as we ought to have done, that we've given up on him too easily, or have allowed him to give up on himself too easily. Not, of course, that it's too late. Nathan hasn't yet been signed, Ted Larkins hasn't yet been, in the great American theatre euphemism, 'let go'.* Perhaps the situation can still be redeemed. No, it can't.

---

* I've heard of an English actress, a jolly and uncomplicated girl, who was cast in a Broadway production. When told by the director and producer, in the middle of a rehearsal, that they were going to 'let her go' she assumed they meant allow her to slip off for a cup of tea. She thanked them both accordingly, thus notching up another one for the myth of the stiff upper lip.

It was in this state of mind that I went off after rehearsals with Mr and Mrs Weisman to a show whose name I've already forgotten, which turned out to be playing at a theatre miles away from the Matrix. The journey was interminable, and the destination, when we at last got there, massively unprepossessing, the theatre being in a complex that contained the kind of car park that people in films drive at each other in, guns blazing. We sat at a counter in one of the restaurants, had some fish snacks and guessed, in a desultory way, at the ages of various long-serving film stars, then went into the show, which was really a kind of *Oklahoma* without the music. People stood about in *Oklahoma*-like togs on a set that consisted of an *Oklahoma*-like log cabin in an *Oklahoma*-like field. The play was co-authored by an elderly and distinguished actor who'd obviously taken on the job with the sole purpose of providing acting work for himself and his equally distinguished actress wife. His own character is meant to be a kind of ghost visible only to his wife (onstage *and* offstage), a conceit taken from *Harvey*, itself a pretty elderly, not to say decrepit play featuring an alcoholic who conjures up a rabbit as his boon companion, a part played by James Stewart in the film. The part, that is, of the alcoholic, not of the rabbit. Anyway, in the *Oklahoma*-without-music play this old ghost is still pottering about the old homestead, even more infuriating than he'd been in life because after all he was meant to be dead, which in a decent society should have meant the end of him. There was one particularly revolting scene in which he and his wife re-enacted the birth of their son, thus giving us the spectacle of the elderly leading lady groaning away on a table, in heavy labour, being tended to by her elderly but dead double-husband who was shouting the baby out as if he were a coach on a football field. Throughout the play the old ghost stood in strange, insignificant* postures or ran nimbly about, with special little skips for ascending to or descending from the porch. Of course what he was really pantomiming was, 'Aren't I in good shape for a guy of seventy-five? Especially for a *dead* guy of seventy-five?' The audience – the theatre is enormous, seating

---

* I think this must be a mistranscription for 'and significant'. Pity. For interesting echo, see *The Common Pursuit*, Act One, Scene One, Nick reading from a letter 'delicate, insensitive poetry – oh, delicate *and* sensitive poetry. Pity.'

about three thousand, if I heard correctly, *and* it was sold out – loved it. There were ripples of warm laughter and sighs of affection at every single cuteness. Fortunately I managed to train such visible malevolence on to the stage that at the interval Sam Weisman suggested we leave. I got myself dropped off in Hollywood Boulevard, saying I'd walk from there, not to worry, thank you for a wonderful evening – no, I couldn't have said that, could I, as we'd left at the interval – then hurried myself to Musso and Frank's, sat on a swivel seat at the counter and ordered myself up a batch of Chivas Regals,* then escorted myself home, in a rather dozy state, watched a bit of television, hit the sack.

Saturday, 11 January

In the morning I dragged myself out of bed with something like a headache. Not a drink headache, but the kind of headache you get at the prospect of the day ahead. I had an ill-judged breakfast and then phoned Nathan Lane. To my horror I got him straight away. I told him, in the solemn tones one assumes for this sort of occasion, that our conversation had to be both confidential and inconclusive. We *were* having trouble, I went on, with the part of Nick. In fact, we were beginning to think we might have to find an alternative, what did he feel about this? He said, 'Great, I'd love to do it.' Just like that. Almost before I'd finished. 'Great, I'd love to do it. What seems to be the trouble with Ted?' I gave a judiciously edited account, then asked him whether their friendship would be a complication. He said, 'Oh well, that'll just have to be something, I don't know, to sort out. That's the way things go. A bit of a problem.' But he made it quite clear that it wasn't a problem that would in any way affect his coming out and playing the part. We left it that all future negotiations would be between himself and Joe Stern. I hung up feeling immensely relieved and slightly sullied. Immensely sullied. But there we were. I then cabbed into the Matrix and reported the conversation to Joe, who managed to look astonished, delighted and distressed all at once. We went in together to watch the rehearsal, standing at the back,

* A very expensive Scotch whisky that I had to make do with at Musso and Frank's, as they don't stock malt whisky there.

in the shadows, like a couple of assassins, all our concentration on Ted Larkins. He was worse than the last time I'd seen him, as if he'd given up even on the ghost of Nick – all he could do was say the words, make the moves.

During a break Joe and I passed the news about Nathan Lane on to Sam Weisman. He received it with the same astonishment, though with more delight and less distress than Joe, but a few minutes later we were into one of those conversations common (I imagine) to most inexperienced conspirators – you know, worring about how Chris Neame (our Peter), who is a great friend of Ted Larkins, will take it; and how John Delancey, a man of evident decency and clear moral views, will take it; and of course how Ted Larkins himself will take it – so forth, on and on, until we backed into a compromise, deciding that we must make one further attempt with Larkins in case he'd simply fixed on some misconception about the part, that a few key words might clear up. This will cost us a few more days, but will make us all feel we're behaving properly.

We resumed the rehearsal, but before it was properly under way the caretaker of the Matrix, who is about twenty-three years old and has a funny little fuzz on his chin, burst in to announce that Sam Weisman's car had been broken into by a large black guy, he guessed, he'd seen running down the alley at the back of the theatre. We went out and surveyed the car.

The front window had been smashed in and the radio three-quarters pulled out, wires trailing everywhere, a real mess. According to the fuzzy-bearded young caretaker, the black guy hadn't been carrying any tools, and as there weren't any rocks around, he must have done all the damage with his bare hands – an extraordinary feat, really. We stood looking at the wreckage for a few minutes, then Kris Tabori set off in his car and Sam Weisman went running off, both looking for the black guy, and I have to note now – something to do with the inhuman, increasingly inhuman, side of my nature – that I was frightened that they'd find him. Frankly I didn't think they'd have much chance with someone as big and powerful as this guy must be – in fact they might get badly hurt or killed even – and where would that leave my play? I didn't want them killed anyway, but I have to admit that the future of the play was really my first thought. Furthermore, I realise now that

I showed not even a courteous interest in the condition of Weisman's car. Being a non-driver, I have no interest in cars, people's relationship to them, even when I'm being driven about in them. I must remember to express sorrow and concern tomorrow.

Both Tabori and Weisman returned intact. Weisman – having to go down to the police station to file a report – called off rehearsals for the day. John Delancey drove me back to the Magic, offering to come up and have a go at fixing my video. It took him a long time – about twenty-five minutes – as most of the plugs were in the wrong socket, while one of the pins in one of the plugs was bent. He had to cut the pin off and insert the naked wires into the set. It's probably been made quite lethal, but I admired the calm dexterity and logic with which he first detected the problem and then solved it. If it is solved. I haven't had a chance to test it. By the time he'd finished I was late for the Roddy McDowall dinner, to which Delancey offered to drive me. I had virtually no clothes, even though I'd got Delancey to stop off at the laundry where I'd left some (so, come to think of it, Delancey functioned first as my valet, and then as my electrician, and then as my chauffeur). But the point is that even with my laundry back, I still hadn't anything reasonable to change into. In fact all I'd got were the threadbare black cords I was in – still am in – a pair of soft brown run-down shoes, and only one light shirt, which I was also in (though I've changed it today). Suspecting that Roddy McDowall's was going to be a smartish affair, I had to phone up in front of Delancey and tell Roddy McDowall I was coming straight from the theatre, wouldn't have time to change out of working gear, hoped this was OK, etc. Delancey listened to these lies and apologies with a sympathetic smile.

Naturally, Roddy McDowall lives miles away. Everybody in Los Angeles lives miles away, not from anywhere, because there isn't actually an anywhere to live miles away from, but from each other. It was therefore a long drive through increasingly lush suburbia – like Surrey on the rampage, both in foliage and in architecture – through gates,* down a short wide drive to a flunkey or

---

* Now I think about it, I'm not sure that there were gates. I might have been confusing my arrival with an arrival once made by Dana Andrews in a movie that I saw when I was ten or eleven years old, the title of which I have forgotten. I've also forgotten the story. and the names of the other actors.

two waiting to park cars, and then into the house to be served a (thank God!) enormous drink by another flunkey, with Roddy McDowall and a group of prosperous-looking guests gathered around a fire. Recognisably present were Coral Browne, Vincent Price, and above all the actress Lee Remick, one of my all-time favourite ladies – on the screen, that is, I'd never met her in the flesh before. She's got these adorable teeth. The thing about them is that they just slightly protrude over her underlip when she smiles, and the effect, on me anyway, is simply annihilating. I go straight to pieces. Whenever I see that smile on the screen I go to pieces, and there she was in the flesh, looking pretty good and smiling that smile on the other side of the room.

I hustled myself shyly over to her and said what a great fan of hers I was, especially in that film – I couldn't remember a single film she'd been in. Not a single film. I stared at her blankly, then managed to dredge one up. 'You know,' I said, 'you know, with Gregory Peck. And Robert Mitchum violated you.' She said that she'd never been in a film in which Robert Mitchum violated her. She wished she had. And smiled her smile.* I blundered on to the effect that the film was made so long ago I couldn't remember it properly, thus indicating that not only could I not remember her through the years, but that there had been so many, many years, how could I hope to? – also giving the impression, I think, that I'd been in short trousers while she'd been playing grown-up parts. A pity, as I really would like to have expressed my – my – anyway, she was rescued by Roddy McDowall, a perfect host in every respect, who bore me away to meet a lady whose name rang a bell. An extremely engaging lady, with a Welsh accent and a very Welsh kind of charm. So I talked a bit about my own Welshness, fishing for her identity, and finally proposed indirectly that she might be an actress. She said no, she wasn't, but her daughter, Kate Burton, was.

Dinner itself was fine. I made amends with Lee Remick, who sat next to me, not by suddenly remembering her films, but by recalling that I'd read somewhere that she'd lived for a long time in London, which gave us a subject to talk about. Then I had a gossip

* I've since remembered that it was Anne Francis that was violated by Robert Mitchum. The film was called *Cape Fear* – a humdinger.

with Coral Browne, that I would have enjoyed even more if I hadn't been conscious of myself chain-smoking away in frayed togs, down-at heel shoes, rather like the Boudu tramp in the Renoir film, only without his insouciance. At least I didn't belch.

After dinner we sat by the fire, drinking. I talked mainly to Vincent Price, avoiding a number of other people I sort of sensed were famous but didn't recognise. It was a really nice conversation – Vincent Price telling me about his early days as an actor/art historian – and I was just beginning to relax, looking forward to my next drink, when people around me began to go. This, as I think I've already noted, is the Los Angeles style. People go early, from anywhere. Perhaps they wake up early. Perhaps they're about their day before dawn. Or perhaps there's simply something in the air that makes them semi-comatose after twilight, I don't know. There was a protracted discussion among the other remnants as to who was to drive me home. I was chagrined to note that there wasn't too much competition for this job, though I was pleased when Vincent Price and Coral Browne finally elected themselves. Off I went in a capacious car, Price driving with gentlemanly dexterity, Coral Browne beside him, I lolling in the back at ease, and feeling rather lively. When I got back here, to the Magic, I watched a bit of *The Godfather* (on a tape lent to me by Joe Stern) on the video, which means that John Delancey's labour wasn't in vain, opened a bottle of champagne – I'd shared the last drop of my whisky with John Delancey – and after getting up in the scene where Sterling Hayden is shot through the forehead by Robert de Niro* in the Italian restaurant, turned off the video, and dictated this. Am now going to bed.

Sunday, 12 January

Woke up feeling like absolute hell, made myself a rather disturbing breakfast of bacon, peppery sausages, toast and instant coffee, and decided over it that if only I could get the right pair of trousers, all my main problems would be resolved. But how in Los Angeles without a car *and* on a Sunday did one come by the right pair of trousers? I put this question to Caroline Lagerfelt when

---

* Or was it Al Pacino?

she phoned to enquire after my health, the state of rehearsals, etc. She said there was a famous mall – 'mull' they pronounce it here – which is open every minute of every day of the year, where I'd be able to find trousers galore. I accepted her offer to drive me to it. Just before she arrived Lucy phoned to announce her return from Switzerland – we'd given her a week's holiday there as a Christmas present. She'd had a wonderful time, she said, why didn't I take up skiing? I explained about the dangerous complications that could arise from broken limbs at my sort of age. She said that I wasn't *that* old. I said that one was as old as one felt, and I felt old, at least when it came to skiing. It was very sort of loving to hear her voice, especially as I'd been worrying about her a bit – Beryl had phoned yesterday (Saturday) to point out that she'd been expected back on Friday, and still hadn't returned. Then Caroline, and off in her car, in the heat, to the 'mull'. (I'm dictating this on my porch, looking across to one of the other porches where I can see an extremely delightful-looking dog, staring through the plate-glass window at his departing owners, who are obviously off for the evening. The dog, with a look of dignified desolation, is now getting up and is walking out of sight. Perhaps to pee in their bed. Reproach or piss – what dogs like to do when you leave them alone when they don't want to be left alone, which is most of the time.)

It was hopeless, of course. Quite hopeless. I either stood about in trousers that came down over my feet at one end, and almost up to my armpits at the other, or in trousers so short and tight that I felt the slightest move would result in popping buttons, a gaping fly. I also suspected that word was getting around the 'mull', and that people were coming from its distant parts to look at me. I gave up, thoroughly demoralised – how can it be that for all my credit cards, and with an absolutely routinely proportioned body (given my age) I couldn't find one, not even one, pair of suitable trousers? I took Caroline through this again and again (though in no way blaming her, let it be said) as she drove me to the Matrix, where Sam Weisman blocked me in the lobby. He wanted a little time alone, he said, with Kris Tabori and Judy Geeson. Did I know what he meant? I didn't, but said, 'You're very welcome,' and felt it, really felt it, because what I wanted to do was to have a quiet sandwich and a glass of wine and not think about anything for a bit.

I went next door to the Café Melrose with a two-day-old copy of the London *Times* which I'd picked up on the way in, and devoured the wonderful drama of Heseltine's resignation. Then I sat back and encouraged myself to grow resentful at Sam Weisman's wanting to work alone with the two actors. What was it he didn't want me to see? Or was it Judy Geeson who didn't want me to be there? It had seemed to me that both she and her husband had been slightly alarmed when they saw me arrive. They'd obviously assumed, I thought in retrospect as I sat over my white wine and some peculiar confection of crab and poached eggs (which turned out to be mainly poached eggs), that I wasn't going to turn up this morning – had they already arranged with Sam to keep me away? I went through my usual procedure, smoking numerous cigarettes, drinking numerous glasses of wine and cups of coffee, finally and seethingly deciding that the culprit was Judy Geeson – no doubt because she wanted to be free to 'explore' and 'examine' and all that sort of stuff without the pressure of the author's presence, etc., and so forth. I rose abruptly, hurried next door, and bumped straight into Judy Geeson in the lobby, who said, 'It's a pity you weren't in rehearsal because Kris and I have the feeling that actually Sam is working a bit against the text.'

The rehearsal for the rest of the day was unspeakable. A clear case of an actor drowning before one's eyes. Poor Ted Larkins. Every time he began to do a scene he would stop, almost at once, and involve Weisman in some irrelevant question – as, for example, when do I see this letter, when shall I move to this chair, what do I do when I get to the chair, what do I do when I sit down, which letter do I pick up – anything that would delay having to give us a performance. And Weisman, instead of being solicitous and helpful, manifested impatience – irascible impatience – almost constantly. Larkins would speak two lines and ask a question which would result in an interminable but ill-natured discussion. Then another two lines, another question, another interminable, ill-natured discussion. The atmosphere was absolutely ghastly.

At long last Weisman gave up on Larkins and ran the whole of the first scene, which gave me a chance to see what he'd been up to with Judy Geeson and Kris Tabori. It was really quite interesting – if one's interested in such technicalities – because the scene, as I wrote it, is constructed so that things happen in stages. First we have a look between Stuart and Marigold; then we have a bit of charged conversation; then we have proximity; and then a kiss, the kind of kiss that leads to bed. Now Sam Weisman has always been keen to *start* the scene with a kiss. So what he'd imposed on it while they'd been working without me is a kiss at the beginning, then another kiss, then some business with coffee, then a further kiss, then the conversation, then a further kiss, followed by bed. In other words, a muddle, because the scene begins where in a sense it should end and simply goes on repeating itself with interruptions for coffee and talk. I shall have to do something about it.

The rest of the run had some good things in it: a very nicely developing Martin (Wayne Alexander) and nicely developing Humphry (John Delancey). But of course the scenes with Nick – Ted Larkins – were dire. It was sad, and rather horrifying really, to have to sit through them. In fact I didn't, slipping instead up to the Mexican bar, where I had a few drinks, then got a cab to Musso and Frank's. I was just settling down to nothing in particular – a kind of self-absence – when I suddenly remembered that I didn't know what the call was for tomorrow. I phoned Sam Weisman who told me that it was for seven o'clock in the evening,* then went on to say that he and Joe Stern had had a dreadful conversation with Larkins. Larkins had kept on probing about his part, what it was he still needed to find, and they'd been unable to help him, Sam said, because they knew he was beyond help, though he had the feeling that Larkins's next move would be to phone me. Well, here I am, just back from dinner to discover a message from Larkins asking me to phone him back – he'll be up until half past midnight. I can phone him any time until then to have a chat. It's only ten thirty but I can't face phoning him.

Monday, 13 January

When I woke up this morning, I brushed my teeth, had a shower, breakfasted on coffee and bacon, hung about for a bit, then finally forced myself into phoning Ted Larkins. I said enthusiastically that I'd got his message, did he want to talk to me? And he said,

---

* The arbitrary-seeming times at which rehearsals began – anything between ten in the morning and seven or eight in the evening – is explained by the fact that the director and some of the actors were also pursuing successful careers in television.

yes, that was why he'd phoned, because he wanted to talk to me. Why else would he phone? And could he come round? I said, 'The thing is, Ted, I'm not really quite up yet, the day hasn't taken full possession of me, can I phone you back after I've had a bit of coffee and brushed my teeth, etc.?' He said that was fine by him – he was very nice, very calm. I hung up and did in fact brush my teeth again and made some more coffee. Then I phoned Beryl, discharging all my panic and resentment at the prospect of having to do to Larkins what, clearly, the producer and the director were unable to face doing. As soon as I'd hung up I phoned Larkins and said, 'Come on, why don't you come on round at ten thirty?' I sat on the sofa, wondering what I should say to him, then suddenly realised that I'd forgotten to shave. It was while I was shaving that the line I ought to take became clear to me. I waited for him until just after ten thirty, then went down to the lobby and there he was, coming up the steps. We walked past the pool, talking about the Astroturf which was causing sparks to fly up from our shoes, and about how dangerous life is in Los Angeles even when passing alongside a pool in the sunshine, and on up into my room. I offered him some champagne which he refused, saying – it made my heart sink – that he had to do some work 'on a certain play'. I poured myself a glass of champagne and said, rather abruptly, 'Shall I speak?' He said, yes, he would like me to speak. So I spoke.

What I said was that it seemed to me that I could talk for ever about how he should play Nick, but it was all irrelevant because, 'What we have here is a basic situation and another situation arising out of a situation.' In other words there were two situations. From then on I managed to become slightly more lucid. He was miscast, I said, seriously miscast, because Nick was an expansive, bizarre, outgoing figure and he, Ted, was by nature rather inhibited, shy – introverted in a word. In trying to think of what it was in Nathan Lane's performance that was so different from Ted Larkins's I'd come to the conclusion that Nathan had only to move an inch forward to be Nick, whereas Ted had to make a jump of miles, forward and to the side, to be Nick. I made a point of stressing that it wasn't Ted Larkins as an *actor* that was the problem, but Ted Larkins in a part in which he had been inappropriately cast. Furthermore, I said, it was clear that he was not getting on with the director. There was so much tension between him and Weisman that every time he tried to perform he went into a state of shock, which led him in rehearsals, as for example, yesterday's, to keep stalling by asking utterly irrelevant questions. I'd like to think that I was both gentle and brutal. *Simultaneously* brutal and gentle.

After a pause he said he would like a glass of champagne after all, he rather needed one. I poured him a glass and handed it to him. There was another pause before he said, yes, this was exactly what he'd wanted to hear, he agreed with all of it. He was miscast as Nick as he was really a shy, diffident, out-of-the-corner-of-his-mouth actor, that was his nature, he couldn't help it, how therefore could he be an ebullient, forward-thrusting Nick, especially with a director who kept shouting at him that he needed basic acting lessons? I agreed that he couldn't, and then virtually repeated what I'd said – one tends to go on saying the same things in these situations because (a) one can't think of anything else to say, and (b) there isn't anything else to say. He downed another glass or two of champagne, we parted on the best of terms, it being understood between us that he was going to withdraw from the production.

I phoned Joe Stern and told him that he was now free to contact Nathan, then went on to Musso and Frank's for some lunch. Came back and hung about on the porch of my apartment with the sun beating down, gazing at the people lying around the small pool below, among them a man I took to be English, handsome and middle-aged, who was pulling on a very fat cigar and reading a book – I above him in my thick clothes, sweating and guilty.

I went in for the seven o'clock run-through. A pointless exercise as without one of the characters it was inevitably lopsided and uninformative. There was of course a rather odd atmosphere, over-relaxed, and at times almost hysterical – survivors celebrating, I suppose. They might also have been celebrating the fact that Sam Weisman is going to be away for the next four days, directing a television show to which he committed himself months ago, and they therefore thought that they were getting that time off. Not so, as I've arranged with Joe and Sam to work with the actors on the text, long stretches of which are still bothering me. I'll also take the opportunity to rearrange the blocking, and have a proper look at Judy Geeson and Kristoffer Tabori in the first scene. Though I believe I forgot, so to speak, to mention that to Sam Weisman.

Tuesday, 14 January

When we began work on Act One, Scene Two, Joe plonked himself down right beside me in the front row of the auditorium. I said, 'You're not going to sit there, are you?' He said, 'Yes.' I said, 'Well, I'd rather you didn't, if you don't mind.' He got up and went out without a flounce. He's not the flouncing kind – but nevertheless making it dramatically clear that he'd taken offence. When I got back to the Magic I phoned him to apologise. Instead of acknowledging what I said, he went off at tangents of rage, not confronting the issue directly until the very end, when he suddenly said, 'OK, you're being aggressive now, I'll accept that. But when we get into previews I'll be aggressive. I get very aggressive in previews. And you'll have to accept *that*.' I said I would, but hung up feeling offended in my turn. Went to bed, still imaginatively on the line to Joe. Probably better that he didn't hear what I had to say.

I walked up to Musso and Frank's thinking about the flabby writing in the scene between Martin and Stuart in the first act. After the meal – I remember absolutely nothing about it – I went for a walk in the vicinity of the restaurant, a sleazy section of Hollywood Boulevard, where I suddenly encountered a chap I've become familiar with since my arrival, carrot-haired and wheeling about on skates. From the back he looks about twelve or thirteen, at a distance from the front you realise he must be older, at least sixteen, but when you see his face close to, you discover that in spite of his carroty hair and boyish body, he's actually about fifty. Tonight he came zooming towards me, then skidded around on his skates and zipped away, whipping around other pedestrians who paid him no attention. I paid him very little attention myself, having become used to androgynous or over-muscled creatures on roller skates zooming, zipping and wheeling up and down the pavements just as I've become used to people lying about in the gutters of this part of Hollywood, lifting their hands for compensation for the blight I haven't personally inflicted on them. I went on walking, turning eventually back towards the Magic Hotel, keeping my mind fixed on the scene between Stuart and Martin in Act One, Scene Two.

Wednesday, 15 January

While Wayne Alexander and Kristoffer Tabori were collating the new script, Joe Stern, Chip Estees – who was fussing about with the theatre computer writing a play or a film script, I couldn't make out which – and I traded Irish, Polish and Jewish jokes. We kept each other amused (for about three hours, in fact) until Tabori and Alexander came into the office, looking rather tired, to say goodnight. They've done a remarkable job, performing not only actors' parts, but also critics' and secretaries' parts, while I've merely performed a playwright's part, and that in an antique style, sauntering about with a cigarette in my hand, altering lines on my feet, getting Tabori and Alexander to perform the cuts and changes so I could hear what they sounded like, but not of course condescending to anything practical as, for example, scribbling changes into my text, getting the text sorted out, typed up and collated. No wonder they looked tired, poor boys, especially when entering an office relaxed and jocular, echoing with laughter.

Joe drove me to Musso and Frank's for a quick supper, after which I came back here to confront the video situation, which is as follows: John Delancey's ingenious wire implant of a few days ago hasn't really worked, because the wires keep slipping out. Chip arranged for an engineer from the video shop to come out and fix it properly. I warned the sunnies at the desk that the engineer would be arriving, and left my key in my box in reception, so that he could be let in. When he arrived the sunnies turned him away, on the grounds that, as there was no key available, he couldn't be let in. On hearing this from the sunnies, I walked ponderously to my box, took out my key, and held it up for their inspection. They smiled at it sunnily, making little exclamations – 'Oh, gee . . .' and 'Well, wow . . .', not so much apologies as cheerful little appreciations of my rather smart conjuring trick. But then the Magic Hotel is named after the Magic Castle, an extraordinary Gothic building a little way up the road, where professional magicians exhibit themselves, so perhaps the sunnies thought I was a Magic member, practising. I don't know. All I know is that the saga of the video goes on. I've had it now for nearly two weeks, and it still doesn't work. In London you could have it installed and working in two hours. In New York I expect (though I've never tried) you could have it installed and working in two hours. In Rome, Paris, Vienna – but here in Los Angeles you cannot get it installed and working in under two weeks, no matter what sort of fuss you make, to whom you appeal. It's now ten past one in the morning. We're hitting Thursday, the day when Nathan Lane gets in from New York.

Thursday, 16 January

At the Matrix Theatre in Los Angeles the actors scarcely ever arrive punctually for rehearsal, turning up fifteen or twenty minutes late, having come from television shows or auditions or love affairs, whatever, and furthermore are likely to leave rehearsals abruptly, for the same sort of reasons. This morning John Delancey mentioned, quite nonchalantly, that he was up for a television series called *McGovern*, or *McGiven* or something, and if he got the part would be out of rehearsals for ten days. I think my face, which, being Welsh, can be alarmingly expressive, expressed quite a few, if not all, of my feelings on this, but I'm not sure he noticed. A part of the niceness of nice people is that they assume you're nice too.

At lunchtime I discovered that Nathan Lane had arrived and was next door at the Café Melrose. I scurried the fifteen yards or so down the pavement and into the Melrose, and there he was, Nathan to the life, sitting at a table with various foods spread in front of him. He'd had to get up at 4.30 a.m. to catch a plane at six. He was full of fun and had his usual corporeal energy, though there wasn't much energy in his eyes, which were half dead from fatigue. Kristoffer Tabori and Joe Stern joined us, and there was a lot of talk about this show and that show, who'd seen what and what they thought of it – one of the things about the theatre, there's always a subject to hand to cover the preliminary social manoeuvres.

We went back to the theatre for a read-through, to give Nathan a chance to slot into the company, and for the company to see how he slotted in. We couldn't start immediately, of course, this being the Matrix. The read-through was to be in the Green Room, i.e. an upstairs attic, very hot, with the sun pouring through the skylight. Christopher Neame and Joe Stern made an elaborate business out of opening the skylight, both of them fussing with cords and sticks and mutual advice until they'd so worked it that a little dash of air came through, accompanied by extra lashings of light and heat. At last, hot and uncomfortable, we began. It went on and on. The only good thing was Nathan, who, given the circumstances of his arrival and the fact that he hadn't done the part for a year or so, was marvellously energetic and ripe. Kristoffer Tabori was still finding his way – not surprising, I suppose, as he has a long rewrite to deal with in Act One, Scene Two. My feeling about the play itself was that its shape was right in that it had a curve and it led to climaxes, but that it was too safe. There was a certain deadness or at least dullness about it, and almost an over-shapeliness to the rewritten Act One, Scene Two. But we plodded on, working our way through to the end of Act Two and there ending the day's work, though I addressed a few rather sharpish words to the actors about the importance of observing the punctuation and the language of the play. Christopher Neame was particularly bad, or good (depending on your point of view), at paraphrasing, getting not only whole passages, but simple sentences, even quite short ones, wrong. In fact was all over the book, as was John Delancey, who seemed so mechanical as Humphry that he gave the impression of being over-rehearsed in lines that he nevertheless hadn't learnt properly – a dispiriting combination.

I went back and had my usual meal at Musso and Frank's, where they've consented to give me a booth, at last, and then shambled up to the hotel, where there was a message at reception to the effect that the video engineer, who this time had been allowed into my flat, had been unable to fix the machine, and therefore proposed replacing it with another, far newer one, though needless to say, hasn't yet done so – there's the old set in its usual place, non-functioning as usual. No, that's not fair, partially functioning. It can throw pictures on to the screen, scarred and jagged, as if they've been in an accident. I phoned home and talked extensively to Beryl about what had been going on in Los Angeles. I was about to go to bed when I was suddenly struck by the idea that perhaps I had failed rather in boldness, let's say heroism, in Act One, Scene Two, and began to restructure it in my mind.

Friday, 17 January

I woke at seven thirty and tried to recapture everything I'd thought about Act One, Scene Two, during the night, writing it down on a legal pad, juggling with lines until it was time to go into rehearsal. I began by addressing myself to the problem of Delancey's slipshod robot of a Humphry, but wasn't helped by Joe Stern coming in and settling down beside me, saying, 'Do you mind if I sit in?' I began to make a gesture of denial, then remembering the consequences the last time I'd done this, said, 'Of course, Joe,' though what I wanted to do, actually, was to take him by the scruff of his neck and the seat of his trousers and hurl him down the stairs to his office below. I proceeded rather haltingly, acutely conscious of Joe's presence – he's got a kind of continuous smile when he attends rehearsals, I've noticed, a cynical and despairing one, and every so often he shakes his straw-coloured head, to signify unspoken but emphatic dissent. His performance, of which I was more conscious than of Delancey's, was interrupted by frequent calls to the telephone. We could hear his voice coming up from the floor below, then the patter of his feet, or rather the stamping patter of his feet as he came back to join us, sitting down beside me in this humid attic of a Green Room and then going off again.

We had to break in mid-afternoon when a lady from the *Los Angeles Times* came to interview me. She was small, about sixty, very intense but perfectly agreeable. We went to the Café Melrose, where I seem to spend most of my life when I'm not actually spending it in the theatre or at Musso and Frank's or festering away here in my hotel room. She'd brought with her a copy of the American edition of *An Unnatural Pursuit*. She seemed, rather oddly, to have a great familiarity with the essays at the back of the book, but none at all with the actual diary, though she kept referring to it confidently and inaccurately. When we'd finished, I had a long session with a *Times* photographer – a young man of very exotic extraction, from the looks of him, and very charming, but with a perverse idea of the kind of picture that would convey the spirit of rehearsals. He insisted on my sitting awkwardly on the knife-edged rim of a seat in the middle row of the auditorium, so I wasn't merely facing away from the actors, I actually had my back to them. He also asked me, even when I was smiling, to smile, so I ended up grimacing – pretty viciously, I suspect.

After he'd left I turned my attention to Judy Geeson and Kristoffer Tabori in their scenes together, re-blocking them in an attempt to discover normality, playfulness and sexual tension. One of the things that continues to depress me about Joe Stern and Sam Weisman is their tendency to think that every scene has to be moved about rapidly, rapidly – people scurrying here and scurrying there, no conversation ever unfolding without scurrying. I took out all the moves in which Judy Geeson was called upon to race about the stage, delivering her lines while, metaphorically, anyway, pummelling her fists against the chest of her lover – onstage lover, offstage husband. I went through it again and again, getting it at least calmer, and I hoped slightly more concentrated, until about seven thirty, by which time I was pretty exhausted.

Back at my hotel I found a message to say that the video engineer had installed an entirely new video that he was sure worked perfectly, and therefore he couldn't understand why it didn't actually transmit pictures on to my screen. He had spoken to his boss, who was prepared to return my money. For some reason this message was left not to me, but to Chip Estees. I tried the machine out. Sure enough, there was no connection between the tape whirring away on the video and the active but blank television screen. Depressed and angry, I set out for a meal at, of course, Musso and Frank's, and was disconcerted to discover the restaurant absolutely packed, I think for the first time in my experience. The only seat available was at the counter, right opposite the grill, where I had to sit with lamb chops and steaks and swordfish steaks grilling away almost under my nose. There was a gap at the counter which I thought at first was to allow me space to swivel about in, but in fact turned out to be for the waiters who swivelled me about as they pushed past me to collect the food. I was also swivelled about by customers, as they elbowed their way past on either side. A miserable evening. On my way back there was the ravaged-faced roller-skater with long red hair jumping, nimbling about on his roller skates and suddenly coming towards me as if intent on rape.

Sunday, 19 January

I woke at about eight, having had the most appalling nightmares, *appalling* nightmares, to do with my family and their safety. I lay in bed, smoking and pondering – fretting. Eventually phoned Beryl to make sure that everybody was all right, then got up and had breakfast. Went down to the Chinese laundry on Hollywood, collected the clothes that I'd dumped there the other day, came back, dumped them, phoned the video people. I was put on to a very Los Angeles chappie called Dave, who kept on saying, 'I empathise with you, I deeply empathise with you, I empathise with you, Mr Gray, over your problem – it's been two weeks now,' and all that stuff. He went on to say that he'd consulted with the manager who had decided that they no longer wanted to have anything to do with me because (a) whatever was wrong was not their fault, and (b) even if it was their fault they didn't want to have anything to do with me. They would rather give the Matrix Theatre their money back. I shouted some abuse and hung up.

Sam Weisman phoned. We arranged to meet at the Café Melrose at eleven thirty, half an hour before rehearsals, so I could tell him about the various changes I've made while he's been away. At eleven o'clock I phoned for a taxi, collected Nathan (who is staying at the Magic, by the way, in a small, dark room, without a balcony, close to the lobby – he hates it) and down we hurtled to the Café Melrose where, as seemed almost inevitable, Sam Weisman was not waiting for me. In fact, surging into the café exactly on time, and finding it full of people who had taken it over for a convention, I had to surge straight out again, to hang around in the theatre until Sam Weisman turned up at five to twelve – he'd forgotten his scripts and had had to drive back home to collect them. We stood on the pavement in the boiling sunshine while I told him roughly what I'd done over the last four days. Then we went in – there was the usual further waiting about, because some of the actors hadn't arrived. But at least the floor is being laid, a marvellous floor, it looks, and soon the set will be going up. The trouble is, I haven't got much confidence in the set. I went over the model when I was here for the casting, and pointed out to the designer – a tiny, intense chap, with a rather fey manner – that the couple of small revolves with which he proposed to make the shift from present to future at the beginning of the play, from present to past at the end of it, won't work as the play needs them to work. David Jenkins managed it (I admit he had a bigger stage, and better facilities) in the Long Wharf production, to absolutely heart-stopping effect, time as well as space seeming to shift about in architectural blocks.

My fear with this design is that the two revolves will carry off some of the furniture, but not all of it; and then we'll go down to black while the rest of the furniture is struck or replaced – in fact, a conventional set change requiring a lengthy pause. Exactly what I don't want, and that I've written into the text mustn't happen. When I'd aired my objections he'd emitted little cawing sounds of recognition and agreement, but I suspected he hadn't listened to a word I'd said – he probably believes that playwrights should stick to writing plays, and not bother their ugly little heads with such technical matters as sets and scene changes. At the end of the session he'd greeted one of my suggestions – it was to do with the placing of a window – with an appalled pause, and then said: 'I dunno, I dunno but there's something about that that just makes my flesh crawl. It makes my flesh crawl. To think of half a window on stage makes my flesh – it just craaawls!' And he did a shake with his whole body to illustrate what he looked like when his flesh crawled. I'd known then that he and I were never really going to be in sympathy – on any matter in life, probably, but certainly when it comes to discussing sets for my plays. But I may have been wrong about him. He may have registered everything I said about what the play needs, and is now coming up with wizard solutions. I hope so. But I don't believe so.

Sam Weisman worked through the play from the top with great effect, accepting with equanimity the changes I'd made in the first act, including the elimination of all the kisses and tousling in the first scene. Best of all Act One, Scene Two, seemed to me, almost for the first time, to be fully alive and vigorous. This was partly because of Nathan, who has had a galvanising effect on the rest of the cast. Several actors – Chris Neame, for example – went quite white when he came on. There they'd been, working on the play for weeks and weeks and weeks, and suddenly enter Nathan, shooting about with energy and wit, thus informing the other actors of what the scene should really be like; and they, who had been plodding along happily, tranquilly, finding a bit here and finding a bit there, now had to deal with a chap who was actually finding it all. Terrific.

Oh, I mustn't forget the one serious interruption – to do with the video naturally. I reported the morning's conversation to Joe, who then set about the phone like a madman, calling up all kinds of people, some of whom seemed to be merely friends, until John Delancey came into the office and did the obvious thing, i.e. phoned up the firm itself. He had a polite but, from my point of view, entirely incomprehensible conversation, and then Joe, Delancey and I sped to the Magic to look at the video. It took Delancey about thirty seconds to see that the video was plugged into itself instead of to the television set, and also that there was something wrong with the plug. So down we went – through the heat, really torrid heat, of Los Angeles, in Joe's car with the top pulled back, to the video shop, where we had a series of extremely comfortable exchanges with the manager. People in Los Angeles seem always to be extremely comfortable, even when they're hideously in the wrong as was this man, who has spent two weeks not putting in my video. Clearly in the wrong but very affable with it, gracious even as he handed over a new plug. After rehearsals I put in the plug in the manner prescribed by Delancey, sat down and at last, at last, was able to watch a film. So, as I say, a really good day all round. I've got nothing more to report except cheerfulness so let's leave it at that for once. Right? Goodnight.

Tuesday, 21 January

It's ten past one in the morning and I'm in the Algonquin Hotel, in New York. The knuckles of my left hand are bleeding, so I must have grazed them. I don't know when or how, as I've only just noticed, but I can't recall any incident on the way from the airport, or altercation down in the lobby that could account for it. I must have done something just now, alone here in my room. I'm lying on the bed – in the bed, as a matter of fact – attempting to staunch the flow of blood while speaking into this machine. I've got two days to cover. Two momentous days I'd no doubt say, if I were reporting on a change of government, or a nation at war.

Yesterday I went into the theatre at twelve o'clock. The day before had been – as I think I reported – cheerful and productive, the atmosphere positively jolly. Sam's first day back. Second day back a slightly different kettle of fish. In fact, all in all, I'd rate it as the worst day I've ever spent in a rehearsal. It began when Sam arrived a trifle late and, without warning or even warming up, launched a fierce moral assault on the actors. I don't know if he was merely in a bad mood and was therefore working on a kick-the-dog principle, or whether there was a strategic intent – that a nice day should be followed by a nasty one, to keep complacency or the gods at bay. Anyway he stood in the middle of the auditorium and went at them, crudely, abrasively, robustly, while they stood about on the stage, too bewildered at first to take offence even. I was pretty bewildered too, but at least, unlike the actors, I could escape – which I did, into the Café Melrose next door, where incidentally I was given a cuddle by the semi-Japanese owner, to whom I've become known as Salmon. Whether he can't pronounce my name properly, or is pronouncing his understanding of it properly, I have no idea; but at least his intentions were reassuringly affectionate. So there in the Café Melrose, over a bottle of white wine and a dish of snails, sat Salmon. During the course of the afternoon, Salmon got through two dishes of snails – no mean feat, as they came in a heavy and tasteless white sauce – and two bottles of white wine. Every time I popped back into the Matrix I caught Sam in the middle of another row – or possibly at a later stage of the row he was in the middle of when I'd first left. It was impossible to tell, as there was no context for me to put the rowing in. So white wine and snails in white sauce at the Melrose for Salmon, rows at the Matrix for Simon, were the order of the afternoon and the evening, until Salmon finally cleared out of the Melrose, and Simon looked in on the Matrix for what he intended to be the last time.

Most of the actors had left, but Sam Weisman was still there, conducting an assault on Nathan Lane. Sam was sitting in his usual seat, his director's seat, with his head half turned over his shoulder, talking rapidly and abrasively. Nathan was sitting in the row behind him, so he could only hear what Sam was saying by leaning forward. It was very odd as well as unattractive – Sam seemed almost to be making a point of not listening clearly to what he himself was saying, let alone to what Nathan was saying in reply. It was over-the-shoulder stuff and not quite over-the-shoulder stuff – looking half back at Nathan, then glaring at the stage, then looking half back at Nathan, then looking somewhere else, then half back at Nathan – his voice rasping on and through Nathan's increasingly desperate interjections. The burden of his message appeared to be this: 'Try and calm down your perform-ance, get it down to something less complete and strong for the moment, because the other actors are having trouble keeping up with you – in other words, you're putting them off, you see.' That was the message, and not one I would have found myself agree-ing with, even if expressed with delicacy, but delivered by Sam with his head turning over his shoulder and his head not turning over his shoulder, it came out something like this: 'Hey, you guy – you guy there that's playing Nick, don't you go giving us your big performance yet, we're not ready for it yet, hold back on your big, big performance, you guy playing Nick.' I don't mean that that was his actual vocabulary or sentence structure, but that was the effect, so off-handedly violent that Nathan could scarcely make sense of it. All that he understood was that he was being ordered not to be the actor that he is, playing the character that he's play-ing – his very soul as an actor was being 'fucked over' in fact was how he put it, though not to Sam, of course, to me afterwards, when we went to Antonio's for a drink.

Being full of white wine and snails, I wasn't up to a drink – just the one made me feel I was going to fall over the counter – but I dimly grasped that it was crucial to calm Nathan down. So we got on to the subject of the Long Wharf production, Nathan reminis-cing about Michael Countryman, who had played the part of Martin, a sublime performance, delicate and funny and *simple*, anyway *seeming* so simple; and Peter Friedman as Humphry, with his brilliantly fussy Scottishness, deeply moving towards the end; and of course himself, although he didn't say it, as Nick.* And

* I still remember Michael Countryman's, Peter Friedman's and Nathan Lane's auditions. Ken Frankel and I had seen lots of actors for each of the three parts, responding on the whole quite positively to quite a few of them, until Michael came in for Martin, Peter came in for Humphry, Nathan came in for Nick. In each case I had that unmistakable stirring at the back of my neck – recognition, iden-tification – that here was my Martin, my Humphry, my Nick. And not because they were 'right' for the part, but because they were evidently fine actors that I wanted

now here he was, at the Matrix, being fucked over, his very soul as an actor being fucked over – he didn't understand it, what was going on, I mean Jesus –! So forth. I said that probably all Sam wanted to do was to protect the other actors, encourage them to come through at their own pace, not make them feel that they had to force themselves along to where Nathan was already, that therefore he was indirectly, and in a somewhat unusual style, actually paying Nathan a *compliment*. So forth. But it wasn't any good really. Nathan had been fucked over in his actor's soul, even if by compliments.

When I got back to the Magic I sat in a heap on the sofa, depressed by the day's white wine, snails, and lethal one drink at Antonio's, and most of all depressed by the way I'd simply withdrawn from the horrors of the Matrix. I wasn't sure what I could actually have done, short of interposing myself between Sam and the actors, and then I wasn't *altogether* sure that such interposing would have been welcome – perhaps in Los Angeles, or at the Matrix anyway, they go in for occasional blood-letting, need it even, would become leaden and despondent without it. In which case Sam was merely fulfilling a part of his duties, his tribal duties – like a kind of witch doctor. Or a group therapist. I phoned up one or two of the actors, to check this theory out, initiating the conversations with a thickly cheerful salutation and an enquiry into health, well-being, etc., to be informed that well-being, health, were all at a low ebb, though tempers had never been so high. In fact, the general consensus was that never before had they been treated! Were thinking of leaving the production! Last time ever at the Matrix! So forth.

to involve in the production, who were also right for their parts. Such moments come very rarely in casting. To have experienced three within a few days justified all the boredom and irritation that invariably attends long sessions of casting, and also justifies in retrospect the morning treks from New York to New Haven, the late-night treks back, on the most sordidly uncomfortable train I've ever had to travel regularly on. It even justifies having to live in New Haven for a week or so, the only town in the States I positively hate (in spite of Yale) – its atmosphere, for me anyway, being a combination of the dreary and the dangerous. I always expected to get mugged there. Of course I frequently expect to get mugged in New York, but quickly, viciously, expertly. In New Haven I expected to be mugged dully. Slowly and dully. So I can scarcely speak more highly of an actor, can I, than by saying that meeting him justified spending a week in New Haven?

I phoned up Joe, described what I'd seen and what had been reported to me, and put it to him that he was in danger of having on his hands six disaffected actors, one disaffected playwright, and as far as I could make out, one completely unaffected director. Joe was upset, above all humiliated, saying, 'Oh shit, fuck. Fuck, shit. What am I gonna do? Oh shit. Oh fuck.' It was an inordinately long conversation, and furthermore it was long-distance – is Los Angeles the only town in the world where some of the inhabitants have to call each other long-distance? – so it was also very expensive, which did nothing to raise my morale, especially as I had in front of me a telephone bill amounting, because of my calls to England, to something like —.* I suppose I then stumbled down to Musso and Frank's for dinner, then stumbled back to the Magic, to bed. I don't remember. Or rather, can't be bothered to.

Anyway, that was my yesterday. When I woke this morning, with the prospect of the flight to New York in the early afternoon, I decided I couldn't face a morning at the Matrix. I phoned Joe and dished out some flimflammery about having to go to the laundry to pick up my clothes, then what with packing, this and that . . . He drove straight through all this by reminding me of my responsibility to the Matrix, the actors, the production, myself, himself, our life-muscles, etc., along with a direct and colloquial appeal: 'Oh, c'mon Si – Big Si – you gotta go in. You gotta. To see how it goes. Hey, Si?' So of course in I went – having first extracted from him a promise to drive me to the airport – to see how it was going. What was going was Sam, full tilt, to an audience that consisted only of the stage management, as the actors hadn't yet arrived. He was storming up and down the aisles, up and down the stage, bellowing away about his scripts, which he'd left in the theatre the night before and now couldn't find. He was also bellowing about the revolve, which he'd come in specially early to check. It refused to work. So there he was, at it when I arrived. I sat down in the stalls and watched him. He was still at it when the actors arrived.

It was really quite eerie – this short, red-bearded man running fumingly up and down the aisles, then across the stage in front of us, demanding his scripts back, demanding that the set be made

* I can't bring myself to specify the sum.

to work, demanding all kinds of other things as well, including, it seemed, the right to exist from a recalcitrant God. Then he homed in on the stage manager, whom he accused of having stolen his scripts or she'd thrown them out with the other rubbish; or she'd buried them up in the California hills – it was hard to make out precisely what he thought she'd done with his scripts, and more particularly why she'd done it. All that was clear was that he'd suddenly located her at the centre of the conspiracy to keep him apart from his scripts. Now the stage manager is an extraordinary girl – well, not girl, woman really, as she must be into her mid-thirties – very thin, hollow-cheeked, chain-smoking, with a kind of desolated look, but extremely efficient. She clearly loves the Matrix and the kind of theatre Joe is trying to produce in it. Sam, seeing her sitting there hunched, gaunt, smoking, aimed himself directly at her, warning her that his scripts should never again be allowed to vanish, that the revolve should never again be allowed not to revolve. At one point he turned, and shook his fist around the auditorium. And there we all were, sitting watching him shaking his fist and bellowing his abuse. Suddenly he stopped. He didn't wind down or deflect himself on to another subject. He simply stopped, mid-bellow, on the subject of the scripts and the revolve, and started up immediately, in mid-bellow, on the subject of Act One, Scene Two. The rehearsal had begun.

Not for long. Act One, Scene Two, the curse of *The Common Pursuit*, had been rewritten so completely during Sam's absence that the two actors involved – Kristoffer Tabori and Wayne Alexander (who'd put the new text on to the computer, and then collated it) – still hadn't had a chance to learn it properly. Nor had Sam had a chance to digest it properly. He turned to me and snarled out an intelligent question about the meaning of some new or changed lines, but in such a way as to suggest that he was snarling at Kristoffer Tabori for having failed to learn the new lines properly. Whereupon Tabori threw his script to the ground, stamped on it, screaming that the speech he was accused of failing to learn had never been in the script before, how had he possibly had time to learn it? Whereupon Sam snarled back – forgetting that he'd originally addressed his snarl to me, and not to Tabori – that the speech had always been in the script. Whereupon Tabori screamed back, 'This speech has never been in the script before.'

Whereupon Sam snarled back, and Tabori screamed back, until they were snarling and screaming simultaneously. Both of them, of course, were in a sense right. Though the speech had never been in the script before (Tabori), a version of it had been (Weisman). Where Tabori was in the wrong was in thinking that *he* was being criticised for not knowing the speech, when in fact *I* was being interrogated about the purpose of the changes I'd made in it. Where Weisman was in the wrong was in giving such general offence so offensively that somebody in earshot was bound, sooner or later, to take it personally.

I don't know how genuine Tabori's tantrum was. His gesticulations and counter-screamings were so extravagant that they were more like an impersonated dementia than the genuine article. Weisman met whatever it was with a contemptuous disdain, finally walking out of the auditorium, saying, 'I don't know what's going on here but I'll wait. I'll go out and we'll have a break while you get yourself together, and when you're ready I'll come back in, yer know what I mean? Yer know what I mean?' Kristoffer Tabori and Wayne Alexander, who are old friends, went slouching off, laughing angrily. I waited a few minutes, then shambled after Weisman, a cigarette between my lips. I found him by himself, goating about with his beard in a corner of the lobby. Having reintroduced myself to him, so to speak, I said, 'Those lines you were asking about, we'd better discuss them.' He said, 'Yeah. Right.' We got into the text for a time, cleared up the point he'd raised, then I said, 'Let's go back and tell the actors what we've decided,' and he said, 'Yeah, right, let's go talk to the actors.'

I went back in to the rehearsal and discovered, after I'd begun to address the actors about the text, that Sam Weisman hadn't come with me. Suddenly Joe Stern came scooting down the corridor, lifted an index finger and said, 'Come with me.' I looked at him fairly steadily* and said, 'What?' And he said, 'Come with me.' I said, 'Why?' And he said, 'We've got to sort this out.' As we shot towards his office he said, 'You've gotta tell him exactly what you think and feel.' So in I went. Sam Weisman was sitting at Joe's desk. After I'd left him in the lobby, he'd come in to Joe to complain about the actors. In return Joe had reported to him what I'd

---

* I don't know what this means, but I like the image – Alan Ladd in *Shane*.

said to Joe the night before about the state of the actors, etc. He sat there, looking utterly defeated, a goat demoralised. We then had a reasonably civilised conversation, though it was prefaced by an illogical, formless but passionate speech from Joe about what it was he wanted from the Matrix, from the theatre generally, from life itself. Then he nodded to me. I said to Sam Weisman that the problem seemed to me that sometimes he forgot to talk to people simply and directly, in themselves – you know, me as Simon Gray, Kristoffer Tabori as Kristoffer Tabori, Wayne Alexander as Wayne Alexander. He talked to me as if I was the 'awther' and he talked to Wayne Alexander as the guy who was playing Martin, and to Kristoffer Tabori as the guy, as the actor guy, who was playing Stuart. I said that what we wanted from him was a degree of patience along with a recognition of our personal identities. He began by flannelling angrily along and then suddenly looked bewildered and then equally suddenly became extremely sweet and talked about himself, and his sense of what was going on in the company and his failure to talk to them – he didn't know what it came from – and at the same time defended himself by claiming that 'they' were all against him. Of course Joe, keeping his own psychodrama going, kept interrupting with diversions to do with his and Sam's relationship and further statements about what it was he wanted from the theatre, life, etc.

Throughout all this I was aware that I really ought to be on my way to the airport, to catch my plane to New York. At the same time I was really desperate to bring the conversation to a proper conclusion. So I said that I thought Weisman should go back into the theatre, not to offer explanations and apologies, but simply to talk to the actors in the same tone as he had talked to Joe and myself, i.e. as if they were there in the room with him. In the end, hesitantly, he agreed to do that. Joe and I left him in the office still brooding, and scampered off to Joe's car. When we got to the airport – a hectic drive – I discovered he'd got me a round ticket that seemed to have cost only $30, and involved my changing at St Louis, travelling steerage. Furthermore he'd failed to get me the aisle seat he'd promised. I found myself sitting in the middle of a row of five seats, deeply uncomfortable and hating every minute of it, unable to read properly because the lighting was so bad, unable to drink properly because the stewardess was always too deeply involved in cooing negotiations with the other customers, mostly florid and travel-practised businessmen, to get to me. Once down at St Louis I checked that the interconnecting flight left in an hour's time, which at least gave me opportunity for a drink. I shambled into the first visible cocktail bar – a very peculiar bar actually. It was crowded, with only one girl serving. She was rather sexy, in a skirt cut almost up to the hip, with a bulging blouse. She was also very sharp with the dialogue. Whenever anyone called for a drink, she would say, 'I hear you, I hear you, I'll be with you in a minute but listen, I go through this 350,000 times a day, wait your turn, if you don't like it, go on to your plane' sort of stuff. She was in her late twenties, I suppose, but she had the command of dialogue of a woman who had been playing this part for forty years. Fortunately she was struck by my English accent and got me my drink – a large Scotch – fairly quickly, which I nursed until ten minutes before my plane was due to leave.

So what was St Louis to me? To me St Louis was an airport with piped music, a cocktail bar and a waitress, which might be a better St Louis than most people encounter, except that the cocktail bar and the waitress were located around Gate 42 and I had to get to Gate 16 in under ten minutes, which meant my running along conveyor belts* and then across lobbies and then further lobbies and then on to conveyor belts again, arriving at Gate 16 just as the plane was about to take off. I'd been told at Los Angeles that from St Louis I would certainly have – no question, they'd already booked it for me – an aisle-seat smoker. But there I was again, squeezed as before in a row of people, smoking angrily – another uncomfortable flight, at least physically. But psychologically the further I got from Los Angeles and Sam Weisman and the traumas of the Matrix the more comfortable I felt. I'd had the foresight to arrange with Phyllis Wender, my New York agent, to have a limo waiting for me at La Guardia which, inevitably, wasn't there. After a long wait for a taxi, a fairly short ride to the Algonquin, I was back in the hotel and in the suite – 310 – in which I've spent so many nights of my life. The card on which I signed in displayed my signature from previous visits over the years. They looked

* For passengers, not for luggage.

identical to each other and my fresh signature looked identical to them, as if I had forged it rather than just scribbled it down. I had had three large Scotches on the plane, I have to own up to that. I was also therefore not only very tired and exhausted but pretty drunk. Nevertheless, the first thing I did here at the Algonquin was to settle into the familiar and comforting lobby, and order myself another large Scotch. I sat there for hours, brooding, then came up here to my room. It is now, I might say, five to – can this be RIGHT? – it's five to fucking three in the morning, my knuckle is bleeding again because I've just ripped off the Kleenex or whatever . . .

Thursday, 23 January

Flew back this afternoon with the two male parts in *Dog Days* cast – Stephen will have to cast the two female parts from Dallas-based actresses as the theatre can't afford living expenses for four out-of-town actors. I had my ticket changed so that I travelled direct, business class, aisle-seat smoker. A very agreeable journey except that I couldn't, alas, resist a glass of champagne when we took off, then another glass of champagne, then wine with the meal and then, I'm afraid, a whisky or two after the meal. By the time I got to Los Angeles at seven in the evening I was pretty drunk. Joe met me and took me to the Magic. On the way he told me that the ghastly row and subsequent conversation that had taken place just before I left had cleared the air, everyone was working very hard, everything was going well, Sam Weisman was working with Kris Tabori and Wayne Alexander at that very moment. At the Magic the sunnies at the desk passed on angry messages left by somebody called Donna at the video shop, demanding to know the serial number of the video, and saying that it was some kind of contravention of the contract (what contract?) to have the machine in the hotel – as it had been booked by the theatre it had to be in the theatre. I don't know if I've mentioned it but I discovered before I left for New York that for some reason I cannot wind the tapes back automatically, I have to sit pointing the remote control at it with my thumb pressed on the backwards scan button for about twenty-five minutes before the tape gets back to the beginning.*

I managed to stay up for a bit but not very long. Reeled into bed.

Friday, 24 January

A lot of stopping and starting as we went through the new text. Chip had managed to lock into it lumps from about five previous texts – apparently he'd got the discs mixed when feeding them into the computer. I had to break to give an extremely exhausting interview to a chap from a local theatre magazine. As he himself is a playwright, the conversation had to be at a high level between two serious artists of the theatre. I could have put up with gossip or anecdotes, but not with having to go through a solemn pretence of being seriously interested in such subjects as construction – especially when in the middle of reconstructing a computer-garbled text of my own.

Back in the theatre there was a prickly passage with Wayne Alexander. I overheard him saying to Kristoffer Tabori: 'I miss it, I really miss it.' Assuming he was talking about a cut line, or even a cut speech, I said what I always say when actors are protesting about cuts, viz: 'I'm sure you're going to miss all kinds of stuff for a day or two. Then you won't even remember it was there.' He turned on me, twitching. 'You don't even know what I'm talking about,' he said tightly. 'You don't know what I'm talking about.' Of course he was perfectly right. He may well have been talking about missing a person, a place or a pet, and not a line or a passage from the play. I should remind myself from time to time that the actors have lives outside the rehearsal room. 'Right,' I said. 'Sorry. But look, for Christ's sake, does everyone have to be so touchy around here?' He muttered something and turned away, and I left the auditorium in a huff for a glass of wine at the Café Melrose. Came back, saw Wayne Alexander spotting me, then saw him bustling around the side of the stage to trap me in the corridor, where we apologised to each other, embraced, cuddled, slapped each other's shoulders affectionately and that was that.

---

* John Delancey – who else? – eventually solved this problem for me by finding the appropriate button on the machine itself. The tapes couldn't be wound back by remote control. So much for American technology.

It really has to be that actually because, you know, if one were to take seriously everything that everyone – I include myself – gets up to at the Matrix Theatre, one would spend one's life planning either homicide or suicide.

Later, I had a long talk with John Delancey, taking him upstairs to the Green Room to be private. I said that what he had to do was to stop imitating or impersonating Humphry and just *be* Humphry. Unprepared, alive to all the possibilities of experience. When he first goes to Stuart's room he should expect to find Stuart there, as had been arranged, and therefore be *surprised* to find Martin instead – at the moment he enters as if he already knows he'll find Martin, thus getting the scene off to what looks like a rehearsed start. In other words, John, live the play minute by minute, don't report on the dialogue and the character – that sort of thing. He went in for being tremendously enlightened, exclaiming, 'Of course what you're talking about here is acting.' 'No, no,' I said. 'I'm a writer, I *never* talk about acting,' although what I was actually doing was talking about acting. My principle (for as long as I can sustain it) is that when I'm hovering about as the playwright I always pretend to be talking about the text and the character, and never about acting – *especially* when I'm talking about acting.

During the afternoon we ran Act One, Scene Two, and I do believe that now – but Jesus Christ, I've said this so often about Act One, Scene Two – but I do believe that now it works. There was a run-through followed by a break before a technical run, which gave rise to one of those great Matrix moments. Joe, assuming that the break would be brief, dashed out to a fast-food store and came back loaded down with pizzas and Coke and beer for the actors just as the actors, having been informed by Sam Weisman that the break would be quite long, were taking themselves off to restaurants for a proper meal. There was therefore a scene between Joe and Sam about the redundant pizzas, Joe expostulating about the waste of money and time, Sam insisting he didn't know that Joe was going out for pizzas, Joe arguing that nobody had told him there was going to be a longer break – it really is like being adopted into a close-knit family of lunatics. All of them lunatic in a quite different way.

Saturday, 25 January

Great improvement from John Delancey. For the first time he came into the room walking and speaking naturally, *actively* listening to people, rather than simply waiting for them to finish so that he could deliver his own lines. Joe watched this, looking extremely pleased with himself. Later I discovered that Joe had also taken John Delancey off for a private talk. One of the things the run revealed to me is that the Epilogue requires rewriting. I shall try to do that on my way to the theatre – I'm off in a few minutes, having arranged to meet Sam to discuss it at quarter to twelve, rehearsals beginning at twelve. It is now twenty-five past eleven so I'd better get a move on. But I shall probably get there and Sam won't be there. He's generally late. Off I go.

Later   I rewrote the opening of the Epilogue in the taxi. It really required not so much rewriting as shifting lines – the best I can do because I'm not up to writing fresh dialogue. It took exactly the length of the taxi drive to do it in. Sam was indeed not there. When he did arrive he went scudding past me straight into the theatre, completely ignoring my greeting of 'Good morning, Sam.' This is one of the minor, but grit-like irritants of the Matrix. People are quite likely not to return a 'good morning' or a 'good evening', unlike almost everyone else in California. Almost everyone else in California says, 'How are you today?' and 'Have a good day,' and even, on occasions, more dangerously, 'Have a good night.' But this is not true of Joe and Sam, and especially of Sam. I followed him into the theatre and said, 'Good morning, Sam,' again, rather forcefully, and this time got a response. We then sat down and discussed the Epilogue. The day passed with fretful lumps of rehearsal here and fretful lumps of rehearsal there. Then we did a run. It went surprisingly well, in that the play seemed to work at last. A great weight off my shoulders. I now have the play that I should have written in the first place (London), or at least in the second place (Long Wharf). So on that score I feel pretty good.

After rehearsals I popped into the shop next to the Café Melrose, to buy some razor blades. It's a curious little shop, which seems to offer for sale almost nothing but a few tins of beer, disposable razors, newspapers, chocolate bars – in fact rather like a shop run by Pakistanis or Indians in London, except that it's run less efficiently and contains fewer saleable goods. There in front of me was a strappingly built transvestite or transsexual, I couldn't make out which, and his consort, who in any other company would have been thought astonishingly effeminate. They were fondling chocolate bars, passing them backwards and forwards to each other, trying to test the texture and even get a whiff of the flavour through the wrapping, all the time talking in what I suppose is a normal transsexual/transvestite manner about which sort of chocolate bar they most preferred. When they went out the woman behind the counter, who is Chinese or Korean, burst into laughter and then sealed her face into a courteous grimace when two oldy-worldy queers came padding in. Now the point about this is that it took place not on Sunset Boulevard or in some other exotic part of Los Angeles, but in an around-the-corner shop where they sold – or didn't sell, as it turned out – G2 razor blades, but did sell disposable razors and cans of beer and a few bottles of appalling wine, warm and sweet, one of which I was fool enough to buy.

Monday, 27 January

Today, coming back from lunch at Musso and Frank's, I made a study of the stars on the pavement. These stars are of metal bronze, I think – set into the pavement with the name of the star on it. I'm told that the stars have to pay for this honour. So one finds oneself trampling across, say, Yvonne de Carlo, then Elvis Presley, then Broderick Crawford, and then one's foot hovers over the name Frank Primrose, for instance. Frank Primrose! I mean who could that be? A producer? A director? A cameraman? Probably a scriptwriter. So what happens is that one recognises three or so names in succession and then there is a name that means nothing and something falls away inside you. You feel that either you ought to know this name or this name is attempting to claim your attention, having no credentials to claim it with – a pathetic call from beyond the grave, though embedded here among the stars.

Tuesday, 28 January

Look, let's come down to the bare knuckles on this one. Today is Tuesday, and from Saturday, Sunday, Monday through to Tuesday nothing has happened in my life at all except that I have gone, when it's open – it's not open on Sundays – to Musso and Frank's for lunch or dinner, depending on what time rehearsals have been called. I've gone into the theatre, observed run-throughs, made my notes and given comments, most of them exasperated because all the technical stuff is days, if not possibly a week, behind. The sound hasn't been properly organised yet, the lighting cues are disastrously unworked out, and as for the set changes – that guy who a month or so, it seems to me a lifetime, ago, when I proposed that the windows should be *there* rather than *there*, said the thought of it chilled his blood, and did a kind of wince and squirmish and smirk, and when I tried to explain to him the dramatic importance of time in the play I could see that he wasn't listening, I could see that he was *not* listening, because all he was thinking of was his monumental sets – has now stuck us with his monumental sets. Not only has he not managed a proper working revolve, managing instead two little revolves that don't work properly, he also hasn't managed *any* system that gets people shunted in and out quickly enough for us to go from one period to another visibly and dramatically on stage. There he is now, fluttering around, looking mildly embarrassed at the fact that his sets not only don't work but actually dwarf the actors with great slabs of phoney masonry. So we have this problem to deal with. Even though I don't believe there is any way of dealing with it. Nevertheless I've gone on whining at Joe and Sam Weisman, nagging and whining and occasionally shouting and pounding my fist against my upper thigh until something is at last being done to try to achieve the shifts in time succinctly, if not dramatically.

On top of which I've been yet again and yet again and yet again rewriting Act One, Scene Two. I'm beginning to wonder if this scene can ever be got right, if there isn't something radically flawed in the construction of the play. I don't know. I do know that it works better than it did in London and at the Long Wharf but I'm not sure that it works better *enough*. We also had costumes on display tonight. Most of them looked OK. The day was full of hiatuses. We'd get through a scene and then have to stop for something like an hour while scene changes and music and lighting cues were worked out. In these intermissions I would gambol up the road and have a drink or two at Antonio's and gambol back extremely ill-tempered to discover that they *still* hadn't sorted out the cues and the changes. There was a terrific moment when Sam Weisman was trying simultaneously both to rehearse scenes and to get the lighting and the set change and the sound cues right, while the actors, one after the other, were protesting at being forced to continue to rehearse the text when they still hadn't got their actual costume changes and their other physical changes, like moustaches added on here and moustaches taken off there, worked out. One couldn't help but sympathise with them, one couldn't help but sympathise with Sam Weisman. His ginger-bearded and balding head sank on to the palm of his hand and he just stared at the ground while Joe took over. It's the kind of situation I think Joe enjoys, dealing with the actors' problems with sympathy and concern and dealing with the director's problem, the director sitting dejected – he looked like a monument to dejection actually – to one side, and the playwright, one has to say, slightly drunk from his trips up to Antonio's, lurching around somewhere at the back. On the subject of Antonio's, by the way – they come before you've even sat down and strum guitars at you and sing into your face. And they continue after you've sat down, with your drink in your hand, singing and strumming at you. It would be quite a nice place to go to if they would only leave you alone.

But to come back to the technicals, all I can say is that it is like almost any technical experience I've ever had in the theatre, only far worse. Everything takes vastly longer. Nothing functions with precision. They can't even let me know accurately when I should arrive for rehearsals – the schedule changes from moment to moment. For most of the time we can't even depend on a full cast, as the actors are also out and about doing their bread-and-butter TV soaps and series. At the moment our leading lady, Judy Geeson, who is trying to get American citizenship, keeps having to go up for immigration clearance with her husband, our leading man, who has to sit beside her and present her case. I don't know what sort of case he has to present. Surely there should be no problem as she's married to an American. Perhaps Tabori has to persuade them that she's innately American enough to be married to him.

Wednesday, 29 January

Spent seven hours in the theatre, two of them in the disgusting early-afternoon heat, hanging about, waiting for Sam Weisman, who had asked me to meet him. Two hours late is something of a record even for Sam Weisman. He had been at the sound studios, too absorbed to telephone, or something.

I suppose rehearsals went all right, and I kept my demeanour, I hope, civilised as I insinuated my notes and got some of the blocking in Act Two changed. But my nerves are on fire with irritation, exhaustion, frustration – I don't know what it is – just the day-in day-out experience of the Matrix, I expect. One of the things that inflames them further – my nerves, that is – is the amount of eating that goes on. What makes it particularly repulsive is that they don't bring in genuine meals, but always something that poses as a piece of natural food, a 'nutritional' salad or a 'slimming' sandwich. Some of this food, or non-food or whatever it is, invariably falls out of their mouths and dribbles down their chins; what they retain in their mouths they eat with almost smacking noises. I have to say this. I mean this won't be in the published diary,* but I do have actually to observe that I have never seen so much eating going on in my life before. All the time. Today, during notes before the technical run, one of the actors sat on the floor in a kind of circle of packages of nuts and raisins and biscuits, little non-nutritional or anyway non-toxic biscuits, and his hands were going into one or the other, his lips smacking away, while lumps of biscuits and nuts and raisins were tumbling out of his mouth on to the floor and were then flicked away by his hands which then went back among the biscuits or the nuts or the raisins. I've developed a kind of counter-attack. Whenever they eat I puff smoke into their faces from whatever angle I happen to be at from them. I also have a goblet – a plastic goblet – of wine in my hand, or late in the evening, like this evening, a plastic goblet of malt whisky in my hand. There I stand amongst them, puffing and

---

* This is demonstrably untrue.

sipping at them, and there they stand, gobbling and slurping back at me.

I left at 10 p.m. in the middle of the technical, Joe having offered to drive me to Musso and Frank's. We were just crossing the parking lot to his car – there's always a parking lot in Los Angeles, you can't get anywhere without crossing a parking lot – when my watch, which I deeply cherish because it has so many associations, just fell off my wrist. Fell off my wrist and dashed itself in what seemed to me an act of wanton self-destruction on the parking-lot cement. The glass splintered, some of it falling through to the face of the watch, preventing the second hand and the minute hand from moving, and this watch, which maintains so many connections to my life back in London – whenever I look at my watch, I remember who I am and where I am, or it seems to me that I do – had suddenly become an utterly useless object. It *fell* from my wrist, *fell* and became an utterly useless object. I took it in to be repaired, of course, and am in the meantime wearing a replacement lent to me by Joe Stern. It's very heavy with a steel strap, and it's the kind of watch that I most object to. I like simple numbers, Arabic numbers, but this one hasn't even got Roman numbers, it's got dashes except for the twelve and the six and the nine and the three. It originally belonged to Joe's father, now dead, and has come down to Joe's son who no longer wears it, but wants it back for sentimental reasons. So I'm under a serious obligation not to lose this watch. I don't know how I could lose it, actually, short of having my wrist chopped off, because it's never going to fall off of its own accord. Its metal is going to stick tightly to my wrist, like half a handcuff.

Joe got me to Musso and Frank's just in time for a meal. I sat in the cubicle with the intention of reading but couldn't because there was an extraordinarily loud and garrulous television star, I assume she was from the nature of her conversation, talking to, presumably, her agent, about why she was shy and found things difficult and how she couldn't stand some other actor in her television series who seemed to her to be cheap in the way that he got laughs. Her agent, if he was her agent, was being soothing and sympathetic. He looked exactly like Woody Allen, only a few feet taller. I became so involved in their conversation that I stayed on and on until we were the only people left in the restaurant.

When I got back to the Magic I was informed by the smiling Californian youth at the desk, who also looks a bit like Woody Allen, that all the telephones in the hotel were out of order. It was impossible to make an outgoing call or to receive an incoming call because the week before or so they had put the telephones on to a computer and the computer, as computers invariably do, had failed them. 'So,' he said cheerfully, 'there are no messages for you, Mr Gray, but then there couldn't be any messages, Mr Gray, because the telephones aren't working,' and he gave me this Woody Allen smile. And I must say I wanted to smash this Woody Allen smile into all kinds of lumps and welts because for one thing it meant I couldn't get a morning call, for another thing Joe was going to phone to let me know the rehearsal time. I therefore dealt with this Woody Allen chap in my least charming and sympathetic manner. In fact I launched an attack on what he must have felt was his private life, his sexuality, his purpose in the world, his right to a place in the universe, I called everything about him into question. At one point – at no stage in this conversation did I raise my voice, by the way, which I think must have made me more disgusting – I kept it at a kind of angry, low, growling malcontented level – at one point he said, 'It's no good shouting at me, it's not my fault,' and I said, in my angry, low, growling voice, 'But I'm not shouting at you, am I? Am I shouting at you?' And of course he had to admit that I wasn't shouting. It was most unfair. But I think it was his Woody Allen smile – which he wore even when asking me not to shout at him – that did it. My consolation for having behaved so badly is that I have at last come full circle in Los Angeles. From a functioning video and a telephone that never worked on my last trip,* through functioning telephones and a non-functioning video, back to a working video and non-functioning telephones. And so from my balcony at past one in

---

* There was an infuriating dummy that sat prominently on the sitting-room table of the Taboris' cottage. The Taboris kept asking the relevant company to reconnect it. One afternoon a gang of men in plastic helmets appeared. They scaled trees, foraged in the undergrowth, then left with merry salutes of 'See ya then' and 'You're very welcome'. The telephone, when I tried it, merely whistled into my ear before falling dead again. What I missed most, of course, was the making and receiving of impulse calls – as well as the making and receiving of anonymous calls. A diminished life.

the morning, recording this, my voice no doubt still growling with malcontent, I offer a mild gesture with my fingers to the soft, muggy, star-dappled sky before taking myself off to bed.

Thursday, 30 January

I spent the morning on the porch reading some Chekhov short stories, hating the sun whose presence seemed to me impertinence, given that it's late January. On one neighbouring porch there was an elderly French couple, he in his bathing trunks, with a kind of masking cup over his nose and various creams on his face, and she in and out of the sitting room with various drinks for him to sip at, with the smells of an elaborate French meal in preparation drifting from their porch to mine. I don't think that anyone in this hotel is a native Californian. They're either New Yorkers or even more foreign. Currently in residence are some black Gospel singers, six of them blind. They trundle carefully around the pool with their sticks but apparently are quite sensational on stage in a spiritual musical about Oedipus. The apartment next to me, on the other side from the elderly French couple, appears to be inhabited entirely by a child of about three. She comes out on to the porch, she goes back in, I hear her squalling, I hear her chortling, but I have never seen or heard an adult in attendance. I suppose there is one. Unless, of course, she's a midget. If so she's an inarticulate midget that chortles and squalls as a means of communication. But I don't believe that, she must be a child. I'm sure she's a child. She looks a perfectly healthy normal three-year-old child – four-year-old? three-year-old? She can't speak, what age does that make her – two-year-old, I suppose, if she can't speak. The telephones still don't work, by the way.

But what do I know of Los Angeles? I know the little stroll down Hollywood Boulevard to Musso and Frank's – I go down Orange Street and turn left into Hollywood Boulevard and there are these freaks – cocaine addicts, drunks, black guys with bangles and leather straps around their wrists, guys sitting on motorbikes revving up, with police cars bunched powerfully beside them – turn into Musso and Frank's, have my meal, come out again and back up to the hotel. Or get delivered from the theatre to Musso and Frank's and walk back up past these creatures. It seems to me the most cut-off and isolated life. I'm DESPERATE to be at home. DESPERATE to be at home, running about my usual life, seeing all the people I want to see, trying to do some writing in my study with Hazel at my feet, away from this almost unendurably boring existence. That's the key word in all this. Boring. All the dramas at the Matrix, all the life lived or not lived in the Magic Hotel, all the tramps down Hollywood Boulevard to Musso and Frank's, or up Hollywood Boulevard away from Musso and Frank's, I've managed to convert into a routine that is dreadfully boring. Though sometimes I quite like it all.

Friday, 31 January

I bumped into Nathan in the manager's office where we were both trying to make phone calls – all the other phones are still out. While he was making his call I signalled that I was going to my room to get my bag. When I came back he'd vanished. I went to his room, he wasn't there. I went back to the manager's office, he wasn't there. I checked back in my room, then back in his room, then back in the manager's office, gave up and set out for Musso and Frank's. Halfway there, along Hollywood Boulevard, I spotted Nathan in one of the public telephone booths. He explained that as his call was of an intensely personal nature, he'd decided that a public booth would guarantee him more privacy than the manager's office, especially as the manager and his assistants sit around listening in on your end of the conversation. What is odd is not that they listen in – who wouldn't? – but that they make no attempt to disguise it. There they sit, not even turning their heads away. They simply smile and listen, and I'm sure one would see them nodding at the points one was making if one didn't find oneself irritably turning one's back on them. Not that turning one's back offends them. When I did it yesterday, in the course of a conversation in which I was arranging to meet Joe at Musso and Frank's, then glared pointedly around at them when I'd hung up, one of them asked me, in his usual sunny style, whether, if anyone wanted me, he should say I'd be at Musso and Frank's with Joe. Of course this may turn out to be a more effective way of getting them to pass on messages than just asking them to – for one thing they seem actually to take in what they're not intended to hear.

Over lunch Nathan told me that after I'd left the theatre last night Sam gathered the cast together and held a conference that lasted well over an hour, in which they were invited to say what scenes they wanted to rehearse today. When it was Nathan's turn to speak, he opted for his two scenes in Act One. Sam's reply was he wasn't interested in hearing Nathan's views, this rehearsal time was for the other actors. This upset Nathan quite a lot. He couldn't see the point, he said, of having to hang about for an hour in order to be asked what he wanted to rehearse, if he was then going to be told that nobody wanted to know what he wanted to rehearse.

We got to the Matrix at one thirty – the time settled on at Sam's conference – and then sat around for forty-five minutes waiting for the other actors and the director to show up. It was then discovered that we couldn't have a rehearsal anyway, because the set designer, who has made such a hash of the set, with his enormous, tomb-like rooms, and his revolves that don't work to any purpose other than to shift the furniture interminably about, was busy on the set. What he'd been busy at was quite incomprehensible to me when I saw the set later. It looked exactly as it had done before and worked in the evening run-through just as badly as it had done before. He'd probably been putting some books in the shelves and arranging some papers on the desks. That's about his speed. Anyway, the main rehearsal was abandoned. Instead, Tabori, Wayne Alexander, Sam Weisman and I went up to the attic Green Room, where we set about examining in detail the new text of the dreaded Act One, Scene Two.

We were making pretty good progress, Sam talking about what resources he thought Alexander and Tabori needed to draw on in a particular passage, I explaining what I took to be the intentions behind the lines, when there was a sudden altercation between Sam Weisman and Wayne Alexander, who, as I think I've already noted, is a rather sensitive sort of chap, and now took exception to Weisman's manner, exclaiming that whenever he tried to say something about a line, a scene, a passage, about anything at all in fact, Weisman would interrupt him. Now it's perfectly true that Sam is one of the world's great interrupters – he finds it barely possible to allow you more than two sentences before cutting across and summing up your sentences for you and then – usually – dismissing them. Wayne, in his sudden breakdown, or outburst, went on to say that he'd had enough of this, he wasn't a complete fool, you know, Sam, he wished he'd be allowed to finish when he spoke. Sam let him go on for a bit, staring at him in a slightly peculiar, hunched, unfocused way, and then cut across him, 'Yeah, but what I was trying to say about the scene,' and so Wayne, expostulating away about never being allowed to finish a sentence, he had contributions to make which ought to be listened to, found himself interrupted in full flow, and everything he'd said disregarded. He rallied, started again on an even higher note, and again Sam just sat hunched, staring at him, and then again cut across him, saying, 'Yeah, but what I'm saying to you about this scene is –' whereupon Wayne threw up his arms in despair, disbelief, and capitulated.

This altercation between Weisman and Alexander was fairly swiftly followed by an altercation between Weisman and myself. I'd just explained the meaning of a line over which Tabori and Alexander had been confused, and they were articulating their new realisation, in the way that people do, with such phrases as 'Oh, I *see* . . .' and 'So that's why my next line never made sense . . .' and so forth, just a casual little interlude, really, a kind of verbal tea break, into which Sam Weisman surged with a long, rasping windy sentence that went something like this: 'Ya know! Ya know, it's very difficult, this is very difficult to sit here like this, doing this, and, ya know, it's very important the author should be here, but it's very difficult for me, ya know, and what I don't want is to have the two actors talking between themselves about something *you've* said to them. Ya know!' And on from there, windily, but raspingly, his point being that if the actors understood each other's intentions, as identified by the author, they would cease to be spontaneous. I became pretty windy and rather rasping myself, asking him whether he meant that I shouldn't be too precise about the purpose of a line or a speech because the actor not directly involved might find out too much about the processes of the actor directly involved. Yeah, he said, that's what he meant, going straight on into one of his statements about acting and the acting process, and what he was trying to do here which was to teach the actors something about acting, instead of paying all this attention to the literals. 'The literals' being, I suppose, the text and its meaning. But they needed to know what it was they were acting,

I said, and as for not informing one actor in the presence of another actor about the meaning of a line, did he propose that we approach the actors *separately*?

I wish I could give an accurate rendering of our respective tones, Sam Weisman's angry, but somehow abstract snarlings, my own fury, intensified by the consciousness of the plastic mug of white wine in my hand, which I felt put me at a moral disadvantage to such an extent that I over-enunciated every syllable, to make it clear, in the characteristic drunk's fashion, that I wasn't drunk – though, in fact, I wasn't drunk. We went on and on at each other, disputatiously, discourteously, with Wayne Alexander occasionally offering to explain Sam Weisman to me, me to Sam Weisman, and Kris Tabori putting in some good, solid work as the embarrassed onlooker, until I finally found myself telling Sam Weisman that his behaviour was unprofessional and improper – I was sick to death, I said, sick to death of these horrendous conversations one always seemed to find oneself in at the Matrix, especially with him. There was a long, brooding silence, interrupted only by little scuffling noises from Joe's office below, which alerted me to the fact that he'd been listening in, and then we carried on, inhibitedly polite to each other, and so made far less progress than we'd been making up to the rows. Over the last few days, in fact, when we'd been in accord almost continuously.

Joe drove me back to the hotel, admitting that he'd heard most of what had gone on, encouraging me to report my anger, and even develop it – full of sympathy and concern, but nevertheless looking rather pleased, as he always does when there's a tempest about.

But, my God, what an ordeal it's been at the Matrix! I suppose the main problem is that nobody is getting paid. When actors are being paid they can accept an ill-mannered director as simply another professional hazard. When they're not being paid they resent any slight – anyway, certainly feel that they should be treated as courteously as they usually are when they're being paid. And Sam Weisman, himself not only unpaid but sacrificing the huge sums of money he could be earning as a television director, doubtless feels the actors owe him respect and total obedience, if not adoration, on that account alone. So what we have here is a ghastly kind of amateur set-up, except that everyone concerned is professional. The worst of both worlds. Or at least so it seems to me, as I sit here on my balcony at six in the evening, the tumbler of malt in my hand not sufficiently softening the prospect of having to be back at the Matrix in an hour and a half's time. We're having a fully dressed run before a small, invited audience. One thing I can be sure of. We won't start on time. The cat that I can't get up to my room is sitting at the edge of the pool, by the way, dipping its paw into the water. It looks worried, as if it's lost something.

Later I got to the theatre on time, to find that they hadn't yet finished a technical run-through. Joe caught me in the auditorium, raised a finger to his lips, then beckoned me down the corridor into his office, where he gravely informed me – apropos our conversation in the car – that Sam had been deeply offended by the things I'd said to him this afternoon. This both surprised me and cheered me up. I'd begun to think that Weisman, who is so prone, whether consciously or not, to giving offence, was unable to receive it. I thanked Joe for the information, checked up on the technical again, popped into the Café Melrose for a hamburger, checked back on the technical, to find it at exactly the same place as when I'd left – even down to the actors' positions, while the stage-hands, running about in the darkness, seemed to be shouting out exactly what they'd been shouting out the last time I'd heard them. The small audience – very small indeed, about ten people – had been invited for eight thirty. We began at half past nine. Apart from that, it went well, I thought. The play certainly works, and the actors seemed to know what they were doing. John Delancey, although stiff and unyielding, has enormous natural authority – he's almost hypnotic – so that one doesn't too much mind the inflexibility of his delivery. I shall never warm to Wayne Alexander's Martin – it's a highly skilled and well-judged performance, but morally wrong, a snaky friend rather than a good friend who does – has to do – something sneaky. Kris Tabori had a fine first act, dropping all his Lee J. Cobb mannerisms (gesturing and strutting about), being instead calm and natural. In the second act the mannerisms returned – instead of a literary editor, we got an actor doing some 'acting'. But then the second act was generally less good. Not surprisingly, as all the effort recently has gone into Act One, and particularly Act One, Scene Two. I think the exchange between Martin and Stuart near the top of Act Two, Scene One, is too long in the writing. I'll have to cut it by a beat or two.

All in all, though, everyone was rather pleased. The sparse audience seemed to enjoy it, at least. Nathan and I decided to go off and have a sandwich alone together, Joe having offered to drive us to a restaurant or café. But then began one of those interminable Matrix discussions about things like moustaches, overcoats, etc. It was now past midnight, everyone hungry and anxious to be off, and yet – it could only happen at the Matrix, I've never known anything like it – no one could escape from this conversation, once it had begun. It was like a net that they'd entwined themselves in. Finally I had to remove Joe virtually by force. Before getting into Joe's car, I had a brief conversation with Sam Weisman on the pavement, saying, 'Look, Sam, about our little dispute. We could have an interminable post-mortem on what you meant, what I meant, so forth, but I'd much rather we both just forget it, do you agree?' He looked vastly relieved, said yes, he did agree, we said fond goodnights, so I was rather surprised when he turned up at Joe Allen's just a few minutes after we did. He worked so hard at being genial that all you saw was the work, which meant that the geniality grated on the nerves – mine anyway. And I suspect I worked so hard at responding to his geniality that all *he* saw was the work, rather than the response, so no doubt I grated on *his* nerves, in turn.

Joe and Nathan, on the other hand, were relaxed. They began to tell theatre jokes, Joe getting into one, rather long one, about a guy who had writer's block, had no money, didn't know where his next meal was coming from. One morning, after a night of tossing and turning, he went downstairs to find the script he'd been blocked on not only finished, but brilliantly finished. He took it to a producer who loved it instantly and paid him half a million dollars for it. A few months later he was tossing and turning with writer's block, although he'd bought himself a house and a new car, and was living in fairly comfortable style. He went downstairs and there, neatly on the desk, was the script he'd been working on, brilliantly finished. He took it to the producer who loved it and this time paid him a million dollars. The next time he was blocked and lay tossing and turning, he heard the typewriter going. He hurried downstairs and discovered an elf sitting at the typewriter, typing furiously away. It turned out that this elf had written all his other scripts for him, so he said to the elf, 'Well, listen, I must give you something.' The elf said, 'No, no, I don't want anything, I just enjoy the work.' He went on typing until he'd finished the script. The writer took it off to the producer, who loved it, paid him one and a half million. This went on for some time, the elf writing script after script, the writer selling them for two, three million, until the writer got rather desperate at the elf's refusal to accept anything in return. He offered him women, and the elf said, 'What would I want with a woman? I'm an elf.' He offered him a house, a car, trips abroad, but the elf would accept nothing, always saying, 'I don't need it. I'm an elf.' Until the writer said, 'Look, this is terrible, there must be something I can give you, let me give you something. Please. *Anything.* For *my* sake. Name it!' After a pause the elf said shyly, 'Well, look. There is – well, a little thing – look, do you think I could have a share of the writing credit?' The writer stared at him. 'Share my writing credit! What do you think I am – fucking crazy?'

I got back here at two o'clock. Just now, in fact. To discover that the phones are still out of order. The sunny at the desk talked of their being fixed in the morning but made, smilingly, no promises. Now that I've got the video working, I'm too tired to watch anything on it.

Saturday, 1 February

Left the hotel with the phones still on the blink, having been told that they'd be fixed by ten o'clock, then twelve o'clock, then three o'clock. Joe had arranged to pick me up at twelve thirty for lunch. He arrived at one fifteen, by which time I was feeling almost ill with hunger, having had nothing for breakfast but a glass or two of champagne. He drove me to Musso and Frank's in the rain. While he parked the car I walked back to the jeweller's to collect my watch. There was a Pole there, a laughing Pole – I hadn't *left* the watch with a laughing Pole – who told me I must have come to the wrong shop because they had no watch there along the lines of my description, try further down the street. To my own triumphant astonishment, and to his evident bewilderment – at least it stopped him laughing – I produced, probably for the first time in my life, a receipt, and further told him the make of the watch, so there was no getting out of it, he had my watch somewhere. He made some phone calls in Polish, then announced that it would be ready in an hour. As his English wasn't too hot I had to pantomime my anger before slogging back through the rain to have lunch with Joe, and a friend of his who'd joined him, an American actor who 'did' English* – a perfectly pleasant fellow, no doubt, but not somebody I wanted to meet at this precise moment in my life, what with non-functioning telephones, my unreturned watch, the first preview coming up in the evening. The lunch seemed to go on and on, the conversation centring mainly on McEnroe and Borg, though shifting now and then to Harold, with whom this actor who 'did' English had once worked. I found it hard to concentrate, Borg, Harold, McEnroe sort of mixing themselves up in my mind into one composite figure on the other side of life's net, so to speak especially as the food had a very dominating personality. I'd ordered kidneys, but what had arrived were not kidneys as we know them, too enormous to have come from any farmyard animals of my experience. They lay there on my plate, seeming to stir occasionally, as if *challenging* me to eat them.

Eventually I got Joe to agree that it was time to go, especially as I had to pick up my watch before heading on to the theatre. Out the three of us went, into the Musso and Frank's car park, where we bumped into a television producer Joe knew, to whom he insisted on introducing me. I stood in the rain in my shirt-sleeves – everyone else, I noticed, had on some kind of rain-defying apparel – while Joe and the actor and the producer, a big black-bearded, shambling figure, reminisced their way back to their early youths. When I was sufficiently soaked I reminded Joe about my watch, plodded off to collect it. I was met by the Pole, his eyes dancing with merriment, who informed me that it would be ready in half an hour or so. I threw a tantrum, heaving about his tiny shop, knocking against things. Because of his limited understanding of English I chose words that everyone in Los Angeles uses all the

---

* That is, specialised in playing English parts.

time, even foreigners. I don't think I actually went as far as 'motherfucker' but I deployed 'shit' frequently and noisily, then wrote down the telephone number of the Matrix, and told him to phone the second my watch arrived. Then back through the rain to Joe in the car park, and on to the theatre, to discover Sam, for the first time ever, not only there before me, but already in the throes of rehearsal. I was half an hour late. He's generally a minimum of forty-five minutes late. But just yesterday I'd made such a point about the endemic unpunctuality at the Matrix, and given Joe, within Sam Weisman's hearing, a lecture about it, that it was particularly mortifying to be late myself the very next day, thus giving Sam Weisman the right to treat me like an interloper, a right he tried to exercise. I wasn't having any of it, stopping him constantly, checking his comments, discussing various points to the full. I have to admit that he dealt with me with remarkable forbearance, and managed to give the actors clear and good notes. When I watch him at his best I believe the play is in safe hands. I just wish that our temperaments and our vanities didn't collide so readily – eagerly, even – and that he didn't so often move from the illuminating to the obscure in half a sentence. What was evident and reassuring was that the two actors, Wayne Alexander and Kris Tabori, have reached some accommodation with him, settling for picking up what they can. Of course, they are now about to go before the public, and *need* the feeling that they are in the hands of a director.

At about five p.m. the jeweller's phoned to say that my watch was ready. I had Chip Estees drive me to the shop, where the Pole triumphantly – rather as if he'd manufactured it himself, he was so proud of having it in his possession – handed it over to me for the sum of $12, a trifling amount given the comfort it has restored to my wrist, to the whole of me, as a matter of fact. I went on to the Magic, but decided not to go into the office to find out whether the telephones were working because I thought that if they weren't the complications arising from the subsequent row would probably lead to violence, the police, handcuffs, gaol. Every day on the way to the theatre I pass a shop that offers bail bonds. I would hate to think that Beryl might have to fly over to Los Angeles and take out a bail bond as the result of altercations I'd had from not being able to reach her on the telephone. When

I entered my room the telephone was ringing. Yes, actually ringing. Rick Quinones, someone I hadn't seen for nearly thirty years, when I was twenty and he a few years older, he a student from Midwestern University in Chicago, taking a course in French literature at the University of Clermont-Ferrand and I, *en route* to Cambridge from Halifax, Nova Scotia, teaching English to French students at the Collège Technique in Clermont-Ferrand. He was married to a beautiful American girl called Laurel, who became pregnant halfway through our year there. The only contact I've had with him since came through the post a couple of years ago in the form of a pamphlet of poems by Laurel, along with the announcement from Rick that she'd died of cancer. He is now lecturing at Claremont College, not far from Los Angeles. We arranged to have lunch on Monday. I'm looking forward to it with some trepidation. It was for such a short time, such a long time ago, that we knew each other. On which note I'll sign off for the evening. I go back to the theatre in a few minutes to the first preview. I'll report on it either later tonight, or tomorrow morning. When I'm either drunk or hungover.

Later   The first preview went off well enough, under the circumstances. The play seemed to hold up strongly, the audience was absorbed, laughing a great deal and also seeming, from time to time, to be touched. The key moments certainly worked better than at the Long Wharf or in London. But the set is an utter disaster. The actors remain dwarfed by the monumental walls and the vast stretches of brown. One of the designer's most ghastly mistakes is that he's used the same door for the two rooms, although the first room, in Cambridge, is back in the sixties, and the one in London goes up almost to the present. But in each room we have the same door, an *enormous* door. The architecture of the stage is such that your eyes go to it immediately, and you are immediately convinced that you are, even after the most elaborate, ponderous and time-consuming set-changes, still in the same room.

The other problem is Kris Tabori. He played the funny bits 'funnily' and the serious bits 'seriously', over-emphasis everywhere, back to Lee J. Cobb, in fact. Now Lee J. Cobb was a great actor, everything he did coming, or seeming to come, from something found and truthful in his own nature. But Kristoffer Tabori was giving a mere imitation of Lee J. Cobb, announcing the mood in every scene with his first line, leaving himself absolutely nowhere to go – Lee J. Cobb always had plenty of places to go. It was as if Tabori couldn't trust the text to make itself understood, or the audience to understand it. He was directing himself, as a police-man directs traffic. Now this way, now that. Go. Stop, watch the lights.

Still, there was euphoria at the interval, and euphoria after the second act, Joe grinning jubilantly, Sam Weisman stamping feroci-ously about proclaiming that we had a hit, 'a monster hit, a fuck-ing monster!', on our hands, though as the auditorium seats only ninety-nine it seems to me that it will be a very small monster of a hit, fucking or otherwise.

But being the Matrix they weren't content to leave the evening at that, in a blaze of celebration and some formal pronouncement to the effect that we'd all meet tomorrow for a general note period, followed by specific notes, followed by rehearsals. Instead Joe and Sam Weisman, in their weird, implacable, devotional style – per-haps it's the house-style – insisted on holding a post-mortem on the props, and where they should be placed. It became increas-ingly Byzantine, this conversation, moving from a consideration of the props to even smaller considerations, until Wayne Alex-ander insisted on discussing the question of whether he should have marking tapes to illuminate the keyboard of his typewriter in the dark, so that he will know exactly where to put his fingers when he begins typing at the beginning of Act Two, just before the lights go up. The idea that Wayne Alexander needs to have the keys he is *pretending* to tap illuminated with tape seems to me preposterous, at least as a subject for a debate that lasted a full twenty minutes, at getting on for midnight.

Driven by all this beyond endurance, I seized Nathan Lane and hurled him into the lobby, where he was gathered up by a friend – a tall, dark Jewish girl in her early thirties from New York, who comes up periodically to Los Angeles to turn a buck or two as a warm-up comedienne for situation comedies on television. The three of us went off to Joe Allen's, where I had a very large Scotch, a piece of pecan pie and a large espresso, while they dealt out to each other spoonfuls of various salads and ordered each other drinks. The warm-up comedienne lady had seen the show at the Long Wharf, felt that the version here went deeper, but also felt that the set was a catastrophe. As we'd asked for her opinion, we had to tolerate her giving it to us. She went through the cast, plus-ing and minus-ing in terms of the Long Wharf production, while the Joe Allen waiters kept skirmishing up with offers of more food, drink, etc., until I suppose after one in the morning, virtually the last ones in the place, we left, the stand-up comedienne driving Nathan and myself back to the Magic Hotel – where I am now, dictating this. I wish she hadn't confirmed all my fears about the set, I'd hoped my reactions were special to myself, paranoid, and that we'd got by. But we simply can't have two different sets creating exactly the same atmosphere in different places and times, especially after we make such a fuss about changing them. The problems with the actor, Kris Tabori, will probably be corrected by a serious conversation or two; but the problem of the set won't be corrected by just conversations, however many of them we have, however serious. Really, we should begin by ripping it down and reconceiving it.

Before dictating this I phoned Beryl – two a.m. my time, ten in the morning her time – to be told, among other things, that Hazel has become almost completely incontinent, seeming to have developed a method of eating and crapping simultaneously. When ushered into the garden, where in her prime she dropped turds at random, she now merely stands sniffing abstractedly for a brief moment, before hurrying in to mess up the kitchen floor, her nose buried in a dish. I can't bear the thought of anything happening to her, even though I know it will and must, as to all mortal creatures, so what I mean is that I can't bear the thought of my life without her. She sits under my desk or lies on the sofa gazing at me with sheer reverence when I write, and has been my friend and confidante for sixteen years now.

Sunday, 2 February

Lunch by myself at Musso and Frank's. Read the English newspapers, three days behind, and ate mushrooms on toast, or tried to. They were disgusting, actually. They have no idea about mushrooms, Americans. They think that you have to pour vinegar and wine over them, when all a civilised eater wants is for them to be fried in butter with a little bit of garlic, some salt and pepper added – true mushrooms on toast. If the toast's OK. But at Musso and Frank's the mushrooms sprawl across the thick, sweet toast, lapping around its edges, smothered in wine and vinegar. And beside it is another plate of mushrooms on sweet thick toast, so that if one runs out of the first load, one has a second load to turn to. Though the prospect of running through the first load and wanting more must surely be remote, even for Californians.

Sam Weisman arrived while I was toying with my coffee, drove me to the theatre. We talked about the actors, the costumes, the props, and above all, the set. Although he hates it too, he doesn't think anything can be done about it. When we got to the theatre, we had a talk with Kristoffer Tabori about the part of Stuart. I put down various cards about my understanding of the character, that he is so much at home in the English language that he never feels the need to colour his words with 'meaning' and 'intention'; that he is always poised, calm, only breaking down once in the play, in a moment of extreme crisis. Tabori nodded thoughtfully through all this, and I left him with Sam Weisman to do some specific rehearsing, while I went along to the office, and found Joe on the telephone, looking odd. He hung up, terminating his conversation abruptly, and said he didn't feel well. He seemed rather puzzled by this. His eyes had a slightly dreamy, almost vacant look, as if he'd been drugged. I suppose he's suffering from a combination of fatigue and tension, the feeling that things are almost there, but aren't quite – it's characteristic of the Matrix that although we've had *two* public previews, everyone has behaved as if both were an official first night, instead of viewing them as mere extensions of the rehearsal period, a time to learn through an audience.

I went next door to the Café Melrose for a glass of wine. Joe joined me a few minutes later, to talk about the set, Kristoffer Tabori, Wayne Alexander, this actor, that actor, how it had gone last night, how it had failed to go, all this with his usual energy but still slightly unfocused, although he did manage to ask if he could be guaranteed some participation, should the play be produced in New York. I said that of course he would be – I do think he's a terrific producer, given the limited resources he has to work with, although I also think that as a producer he continues in many respects to be an actor playing the part of a producer, and is sometimes in need of a good director.* I went back to the rehearsal, where I immediately found myself in another altercation with Wayne Alexander about a line that I felt he was delivering as if he'd learnt it, that *he* felt he was delivering as if it were spontaneous. 'I don't understand what you're saying,' he kept saying. 'It was spontaneous. It felt spontaneous.' 'But it sounded,' I kept saying, 'rehearsed. As if it had been rehearsed.' Back and forth we went, he getting pricklier, I more ponderous, Sam Weisman saying nothing, watching with a kind of vacant impatience until we got back to work, then broke for a pre-preview meal and rest. I dashed off for a drink with Antonia Pinter's daughter, Natasha, to exchange views about Los Angeles, then back to the theatre just before the lights were due to come up, to find the actors hanging about looking listless, accident-prone, riddled with anxiety in the Matrix manner. I went next door to the Café Melrose, ordered a glass of wine, where I was joined by a Joe even more frantic and unfocused than before, wanting to talk, though it wasn't clear about what, he was so fretful. He sat down, got up, sat down, got up, finally sat himself down for about four long minutes before getting up again and going out, saying he'd see me in the theatre. During all this he scarcely spoke. It was as if Joe – the fertile-minded, imaginative, joke-making Joe – had been abruptly drained, while his body continued to behave with remembered energy. It made me uneasy.

I got into the theatre just as the play was starting. At once it was obvious that we had a rather different Kris Tabori on stage, much more in control, much calmer. As he's got natural presence he therefore became vastly more eloquent than when dramatizing every line with his body and his voice. There were the usual technical problems and of course I found myself from time to time staring angrily at the set, particularly at the double-duty door.

At the interval I nipped into the Melrose again to stay out of earshot of the audience, then went back to the office just as the second act was about to begin, to find Joe and Sam sitting silently in an atmosphere of strain, as if they had been having, or were on

---

* Which reminds me that Joe's production company is officially (and ominously) entitled 'Actors for Themselves'.

the verge of having, a row. I stared at them both, then hurried out into the auditorium for the second act, fixing my attention on four old ladies in the front row, on whose faces there wasn't a flicker of surprise, concern, amusement, interest of any kind. I suppose they'd only come back from the interval because they had ordered their limo to return at the end of the play. Just before the change to the Epilogue the audience burst into what I would have taken as heart-warming applause if I hadn't known that a few seconds later – quite a few seconds later, as a matter of fact, because of the elaborations of the set-change – the audience was going to find itself back in a strikingly similar room, with all the actors assembled, and the Epilogue still to get through. They took it on the chin, when they at last discovered that the play was going on past the point at which they'd complimented it for having finished.

So that was that. I scurried, as is my wont, around to the office, to find Joe and Sam already there, having a row – the row that had presumably not quite started, or that I had interrupted, at the interval. Joe was not only shouting at Sam Weisman but – between sentences – also shouting at the stage-hands for their incompetence. It was the first time I'd ever seen Joe angry, really angry. Sam kept intervening, ordering Joe not to shout at the stage-hands, they were doing their best, which of course further incensed Joe, who has had to spend, as he loudly pointed out, the last month or so attempting to pacify everyone with whom Sam has come into contact – having Sam now publicly telling him to calm down and to behave with better manners was more than he could endure. Sam actually developed a very good line in the middle of the row, sitting down and smiling gravely at the folly of mankind, or more specifically Joe's folly, which had the (desired, I assume) effect of enraging Joe even further, until Sam suddenly got up, said he had to get to his television studio to look at some stills, and went, leaving Joe fulminating into emptiness. Then, noticing me, he began to fulminate in my direction, though not precisely at me, saying that the work 'you guys' had done on the first scene had turned it into a pile of shit. And the whole play goes down the toilet. 'And the whole play goes down the toilet!' he bellowed. I always find it very hard to be angry with Joe when we're face to face, and even in these circumstances, melodramatic though they were, I found myself trying to pacify him. I dimly understood, I think, that his fury had in some way to be spent. He went on lashing out at Sam and myself (this package deal was rather hard to take) like a minor heavy in a Clint Eastwood film, every other sentence containing 'fucking' and 'fuck', with 'shit' bobbing about on the surface as well. He didn't so much calm down as wind down. He stared at me blankly for a moment, gave a feeble laugh, offered to drive me to Joe Allen's, then was overwhelmed by a fit of the shakes. He stood in his office shaking, looking extremely perplexed by the shaking, saying he couldn't understand what was the matter with him. Chip Estees and I got him to lie down on the sofa, and covered him with a blanket. He continued to shake and tremble under the blanket, looking utterly befuddled, while I phoned Pepe to come and fetch him.

I wasn't really as worried as perhaps I ought to have been because I felt that the shaking and the trembling were intimately connected with his rage, as if a very strong tempest had passed through his body, leaving his will unable to deal with the complete exhaustion that followed it. I got the stage manager, the young guy with the wispy beard, to drive me to Joe Allen's, where Nathan, already ensconced, had his own drink in his hand, and another on the table, waiting for me. Before I could tell him about Joe, the door swung open. Sam Weisman stood there, framed in it, like some kind of goatish gun-slinger from an old B-movie. His eyes scanned the room, he picked out our table, over he came. Nathan and I, who had been going to spend the evening celebrating his birthday – it was his thirtieth – along with old times past and old times to come, found ourselves instead having to deal with an absolutely obsessed director, who wanted to talk about the set, and how he was determined to make its changes work, some awkward moves and how he was going to change them to make them work, on and on and on, until I was too drunk to listen to him properly. Nathan sloped off, gesturing that he was going to the lavatory, came back again, then after five minutes, glancing out of the window, said, 'There's my taxi.' I said, 'Your taxi?' He said, 'Yes, my taxi. Somebody I want to see. I'll drop you off at the Magic on the way there.' I began to say, 'Yes, fine,' but Sam Weisman cut across – he being in full flow – and said, 'I'll take him home, I'll take him home. Don't worry about him, I'll look after him, you go off, Nathan!' Nathan went off, I don't know where to, but I hope to someone with whom he had a night of passion.

I sat on with Sam Weisman, my concentration gone, my focus gone, sat with my chin on my fist, staring dully at him as he talked very emotionally about all the things he intended to do, to the set, to the blocking, to make the production work. Joe Allen's cleared, the restaurant was empty, the kitchen was closed, the bar was closing, the waiters were desperate to get rid of us, and I only wanted, it was all I wanted, to get back to the Magic, and into bed. But Sam Weisman talked on until, in the middle of a sentence, he got up, said, 'Listen, I'm very tired so you'll have to find your own way home, I can't make it, I've got to get home myself so see you,' and went off. I went to the bar where I asked for a taxi. 'The guy here wants a cab,' one of the two remaining waiters said. 'Well actually not a guy,' I said. 'It's a gentleman here asking for a taxi.' There was a pause, then some merriment between the two of them at the proposition that the guy who wanted a cab was actually passing himself off as a gentleman who wanted a taxi, though a taxi arrived almost at once, and I was brought here to the Magic to end my day by reporting all this into the tape recorder.

Monday, 3 February

Awoke at ten thirty this morning, a rest day and therefore no rehearsal. I lay in bed, rather numbly, unable to get going until I forced myself to the telephone and called Joe to find out how he was. He sounded a bit enfeebled but said he felt he was OK, really. Then Nathan phoned to say he was going out to lunch, would I like to come with him? I said yes but explained that we couldn't have lunch, as I'd already arranged to have lunch with Rick Quinones, the guy I'd last seen twenty-nine or thirty years ago in Clermont-Ferrand. Nathan and I strolled down to Musso and Frank's, sat down at a table and ordered a drink. I kept checking people as they came through the door, occasionally thinking I half recognised Rick Quinones, until suddenly at exactly one o'clock I looked up and there was a man, whom I'd last seen beardless and with quite a head of hair, coming through the door, almost bald with a beard. He came over to the table, I introduced him to

Nathan, who then withdrew to another table, leaving us alone to talk. The last time I'd seen him he'd also been with his beautiful and pregnant wife, and now I learnt that not only was Laurel dead from cancer, but that the son with whom she'd been pregnant had been killed, a month before Laurel died, in a car crash. We talked our way through that, all the way back through our respective careers as university teachers, to what we wanted to remember about Clermont-Ferrand, the friendships formed between the English and Americans, various incidents, as for example Laurel's telling me that they were having trouble getting to sleep at night as their mattress seemed to move under them – they later discovered that a couple of large rats were nesting in its stuffing. We began our lunch at one, ended it at five, not long enough to cover so much time, so much life, so much grief. He drove me back to the Magic, accompanied me to my rooms, looked around them as he pulled at his beard, left, leaving me on the sofa, in tears at the memory of Laurel, triumphantly pregnant, resembling in fact a large and proud robin, two deaths ago, thirty years ago, in Clermont-Ferrand.

I think I would have sat on there for hours if Nathan hadn't phoned from his room on the other side of the pool to say he was going to have dinner with his audience-warming comedienne friend, would I like to join them? She picked us up at about seven, and drove us to an Italian restaurant in Melrose Avenue – near the theatre, in fact – where we ate extremely badly. We were joined by Ted Larkins, to whom nothing had happened professionally since he'd left the company. Conversation was rather strained. There we were: Ted Larkins and his replacement, Nathan Lane; the author who'd done the replacing; the warm-up comedienne who, though chattering brightly, seemed to have her mind on other things; all sitting side by side with bad food in front of them. Suddenly the warm-up comedienne said, 'I've got to go,' and rose to her feet. 'What?' I cried. 'Where?' 'To a club,' she said. 'What club?' She replied, 'Just a club,' but she had to get to it straight away, rather as if she had an appointment with her doctor. 'Well, it sounds very interesting,' I said. 'Let's *all* go to this club.'

So Nathan and I, minus Ted Larkins, who suddenly discovered a previous engagement, clambered into her car, and were driven smartly to the club, a mere few minutes from the restaurant. She parked the car in the car park, and we ascended in an elevator to a disco, where a few men were dancing with each other, one man dancing alone in the middle of the floor, others huddled together, not so much dancing as responding to the music with their feet and torsos while engaged in private conversations – they were dressed in jeans and vests, and they danced extremely closely, touching each other as they jogged up and down. We went on through, past this lot, into an enormous room with a bar where there were about seventy or eighty people sitting on stools at tables, at the end of which was a stage with a microphone. Nathan's comedienne friend walked on up to the stage, picked up the microphone, and went straight into a number about what it was like to be a Jewish New York princess loose in Los Angeles, a comic monologue in fact, for which she was being paid, Nathan whispered to me, nothing. She was doing it to be *seen*, in the hope that her name would be passed on to agents and producers who'd get her into television series. Nathan and I, full of drink and friendship, thought she was very funny indeed, rocking with laughter on our stools, and signalling congratulations every time the audience appreciated one of her jokes. When she'd finished we went on to Joe Allen's, where we had a few more drinks, until Nathan rose, saying his taxi had arrived 'to take him on' – really, I don't know how he arranges these taxis; this time he seemed to have done it without even leaving the table – and tumbled off into the night. The comedienne and I had coffee, then she drove me back to the Magic. I tottered in, treading across the Astroturf, made slushy by recent rain, and wove my way up the stairs to my flat, pitched myself into bed.

Tuesday, 4 February

Met Phyllis Wender, my New York agent, at the Café Melrose, just before the preview. We took our time, sipping glasses of wine, as I'd discovered that we were going to go up late – the handle had come off the double-duty door, so it could be neither opened nor closed properly. We drifted into the theatre half an hour late, a few minutes before the play began. It got off to a good start, and remained good throughout the first act, Kris Tabori and his wife being especially simple, direct and therefore touching. The only actor who had lost it a trifle was old Nathan, who'd gone meta-phorically right back to the large auditorium at the Long Wharf, booming and rasping his way through his scenes as if unaware of how close he was to the audience. The audience, not knowing the play and therefore not knowing that they were free to leave for a cup of coffee (all the Matrix can provide), remained in their seats. Knowing better, and anxious as always to avoid hearing the audi-ence's comments, I made my way up the aisle in the pitch black, my hands held in front of me and so inevitably jammed my fin-gers straight into Sam Weisman's eyes, at the head of the gang-way. I heard him barking with both rage and physical distress as I swivelled smoothly around him, down into the hall, and out to the Café Melrose, trusting that he hadn't identified his assailant.

The second act went as well as the first, though the set changes are, of course, interminable and the Epilogue struck me as a bit ponderous – probably the fault of the writing. After the show I raced up the aisle and into the office. Phyllis came in a few seconds behind me, and then Joe came in, having recovered from his hysteria, flu, breakdown or whatever it was, but looking distinctly lighter and yellower. He was in characteristic form, demanding that I should stay on to help him with the press photocalls for the pictures that would accompany the reviews.

I refused point blank, and went off with Phyllis to Joe Allen's, where we were joined by Michael McGuire, an old friend of mine. I first met him during rehearsals of *Quartermaine's Terms* in San Francisco.* He'd been brought in as a replacement for the part of Windscape about a week before we were due to open. Now Wind-scape is a solid, cheerful, dedicated teacher of English to foreigners, of the English English and middle class, academical with it. What we had in Michael McGuire was a thin, almost cadaverous Mid-western American, wearing high-heeled boots, and with a nasal, Midwestern accent. Not so much a non-Windscape, an anti-Windscape. Or so I thought. But what became clear very quickly was that he was a highly intelligent man, and a real actor. Within a few days he'd not only learnt his lines – there are a lot of them – but he'd moved closer and closer to a Windscape that made complete emotional sense. By the first night his accent was

---

* The following, rather extensive account of my relationship with Michael McGuire is, I hope, justified by his dramatic reappearance in the last section of this book.

impeccably English, his Windscape entirely his own. And all this achieved in really desperate circumstances. We also hit it off off-stage. Having spent most of his adult life drinking very heavily, he'd given up drink, but he still had the conviviality, the *esprit* of the drinker – to such an extent that though he merely sipped genteelly away at Perriers and club sodas, I always remembered him as a chap with whom I'd shared many bottles of whisky. In fact, what I still recall most vividly and with most affection about San Francisco were the late nights he and I spent with Jack McQuiggan, who was overseeing the production – he had produced the play in New York – and who was, like Michael, an ex-drinker. We hung out in a deeply sleazy hamburger joint, Michael tippling away at his bottles of water and chain-smoking, Jack, an ex-chain-smoker, knocking back the coffees, I chain-smoking and at my whiskies; all three of us shouting out anecdotes and rocking with laughter until two or three in the morning.

The next time I bumped into Michael was when I came over here six weeks ago, to help cast *The Common Pursuit*. He's an old friend of Kristoffer Tabori's – no, that isn't right. Kristoffer Tabori isn't old enough yet to have old friends – he was Tabori's mentor and protector when Tabori first started out as an actor at the age of sixteen or so, when Michael was in his early thirties or so. Tabori and Judy Geeson invited him to dinner so that he and I could renew our acquaintance. Since San Francisco he'd given up smoking, which made him (like Jack McQuiggan) an ex-alcoholic ex-chain-smoker. He'd also separated from his long-term girl-friend. He said he was depressed – 'liberated but depressed' – by all this cutting down in his life, but within minutes he was telling a story, yelping with laughter, the same old Michael. A few days later – he'd acted at the Matrix, and knew Joe Stern – he came in to help us with auditions, reading the most unlikely parts, twenty-year-old Cambridge undergraduates, for instance, in his flat, nasal Midwestern accent, but still making enough sense of the lines to give the actors who were actually up for the parts of twenty-year-old Cambridge undergraduates a genuine understanding of what was expected of them.

And now there he was in Joe Allen's this evening, standing at our table, still elevated by his cowboy boots, sucking his chest in and throwing his arms out as he talked passionately about what he'd seen on the stage of the Matrix. I pulled him down into a chair, and allowed him to soliloquise flatteringly on and therefore *intelligently* on, until he expired into his Perrier or club soda on a final few compliments. Exalted, I decided the stage was mine. I launched into a monologue about my immediate future as a playwright, my future as a playwright after I was dead, the state of acting in Los Angeles (cutting off any interpolations from Michael, who laboured under the double disadvantage both of knowing far more about the subject than I did, and of being completely sober) until Phyllis drew my attention to the fact that (yet again) Joe Allen's was beginning to clear, and that I was yet again among the last to leave. Phyllis and I accompanied Michael to his car, one on either side of him, in a rather bizarre role reversal – after all, we'd both been drinking and he hadn't. He clipped along contentedly between us, embraced us both, climbed into his car, drove off to the far Los Angeles canyon he lives in. Phyllis and I then tumbled into her car. Phyllis is about my age, I suppose, a small, neat, methodical lady with a frequent and exceptionally pleasant laugh. Most of all she resembles a successful High School teacher – perhaps, more accurately, a Principal – and is a very sharp agent indeed. Now Phyllis is a New Yorker, doesn't know Los Angeles particularly well, and didn't have a road map to refer to, yet she drove at exceptional speed, unnerving speed, up and down streets she'd never travelled before, depositing me by instinct, it seemed, at the doors of the Magic, then drove off into the night. A pretty good evening, as evenings go in Los Angeles. At the Matrix, anyway.

Wednesday, 5 February

Did what I normally do when I'm free in the morning. Pottered about the flat, watched a bit of television, listened to some music on the radio, tried to do a bit of reading, then shambled down to Musso and Frank's, where I had an altercation with the elderly guy, the bespectacled figure who looks rather like a dentist to the Mafia, who refused me a table on the grounds that tables were for two and I am only one. I pointed out that I'd booked (true), and that I was going to be joined by a friend (a lie) but this old Mafia dentist figure, who's seen me virtually every day since I arrived in Los Angeles, first of all insisted on my telling him my name, which he made an elaborate show of finding confusing and making me spell, then pointed me to a swivel stool at the counter, where I could wait, he informed me, until my friend (actually he said 'fran') came. I've come to hate the counter, because it's quite obvious that anyone sitting at it is by himself, somehow for ever unpartnered, and I can no longer bear to add myself to this poignant line-up of swivelling solitaries, but instead of engaging him in combat – the demons for once being passive – I plodded to the bar and found myself facing a guy who was the image of benevolent authority. I explained that I needed a booth. He immediately conducted me to one. I've no idea where he is in the Musso and Frank's hierarchy. He may not work there at all. But the fact is, he escorted me to a table, and I read my papers, comfortably if rather slowly and carefully as a dyslexic might, actually mouthing some of the words out loud. I spent hours studying the cricket columns.

In the evening I went along to the theatre, arriving in good time for rehearsals. I gave my notes, worried aloud about the Epilogue, complained about the set changes, etc., usual sort of stuff. Except nothing is usual in the Matrix. There is now an atmosphere of frenzy in the auditorium that increases the moment Sam Weisman begins to speak, and will obviously never abate until he's no longer on the premises. It doesn't matter how intelligent he is about the previous night's performance, the actors sit there enduring his notes while making it clear that they can't stand him. And the most astonishing thing is that he goes on, implacably, grindingly, giving his notes, quite unaware of what the actors feel about them and him. About them because of him.

The preview went OK, though Kristoffer Tabori had slipped back to his pantomime performance. Such an odd thing because he's very effective when he's calm and still – the more he 'acts' the less effective he is – and yet there he was, after his wonderful performance on Tuesday night, going right back to it all, as if anxious to show the audience that he is determined to give them their money's worth. It depressed me deeply. After the show Nathan and I went to Joe Allen's. We were having quite a jolly evening when the door opened and in came Sam Weisman, to join us.

Thursday, 6 February

Nathan and I went to Musso and Frank's for lunch, and found bedlam. Not only was every table taken, even the counter was packed, with a crush of people jamming the entrance, desperate for any kind of seating. There was nobody in attendance, the Mafia dentist who generally stands guarding the route to the tables and counter had vanished, presumably having given up. People were just milling angrily about, hungry. We went back along Hollywood Boulevard to the Hamburger Hamlet, which would have been tolerable if it hadn't been crudely segregated – non-smokers being conducted to a light and airy room, smokers consigned to a dark chamber in the back, with grubby booths, like a speakeasy. We talked, as we so often did, about the good times in New Haven in the raw and brutal cold, as opposed to the bad times in Los Angeles in the balmy sunshine, recalling the train from Grand Central to New Haven, and back again, arriving at Grand Central at two or so in the morning, anything from an hour to an hour and a half late, all of us slightly to extremely drunk from Michael Countryman's hip-flask full of whisky, and then the trudges through the snow for cabs, then back to New Haven the next day. Nathan went on to complain about the lack of any kind of theatre community in Los Angeles, the obsession here with films and television, the sheer sunshiny dullness of the place.

After rehearsals I went off to meet Natasha Fraser, treated her to a glass of the Café Melrose white wine, escorted her to the theatre, where she met up with two young and attractive (girl) friends of hers. It went, the play, just about OK, no better than the previous preview, no worse, though once again Kristoffer Tabori's tendency to posture was troubling. Natasha and I went off for dinner, over which we gossiped about the performance, then she drove me to the Magic. And I thought as we drove back that here I was, at the sort of age when I escorted to dinner girls whom I'd first known when they were ten or so. But then, I further ruminated, these girls had also reached the age when they were escorted out to dinner by middle-aged men they'd first known when they were ten or so, and that they, in their turn, would one day be escorting out to dinner boys of ten or so – no, that can't be right. Forget it.

Friday, 7 February, First Night

After breakfast I phoned up all the actors and gave them my notes. I've taken to doing this as a regular morning activity; first breakfast, then phone the actors to discuss their performances. A number of them informed me that they'd had enough of the Matrix, they'd never work there again, they resented Joe for his continual interferences, Sam Weisman for his manner. They didn't say how much or why they resented me, although I expect they do. Sat in a torpor on the balcony for a few hours, a bottle of champagne to hand, then off to M & F for lunch.

Most of the afternoon I spent crouching by my bedroom window, staring through a gap in the curtains at a man sitting on a bench, across the road from the hotel. Tall, ginger-bearded man, about thirty, wearing a tartan shirt, tight jeans, cowboy boots, with an enormous knife strapped to his left buttock. He followed me back to the Magic from just outside Musso and Frank's – the second time he's followed me. The first time, a few days ago, in the early afternoon, also when returning from Musso and Frank's, I found myself standing beside him at a crossing. When the lights changed he waited for me to get ahead, then settled in behind me. I could hear his boots tapping along in time to my own tread, which I kept measured and confident, at least until I got to the hotel steps, up which I shot like a whippet, if you can imagine a portly, forty-nine-year-old whippet, on two legs and with poor wind. That time it didn't occur to me to check whether he lingered on outside, keeping watch. But today the whole business seemed even more deliberate. When I came out of Musso and Frank's he was coming towards me on the crowded pavement. His face registered nothing, but I sensed him turning, settling down behind me again, and once out of Hollywood Boulevard, on the deserted street – Orange Street – that leads up to the Magic, I could hear his boots again, tapping rhythmically along. Again I whippeted up the steps into the lobby, but this time I turned and watched him through the glass doors. He crossed the street to the bench, sat down on it, folded his arms, and stared towards the hotel – or putting it in more personal terms, stared towards *me*. Of course I can't see the bench from my sitting room or balcony, but I can from my bedroom. Hence my crouching there, peering through the curtains. He must have spent several hours virtually immobile, and eventually left when I wasn't watching him. Given my behaviour it's no good pretending that I don't find him, the thought of him, the *image* of him following me back to the Magic, then sitting outside on a bench in the sun as if waiting for me, quite unnerving. He corresponds almost exactly to my vision of the ruffian on the stair, in the W. E. Henley poem.* On the other hand he might simply be a sort of stray, who likes a bit of company when roaming the streets – pedestrians lead a lonely life in Los Angeles. But why the knife? Can it possibly be legal, even in a town like Los Angeles, to go about publicly with a knife that size clamped to your buttock?†

At about six I phoned for a taxi, then hung about on my balcony, keeping an eye on the lobby. The sunnies there sometimes forget to ring you up to let you know that your taxi's arrived. On one occasion, a couple of evenings ago, they actually sent the taxi away, on what grounds I couldn't fathom. Perhaps that I don't exist. Or was curled up with a cat, and shouldn't be disturbed. This time I spotted the driver going to the desk, so I scooted down while he was still on the premises. He and sunny were having a pleasant conversation, though clearly not on the whereabouts of the prospective client – at least I hope not, as there was a lot of headshaking laughter, and exclamations of 'You don't say!', etc. I got to the Matrix at six thirty, an hour and a half before lights up on our official first night. I zipped up the road to Antonio's for a drink and a song in my face, then sauntered fairly calmly back to the Matrix, where Joe informed me I'd have to stand through the performance, as all the seats had been allocated to critics.

According to Joe the word of mouth from the previews has been 'terrific, just terrific', which is not always to the advantage of a first night, as critics like to think that they generate the word of mouth, and certainly don't like to think that they're being usurped by it.‡ So it's not surprising really, that I detected pockets

---

* 'Madam Life's a piece in bloom /Death goes dogging everywhere; / She's the tenant of the room, / He's the ruffian on the stair.'

† I wasn't able to put this question to him as I never saw him again.

‡ A New York producer, who knew his show was a bummer, was astonished to read rave reviews after the first night. 'Now,' he is reported to have said, 'all we got to do is stop the word of mouth.'

of resistance here and there, some ostentatiously unimpressed expressions on the heavily suntanned faces. Nevertheless I thought the show was good, really very good, and afterwards hurried around to the dressing rooms (some of which are merely alcoves with coat hooks) to dish out thanks to the cast, each one in turn. For the first time in my experience of the theatre I felt this was merely a ritual. No, worse. A courtesy. I suddenly realised that though I liked this actor, respected that one, I had no sense of intimacy with any of them. Except for Nathan, of course. Him I gathered up and bore off in a cab to Joe Allen's, where we were joined by friends of his, a husband and wife who failed to observe the first night conventions, and talked about the play and the production only in qualifying details – what they felt wasn't clear in a scene here, what went wrong in a scene there (Act One, Scene Two). We were interrupted by Sam Weisman, who burst through the door, stood for a moment checking out the room, waved to us that he was coming to our table, then sped past us with a late swerve, to join a clutch of people at a large table at the end of the room. Friends, I assume. Or anyway, people with whom he has some acquaintance. While he rampaged amongst them, stabbing his fist into the air with triumph, I went to the bar, ordered a taxi, came back to the Magic, where I now am, out on the balcony, dictating this.

Another first night gone. The third for *The Common Pursuit*. I don't remember the previous two. Soon I won't remember this one – though perhaps I'll remember the next, which is tomorrow. I don't quite know why there should be two official first nights at the Matrix, except of course that as you have to say everything at least twice here, why shouldn't you have to do everything at least twice, too? It's a still night, very quiet for the Magic. Most of the lights are out. No televisions or radios on, that I can hear. Perhaps all the other guests are in bed but awake, listening to my low, disappointed drone, occasionally quickened by a spasm of spite, as I talk on the balcony into this machine.

Saturday, 8 February

Got up just in time for lunch at Musso and Frank's, over which (though what, I don't recall) I read the English papers. Came back, listened to some music, then went to our second first night. All the critics that didn't come (couldn't get in?) to our first first night had appropriated every seat in the auditorium. This would seem to mean that there are nearly two hundred theatre critics in Los Angeles. More than enough, when you consider that there aren't many theatres, and that very few of those are visited by plays. I shambled around the dressing rooms, looking shy but dishing out notes to the actors, then went up to Antonio's for a drink. A drink and a half (a double and single, to be technical. An Antonio double is about the size of a London sextuple) – two songs smack in the face, and a platter of hors d'oeuvres that were simultaneously fiery and heavy. Rather like the songs, come to think of it. Then back to the theatre about ten minutes before the show began. I had to stand at the back again, as a critic, a small bearded woman wearing bombazine and shades, was in my usual seat.*

The show was the best it's ever been, controlled, intelligent, sensitive. I could have made forty notes about the performances, but then at a certain stage of a production one could make forty different notes every night. On the next night the actors themselves would have corrected those forty, while doing forty other things one could note. The real point of continuing to give notes is to make sure they don't become stale, lurching by degrees into habits that usually manifest themselves early in rehearsals, from the something intractable that is in all our natures. Nevertheless I was delighted with the play and with the production, as was the producer and the director, though they were also apprehensive, having observed that the theatre critic for the *Los Angeles Times*, one Dan O'Sullivan,† sat cold-eyed through the evening, apparently totally uninvolved. I said that perhaps he was merely on heavy medication. Or had a hearing problem. Or was bored.

We went on to Joe Allen's, where I found myself at a table of about fourteen or so, Sam Weisman on my left, Joe Stern on my

---

* Sheer fantasy. My usual seat was occupied by a moustachioed man in swimming trunks and shades.

† It might have been Don. Don O'Sullivan. But for some reason I think of him as Dan. Perhaps because it's his name. Dan O'Sullivan. But now it comes to it I'm not too sure of his surname either. It could be Sullivan without the O'. Possibly Don Sullivan then. For the purposes of clarity I've decided to stick with Dan O'Sullivan.

right, both still glumly assessing the reactions, or rather lack of reactions, of Dan O'Sullivan. As I'd already offered my analysis I left pretty quickly for the Magic, where I am now, dictating this. I can't WAIT to get out of Los Angeles, away from the Matrix to Dallas, and then, after Dallas, home. I only hope that somewhere else, but preferably in New York, *The Common Pursuit* will continue its new life. If only to justify the way I've spent the last six weeks.

Sunday, 9 February

I was awoken at about eight this morning by a marital quarrel, full-throated, in the rooms next to mine. I gathered that the man had come back about an hour before, with the woman up waiting for him, demanding to know where he'd been. As their voices were blurred with rage and emotion, I couldn't get the details, though I did catch the following exchange:

From him: 'You've ruined my fucking life.'

From her: *'You've* ruined *my* fucking life.'

They went on for about an hour or so in this vein.

Had lunch with Kristoffer Tabori. He talked for the first time about what it had been like to go from director to leading man, and above all what it had been like to be directed by Sam Weisman, who hadn't consulted him when he took over on any aspect of the production. I took the opportunity – frankness being our agreed mode – to say that I had always believed it was a mistake for him to cast his wife, especially when the playwright was going to be around. He agreed that it had been a mistake, one he intended to avoid in the future, but added that he was certain she was by far the best Marigold available in Los Angeles. I couldn't argue with that. I think her performance, which I realise I have scarcely discussed in these reports, is quite superb. Simple, direct, unaffected. The other performance I haven't discussed is Chris Neame's as Peter, mainly because from the moment he got it right there was little to be said – he is the definitive Peter. If the play goes to New York, I would like to cast Kris Tabori, Judy Geeson, Chris Neame and, of course, old Nathan from the Matrix production, and get Michael Countryman and Peter Friedman from the Long Wharf production to play Martin and Humphry. Not that I think John Delancey, who has great presence, or Wayne Alexander, who is a very skilful actor, are bad, but I believe the other two would be definitive in the way that Chris Neame is definitive. Kristoffer Tabori and I also agreed – we spent a lot of time citing examples – that the Matrix production lacks fine tuning. Plenty of cues are either being rushed or not picked up quickly enough. I didn't say, my frankness not extending that far, that his own performance required considerable fine tuning and there are still moments when he is ponderous, explanatory, and even melo-dramatic. It was a very friendly lunch.

When I got back Joe phoned. He had nothing particular to say, just wanting to make contact. He sounded slightly depressed, so I suspect he has picked up something about the *Los Angeles Times* review which he doesn't want to divulge, for psychological reasons presumably. I can't say I give a damn, as long as it doesn't affect the run of the play. I shall be in Dallas when it comes out.

Monday, 10 February

Last night was my last night ever, I trust, at the Matrix. Before the show I dispensed a few subversive notes to the actors, and then up to Antonio's for a quick large Scotch on ice, then back just ten minutes before the show came up. At the interval I hustled into the Café Melrose, also for the last time, and had a quick farewell cuddle with the Japanese (actually I'm still not sure of their nationality) daughter of the owner, who has waited on me these last six weeks. Then went back for the second act, which I thought was in excellent nick. There was a party in the theatre after the show – really, I suppose, a postponed first-night party. Anyway, it was typically first-nightish in that people one doesn't know and doesn't really want to talk to come up and talk to one knowingly. After an hour or so of just cruising about with glasses of bubbly in my hand, I made it to Joe Allen's, where I was joined by Kris-toffer Tabori and Judy Geeson just after I'd phoned for a taxi to take me home. I sat with them for about five minutes, then Nathan Lane arrived with the warm-up comedienne. Nathan escorted me outside – I think I rather needed an escort – put me in a taxi, and back I came. Joe is picking me up tomorrow morning to take me to the airport, and then I shall be away from Los Angeles at last, though not comfortably or easily as I shall have to drag with me all my first-night gifts of bottles of champagne and bottles of malt whisky. And I shall be wearing heavy trousers, a thick shirt and carrying my raincoat and my sweater. Dallas is just as hot as Los Angeles apparently, if not hotter. I shall also be very tired, as I am now.

Sitting on the Right Hand of God,
or Was It John Wayne?

Tuesday, 11 February 1986

I'm reporting into my machine from Room 328 of the Hyatt-Regency, or the Regency-Hyatt Hotel – I can't remember which way round it is – in Dallas, where I arrived yesterday evening. I spent part of yesterday morning (about ten minutes) packing, and the rest sitting on the balcony in the sunshine, finishing off a bottle of champagne and taking a long, dazed leave of the Matrix, Los Angeles, the Magic. Now and then I told myself that I ought to phone people – members of the cast, and so forth – to say good-bye, but somehow couldn't bring myself to do it, lacking both the natural impulse and the will. Nathan popped in and joined me on the balcony, but for once there didn't seem much for either of us to say. We looked down at the pool together, made a few comments on the personnel around it, he drained off his glass, then left. I lingered on until a few minutes after Joe was due to arrive to take me to the airport, then pausing only to stare at the winking video – I was leaving it to the fates, or Chip Estees or Donna from the video shop to deal with – I trudged for the last time out of the apartment, down the steps, around the pool, into the lobby where one of the sunnies was waiting for me with an enormous telephone bill. Presumably he was saving it up until a few minutes after I ought to have left in the hope of witnessing a final tantrum. It took ages to sort out, of course. They have computers at the Magic that are slightly slower than most human beings but might be faster than most Californians. We were still at it when Joe arrived, bearing with him twenty-five posters which he wanted me to sign and proposed to sell in the foyer of the Matrix. This seemed to be a more imperative piece of business, as far as he was concerned, than getting me out of the Magic and to the airport in time for my plane. I signed several on the counter – Sunny sunnying interminably about with my American Express card, actually losing it for a few minutes – and the rest in the car. Joe had to drive at such speed, darting around corners into short cuts, that I have a suspicion that my signature will look like the work of a man unused to writing his name.

On the way we discussed the experience of the last six weeks. I said that my main feeling was that no production of a play, even one by me, was worth all the pain we had gone through. To my surprise, Joe agreed and went on to prognosticate yet again a poor review in the *Los Angeles Times*, saying he suspected that the critic, Dan O'Sullivan, would fail to allow himself the full experience of the play, taking it on instead as some kind of intellectual challenge. I said – I don't think it was much comfort to him – that my plays tended to get that kind of treatment, as the reviewers always seemed to think that they had in some way to square up to me, though more so in London than in the States, perhaps because my characters came from the sort of world London reviewers themselves inhabited. It was a kind of 'who-does-he-think-he-is?' syndrome. So we chatted, the usual kind of chat between a playwright and producer (except that we really do feel very comfortable with each other) all the way to the airport. When we got there I had to change my ticket. Joe had got me another of his cheapos, which this time seemed not even to be valid. He was parking the car and thus missed out on the acrimonious exchange at the counter which culminated in my handing over my American Express card. We walked to the gate together, touched each other on the arm, and then I was in the plane and off to Dallas for *Dog Days*.

I spent the journey in a kind of doze, an unpleasant doze actually. I was very tired, unable to think coherently, unable to read, without even a glass of champagne as there was no champagne about, even though I was travelling first class. I felt very bitter about this as I had been looking forward to two and a half hours cocooned in luxury, champagne in my mit. Stephen met me at the airport and drove me to this hotel. I must have asked all the correct and courteous questions, as he talked about how the rehearsals were going, but I wasn't really listening to him or to myself, I was still somewhere quite different, in fact still at the Matrix and *The Common Pursuit*. I did, however, manage to take in the Dallas skyline – enormous slabs of office buildings and hotels rising into the air in different forms, some of them seeming actually to be one-dimensional. It isn't unattractive, in fact it's rather stunning. The Regency-Hyatt or the Hyatt-Regency turned out to be one of these slabs made out of marble, glass and concrete, quite graceful and certainly one of the most modern-looking buildings I've ever seen, let alone been inside of. The lobby is like an enormous shopping arcade, with restaurants, cafés, bars, shops and fountains, the whole enclosed in glass, with an escalator to take you to the car park below and glass elevators to take you to the forty or so floors above – the antithesis of the Magic, in fact, with its small swimming pool surrounded by Astroturf, and its minute lobby.

But in spite of its atmosphere of opulent high-tech efficiency, it took me nearly half an hour at reception to check in. Apparently a convention had just arrived and the computer had either broken down or was very slow, we couldn't make out which. The clerks were infuriatingly friendly, meeting my increasing impatience with bright smiles and warm Texan drawls. I was finally given the key to a room by a pretty blonde clerk (female) and as I turned to leave, was given the key to another room by another clerk (male) – the computer having booked me in twice. As I now had two rooms to choose from, one on the twenty-seventh floor, one on the third floor, I asked the second clerk which one he recommended. He plumped for the twenty-seventh, 'because it has a view'. So up we went to the twenty-seventh. As the elevator stopped at every floor, I had lots of time to summon up a memory of that film, *The Towering Inferno*, in which a hotel much like this one blazed to the ground. I found the film deeply satisfying at the time, being almost completely on the side of the fire and regretting only that it didn't manage to make a clean sweep of all the special guest stars, but in the elevator, climbing up in staccato bursts, like a maimed helicopter – they talk of 'riding' the elevator here – with my natural terror of heights somehow intensified by the receding and diminishing shops, bars, cafés and fountains in the lobby, the people turning into brightly coloured specks, like a nasty rash, and surrounded by threateningly affable Texans, most of them tall, all of them fat, I found myself not only recalling the film with deep distaste, but also on the very edge of a scream – I think I was actually in the grip of two terrors simultaneously, agoraphobia *and* claustrophobia. I knew, before we even saw the room, that the twenty-seventh floor was not for me, especially as the view it provided was not for me either – consisting of the most ghastly combination of flyovers, spaghetti junctions and car parks that I've ever seen. Back down we went, I riding with my eyes firmly shut, to the lobby, where after a bit of a wait and altercations rising there from, I got the key to the third-floor room – 328 – from which one can actually *walk* to the lobby. The room itself is identical to the one on the twenty-seventh floor, functional and comfortable, with an enormous bed facing a television set. Except in smell. Twenty-seven had no smell. Three-two-eight smells distinctly marshy, as if fetid waters have recently passed through it. Also, being up to date in all its details, it has windows that can't be opened, and an air conditioner that howls lightly while chilling you to the marrow. Oh Magic, my Magic . . .

I ordered up a fridge, a complicated business, naturally, involving much discussion with hostesses, engineers, stewards, clerks. When it arrived, I installed in it all the champagne that I'd lugged from Los Angeles, so that it would at least be cold, then opened one of the bottles of Glenfiddich, had a few drinks, lay down on the bed, phoned Beryl, passed into a light coma. From which I was disturbed by Stephen, returning from the theatre to take me out to dinner.

I was, of course, wretchedly tired from my six weeks at the Matrix and from the airplane journey, and quite drunk from airplane wine and large, self-administered malts. The last thing I wanted was to go out to dinner. But out I went, with Stephen and his assistant, a chap called Michael Yorda, who is half German, half Cherokee Indian, and on a first, blurred viewing, very pleasant – at least he took the cheque Joe had given me to cover my Los Angeles expenses and said he would give me cash for it, which seemed to me a very pleasant thing to do. The truth is, the pitiful truth is, I don't remember much about the evening except the bad bits, like having to focus on three or four versions of Stephen and Michael Yorda, trying to force the restaurant to settle

349

down while I got food from my mouth to my stomach, then wavering to my feet, demanding to be taken back to my hotel, where, fortunately after I'd made it to my room, I was attacked by the squitters. A savage bout. Went to bed but – Dallas is three hours behind Los Angeles so my system is out of kilter – though I felt very tired, and was drunk and comatose, couldn't get to sleep. Instead I lay fretting and fuming about the Matrix and *The Common Pursuit.* Then when I did get to sleep at last, at about five in the morning, Stephen woke me with a call from the lobby five minutes later it seemed, though in reality it was a quarter to ten, time to go to the rehearsal – my first rehearsal – of *Dog Days.* I told him I simply wasn't up to it, bad night, squitters, monomania, etc. – almost the first time in my life that I've skipped a rehearsal as an author; and on this occasion I'm also meant to be the director, co-director, anyway. We arranged to meet at lunchtime, for a run-through in the afternoon.

I went back to sleep, was awoken by Joe, in an absolute frenzy because O'Sullivan, the reviewer for the *Los Angeles Times*, had come up with a review that was exactly as Joe had predicted: ponderous, dull, telling the whole story of the play, recounting every twist, however minor, of the plot, analysing every character in clotted detail. It wasn't exactly an unfavourable review – did he want me to read it? (I didn't.) It paid me compliments which it then dumpily qualified; the trouble wasn't that it was unfavourable, but that it was boring and unhelpful, the most boring and unhelpful review he'd ever read. And sedentary. A sedentary review. He was particularly incensed because O'Sullivan had gone out and bought a copy of the London version of the play, and quoted a line from that text – a line I'd hated so much that I'd cut it *before* we opened in London* – as proof that the London version was better. At which point I, who'd gone in for soothing Joe, became incensed myself. I mean, here is this chap O'Sullivan, who'd read but not seen the London production, preferring its text to the text of the Matrix production, which he'd seen but not read – and adducing as evidence a line that hadn't even turned up in the London production. Since the London production I'd worked on the script for the Long Wharf, worked on it again in London before the

* The first Methuen text, which was published to coincide with the opening of the play, could not therefore include cuts and changes made in rehearsals or previews.

Matrix production, worked on it in Los Angeles while casting the Matrix production, and worked on it during rehearsals of the Matrix production, and if I knew anything in my bones, *anything*, it was that the current version of the play is vastly superior to the Long Wharf version, which in its turn was vastly superior to the London version. And yet O'Sullivan, with a lax, no, imbecile clatter of his typewriter, negates all those weeks of work . . . And so forth. So forth. So forth. Normal sort of response on receiving news of a review. The other main review was very good for the play, less good for the production, going after Kristoffer Tabori especially, but was at least, Joe said, written with a certain liveliness, and would make people want to go and see for themselves. So back to O'Sullivan – various other critics had phoned Joe to express their indignation, Joe himself was going to phone him up and have it out with him for being so boring, what did I think about writing in a complaint myself? I said I really didn't see the point, nothing I could say would stop O'Sullivan from being O'Sullivan, he might even enjoy opening what he'd no doubt call 'a dialogue' between us, and besides, it sounded like the usual sort of review, *my* usual sort of review. He agreed, reluctantly, and then went on to admit that it probably didn't matter too much, as the show was an established success, the word of mouth was 'great', and on that note – in rather high spirits, actually – he hung up.

I lay on in bed, obliterating all thoughts of tossing lumps of O'Sullivan to the hounds for their breakfast, and didn't, finally, drag myself up, out of my room, and down to one of the smaller hotel bars until one in the afternoon, that bar and that time being where and when I'd arranged to meet Stephen. A mistake, as it turned out, as that particular bar doesn't open until four in the afternoon, which seems to me a most eccentric hour for a bar to open, being the only time in the day when I don't want a drink. So I went to the main bar, which is right out in the concourse, in the open, ordered up a glass of champagne and some smoked sausage, and kept an eye open for Stephen, already late by my reckoning. In fact, he arrived an hour later, at two o'clock, checking my indignation – 'The hours of my life I've wasted by being on time,' I quoted* – with the assurance that I'd got it wrong, he'd

* Bernard Malamud.

explained on the phone that though he'd break rehearsals at one, he had other theatre business to attend to and wouldn't get to the hotel until two. Actually I'd enjoyed my hour in the lobby, watching the men in their stetsons and boots, the women in their furs. Furs. To combat the air conditioning, I suppose, as it was hot and humid outside.

We drove down a number of ugly streets, to a rather nice section of town – the *only* nice section of town, Stephen informed me – where the theatre is. He introduced me to the stage management, the lighting designer, the set designer, etc., and to the actors, and then we crossed the street, cut through a parking lot, and went into the large rehearsal room, situated on the ground floor of a mostly unlet office block. Stephen started the run immediately. It was a bit tight and choked – the four actors were evidently nervous – but I was more pleased with the play than I'd expected. It struck me as an odd piece; written by a self (fifteen years ago) that I am no longer in touch with, but it has its own character all right. Anyway it certainly isn't the nasty little specimen I'd worked myself up into hating in London and in Los Angeles.

We broke at about five thirty, and went to an Irish bar around the corner for a drink, where we were interrupted almost immediately by the theatre critic of one of the Dallas newspapers, also called Dan, as in O'Sullivan, whose second name I didn't catch. He was youngish (i.e. younger than me) and leanish (i.e. leaner than me), saturnine, serious and seemed to be favourably disposed, claiming to believe, without serious prompting, that there was a general critical consensus to downgrade my work, a conspiracy almost, of which – he assured me – he wasn't part. I had a sudden vision of this conspiracy, literary-looking men in capes, scuffling at midnight through the streets to anonymous bars where they laid their further plots to downgrade me – it made complete and satisfying sense. He went on, though, to make it clear that he was familiar with the text of *Dog Days* – he'd read it several times – believed that it was a good play *in embryo*; but was alarmed to discover (from me) that I'd cut the Prologue and the Coda, in many ways his favourite scenes. He hoped, very much hoped, that I could transform the embryo into a mature adult, though sombrely hinting that I might have hampered myself somewhat by lopping off its head and balls.

After the interview Stanley Wilson (playing Peter), Karen Ratcliffe (playing Hilary), Stephen and I went to a nearby Italian restaurant called Lombardi's for dinner. I didn't enjoy the occasion much as I was still tired, gastricly shaky, and full of Scotches imbibed before and during my session with Dan the Critic. I got a taxi back to the hotel, slouched into the bar for a last malt, then came up here, lay down on the bed, fell asleep. I woke up half an hour ago, and began dictating this. I'm now lying full-length on the bed, still dressed, the tape recorder still to my mouth as I watch a girl undressing in a slow, unstately fashion. She's now caressing somewhat dappled breasts, which she is thrusting at me. So this is the sort of thing that goes on, on television, in the Regency-Hyatt or Hyatt-Regency in Dallas. In room 328, anyway.

Wednesday, 12 February

Slept badly. Was woken at seven by music from what I took to be the radio or television in the next room. Lay in bed cursing this extraordinary hotel, with its high-tech wizardry and its transparent bug-like elevators, that yet can't provide soundproofed rooms for their guests. Cursed also the people next door for playing their radio or television at such an hour, heaved myself out of bed, put on minimal togs, left my room with the intention of beating on the door of theirs, and discovered, by looking over the rail of the passage outside my room, that the music was coming from the lobby – there was a chap at the bar playing the piano. There he was, in a suit, playing the piano, at seven in the morning. So porno films at midnight, piano players at dawn, at the Hyatt-Regency in Dallas, Texas.

When I went down to have breakfast at ten, the pianist had gone. Presumably home to bed, for a decent morning's sleep. I sat at a table, sipping coffee, contemplating the amazing lobby, my eye tracking one of the transparent bugs sliding up the wall, the people in it looking like the bug's innards, and then tracking up past the last stopping place of the bug, right up to the ceiling, where there is a network of iron rafters, and saw – I nearly threw up – a child sitting on one of the rafters, playing with a balloon before popping it. I couldn't get myself away from him – I kept trying to fix my eyes on my coffee, but they lifted immediately to this diminutive figure, a hundred feet or so above me, on a strip of metal, playing with a balloon, popping it, scampering on his buttocks to another balloon, reaching out for it, cuddling and patting it, popping it, then off after another one – there were about twenty balloons bobbing about up there, in all. My main impulse was to bellow out warnings both to the boy and to officials down below, but deciding that this was after all Texas, and I hadn't yet had time to acquaint myself with the customs, I enquired casually of the waitress who that was up there, doing what, eh? He was the window-cleaner, she said. Clearing out the balloons that had drifted to the rafters during some festivities down here last night. And of course he wasn't a child, he was a grown man, attached to the rafters by ropes and a pulley I couldn't see from where I sat.

Stephen arrived. We went to the theatre and I began the day's rehearsals, the plan being that Stephen should absent himself until I'd had my way with the actors. We spent the day working from the top of the play. It is the first session in the theatre that I've actually enjoyed since arriving all those weeks, ago in Los Angeles. The actors were eager to get on with it, seeming vastly to prefer work to conspiracies and explosions, while I enjoyed exploring the play, finding myself obliged to direct it as if it had been written by somebody else, which in a sense it was. I couldn't *remember* any of the intentions in the lines, which therefore had to be found as if for the first time.

Stephen suggested that we all go to a show in the evening, but I couldn't face it, feeling tired and limp. I came back to the hotel, lay on the bed, and watched on their cable television one of the foulest films I've ever seen – *Deathwish III*, with Charles Bronson – about a pack of hooligans beating up people in a run-down residential neighbourhood in an unspecified American town, and then being beaten up in their turn by Charles Bronson. The director scarcely bothered to motivate the violence. I was so drugged with fatigue – I had a large Scotch in my hand, needless to say – that I kept slipping into a doze and swimming out of it, to find Bronson smashing somebody's face, or somebody smashing somebody else's face which would then be Bronson's excuse for smashing his face – these unspeakable images no doubt woven into the fabric of a nightmare. I went down, had a pleasant, solitary dinner, reading Sidney Sheldon,* came back and read some more, turned on the television set, immediately fell into a doze again. Woke at midnight, tried to sleep and couldn't, kept on reading until two or three. It must have been three, I think, when I turned my light off. Was woken again by the bloody pianist. 'Shoot the pianist' is becoming my slogan. As we all know, guns are easy to come by in Dallas.

Thursday, 13 February

Another normal and sensible working day interrupted only occasionally by the alarming behaviour of our non-Equity actress,† Cindy Vance. It's irritating enough that our rehearsals frequently have to be organised around her drama-school timetable – she either can't or won't come in when she's got a workshop, seminar, whatever – but what makes it worse is that nobody seems to have taught her any of the basic acting stuff.‡ She certainly hasn't been taught, or anyway hasn't learnt, that the simpler her performance the more effective it will be. She delivers almost every sentence either quaveringly or with a trill of laughter running through it (thus rendering the words incomprehensible) and accompanies it with gestures of the hand, twitches of the shoulders, tappings of the feet – quite hard to take, especially as she has a brazenly democratic attitude to the rehearsal process – the consequence, I suspect, of a confidently Republican upbringing. At one point she stopped in the middle of the run of a scene, to denounce my placing of her – 'I don't like this. I don't feel comfortable doing this. I'll do something else here' – leaving her accomplished and professional colleagues (Stanley Wilson and Michael Rothaar) dangling while she tried out a series of new positions that bore no relation to the purpose of the scene, or to the positions of the two other actors involved in it. I stood, dumb with disbelief, watching this, then heard myself croak out that 'We'll get on with it, shall we,

* I hope that this was a different Sidney Sheldon from the Sidney Sheldon I was reading in Los Angeles.

† The New Arts Theatre had a deal with Equity which allowed them to use one non-Equity member in every so many productions.

‡ An echo here, I now detect, of Sam Weisman.

from where we were when we stopped, all right?' and waved Stanley Wilson and Michael Rothaar back into action. I thought that that would be the end of *that*, but a mere few minutes later she introduced without warning a piece of business that was neither in the script nor had been hinted at by either of her directors.

I broke rehearsals immediately, went for a brief but brisk walk around the room, out of the door, along the corridor, back into the room and around it once again, attempting to calm myself down by telling myself that after all Cindy Vance was a mere girl (actually in her mid-twenties, and working for her MA degree – so not a mere girl, merely an unqualified actress playing a mere girl), jolly lucky to have her, important not to create an atmosphere by losing my temper, etc., and finally returned to the group to find Michael Rothaar and Stanley Wilson sitting apprehensively to one side, while Cindy Vance, bubbling with good spirits, demonstrated some aerobics, or gymnastics, anyway some sort of relaxing exercises that she said everybody – presumably she meant *me* as well – ought to take up. But there must have been something about me – perhaps simply my cheeks, swollen and empurpled with suppressed rage – that had an effect, because from then on the rehearsal proceeded without Cindy's improvising new business or rearranging the blocking. By the end of the afternoon I'd got her to play her scenes with her hands, metaphorically, in her pockets. The next time she can manage to squeeze in a rehearsal I'll try to find the equivalent to a pocket for her voice. I have an idea that she's quite talented, and will turn out to be rather good. Patience. Yes, patience. That's all that's required, really, for harmony and progress.

After rehearsals Stephen drove me back to the hotel, where we had dinner in a restaurant perched at the top of a tower. In fact, having a restaurant perched on its top seemed to be the tower's sole reason for existing. The glass-sided elevator that took us up to it was run by a young woman called Marj, according to a button on her lapel, who pointed out vertiginous views of some of Dallas's car parks. I felt pretty sick by the time we stepped into the restaurant, which turned out to have a revolving floor and glass walls, so that after a girl called Robyn ('Hi there, I'm Robyn and I'm going to look after you') had led us to a table, we could by degrees take in vertiginous views of *all* the Dallas car parks, which seemed to be the sum total of what Dallas amounts to, at ground level seen from high above. I still hadn't recovered from my elevator nausea when Stephen began to succumb to a nausea induced by the revolving floor. Not an altogether successful dinner, in fact, for all of Robyn's epigrams and *bon mots*, but we hung on there for hours, lacking the will to escape.

Back in 328 I slotted a tape of *Criss-Cross* into the video – I'd brought the tape from Los Angeles; the video had been hired for me by Karen Ratcliffe (our leading lady) and installed, in a matter of minutes, by the hotel electrician – lay down on the bed, to watch it. I woke some time after midnight to find myself fully clothed on the bed, the tape humming in the video and a sinister crackling sound coming from the screen across which dots and blobs were racing. I wound the film back, put myself slowly to bed, fearful that I was going to fall asleep while still standing, turned off the light, and promptly became wide awake. By three in the morning my mind was humming along familiar tracks of resentment, some of which led right back to childhood, and a swine of a prep-school master called Mister Brown, who used to beat me savagely and regularly for reasons so arbitrary that he eventually stopped bothering to offer them.

Friday, 14 February

A good morning's work, Stanley Wilson (our leading man) finding charm and humour in the perilous long scene at the beginning of the play. At the break I took him out to lunch – I gather that he's currently a trifle short of funds – and talked, gossiped, really, about his part. It was very pleasant and relaxed, perhaps too much so, as the wine I allowed him to consume induced a very different mood in the afternoon. No charm, very little wit, but a great deal of snarling ill-temper interspersed with bouts of melancholy. I was struggling to recall him to his pre-lunch lightness when the door burst open and a rather plain girl, short and stocky, strode in. She was wearing high-heeled shoes, tights, a little skirt, and above her waist, on her bosom and her back, two red, heart-shaped cushions. She was also carrying about thirty balloons. 'Which one of you gentlemen is Mr Rothaar?' she demanded. I pointed – as did

Stanley Wilson, Karen Ratcliffe and Cynthia Vance – at Michael. She advanced on him, tunelessly singing a song of love, even of adoration. She sang several further songs, her face pressing closer and closer to his, told him three dreadful jokes, pressed the balloons into one hand, a telegram into the other, kissed him on the cheeks, and left. Throughout it all Michael stood there with his jaw dropped – this is a literal description. His jaw fell away from the upper part of his face, and stayed down. But there was something else in his look, his posture – a kind of awkward, shy pleasure at having been remembered on Valentine's Day, I suppose.

When I popped into the theatre later I found a message from Joe, asking me to phone. I caught him at the Matrix, positively jubilant. He told me that he was thinking of coming to Dallas to see an early preview, how was I, how were the rehearsals going, and then got to his main course which was that everything was humming in Los Angeles, *The Common Pursuit* was a big hit, sold out for days ahead, and that all the reviews except the two that he'd phoned me about the last time had been 'raves'. He also said that O'Sullivan of the *Los Angeles Times* had been besieged by telephone calls and letters. When Joe himself had rung him up to remonstrate, he had replied that he was very proud of his review because 'he had conducted the analysis on a high intellectual level'. On the other hand some guy had phoned the theatre to reserve tickets – quite a few tickets – and when Joe had asked him why he had decided to bring a whole party, had said that anything that O'Sullivan wasn't passionate about was for him.

I went back to Lombardi's to have a drink with Stanley Wilson who dropped me at the hotel after initially mistaking the route, and driving off across a bridge that threatened to carry us to somewhere even more Texan than Dallas. We went at least twenty miles out of the way, and when I finally made it to 328 I discovered that the video had been disconnected – all the wires were out – and none of the lights worked. I phoned down to the chap who'd installed the video. He came up, reinstalled it, got the lights working, and informed me that as my fridge was connected to one of the light plugs, it functioned only when the light was on. For hours during the night, therefore, the fridge stopped freezing and all the food – not much food, some grapes and a strange bowl of something that looks like gelatine which the management sent up with the fridge, compliments of the house – had been rotting away. Which explains the smell. I'd been beginning to wonder whether it might be coming from my feet, as I haven't changed my shoes for something like six weeks.

Sunday, 16 February

I was woken before dawn by a nightmare to do with the safety of my family. I phoned home to make sure everyone was all right, and got Lucy, back from school for the weekend, who was extremely cheerful and I think a mite perplexed to hear a kind of grave but unexplained undertone of worry in her father's voice. When I spoke to Beryl, she asked me not to phone again at six in the morning Dallas time (midday London) as my voice was sluggish, and the pauses between my sentences were rather taxing on the attention. I coasted back to sleep and had another nightmare or dream – it was part nightmare, part dream. I was trying to get into a memorial service at the Albert Hall (Beryl had told me that there had been a memorial service that morning for Philip Larkin, and that she'd seen Harold right in the centre of the congregation on television) but the auditorium was packed. I finally managed to climb up to the top tier and was walking along it on the outside when I brushed against a boy who was standing on a kind of plank, so sending him tumbling to his death in the crowd below. I think I was identified, and also identified as being drunk, which I might or might not have been – how does one know in a dream? – got back out into the street, above all being shaken by not being shaken at having caused a death. Suddenly something zoomed into the ground – it was a kind of disc – a turret shot out, some stuff was puffed into my face and I sort of froze. My face froze and I froze. People screamed, ran to call the police. An old-fashioned bus with rocket-like exhausts arrived. I was escorted aboard, shown to a small room with a chair in it, and was told by two very pleasant men that I was being taken off to a planet, whose name I can't recall, to serve three and a half years in the penitentiary there. I began to expostulate – in a deeply depressed way, because I knew that somehow this was my proper fate – that I should surely let my family and friends know what was happening to me. They explained that this, on the whole, was not allowed. They were perfectly affable. We sped off through the air and I said, but I can't spend all my time sitting in this room on this seat. They said not to worry too much, some kind of gas would render me unconscious for most of the journey, and that anyway I would find my three and a half years of servitude in a penitentiary extremely pleasant ones as they were going to call on my particular gifts as a writer and a teacher, had I ever thought of doing the lecture circuit in America? – this is all absolutely as it went – because I could make an enormous amount of money. But they also kept on saying at interludes, as I recall, that three and a half years was a very long time, I must have done something serious. They couldn't imagine why somebody of my nature and status should be serving three and a half years in a penitentiary on this other planet. I didn't formulate it then – because of the wisdom of their manner – that it seemed to me an impertinence to impose their penal or moral code on aliens. After a while we had to stop to pick up a baby with a deformed skull, who was put down beside me. I couldn't think what its offence might have been, or was it perhaps going to this other planet's casualty ward? We also stopped for refuelling somewhere where Marlon Brando was acting in a film. We went for a walk down the street in which there were humming-birds and squirrels singing, as in one of the old Walt Disneys.

There the dream ended. But it hung around inside me, in my nervous system it almost seemed, so that all my perceptions were slightly odd, even in rehearsals, which began at midday. The scenes we worked on struck me as quite unreal, as did the actors, the props, the walls of the room. But I plugged on, plugged on, stopping scenes, starting them, running them through until everything gradually slipped back into a kind of sense, and I began to enjoy myself. By the time we broke, at seven, I felt fairly normal, anyway no longer dream-ridden, nightmare-haunted, whatever it was, and by the time I was in Lombardi's settling into the malts, I felt comfortable, tired and pretty good. Stephen came in, looking alarmed, to say he'd been waiting in his office, had I forgotten the party? I said I didn't know anything about any party, except the small one I was holding by myself, of course. He said I had to come, we had to leave now. This minute. 'Not on your Nelly,' I said. Hard day. Needed a rest. Another drink or two. Quiet dinner.

Video. Sheldon. Early night. He explained, slowly, gravely, not to say imploringly, that the party was being given by rich patrons of the theatre, that I was the guest of honour, that my absence would give enormous offence.

Off we went, to the upper and monied reaches of Dallas, where the houses were enormous, some of them the size of little castles, but the surrounding countryside was parched and drear. We arrived late, having started late and then getting lost on the way, and I didn't realise until I was through the doors and inside the massive living room, packed with dinner jackets and long gowns, that I was still in my rehearsal clothes, scruffier even than I'd been at Roddy McDowall's dinner party, and no doubt flushed both with ill-temper and the couple of drinks I'd already downed. Somebody – I suppose the host, though it could well have been a waiter – pressed into my hand the largest glass of Scotch I've ever seen. In fact it looked like a glass of lager. I swayed at the very sight of it. Around me the dinner jackets and long gowns clustered, engaging me and each other in conversation of exotic banality – I mean the subjects were banal, but the accents and vocabulary were exotic. I expect I cut a pretty disturbing figure back at them, down at heel, gruffly monosyllabic, my tankard of whisky dwindling by the second.

The only person – a middle-aged woman – with whom I managed to have what seemed to me a reasonable conversation turned out to be from New York and Jewish, running a large theatre in a nearby city, or was it state, but before we could settle properly into comparisons and gossip she was elbowed aside by a strange-looking and adhesive Pole, who'd just escaped from Gdansk. He had been a teacher of theatre there but now, by routes too complicated to fathom, was lecturing in a college in Dallas. Frankly, though I would wish no one in Gdansk who doesn't want to be there, I did wish that this particular chap hadn't made it all the way to Dallas – couldn't he have been stopped in Mesquite, a place outside Dallas that I don't like the sound of? It wasn't only that he was boring, noisy and mainly incomprehensible, but also that he covered me with his spittle, some of which got into my whisky. Which I drained off anyway. At that point Stephen reappeared, took in my swaying figure; my large, ominously empty glass; my frenzied companion; then summoned Stanley

Wilson and Karen Ratcliffe, and got us back to a restaurant near
the New Arts, *not* Lombardi's. I began to go very fast. I was both
exhausted and drunk. I have a dim memory of attempting to
describe my dream, a dimmer memory of being deposited back at
the hotel, but have no memory of what transpired in my room.
Whether I watched *Criss-Cross* or what.

Monday, 17 February

Stephen phoned me before I was properly awake to remind me
that we were expected to give a couple of talks – one at lunchtime,
one in the evening – to students at a college with a Shakespearian
pastoral name, Arcadia perhaps, outside Dallas. I said I'd have to
cancel, too busy with rehearsals, etc. He said, 'Today's Monday.
No rehearsals.' I said, ah, well in that case I'd spend the morning
in my room meditating, in the afternoon perhaps a stroll downtown, where I'd chat with the natives on such subjects as Karl
Marx and transsexuality, while poking mild fun at their accents
and clothes. He said, 'They're paying you a lot of money for these
talks. It's an hour's drive. I'll pick you up at 11.15 on the nose,'
thus allowing me a mere forty-five minutes to bath, shave, get
dressed, drink some champagne. In twelve minutes flat, spruce
and thirsty, I sped in a dignified way down to the bar, where a
splendid-looking Indian or Pakistani, polishing glasses behind the
counter, greeted me as follows: 'Hello there, how are you today,
nice to see you, sorry I can't serve you yet, bar doesn't open until
eleven.' I sped back up to my room, paced about fuming – in both
the English and the French senses – until one minute to eleven, then
sped back down to the bar, arriving just in time to see the Indian
or Pakistani strutting rapidly away from it, off across the foyer.

I sat down at a table and fixed my concentration on the only
other customer, a small, thin, middle-aged man with spectacles
wearing civvies (ie. no stetson, no high heels, just a business-like
suit, black shoes) who was working his pocket calculator as he
checked through some accounts or something. At seven minutes
past eleven by my watch the barman returned, carrying a tray of
money, which he then organised into his till, patting the different
denominations into their compartments, rolling the coins into
their troughs. When he'd finished he turned to the computer-

accounts chap, listened closely to his order, and to my amazement strutted rapidly off again, his figure dwindling into the lobby's distant reaches. Four minutes later he returned with a pot of coffee, presumably fetched from one of the many places in the lobby that serve it, placed it before the computer-and-accounts bugger, then took my order for a glass of champagne – two glasses, actually, as they're diminutive at the Hyatt. Of course he had trouble opening the bottle, trouble locating the glasses, trouble slicing the strawberries, trouble getting the strawberries to perch on the rim of the glasses, trouble remembering who it was he was going to all this trouble for, finally bringing the drinks to me at the very second that Stephen arrived to take me away from them. I swilled them down on my feet, then jogged across the lobby, down some corridors, around some corners, into a lavatory all of whose urinals were blocked except one which, I'm proud to report, was the one I chose to pee into, jogged back to Stephen waiting at the car exit, and off we went, through the sleaze of downtown Dallas, through one of its wasteland suburbs, along a freeway and on to a ribbon road and eventually off that into a car park that encircled the Arcadian-sounding college like a moat. A pleasant lady of about fifty in a white suit greeted us at the reception bunker, and guided us to a younger woman, small, dark, intense, who claimed, as she led us towards the lecture room, to be familiar with all my works.

In the car Stephen had told me that we would be addressing a smallish group, almost a seminar, of two dozen or so. Waiting in the vast hall were something like two hundred people, sitting or standing in rows around a stage on to which we were led. There were no chairs, no table, only the small, intense woman who was now holding a microphone. She spoke into it, droning and garrulous, sketching out a theological scheme in which Harold sat plumb at the top as God,* I down on his right as either Jesus Christ

* Evidence that Harold's status, if not actually divine, is unusually high in the order of things was provided shortly after my return to London. We were having dinner out *à quatre* – i.e. with wives – when we fell, late in the evening, into a dispute. A rather fierce dispute. It was still unresolved when Harold declared himself too tired to continue. I offered to call him up a taxi while calling up one for myself and made a specific point to the dispatcher of demanding my taxi immediately, the one for Mr Pinter to follow in due course, without urgency – 'in twenty minutes or so would do' – my plan, of course, being to exit with dignity, rather than to be exited from by a dignified Harold. It was hard to believe it, therefore,

or the Holy Ghost, I couldn't quite make out which, though I suspect that if I hadn't been present in the flesh I'd only have scraped in, if at all, as one of the minor prophets. She then handed me the microphone, informing me that when I'd finished speaking I was to hand it to Stephen, then informed Stephen that when he'd finished speaking he was to hand it back to me, which meant that in the unlikely event of our dialogue turning snappy, we'd end up passing it back and forth like a couple of old-style comics in a radio skit. I led off by saying here we were, Stephen and I, nice to see them all, wasn't it, Stephen? Had they any questions, be happy to answer them, wouldn't we, Stephen? The first question – 'What do you use to write with?' – wasn't the most stupid; the second – 'What about your personal life?' – wasn't the most impertinent. It went on and on, the questions so valueless that eventually we took to answering on a kind of rota system, doing ten minutes or so each, without concern as to which of us was being addressed.

After well over an hour, the small, intense lady, who thought (and almost certainly still thinks) that Harold is God, took the microphone back, introduced us all over again, then closed down the proceedings by inviting us through the microphone, and therefore publicly, to a brown-bag lunch. Stephen, whose mind can work with the speed of a cornered rat in this sort of situation, explained smoothly that, alas, we had to get back to the theatre where there was a crisis over the set, but we'd have everything sorted out before our second session in the evening. 'Now there's a little problem there,' she said. 'Our evening session won't be in here, it'll be in the large theatre, there are always two or three times the number in the evening, about, well, four or five hundred you'll be talking to, I won't be there myself, I've got other festival duties. But somebody will look after you. Thank you, thank you so much, hope we meet again some time.' So back we went, Stephen and I, around the car park, down the ribbon road, on to the freeway, through the sleaze, past the Wendy Inns and hamburger joints and wasteland to the New Arts, where we did

when his taxi arrived almost before I got back to the table, while mine turned up in not much under half an hour. It's just possible that there was nothing miraculous about this – taxis no doubt preferring to go to Holland Park than all the way up to Highgate – but at the time it felt like an intervention of some sort.

indeed look in on the set – in the earliest stage of construction and therefore virtually indecipherable – and then to Lombardi's for a leisurely meal, over which we tried to guess at the contents of a brown-bag lunch, then back I came to the hotel for a brief nap, and then back we went, Stephen and I, through the sleaze and wasteland to the freeway, on to the ribbon road, into the moat-like car park of the Arcadian college.

We were met by – actually I don't know who the hell we were met by. I don't have the slightest recollection of anything about her but a mop of ginger hair and pendulous green slacks, seen from behind as she led us off to the lecture hall – not the larger one we'd been warned about, but a much smaller one, classroom sized, in fact, where we found ourselves confronted by rather fewer than the five hundred we'd been dreading. Four hundred and ninety-three fewer, to be accurate, as there were seven people in the audience.

Tuesday, 18 February

Stephen collected me at ten o'clock, and drove me to a local radio station, where we were scheduled to give a joint interview. The station was located in the usual devastation of vacant lots and car parks, in which Stephen got lost, driving out of them on to a motorway that led back several minutes and miles further on into what looked like the section we'd driven away from. Arrived late, therefore, having parked in a patch of marsh (the result of over-night rain) and then having had to pick our way through partially cemented paths into a deserted lobby. We pressed a buzzer, banged on the counter, shouted hellos, then wandered down a corridor to a small studio, where a tall man with a grey beard was waiting for us. He beckoned us in through semi-opaque windows, then sent Stephen straight out again, saying he didn't want him to be in the interview. Stephen went back to the lobby. I asked the grey-beard if he minded my smoking. He said yes, he did mind. I said, 'Sorry, but I smoke, OK? What about you?' I asked the engineer. 'Do you mind?' 'Yes,' he said, 'I mind. But thanks for the courtesy of asking.' 'Not at all,' I said. 'Not at all.'

The engineer went behind his partition, the greybeard tested his mike, I lit up a cigarette, the interview began. It went on for twenty minutes, stopping when the engineer signalled despair to the interviewer. Apparently my voice had been so faint, so enfeebled and vitiated by life in first Los Angeles and now Dallas, that almost nothing I'd said had been audible. Start again. Greybeard took me through exactly the same questions as before, though introducing me in strikingly different terms. The first time round he'd described me as the most prominent playwright in the country (my country, I assumed he meant). The second time round he introduced me as 'one of the more prominent playwrights'. So, in the course of two virtually identical interviews, I'd succeeded in having myself substantially downgraded. We then plodded through the same set of questions, getting halfway to where we'd been the first time, when the door swung open and a man, also with a grey beard, wearing laundered blue jeans and an odd jacket – I don't remember what was odd about it, I just remember noticing that it was odd – and with a clutch of keys dangling from his belt, staggered in. Greybeard ordered him out. Alternative greybeard stood in the studio shouting defiance, then turned, and went out, around to the semi-opaque window, through which he mouthed abuse. Greybeard mouthed abuse back at him, then told me to ignore him – 'Just a guy who runs a local bookshop. He buys advertising time, thinks he owns the place. Let's get on with it, eh?' But there was nothing to get on with, as he became suddenly rather listless, couldn't be bothered to ask me any more of the questions he'd already asked me, and ushered me out of the door with the warning that when the interview was broadcast it would be followed immediately by his review of the play.

In the lobby the bookseller was sitting on a sofa, jangling his keys and muttering. Stephen was standing by the door, rueful at the waste of his time, desperate to be off. He had some trouble getting out of the parking lots, but eventually made it to Lombardi's, where we had a quick lunch. Then into the theatre for a technical run, during which I tried not to concentrate on the set, which nevertheless struck me as ghastly, having in common with the Matrix set for *The Common Pursuit* a high and dominating, i.e. actor-dwarfing, effect, but was unlike the Matrix in that it was so flimsy – almost to the point of transparency – that I felt I could have looked right through it if I peered hard enough at its drably painted walls, which shook when the actors moved. I was pretty sure that the floor shook too.

Stephen and I had a dejected dinner at Lombardi's, discussing the set and what could be done about it, the set designer and what should be done to him, and then back to the New Arts for another technical run that at least, now and then, gave me an opportunity to do some work with the actors. I got back to the hotel at about midnight, slunk into the bar for some malts, then came upstairs, lay on my bed and watched a film Karen Ratcliffe had lent me – a John Wayne/John Ford film that I'd never even heard of, let alone seen – a kind of Victorian melodrama about three desperadoes redeemed by a baby that they have rescued by mistake, and are toting across the desert. Two of them are taken out by a combination of Indians, snakes and thirst, but Big John Wayne, looking both curvaceously masculine and overpoweringly maternal, struggles on to salvation, the babe in his arms. Throughout John Ford had his chorus singing away as usual, only more so. The experience of the film was so bizarre that I couldn't help wondering whether I wasn't making it up. I mean could anyone, even John Ford at his peak, seriously make a film like *The Three Godfathers*? It made me cry a bit, of course, but I cry at almost any film that has choruses singing old Western songs. And John Wayne carrying babies. Though I prefer him carrying guns. After the film I settled into a coma.

Wednesday, 19 February

Woke up pretty late, and lay on in bed, coasting seraphically, until Beryl phoned. I told her about my life here in Dallas, she told me about hers there in London, we agreed that I'd be home by Tuesday – I'd already told someone at the theatre to book me on to a plane on Monday. I hung up, sinking into a positively voluptuous drowsiness, before getting around to confronting the real facts, the hard facts, about my immediate future, which were: that I had to shave; I had to shower; I had to wash my hair; I had to cut my fingernails, which are beginning to curve around my fingertips like talons; I had to find some way of sawing off my toenails, which are threatening to slice through my soft leather shoes (only pair). I started on my hair in the shower, then had a long, hot bath in the hope of softening my nails down to the clippable. In fact,

I was just climbing out of the bath to deal with them, when the phone rang. A woman from the New Arts publicity department to say that she had just sent a journalist over to the hotel to interview me, she would be arriving in fifteen minutes, was that all right? All right? My hair was wet, in fact I was wet all over, and yet in fifteen minutes, without having had any breakfast let alone a glass of champagne, I was going to have to cope with some woman journalist. I said no, sorry, can't, I'm drying myself, I've got to get dressed, I haven't had breakfast, put her off. OK? But of course it was too late to put her off. She was already on her way.

I went down to the bar and downed a glass or two of champagne, my main thought being that it was up to her to find me, and who in the world, apart from anybody who knew me, would think of looking in the bar at that time of the morning? She arrived within minutes, flanked by officious personnel from both the theatre and the hotel, who led her straight to my table, without even having checked out, as far as I could tell, either my room or the various coffee shops. She plonked herself opposite me, and there she stayed. She was a bit older than me, handsome, with a sort of wart on her lip – to the right side of her lip. Spectacles, over which she peered in the manner of a flirtatiously reproving school teacher. A widow. I can't remember what particular questions she asked me, though I do remember that several were highly personal. I also remember that I kept summoning more champagne for both of us while she kept independently summoning more champagne for herself, so that in no time she was drunk. Among the signals she sent out, even though drunk, was that she had no intention of paying for her own champagne, let alone mine. After two hours of champagne and impertinence, she announced that she was hungry, where would we have lunch? I said we couldn't possibly have lunch, I had to get to the theatre, which was a lie, of course. But I was desperate to get away, especially as she'd become libidinous, rapping me on the knee and stroking me on the wrist. No, no, must have lunch, she insisted. Must. I said it was impossible, out of the question, but just to confirm I'd phone the New Arts, check up on my schedule.

I lurched up to my room and hung about, smoking a cigarette, then lurched back down to the bar where she had ordered another glass of champagne, both for me and for herself. I informed her, standing swaying on my feet, that yes, I *did* have to be at the theatre, damn it! The actors were waiting for me. Oh, she said, well in that case she'd drive me. This seemed a prospect more frightening even than lunch, but short of knocking her unconscious I couldn't see how to refuse.* We went to the car exit. While we were getting her keys from the high-booted, tall-hatted bellhop – I could see the two of us, by the way, reflected in the glittering slabs of pseudo-glass that make up the wall of the hotel, teetering towards each other, swaying away from each other – she informed me that she had to find a toilet. She returned her keys to the flunkey from whom she'd just received them, reeled off into the hotel. Although she wasn't gone long she came back more drunk, as if she'd grabbed another glass on her way to and from her pee. She wavered straight to her car, and tried to get in. I explained that she needed her keys, so back we went to the flunkey, back to the car, into it. We veered and swerved and rolled drunkenly off, watched by the completely impassive flunkey. The journey, which normally takes about four minutes, was an absolute nightmare. She kept going down the wrong streets, her reflexes contradicting my instructions, right for left, straight on for turn. Also she went in for dramatic changes of speed, accelerating whenever she saw a car ahead, whether it was going the same way or coming towards us, but slowing down whenever the street was empty. She braked at traffic lights or passed through them without reference to their colour. We clocked up seven near-accidents on a journey that in real time lasted only fifteen minutes, but in true time lasted a couple of months, to be deducted in due course, no doubt, from my personal account.

When we got to the theatre I tried to behave affectionately – 'If you're ever in London,' I said, kissing her just to the side of the wart, 'Look me up in the phone book. If I'm ever in Dallas, I'll give you a ring' – as not only is she going to be writing up the interview (assuming she made it safely to her home, or her office, or the police cells) she's also, like greybeard of the radio, going to be reviewing the play. Jesus Christ! The last I saw of her she was swerving crazily away from the New Arts, up through the western

* I suppose I could have said, 'No thanks. You're too drunk to drive,' and taken a cab. But I'm a man of extremes. Either blows or acquiescence – anyway, when full of champagne.

patch of Dallas, while I, pretending to go into the theatre, was in fact swerving out of it into Lombardi's, where I ordered lunch. It was now nearly two o'clock, and I felt quite ghastly. I was stuffing some food down myself when Stephen appeared with the cheque for our lectures at the Arcadian college. Its size cheered me a bit, but not enough. We went in for a technical run, hung about for a few hours doing the lighting and sound cues, then went back to Lombardi's for a drink – it was now about six – and then back to the theatre for the first dress rehearsal.

The show was so hideously lit that the actors seemed to be pushed against the walls, featureless, virtually faceless, but possessed of enormous shadows, sometimes double shadows. At times there seemed to be nine or ten people on the stage, six of them silhouettes. The actors struggled gamely, but the great pall of darkness surrounding the sets seeped into their playing. The sets themselves continued to shake and gibber, bits of them seeming to be on the verge of falling down every time an actor moved, while the closing of a door caused the room to sway for about thirty seconds afterwards. The sound effects were equally preposterous. The unseen child, who is meant to be about six, reasonably bright and articulate, made the kind of noises appropriate to the vegetable infant in *A Day in the Death of Joe Egg*. There were a few guests, or volunteers would be the better word, present who laughed politely and applauded politely, but we all knew that they'd had a dreadful evening, though probably not as dreadful as the parties responsible, Stephen and I, had had.

Afterwards, at Lombardi's, I tried to reassure the actors that we would resolve all our little technical problems and, anyway, they were so wonderfully and deeply rooted in their parts . . . I suspect I wasn't very convincing. Anyway they didn't look convinced. Stephen drove me back to the hotel, breaking the news *en route* that I wouldn't after all be flying to London on Monday as there is no plane from Dallas to London on Mondays. So I shall have to leave on Tuesday, arriving back on Wednesday. I had a drink at the bar as usual. When I stood up I found myself tottering, but I tried to keep a certain dignity of demeanour and gesture as I strutted up to my room. Since then – it is now twenty to two, 20 February – I have dictated all this. Tomorrow we have our first preview. There's another preview on Saturday and two on Sunday. Monday, the day I can't go back to London, is the cast's official rest day so I shan't be able to do any work either. But Tuesday, home.*

Thursday, 20 February

I rolled out of bed at eleven, went downstairs, had my two glasses – he's now actually understood this, the Pakistani, that I have *two* glasses – of champagne while waiting for Stephen to arrive. I don't know if I've said this, but their champagne is actually quite good, though I still haven't got used to the strawberries perching on the glasses' rim. I invariably take the strawberry off and eat it, forget all about it, then when I begin to address myself to the drink I suddenly see the stain, a splash of red, that's left on the rim and start back in alarm, thinking it's either lipstick or blood. When Stephen came, we sat on in the bar discussing aspects of the text, the play, the production, then went and had lunch. Anxious for something light on the stomach, I ordered chicken noodle soup, which arrived in a bowl so large that it made me think of a trough. We went to the theatre, keyed up for the last dress rehearsal before the first preview, to discover that in fact there was to be no dress rehearsal as there were no costumes, somebody in wardrobe having removed them from the actors' dressing rooms to have them cleaned. There was however a photographer, who was determined to take pictures whether the actors were in costume or not.

Deciding that the whole enterprise would be a waste of time, I came back to the hotel and watched *Shenandoah.* Then went back in a cab – the temperature has suddenly plummeted, by the way, from the seventies to the thirties, so that for almost the first time during this six weeks or so in the States I find myself appropriately dressed – and at the theatre found Stephen hoovering the floor of the auditorium, one of the duties of the artistic director of a theatre in Dallas. He asked if I would like to help. I said no,† and

---

* *Wednesday* home. But even if I'd got it right, I'd have been wrong, as it turned out.

† Stephen, as he occasionally points out, is younger than me. If it hadn't been for his one or two physical impediments, he might have become a top athlete. I was in no shape to handle a Hoover. Besides, I didn't want to.

went over to Lombardi's, where Stephen – his humble tasks performed (I trust) – eventually joined me. We had the usual pre-first preview kind of conversation, airing our worries about the play, the actors, the set and the lighting. Then back to the theatre, where I briefly inspected the floor and seats for signs of dust, then upstairs to the dressing room to cuddle the four actors and to tell them that they were looking forward to it as they were desperate for an audience, etc., then down again to the auditorium, and up to Stephen's office where, over a glass of white wine so disgusting that I refuse to believe it can have been alcoholic, one of the assistants told me she'd arranged my plane ticket for Tuesday, Super Executive, provided free by British Caledonian – their way, and a splendid way, it seems to me, of helping to subsidise the theatre. Nevertheless, I rejected it, telling the girl to demand a free first-class ticket instead. British Caledonian is throwing a party in my honour on Sunday night, which I have no intention of being present at unless I go back to London in proper style and comfort on Tuesday, OK? The girl said OK, she'd pass the message on. Then we went down, took up our seats on different sides of the auditorium, watched the play.

Two vital facts emerged from the experience. One, that from our point of view, the play was fully alive, funny and touching. Two, that from the audience's point of view, it wasn't. They weren't actually hostile. They didn't rustle their programmes, whisper among themselves or jiggle their buttocks about. They sat in stillness, impassively polite, rather like members of the Royal Family sitting through yet another rain dance or fertility ritual.* They made a noise at the end – it sounded like a light rainfall which I took to be applause. Then they rose, they left, without comment. All quite unnerving. Nevertheless Stephen and I raced up to the dressing rooms, flung out our arms, drew the actors triumphantly into them, then raced over to Lombardi's and set up the drinks. When the actors joined us we celebrated away as if we'd just picked up a clutch of Tonys.† Michael Rothaar, whom

* When travelling the far reaches of what used to be the Commonwealth, I mean. We don't do rain dances or fertility rituals in England, although I suppose we might if tourists expressed a demand for them.

† The major New York theatre awards, named after Antoinette Perry – I don't know why, as I don't know who she is, or was. The Tony is in the shape of a statuette

previously I'd only seen sipping at Perrier water, proved that he's not an alcoholic by swigging down vodka after vodka. I set about concussing myself with some malts, but was still conscious when I had Stephen drive me back to the hotel. I managed to put myself to bed, and was just trekking towards sleep when Sam Weisman phoned. There was a dreadful second when I thought he was downstairs in the lobby, wanting to come up, but he was of course in Los Angeles, *The Common Pursuit* was going well. Last night the little Matrix had been packed with Hollywood celebrities, he said, *big* stars, really *big* stars. The trouble was the electrical system had cut out just as the play began, so the really big stars had had to sit in complete darkness until Joe passed some candles out. They sat for twenty minutes or so holding the candles aloft, and then departed. One or two of them had said they'd try again, some other evening.

Friday, 21 February

For the second night running, one couldn't see the actors' faces properly and therefore couldn't follow their emotions, although, on the other hand, who really gives a fuck? The audience probably only vaguely noticed that they couldn't quite see the actors' faces and therefore only vaguely noticed that they weren't following the emotional line of the play, which they probably wouldn't have liked anyway as in one sense it's about a man being unmanned by women, a prospect not truly, I suspect, in the Texan scheme of things. Nevertheless I have never felt such loathing for a lighting man, who is probably very sweet in his personal life. The fact remains that he's buggering up the play. However little that matters to anyone else, it matters to me. After all I have to keep sitting through it.

Saturday, 22 February

Woke up with the shivers, utterly miserable, but was cheered by a telephone call from James Hammerstein, who read out a review that

conferred each year on the most successful musical, play, actor, etc., on Broadway. Its only value to the straight theatre is that it ensures that at least one play gets to Broadway each year, so that the award can be conferred.

has appeared in today's *New York Times* of my book, *An Unnatural Pursuit*. A warm, indeed glow-making review, and he read it out in a voice, at once leisurely and dramatic, which made it all the more enjoyable, though he faltered when I asked him to describe the photograph of myself which appears with it. In fact I was sure I heard him laughing slightly, which leads me to believe that once again I come across as a plump and degenerate lesbian. Morally galvanised but still physically enfeebled, I went down to a late breakfast, for which I foolishly chose catfish in batter (which arrived with a mountain of French fries) and a few glasses of wine, having even more foolishly, I must admit, gone through a few glasses of champagne previously by way of aperitif. Then, my stomach heaving, got a cab to the theatre, where Stephen was attending to the sound and the lighting, and manoeuvring the actors around, perhaps a fraction more rapidly than I cared for – we always come to this directorial problem with my plays. Speeding the actors up won't speed the play up, in fact slows it down, because the audience stops listening even sooner than when the actors move only when there is a reason for doing so. But I left him to it, knowing that in the end the old moves would somehow reinsert themselves.

Went to Lombardi's for a glass of white wine or two, and then sauntered unsteadily back to do my share of the rehearsing, i.e. unblocking and re-blocking Stephen's blocking, Stephen viewing me at it with sardonic equanimity. Later, at Lombardi's, he was full of worry about his future, both at Dallas and generally. We discussed his life, moved on to discuss the meaning of life, then the meaninglessness of life, then went back to watch the performance.

It was a pretty full house and a responsive one – in fact the evening went quite well. The lighting was vastly better but the sound effects still dreadful, though in a quite different way – the offstage noises of children playing in the garden at the top of the first scene, which previously had been almost inaudible, now made them sound like a gang of football hooligans on the rampage. Furthermore their voices, instead of just coming up briefly, then going down and then returning even more briefly and then going down, stayed there, shouting and hollering right through the onstage actors' lines, drowning them out. The music we'd chosen to cover the scene changes, 'And did those feet', came in and out in the most eccentric way, so that sometimes we got the thunder of an organ without voices and sometimes the voices but no organ; sometimes we didn't get anything at all because the chap in the sound box had forgotten to put the record on. And so it goes and so it goes . . .

Anyway, after the show, I scurried across to Lombardi's and booked a table, then went backstage with Stephen, collected the cast and took them to dinner. We sat there, drinking, eating, gossiping, joking, reminiscing about old films and plays and rehearsal experiences, etc. – one of those delightful evenings that come so frequently in the theatre.

Sunday, 23 February

Slept late, finally being pounded out of bed by the lobby piano at about eleven. I sat at the bar sipping champagne and observing – not for the first time – the waiters' obsession with ashtrays. The moment you tap a bit of ash into it, they (actually only one of them) whisk it away and replace it with a fresh one. You thus find yourself getting through about five ashtrays in the course of a single cigarette. I find this exceptionally irritating as it (a) messes up a conversation or a train of thought or even a state of comfortable vacancy, and (b) messes up one's relationship – ideally so uncomplicated that one doesn't notice it – with one's cigarette. At times I feel like demanding the ash back, insisting that it belongs to me personally, they have no right to remove it.

I decided over my third, or possibly fourth glass, that I wouldn't go to the matinee, having had enough of plays of mine at the moment, so I stayed on and had brunch in the hotel – on Sundays they lay out tables and counters of cold crab, cold prawns, cold lobster, lumps of chicken, and quite a lot of food that I couldn't identify. I padded about piling my platter high with a visually stunning assortment of what turned out to be nearly tasteless delicacies, then sat down to read an interview I'd given in one of the local papers. There I was, portly and lesbian, half smirking and half glaring out. The interview was friendly enough but quite pointless because – as the interviewer explained – since I'd refused to discuss the 'meaning' of my plays, or to consider them in any aspect whatsoever, there was nothing much for either of us to say.

At about two thirty I thought I'd better look in on the matinee after all, or at least what would be left of it by the time I walked to the theatre. I passed down the escalator and along an extra-ordinary underground corridor, the walls of which were lined with photographs of ex-Presidents of the United States. Both Roosevelts were there, I think; Truman, Eisenhower, Johnson, Reagan (no satire intended, I'm sure, in placing him among the dead) but no photograph that I could see of Kennedy, who'd been gunned down not a mile from where I was walking. Anyway, along this peculiar, carpeted corridor, around the corner of Union Station, into the boulevard on which the hotel is situated – the least boulevard-like boulevard in the world, I imagine, being really a sort of freeway, with car parks and grandiose but mostly empty buildings on either side. Not a bar, not a café, not a shop and scarcely a human being in evidence. Very few sounds, too, and those in the distance, mainly sirens denoting mishap and death. I got to the New Arts just as the audience was coming out at the interval. I sat on a bench opposite, surveying them as they stood chatting, rather angrily it seemed to me, about the play, though it might have been about their parents or their children or the lapses of God.

The second act was poor, full of unnecessary gaps – well, not quite gaps so much as extended pauses that achieved gap-like effects. This didn't depress me too much – after all, a Sunday matinee, the temperature up again, the theatre hot, the actors exhausted from their week – but I made a few notes, especially about Stanley Wilson, who had lost his edge and seemed to be in a dallying mood. After the show I sent a message around to his dressing room, asking him to meet me in the only restaurant in the vicinity – Chinese, naturally – that was open on a Sunday afternoon. I crossed to the restaurant, and was surprised to find myself half accompanied by a short, tubby man with a red beard,* wearing peculiarly patterned, tartan trousers and a looping leather jacket, the pockets of which looked as if they were bulging with marbles. He stopped on the pavement when I entered the restaurant, and stood swaying, staring after me. I sat down and

* Sam Weisman has a red beard. So did the man with the knife who followed me in Los Angeles.

peered through the window, keeping a lookout for Stanley Wilson but also watching tartan-trousers, who was continuing to watch me, amiably, indecisively, rather in the manner of a well-disposed dog who hasn't yet made up its mind to pick you up. When Stanley appeared, he followed him into the restaurant – large and virtually empty – and when Stanley sat down opposite me, sat down himself, at the next table. We had drinks, he had drinks and a bowl of food, and all the way through our note session he kept his good-natured intoxicated attention on us.

We left him there, Stanley going back to the theatre, I back to the hotel. Dozed for a while, then went down to the bar for a single malt. I was determined to be sober for the evening, as the show was to be preceded by the big-deal, British-Caledonian-sponsored reception. So I sat watching the bugs of elevators sliding up and down the walls, and the men in their stetsons and high-heeled boots and the women in their fur coats throwing coins into the bizarre concoction of a fountain that isn't a fountain but a great inverted bowl with something sliding up and down its side that looks like water but isn't. In fact the whole thing is a *trompe l'oeil* perversion of a wishing well. There's no gap for the thrown coins to fall through so they simply bounce off the top of the bowl and tumble down into the basin, visible but unretrievable.

I stayed on and on, entranced by so much opulent triviality, until I suddenly realised that it was past seven and that Stephen, who was going to collect me and take me to the reception, still hadn't appeared. I dashed out in a panic, got the flunkey to whistle over a cab from the long line that waits, like a kind of dole queue, outside the hotel, and got to the theatre a quarter of an hour late. The lobby was jammed with the usual tuxes and long gowns. I had to push my way through them, quite brutally really, swinging my bag from my shoulder as a kind of flail, to get into the office. There I put on my coat, fished my tie out of my bag* and put it on, then slid back out into the lobby, where I bumped

---

* I began the practice of keeping a tie in my bag when I was made a member of the MCC (Marylebone Cricket Club). For reasons that make no sense to any intelligent human being, you have to wear a jacket and tie to get into the pavilion. I always try to wear a dark blue tie against a dark blue shirt in the hope, regularly satisfied, of luring one of the noisy, ill-mannered and officious stewards into the kind of error for which even they have to apologise.

directly into Stephen, forcing his way through the packs of Texans towards the door with the intention – or so he claimed – of collecting me from the hotel. He hadn't forgotten me, just forgotten the time, he said, as he took me around and introduced me all over the place. I was smiling and nodding and showing what's left of my teeth in merry grins, when I spotted old tartan-trousers, pulling at his red beard with one hand, his other loosely encompassing a glass of champagne, swaying uncomprehendingly on the other side of the lobby, the only person with quite a lot of space around him. He'd got in, Stephen told me, because anyone who was prepared to spend twenty-five dollars on a ticket to the play could get in. In a fit of something or other – perhaps merely spite – I went over and introduced myself to him, then introduced him to every tux or gown whose name I could remember. He didn't speak a word, just stood there swaying and burping and nodding, possibly on the point of throwing up. The tuxes and gowns dealt with him perfectly politely – perhaps they took him for a relation of mine, and certainly, sartorially and possibly in other respects too, we might have seemed to have more in common with each other than with anyone else in the lobby. What I couldn't understand, what I still don't understand, is why he should have wanted to come. Surely he could find something better to do, even on a Sunday afternoon in Dallas, than to attend a performance of *Dog Days*? The last I saw of him he was gaping dangerously at a couple of tuxes and some fur coats, all of whom had the sense to stand well away from him.

We were summoned into the theatre inexplicably early – at about a quarter to eight. I took up my usual seat at the back of the stalls, and prepared to take notes. I was slightly depressed, actually, as I'd become quite fond, through all the work I'd put in, I suppose, of this odd, flawed little play, and felt that I still hadn't done right by it. I don't mean in the production – though I'd made some major mistakes there too, not least in the use of 'And did those feet' as the musical theme, which, in the only version available in Dallas, provided a downward pulsing effect, like an ill-tempered dirge, rather than the rousingly ironic commentary I'd intended* – but in the text. Above all, it was in the text that I

* We eventually substituted some jolly, but non-committal (in terms of the play) Mozart.

hadn't really pulled *Dog Days* off. I was brooding away like this, waiting for the lights to go down, the curtain to go up, when the curtain suddenly went up, without the lights going down. A young civic dignitary, possibly the mayor, wearing a tux of course but with a white silk scarf wrapped carelessly about his throat, stepped forward and gestured towards the wings, out of which stepped a middle-aged chap, the chap who runs British Caledonian in Dallas, as it turned out, who came in for a little peroration of thanks from the youthful mayoral figure for his contribution to the evening – the contribution being, as far as I could make out, to provide ticket-holders with free champagne, and to fly me free first class back to London – in other words, an extremely important contribution, especially the back-to-London part. The chap who runs British Caledonian in Dallas then made one of those speeches that sponsors make about his pride and pleasure in being behind the evening that we were about to see although he'd probably have been better advised to wait until he'd seen the evening before boasting about his responsibility for it.

When he'd finished somebody else was called out of the audience to be awarded accolades for something or other, I really wasn't paying much attention, wishing really that we could get on with the show, but when *he* left the stage the mayor launched into a five-minute tribute to yet another chap – myself, as it happened. He finished by gesturing me up to a spot beside him. I felt quite easy about all this, the whole affair seeming quite unreal, dreamlike. So down the aisle I coasted, floated down the aisle, up on to the stage, took up my place beside him with a shy little stumble of feet, and stood through a few more minutes of acclaim which concluded with my being made an Honorary Citizen of Dallas, and being presented with a plaque that apparently entitled me to drive anywhere I like in Dallas without being impeded by the police, and to park anywhere I like without being given a ticket – though presumably not in the grounds or garages of the sort of people sitting there watching me receive it. In fact the plaque wasn't something I'd care to hold out for close inspection, even to the Dallas police, as it looked like an enormous wallet made out of balsa wood and plastic, and covered with varnish, though it's true it had attached to it a sheet of official paper, with some writing and quite a few signatures on it. I accepted it with what

I hoped was an overwhelmed smile, made an under-energised joke about my financial condition already announced by my appearance – but how delighted I was to be received into the very bosom of Dallas (its car parks), what a pleasure it had been to work with Stephen at the New Arts, scooted back off the stage up to my seat, then as soon as the play began, scooted along to the lavatory for a pee, then scooted back, and settled down to the first act.

It was all right. I tried to avoid being irritated by the text by concentrating on being irritated by the sets and particularly the interminable scene changes. The performances were in good nick, especially Karen Ratcliffe's. I really adore her acting, not only her innate delicacy, but what she does physically. I often watch her feet because they act out her emotions almost independently – doing little jumps or turning inwards or pointing towards the character that's talking to her even when her body is turned away – I find her feet very eloquent, very charming.

At the interval I went up and joined Stephen in his office. We congratulated ourselves on the way the act had gone, although worrying a bit that the laughter was coming where it had never come in the previous productions in Oxford and Vienna, nor in the other previews in Dallas. But it was a relief, I suppose, that the befurred and tuxedoed gathering had managed to find amusement, even if it was theirs rather than ours – though I now remember that a couple had left halfway through, the young woman leaning heavily on what I assumed was her husband's arm, either courteously pretending serious illness, or seriously ill.

The second act would have been all right, too, if it hadn't been marred by the interminable set change back from seedy bedsitter to middle-class Muswell Hill – even longer than the other-way-round change in the first act. I pondered this as I made my way back to the lobby, where I found myself barricaded away from the office by the audience, who wanted to shake hands and drawl out Texan compliments to this newly elected honorary citizen of a city which, frankly, mainly looks as if it's been nuked. What struck me yet again was their dress, or rather the contradiction between their opulent dress and their semi-educated speech, unlike the characters in the play, who are exactly the opposite, dressing shabbily and speaking literately – yes, this is the nub of it, the audience dressed to the nines and speaking down there in the twos, or even the ones, while the play is dressed up verbally to the nines, but is right down in the ones, or even the minuses, in dress.

We – Stephen, the cast and myself – eventually made it across the road to the only restaurant open in the neighbourhood on Sunday nights, to find that they stopped serving food at nine thirty – an excellent policy when directly opposite a theatre that doesn't come down until ten. The mayoral figure was there, at the bar, with an enormous cigar added to the white silk scarf and the tux. He looked, with a lock of dark hair straying over his forehead, like yet another version of the Great Gatsby. He was, in fact, searching for me, having neglected to present me with a plastic key set in a block of plastic wood that completed my honorary citizen's kit. More to the point, as the bar was extremely crowded, he furnished us all with drinks, seeming to have the kind of relationship with the barman that one would like to have with barmen all over the world. In the meantime Stephen had found out about a wine bar some way off, to which we repaired after I had ceremonially thanked the mayoral figure for having presented me with the Freedom of the City. The wine bar was pleasant, the food OK as far as I remember it, and there went another evening.

Monday, 24 February

A rather strange woman, semi-oriental, possibly Filipino, squat, ill-tempered, speaking almost no English, cleans my room. She completely ignores the 'Do not disturb' sign and glowers indignantly when I explain, with smiles and deferential gestures, that I am actually in my room, intend to remain in it for a while, and would she come back later? She stumps off, and when she comes back after I've gone, evidently turns on the radio, then forgets to turn it off, so that when I return at one or two in the morning, already sufficiently unfocused, I open the door either on voices gravely talking or to an explosion of music. It must be she that's fiddled with this recorder, turning the tape over in the hope of finding something interesting, and leaving it there. The result is that I've recorded over myself – about five minutes wiped, and the five minutes I wiped it with now in the wrong context. Thanks, Filipino lady.

But this has turned out to be an extraordinary day, the break day on which the actors can't be called on to rehearse and no plane flies out of Dallas to London. My plan was to spend it doing things that normal people sometimes do – as for example a film in the evening, in the company of Stanley Wilson, Karen Ratcliffe and anyone else – tartan-trousers, for instance – who wanted to tag along. But first I had lunch with Stephen, to discuss various notes I wanted to give the cast before leaving on the plane tomorrow. Halfway through lunch I suddenly found myself saying, 'I wish to Christ, I wish to Christ, that I'd set this play in one room. The set changes are destroying the production, they're all wrong for the rhythm of the play – I just wish I'd found some way of doing it.' Stephen said, 'I wish you had, I can't stand the set changes either.' From that moment everything turned on its axis. It suddenly became a positive, a powerful ambition in me to rework the play into one set – I suddenly realised I'd been edging unconsciously towards an attempt to do so ever since I'd seen the first run. I began at once, on the paper table-covering at Lombardi's, where they also thoughtfully provide crayons – for precisely such emergencies, I assume – scribbling out new lines of dialogue, adjusting old ones, changing the end of scenes, the whole operation taking three hours, including a short break for a telephone call home, in which I told Beryl that under the circumstances I'd better come back on Thursday, giving myself a necessary two days to put in the changes with the actors and see how they worked – news that she received with generous equanimity, relieved that at least I'd be in time for the opera on Friday, for which she'd got a couple of very expensive tickets.

When I got back to the table and the crayons, Stephen, who'd been guarding them, went off to rearrange my flight, joining me half an hour later with the news that there was no plane out on Thursday either – no plane on Monday, which had turned out to be a blessing in that it had led to the decision to rework the play; no plane on Thursday, which was a curse – another example of life's quite superfluous swings-and-roundabouts policy, I suppose. And so back to the telephone, and a slightly less fluent conversation with Beryl about how I'd have to miss the opera after all, damn British Caledonian, what was the point of free tickets if the plane didn't actually go when you wanted it to, sort of stuff; and then back to the table, very depressed, because having to stay on and on is very depressing, especially when one adds to that having to give explanations to loved ones about having to stay on and on. The only nice thing was that somebody in the office told me there'd been a nationwide rave for the Matrix *Common Pursuit* on the radio, she'd picked it up over breakfast – ah well, a further, but altogether more laudable, example of swings and roundabouts, especially as there was a double ration of the roundabouts in the form of a phone call from Joe Stern, confirming marvellous feedback, floods of favourable reviews, so forth. But I can hardly recall the days of Joe Stern and Sam Weisman, not even the ugliest days of rehearsal. One good thing about the theatre. It keeps you in the here and now. Which seems to suit my temperament.

The actors, whose break day this is, nevertheless came over to Lombardi's, where I took them through the changes, pointing to this section and that section of the paper table-covering. Then we made plans for tomorrow's rehearsals. I love it about actors that they too seem to live in the here and now. Mine.

Tuesday, 25 February

Got up about ten, went downstairs to the bar at about twelve, had the usual two glasses, then went to the theatre and rehearsed the alterations with the actors. The physical changes involved very little for the stage management to come to terms with, being almost entirely a matter of elimination – above all, the elimination of the lumbering set changes. But, as always, even minor physical modifications seemed to require endless adjustments of lights, sound, props. After standing impatiently about for an hour or so, I walked back to the hotel, lay down for a while, then went down to the bar, where I kept an eye on this exceedingly tall, let's say about seven foot two, black chap with a relaxed, easy, almost sloppy manner, strolling around the lobby in a tracksuit, being accosted first of all by an elderly Texan in a trim suit, with a white moustache, who seemed to want his autograph – anyway, he held out a little book, which the black chap signed – and then by a little gaggle of women, giggling, who seemed to want to press the flesh, taking his hand, holding it, passing it about amongst themselves.

And still he strolled, the only creature I've ever seen in the lobby of the Regency-Hyatt or Hyatt-Regency who has been in proper proportion to it. I got up, and for no reason I could understand, began to follow him about, just plodding along behind him, watching as various other people came up, spoke shyly to him, went away from him waving and shouting good lucks, until we got to the elevator section, where there were two middle-aged women and the elderly Texan with the white moustache who'd already got his autograph. The two women asked for his auto- graph just as the elevator arrived. They all got in, the elderly Texan now looking angry, angry and puzzled, as the black guy bent over the ladies. I stood watching from the lobby as the bug climbed up the wall, I could see them through the glass, and the thought occurred to me for the first time – I'd been a bit slow because it's a sport that's never interested me – that the black guy was prob- ably a basketball player, a famous basketball player, which was why, of course, they all wanted his autograph. What I couldn't understand, though, was why the white-moustached Texan should be angry with the two women collecting his autograph, having collected one for himself. Unless, of course, the black guy wasn't a famous basketball player, but a famous stud.

I went back to the bar for another drink, Stephen arrived, we went to the theatre, and I was pleased to see that the play, at least as a play, worked better than before, flowing much more smoothly without the set changes, and was correspondingly better received by the audience, who were, I think, composed mainly of a con- tingent from Delta Airlines – they, like British Caledonian, have their evening too, but without offering up either free champagne or free plane tickets or the Freedom of the City. But if the play had improved, the performances had deteriorated. Karen Ratcliffe had lost her bite and authority, especially in the last scene, when she boots – according to the script – her husband back out on to the pavement. She kept giving him tender, loving glances against the run of the text and the production, as if playing a scene of a different spirit in a quite different sort of play. And Stanley Wilson, as the booted-out husband, responded in kind, turning lines we'd rehearsed as acid and dignified into pleas for forgiveness in a shared bed. All it needed to be completely disgusting was violin music. So roundabouts and swings again, though again I felt I was up – preferring an improved play to improved or even accurate performances. I whisked the actors off to Lombardi's, manoeuvred the seating to be next to Karen, discussed the scene with her; manoeuvred Stanley Wilson into driving me back to the hotel, discussed the scene with him over a drink at the bar, came upstairs where I am now dictating this.

Wednesday, 26 February

Woke feeling terrible – tired, hungover and headachy. Took me hours to get up, but I finally managed to get down to the bar, picking up the two Dallas newspapers on the way, to read about the overthrow of President Marcos of the Philippines, then idly turning the pages of one of the newspapers was suddenly confronted by a large Technicolored photograph of myself, under which there's a caption reading 'Playwright Simon Gray has a passion for cinema, especially American movies, but loathes rude movie audiences.' In the article itself he reports on my rumpled appearance, grey hair, pouched eyes and trembling hands, then describes at length my attempts to secure a decent glass of white wine at the restaurant where we met – presenting me, in other words, as both an alcoholic and a snob. By the time I'd finished reading this my hangover had intensified, my head was pounding with a kind of soft, genial dreadfulness. It was pounding softly, pounding genially, killing me. I went up to one of the shops in the lobby and bought a tin of aspirins, which I was unable to open. There was a little message on the lid, that I had to squint at to read, ordering me to press my thumb on the two red spots, but no matter how I squeezed my thumbs down on the two red spots, the lid didn't snap up. In fact, nothing happened at all. It seems to me characteristic of modern life that when you have a hangover and a headache and therefore need to buy an aspirin, you should be provided with aspirins you probably couldn't get at when you are at your most sober and supple-thumbed. I finally gave the tin back to the girl who'd sold it to me, pointing out the problem in strong but controlled terms. She looked puzzled, tried to open it herself, couldn't, passed the tin on to the responsible-looking chap in charge of the shop, who struggled for a while with his thumbs, then with an exclamation whipped off a completely invisible wrapping, and proceeded to thump away until the lid flew up. I got some water from the bar, dropped some aspirins down my throat, and got a taxi to Lombardi's, where I had two plates of carpaccio, a marinated, uncooked beef, served with grated parmesan and a vinaigrette dressing – they offered me a third, on the house, but I wasn't up to it, and anyway had to get across to the theatre, where the cast was waiting.

We rehearsed for three hours, and then Stephen and I went through all the physical changes with the stage management, and then I came back here, feeling distinctly ropy but at least without the headache, and tried to dictate the above. Something had gone seriously wrong with my tape recorder – as I talked into it, it grew first warm, then hot, until finally, with smoke leaking out of its sides, it began to burn my hand. I went down to the shop where I'd bought the aspirins, bought some new batteries, put them in, started again. The same thing happened, although more quickly this time. It was really rather alarming, having the machine with which and into which I've been so intimate over the last seven weeks, smouldering violently away in the palm of my hand. I suppose its little heart had just given out, worn down by all the worry and anger I've poured into it. Or it was a cheapo to begin with, with a built-in failure system. Either way, there was only one place for it, the wastepaper basket. I phoned up Michael Rothaar, from an instinct that he was a machine-type chap, and got him to agree to lend me one of his tape recorders, then went in for the evening show, the (for me) penultimate performance, and the last preview.

Everything was going swimmingly along – I wasn't even paying much attention, really – until the reorganised scene between Peter (Stanley Wilson) and the girl he picks up (Cindy Vance). In the new version, in order to eliminate the protracted set change, it takes place in Peter's Muswell Hill sitting room, rather than in a borrowed bedsitter. He fails to fuck the girl, denounces her for his failure, shows her out, then picks up the bags he's already packed, glances around the room in which he's spent so much of his young husbandhood and his fatherhood, leaves for pastures new. That's what I wrote down on the paper tablecloth at Lombardi's, and that's what they did last night. Tonight, the lights went down abruptly before he'd shown the girl the door, let alone before he'd had a chance to pick up the bags, bid farewell to the room. Stanley and Cynthia had to blunder off the stage in the dark, leaving the bags on stage. The lights came up almost at once, seeming positively to glow over the two unremoved bags as Peter's wife and Peter's brother discussed the implications of Peter's departure, a dramatic event which the onstage bags emphatically contradicted. Karen Ratcliffe and Michael Rothaar kept darting their eyes towards them, and then imploringly towards the spot in the stalls where they knew Stephen and I always sat. There was of course absolutely nothing either of us could do except what we did do, which was to hurry down into the lobby and have a sullen row, one of the few we've ever had, in which I denounced the stage management of his theatre for their incompetence, and he defended them on the grounds that they were doing their best in exacting circumstances, bound to be mistakes when changes had been made so rapidly, little time to practise them, so forth. We stopped when we'd exhausted ourselves, went to Lombardi's, had a mutually pacifying drink, went back to the theatre, watched what there was left of the play to watch, both of us dejected, and therefore both of us surprised by the warmish response from the audience, anyway a response which suggested that they'd noticed nothing amiss, certainly not an unremoved suitcase, stage left.

After the show Stephen and I hustled back to Lombardi's, waited over drinks for the cast, who joined us for further drinks and a meal, then I came back here, dictated this into a tape recorder furnished by Michael Rothaar, a sturdy, simply func-tioning thing (the tape recorder, not Michael Rothaar) and am now contemplating going down to the bar . . . The temperature today was up in the nineties, by the way. The nineties. In February. And tomorrow is the first night of *Dog Days*. An event I'd intended to miss by some days or so. I really don't want another first night so soon after the last first night, especially when that one was in Los Angeles, at the Matrix, and happened twice.

Friday, 28 February

The morning after the first night before. And yesterday was very conventional, almost like a little model of a first-night day. After spending a couple of hours, woozy hours, watching the glass bugs slide up and down the walls, attempting to overhear various Texan conversations – there was a Manure Marketing Convention in – I tore myself away from the lobby and over to the theatre, rehearsed all the scenes which seemed to me to have been off the previous night, which meant almost all of them actually, had some confidential words with Stanley about the actor's husk he adopts from time to time, had coffee with him and with Stephen at Lombardi's, came back to the hotel, lay down for a while, went back to Lombardi's, where I had a large Scotch, and waited for Stephen. When he arrived we both realised we hadn't got any good luck cards to give the actors, so we set forth in Stephen's car. We drove for about ten minutes in the general direction of a card shop which he believed might still be open, then gave up, came back to Lombardi's, had another drink, then over to the theatre for the opening.

It went OK, I thought – a responsive audience causing the only real confusion, in that they laughed more than previous audiences, louder and longer. The actors didn't quite cope with this, so that some of the better lines were buried under laughs trailing over from a previous line and weren't resurrected by the usual professional means, i.e. repeating them. There was also a dreadful moment when Stanley dried, but then the youngest member of the cast, Cynthia Vance, drama student, came to his rescue by feeding him the information he needed in the form of a question, thus getting him going again. But the curtain came down to decent – no, positively generous – applause. Afterwards the company went on to a bar-restaurant called the Green Leaf, which likes to honour the New Arts after every first night, and did so with us by issuing us each, as we went through the door, with a ticket that entitled us to one free drink each. The bar was badly lit, full of people who'd obviously never needed a free drink in their lives. I drained off my own as I roamed briefly through the shadows in search of Truth, Beauty or even a recognisable face, then got Stephen to drive me to the hotel, came up here to 328, dictated this.

I packed my bag, got the video into its case – obviously the wrong way around, from its distorted shape – and went down to the bar. There I sat, smoking and sipping champagne, while I watched for the last time the bugs sliding up and down the walls; the men in stetsons and the women in furs tossing coins and

dollars into the bogus fountain; the platoons of fat women wad-
dling to their conference rooms and banqueting halls; the children
among the rafters, riding on balloons; the cops crouching behind
the plastic ferns, guns ablaze; John Wayne stumbling towards the
down escalator, his arms full of babies; a chorus of holy ghosts,
led by Harold, offering up the yellow rose of Texas; Stephen
Hollis, standing above me, suggesting it was time to check out.

At the counter I set one of the bell-hops, a grizzled veteran of
some twenty summers, an initiative test by sending him up to 328
for my bags. He passed triumphantly, returning with them in
twenty minutes rather than the mere two or three that less experienced mortals would have required – though I admit that his
coming down twice, once to check on the number of the room, the
second time to collect the key without which, he discovered, he
couldn't get in, might have struck a less ardent fan as a form of
cheating. Then into Stephen's car, and off – with a majestic salute
to the high-booted, tall-hatted flunkey who keeps the doors of the
Hyatt-Regency or the Regency-Hyatt – to Lombardi's, for a last
lunch with the cast. We sat at a round table by the window, looking out at the only bearable part of Dallas, talking over our memories of rehearsals, hoping we'd all meet again, work together
again, possibly do *Dog Days* in New York one day – relaxed and
nostalgic, ending the experience in the way in which these experiences should always end. There was one stomach-lurching moment
when I thought I saw the small, arm-swinging, red-bearded figure
of Sam Weisman crossing purposefully towards us, about to appear
at the door as he used to appear at the door of Joe Allen's during
the preview nights in Los Angeles. But it wasn't Sam Weisman,
of course, and whoever it was went on past the restaurant, down
the pavement, in the sunlight.

There was a spot of trouble at the airport, when an exceptionally handsome, broad-smiling chap at the check-in tried to fob me
off with a Super Executive. I explained his error in my most civilised manner, and within minutes I had my first-class ticket in my
hand, was through the screening, and was just settling down to
a last glass of champagne when I was called back to check-in over
the public address system, and informed by the magnificent Texan
that he'd made a mistake, first class was full. I said I was one of the
people who made it so, had in fact been guaranteed a first-class

aisle smoker by British Caledonian's most senior executive at the ceremony at which I'd been made an Honorary Citizen, recommended he phone said Senior Executive before we found ourselves on the way to an international incident, etc. I stood there resolutely, possibly tramp-like in appearance but indisputably aristocratic – Welshly aristocratic – in manner, managing to keep my bags in the way of other riff-raff struggling to check in until his nerve broke. So that was that. I got on to the plane, settled into my aisle smoker, noting sorrowfully as I did so that the magnificent Texan's claim that first class was full was a lie. It was half full. Or half empty, depending on how you choose to look at it. The seat next to mine was unoccupied, so I had, as these things go, an extremely comfortable flight, reading most of the recent Orson Welles biography, and didn't mind too much that we were in the air for an hour longer than scheduled because Gatwick was frozen over. From Gatwick to Victoria by train, and then across London by taxi, taking in the sights that at various times over the last two months I'd thought I might never see again, all of them covered in snow, which made them for some reason all the more endearing, arriving home just as Beryl was stepping out of the door, on her way to a George Eliot Fellowship meeting. Talked for a while to Hazel, who has become slightly less incontinent, I gather, but sometimes stands for minutes at a time, facing no particular direction, from which I assume that she is now almost blind. Looking at her when she does this makes my heart pinch, but I feel OK, that she'll go on for ever, when she is under my desk (which she is now) stirring every so often.

First a Body Count, Then
On with the Show!

[1]

I began writing again almost as soon as I got home, working in succession through three film scripts that I'd left in varying states of suspension.* By the time I got to the third I'd managed to give up smoking, taking up nicotine chewing gum at last, which made early script conferences with the director something of an ordeal. A thoughtful, imaginative Irishman who chooses his words with fastidious care, he is also an infuriatingly eccentric smoker – treating his cigarettes as finger aids to concentration, sort of worry beads, really. He would take one out of a packet as he searched for a phrase, fondle it, put it back, stare at the packet, revolve it in his hand, take the cigarette out again, put the packet on the table, massage the cigarette, place it between his lips, extract it, revolve it, before lighting up slowly and ceremonially, as if treating himself to an enormous cigar at the end of a banquet. The whole ritual, *sadistic* ritual as I saw it, sometimes took him half an hour to perform. Through it I sat stiffly, concentrating not on what he was saying about the script, but on the effort of not hurling myself across the room to relieve him of the cigarette by force, and smoke it myself. It wasn't until our fourth or fifth meeting that I'd become sufficiently experienced in his ways, and sufficiently habituated to the gum, to enjoy both the work and his company. In fact, it turned out to be a very happy collaboration that demanded tolerance on his side too. He was after all dealing with an impatient, frequently fretful colleague

---

* These were *After Pilkington* for the BBC; an adaptation of *Quartermaine's Terms* for the BBC; and a version of J. L. Carr's novel *A Month in the Country*, for Channel 4 and Euston Films.

whose jaws only stopped working when one piece of gum was being replaced with another.

In early May Beryl and I went to Lucerne for a holiday. I took with me a throbbing pain, that now and then soared into a piercing pain, in my left ear – the result, I subsequently discovered, of the incessant gum-chewing. All I remember of the holiday now is going about the lake in big boats, muffled against the wind, the sleet, the snow or merely the rain, or whipping through valleys in trains, my head bent over a book in order not to notice the throb in my ear. A perfect companion as always for my wife. When we got back I started a new play, writing demonically through May, June, July, frequently day and night, the cellophane strips from the gum piling up as the cigarette packets had once piled up, the dead pieces of gum filling my black metal wastepaper basket as the cigarette ends had once filled it. There was a brief spell of about three days when I gave up the gum because I was convinced that it was leaking a stagnant pool of nicotine into my stomach which would poison my whole system. But without either cigarettes or gum I found myself in a state of continuous and unbearable agitation, unable to write, unable to read, and of course unable to sleep. I spent hours sitting jumpily in front of the television set, on one occasion staying up until two in the morning, a bottle of Scotch at my side, just to watch the fight, transmitted from Las Vegas, between Barry McGuigan and some no-hope Mexican called Cruz. Both the Irish champ and the Mexican chump insisted on going the distance, which meant I didn't have to go to bed and try to wrestle myself to sleep until nearly four, by which time we had a Mexican champ and an Irish chump. Cruz, a rather blandly smiling brown boy, slipped coolly about on the shady side of the ring; McGuigan, the tough little towser from County Down, scampered about on the sunny side, looking rather like the infant alien from the film of that name, all claws and knobs, though skewering away at nothing. The whole experience was so unnaturally vivid, almost hallucinatory – the consequence, I suppose, of my nicotine-deprived, over-alcoholed condition – that I've wondered since whether it wasn't my equivalent of a trip on acid.

Either the next day or the day after I went back on to the Nicorettes, and so got back into the play. A few days before I'd actually finished it, but when I knew that it was about to be finished,

I went to Lord's* for the afternoon. After an hour or so of listless inattention, I went up to the bar, where I sat for a time speculating about the bizarre little man who always sits on a chair in a corner by the window, never turning his head to look out of it and see the game. He's about seventy, with spectacles and a hearing aid, his scalp visible through strands of (dyed, I believe) black hair plastered thinly back, and an odd little thick black moustache (also, I believe, dyed). He wears a heavy suit even on the hottest of afternoons, with his member's tie knotted right up under his chin, and he always has a drink in his hand. That afternoon there was the usual coterie of teasers gathered around him, with whom he was swapping the usual badinage, very loudly as usual. I was trying to imagine him in some other environment – where and with whom did he live? What did he do (had once done) for a living? How did he spend his days during the long months when there was no cricket and the bar was closed? Did he, in fact, exist except in that corner, that chair – when I suddenly found myself hurtling out of the bar, down the steps to the telephones, which, at Lord's, are to be found in antique wooden cupboards that seal you off from the world and its air so completely that by the end of a medium-length conversation you feel on the verge of death by suffocation.

I phoned Michael Codron and told him that I had a new play. He went in for being delighted, urged me to get it to him before I went off to Sestri Levante for the annual family holiday, and fixed an appointment for two days' time, at four p.m., in his offices, for the ritual transfer of the script. I spent the next day and a half messing about with the text, mainly cutting, though deciding not to worry about its comparative roughness, both in the writing and the typography. In fact, I rather *liked* its roughness, comparing its effect to that of a violent, but life-enhancing tramp – a tramp of the old school. I arrived at Michael's office, punctual to the minute. In the reception area a girl reading what looked suspiciously like a script by Tom Stoppard or Michael Frayn or Alan Ayckbourn† told me that Michael wasn't ready to see me yet, and invited me

---

* For the benefit of American readers: Lord's is one of the larger cricket grounds in the London suburb of St John's Wood. As it is a predominantly Jewish neighbourhood Lord's is frequently referred to as the synagogue of cricket.

† Three English playwrights.

to sit on a peripheral sofa, would I like tea or coffee? I sat down, took out of my bag a copy of the *Spectator*, which was nestling beside my play, and with a cup of tea beside me, my mind really full of the impending interview, began to thumb through it. After about ten minutes Michael appeared. Seeing the *Spectator* in my hand, he said, 'Oh, you're reading the *Spectator* too, I was just reading it in my office.' So there we'd been, he in his office keeping me waiting while he read the *Spectator*, I in his foyer reading the *Spectator* while he was keeping me waiting. Quite a coincidence when you think about it.

Once in his office, I took the play, which was packed in a cardboard box, out of my bag, and handed it over with a little bow. He put it down on his desk rather hurriedly, then, with his eyes averted from it, went behind the desk, sat down. Though his noble and hawk-like face looked as noble as ever, and slightly more hawk-like, I noticed that his eyes resolutely refused to rest even fleetingly on the encoffined play, nor did his fingers stray absently towards it. We sat there, gossiping vivaciously along, eventually settling on a little incident in which Beryl and I had left at the interval of a play he'd produced at the Aldwych fairly recently. The reason we'd left was not precisely that we'd thought the play bad, but that we couldn't make out whether it was or wasn't, not being able to hear more than the occasional word. We were sitting quite a few rows back in the dress circle (house seats, though I'd paid for them) of a theatre far from full, but the extraordinarily cavernous sets, for what was virtually a conversation piece about sex as far as one could gather, soaked up the actors' voices while diminishing their physical presences. Good actors too, with good voices and presences, there miming dutifully away to thin trickles of meaning. So why stay, once there was an interval to leave surreptitiously in? Unfortunately some people sitting right behind us reported to their friend the director our failure to return, who reported it to the author, who mentioned it to the producer, who was now discussing it with me, in phrases that indicated forgiveness and forgetfulness in counterpoint to my blustering explanations and apologies. We got through all that eventually, on to a bit more gossip briefly, then Michael said, as I was raising my cup to my lips, 'Don't you think that you ought perhaps – I mean, the longer you stay, the less time I have to get to this,' somehow indicating my play without either gesturing or even glancing towards it. And then went straight on to warn me that as a matter of fact he wouldn't be able to read it for a couple of days as he was about to open a new Ayckbourn in Richmond. As he said this he got to his feet, terminating the interview, seemingly unaware that in consecutive sentences he'd established two completely contradictory positions. To wit: that he was desperate to read the play, please therefore would I go; that he couldn't read the play for a couple of days because he was opening a new Ayckbourn in Richmond, nevertheless please would I go. Both positions, however, succeeded in containing the same conclusion – I was to piss off. So back through his reception I went, down the endless stairs, out into the Aldwych, into a taxi, and home.

A week later, on holiday in Sestri Levante, I heard from Judy Daish that Michael had rejected the play, finding it 'too big' and 'too upsetting' – producer's synonyms, perhaps, for too expensive and too uncommercial.* The holiday was further marred by the news from our house-sitter that Hazel, who had fallen down the steps to the back garden, was seriously ill. My brother Piers, who had joined us for a week or so at Sestri, got back to London in time to see her through the vet's visit, into death. I shall always regret that neither Beryl nor I was there at her end, although from Piers's account she was probably past caring. She was over seventeen years old when she died, which is OK for a dog, I suppose, and she was never very bright, and in her prime exceptionally greedy. She was also a coward, a reckless coward, as she would often start fights by yelping belligerently at a passing dog, and then, when the passing dog took offence and yelped back, would try to scale up the nearest human body for safety. She was deeply affectionate, had soulful brown eyes, and stuck by me, under my desk, night after night, when I was at work. Her portrait, done in oils by a friend, hangs above my desk, slightly idealised, as is appropriate for a portrait, and so missing out on her innate gift for the comic gesture or the foolish utterance, but catching something of her lurking spirituality.

---

* This play – *Melon* – was eventually produced by Duncan Weldon at the Theatre Royal, Haymarket, with Christopher Morahan directing and Alan Bates in the lead.

[2]

Throughout the spring and summer while I was writing the new play, there was also, of course, *The Common Pursuit* and the question of its future. Some time in mid-March Jack McQuiggan phoned from New York to say that finally, on his fourth attempt, he'd made it to Los Angeles to see the Matrix production, his three previous attempts having been foiled by, respectively, an ailing mother; a back injury actually incurred on the way to the airport; a crisis in the show he was currently producing Off-Broadway. He liked the play very much, could see that it worked well on stage, and wanted to produce it in New York. What did I say? I said yes, delighted – which I was. When he'd done *Quartermaine's Terms* I'd thought him the best producer I'd ever worked with. After we'd exchanged a few 'greats' and 'wonderfuls' at the prospect of being in business together again, he went on to say that as far as he could see, there were only two problems: (1) he didn't want to move the Matrix production, being unhappy with some of the casting, and of course the sets, and (2) he wanted me to direct it myself. I was in complete agreement on (1), but not on (2), claiming that I'd dug myself so deeply into the text when rewriting it for the Matrix that I wasn't sure I could keep a cool and detached eye on it yet, but that I'd be happy to co-direct it. OK, Jack said, but who with? What about Ken Frankel, I said, from the Long Wharf production? After all, he had a pleasant personality, so that at least there'd be a relaxed atmosphere in the rehearsal room. I would come over for the last two weeks of rehearsals and all the previews, do everything I'd done with *Quartermaine's Terms* to make sure the show was right, and this time appear as official co-director. Jack finally agreed, though not very enthusiastically – he'd worked with Frankel since *Quartermaine's Terms*, when no other had been present to take charge. We left it that I'd phone Frankel and invite him to co-direct *The Common Pursuit* in New York.

As it turned out, Frankel wanted to resume our previous arrangement, viz. that I'd continue to do a great deal of the work, while he'd continue to take all the director's royalties and the credits. I passed this offer back to Jack, who turned it down with what sounded suspiciously like exhilaration. 'What about Sam Weisman?' I asked. 'But you hated working with him in Los Angeles,' Jack reminded me. Yes, but – but what? Well, he *was* good on the text, and let's hope that he now realises the importance of a happy rehearsal room. On in this vein until we left it that I'd phone Weisman and put it to him.

But first a call to Frankel, saying he was out, Sam Weisman was in. 'Weisman? In as what?' he asked. 'Well, as director.' How did this make sense, he asked, he only as co-director, Sam Weisman as director? 'Well, you see –' though actually I hadn't quite worked it out, partly, I suppose, because I hadn't thought about it. What I came up with was that as Sam Weisman had only a month or so previously appeared in Los Angeles as sole director, it would seem a trifle odd if he now turned up in New York as co-director. Whereas he, Ken Frankel, had been involved in *The Common Pursuit* a year and a half ago, a script and a half ago, he'd be dealing in some respects with a new play, so questions wouldn't be asked about his personal demotion, in fact what could be more natural? It all sounded pretty persuasive to me, but didn't persuade Frankel, who cut across to tell me I was being 'stupid' not to do it on our old terms. No good, I said, Jack won't have it. He said again that I was being 'stupid'. I took him, as soothingly as I could, through my arguments again and we ended by exchanging pleasantries, no doubt both of us wishing that there was a reason or a season, like Christmas, to hang them on.

After Frankel, Weisman. Actually not quite. Weisman was directing a production or something or other on the West Coast, couldn't be contacted direct, but as he was in the habit of phoning Joe Stern almost every evening I asked Joe to pass on my message. A few days later Weisman phoned to say he'd love to do the play in New York. I gave him my thoughts on casting – Kristoffer Tabori (Stuart), Judy Geeson (Marigold) and Christopher Neame (Peter) from the Matrix production; Nathan Lane (Nick) from the Long Wharf and Matrix productions; Michael Countryman (Martin) and Peter Friedman (Humphry) from the Long Wharf productions. What did he think? Fine, he said, great – so what was the next move? I said I supposed it would be for him to come to an agreement with Jack, then to meet – or at least talk with – David Jenkins, who'd designed the set for the Long Wharf and would now,

I hoped, be designing it for us. Right, he said, he'd get on to Jack and Jenkins straight away. Great. Fine. Thanks. And that was that.

For about a week. Then Jack phoned, to say that he and Weisman had talked, there was one thing he needed to get absolutely clear, Weisman and I would be co-directing, sharing the royalties, the billing, right? Wrong, I said, Weisman was to be to this production exactly what he'd been to the Matrix production (except in manners and behaviour, I hoped). In other words, the sole director. 'Ah,' said Jack doubtfully, 'that's the arrangement, is it?' Well, if I was *sure* that that was what I wanted – was I sure? I said that on balance I *supposed* I was, then moved the conversation to the question of casting, the need for David Jenkins to do the set, the need for a good lighting man, sound man. And that was that.

Some weeks later Jack came over to London, bearing with him two large trophies won by *Quartermaine's Terms*, one for heading the Off-Broadway baseball league, the other for getting to the finals of the Off-Broadway baseball knock-out competition. He wanted me to have them in my collection rather than his, not because they were endearingly ugly, but because he, along with the director and the cast, had won trophies for their part in the production of the play, while the play itself had won nothing. I deserved *some* reward, he said, for being the cause of rewards to others. We had lunch together one day, dinner the next. It was clear that he was already enjoying getting the production under way – he was negotiating with the actors, with David Jenkins, with a top lighting chap (female) and with an excellent sound man. Would I please reconsider my decision not to co-direct? Even better, would I please reconsider my decision not to direct on my own? I said I wouldn't, why? He said he just had a feeling, that's all.

A week or so after Jack had flown back to New York Kristoffer Tabori and Judy Geeson turned up in London. Over lunch at Groucho's* we had a rather formless discussion about Jack's desire, of which they'd got wind, that I should direct the play on my own. They seemed to have no feelings on the matter, let alone views. Very perplexing, considering the extent to which they were both prepared to relive the horrors of the Matrix, Tabori enacting

---

* A club in Soho, London.

the several occasions when he'd almost flung himself bodily at Sam Weisman. Perhaps they were just pleased to be doing the play in New York, let who was going to direct direct – Gray, Weisman, Himmler. All my attempts to grill them more closely ended when Judy, either from innocence or guile, deflected me with photographs of myself with massive, shoe-groping dog Digby taken in Los Angeles those months back, myself with their cockatoo those months back – until we ended up in pleasant little rivulets of talk about nothing in particular.

Anyway that was that, and went on being that, until Phyllis Wender (my New York agent) phoned one night in late July, perhaps early August, to tell me that Jack had finally decided against Sam Weisman. As I was deep into the last draft of the new play, I received this information almost absent-mindedly, returning to the typewriter the moment Phyllis hung up, and mentally staying there until Sam Weisman phoned me a few nights later, from a television studio in Hollywood, to inform me that his lawyer in New York had just received a letter *by hand* from Jack McQuiggan (or was it from Jack McQuiggan's lawyer?), announcing that he, Sam Weisman, would not be directing *The Common Pursuit* Off-Broadway, other plans entirely were being laid. There was obviously some mistake here, Sam Weisman said, would I find out what was going on? 'Right,' I said, 'and oh, by the way, I'm just finishing a new play and –' 'Great,' he said. 'Fine. So if you'd give Jack a ring. And clear this up. Know what I mean?' I gave Jack a ring. Yes, Jack said, that's right, Sam Weisman was off the show. It was a producer's decision, which was why he'd taken it without reference to me. 'Any particular reason,' I asked, 'for taking it?' Well, Jack said, he'd met with Sam Weisman in New York, made a few enquiries about him here and there, thought about him a great deal and come to the conclusion – I could call it a hunch if I wanted – that Sam Weisman hadn't the right sensibility for the New York production, there would be a risk of discord in the rehearsal room, other people involved in the production felt the same, and anyway, right or wrong, there was nothing anyone could say, that Sam Weisman could say, or Sam Weisman's lawyer could say, or I could say, that would change it. Sam Weisman was out, Michael McGuire was in. Michael McGuire was in? Yes, Michael. He liked Michael, he knew I liked Michael. Michael liked the play, and furthermore had trained as a director before becoming an actor, so Michael McGuire* in, Sam Weisman out. *His* decision, as producer.

I sat at my desk, Hazel dotingly under it, and contemplated the history to date of *The Common Pursuit* in America. There was no doubt that its most sensational feature was its high body count. I ticked off the corpses, first from the Matrix in Los Angeles, then from the Long Wharf in New Haven. Twelve in all, if one counted the three discarded directors – Frankel, Tabori, Weisman; and counted Chris Neame† among the discarded actors. I tried doing it the other, more cheerful way around, with a checklist of the survivors. Kris Tabori and Judy Geeson from the Matrix; Michael Countryman and Peter Friedman from the Long Wharf; Nathan Lane from both. And now of course Michael McGuire, from nowhere relevant, who so far hadn't had anything to survive. But whichever way round I did my adding up, it remained horribly clear that in New York there would be more ghosts hovering in the wings than players on the stage.

I thought a bit about Sam Weisman, recalled some choice moments from the Matrix rehearsals, wrestled briefly with my conscience,‡ then phoned him and broke the news. He was appalled, angry, disbelieving. I said Jack had said – wanted me to know – that the decision was irreversible. Sam Weisman then asked me to put his case to Jack for him. He would fly to New York at his own expense, if Jack wanted. I agreed, though suspecting that the last thing Jack wanted was Sam Weisman flying to New York, at anybody's expense – especially to see him. I phoned Jack up, and made a coolish and clearish statement of the Weisman entitlement, throwing in one or two rhetorical flourishes. I think I did all right by Weisman, at least I can't think, even now, of a moral stone I left

* For information about my previous relationship with Michael McGuire see pages 334-6.

† Chris Neame had phoned to say he couldn't, after all, be considered for the New York production because as a British national he was unable to get a green card, without which he couldn't work in any theatre except a waiver one, like the Matrix. He would have qualified for a card if he'd married the American girl with whom he lived, but we agreed that no one should use the opportunity of appearing in a play, even a play by me, as an excuse for getting married.

‡ When Richard Nixon said the same thing, it was assumed the fight was fixed.

unturned. And there really was some fervour in me, as a consequence of a conversation I'd had a few hours earlier with Joe, whose distress on Sam Weisman's behalf certainly made me anxious to do right by *him*. Jack listened to me, courteously, patiently, restated his own case, which my advocacy hadn't changed a jot, but offered to write a further letter to Sam Weisman's lawyer, giving a fuller account of the reasons behind his decision – his fear that Sam Weisman would jeopardise the atmosphere in rehearsals, that hiring him might cost us David Jenkins, who was crucial to our plans* and had already announced himself out of sympathy with Sam Weisman's approach and manner – and that everybody else connected with the production who'd met Sam Weisman in New York felt as Jack and Jenkins did.

I didn't really believe that the information that *nobody* in New York wanted him to direct *The Common Pursuit* would bring Sam Weisman much comfort, especially when conveyed in a lawyer's letter. All I myself said when I phoned him was that I hadn't been able to change Jack's mind, give up, Sam. He said he wouldn't. Joe Stern phoned me again; Kris Tabori, in tandem with Joe Stern, in one of those Los Angeles link-ups, phoned; Sam Weisman phoned; Jack McQuiggan phoned – all this after I'd handed my new play over to Michael Codron and was waiting for his response, and at two, sometimes nearly three in the morning. But really, given the finality of Jack's decision, all the calls were a waste of time and money, and just a day or so before I set off with my family for Italy, they stopped.

In Sestri I received just one phone call relating to *The Common Pursuit*. It was from Jack. He wanted to tell me the schedule (we would rehearse through September, open to previews in early October, have our first night on 20 October – the night before my fiftieth birthday) and to discuss various actors he'd lined up to audition for Peter, the Christopher Neame part. 'Oh,' he said, when we'd finished, 'and one other thing. You and Michael McGuire to have equal billing as co-directors. All right?' I said no, surely the arrangement was the usual one, that I'd come over for the last two weeks, and all the previews, and see to things in my capacity as

---

* I'd asked him to repeat his Long Wharf design, with necessary adjustments, given more limited stage space in New York.

author. 'No, not at all,' Jack said. 'You and Michael are co-directing. I never asked Michael to direct. Only to co-direct.' I said that this was the first time I'd been told of this, or anyway understood it. He said, 'Well, I suppose I just took it for granted that you'd understand that that's what I meant. I mean, how else would it make sense?' I hung up, reflecting that Jack, whether consciously or not, had got most of what he'd wanted from the beginning. Which, of course, further increased my respect for him, in that it's always good when producers not only know what they want, but also succeed in getting most of it. On the other hand, I didn't feel so good about being what he'd mostly succeeded in getting, as it meant that I wouldn't be able to turn up at my pleasure and leisure, halfway through rehearsals; nor would I be able to turn up in rehearsals only when I felt inclined (admittedly that was almost all the time). I would have to be there from the very beginning, and turn up at the rehearsals, promptly, at whatever hour Michael McGuire and I called them for. On top of which, taking the credit (which I didn't mind) meant that I also had to take the responsibility (which I might mind) and even the blame (which I would mind). On the *other* other hand, for too many years I had been private director of my plays in the States, going public was perhaps what I secretly wanted, let's do it. It all seemed quite simple, when considered calmly from the terraced restaurant in Sestri, overlooking the harbour at sunset, with a fine Italian meal before me, bottles of wine to hand, nicotine chewing gum on the go, and my family around me. Although the stomach did lurch a little at the prospect of nearly seven weeks in New York, lived through in a double state of frenzy, given that I was now doubly at risk. A bum play directed by a bum director were the headlines I envisaged. To which I could make the comforting amendment, a bum play directed by *two* bum directors.

During the week between my return from Sestri and my setting out to New York, I received a phone call from the joker in the pack, Michael McGuire. He caught me at a bad time – very late in the evening, when I was full of Scotch, grieving over Hazel's death, waiting anxiously to hear about the fate of my new play,* and in

---

* It was currently with Sir Peter Hall at the National. Although he seemed keen to do it, he was unable to offer dates in any future that I could foresee. There was also the usual problem, with the National, of communication, i.e. plenty of phone

the middle of watching *The Cincinnati Kid*[†] on television. He was concerned about how we would proceed in rehearsals – how did co-directors actually work together, he wondered. I said, one eye fixed on the screen, one hand wrapped around a glass, 'Well, we'll just say whatever seems appropriate, surely.' Well, no, he said, he'd been giving the matter a lot of thought and he was unutterably opposed to any system that led to our disagreeing openly in front of the cast, they'd lose confidence, not fair on them – 'But don't misunderstand me,' he also kept saying. 'I don't have any ego problem with this play.' A chilling phrase, 'ego problem', as I'd first heard it from Ken Frankel, when he was about to direct the play at the Long Wharf; then from Kristoffer Tabori in London when he was about to direct the play at the Matrix; and then heard it from Sam Weisman in London when he was about to take over from Kristoffer Tabori at the Matrix. I couldn't say, though I wanted to, that I *did* have an ego problem with this play as it was by me. Instead, I babbled on incoherently, sometimes drawing on experience so past I could scarcely remember it, sometimes being, or attempting to sound, curtly professional, cutting across his uncertainties with a slurred epigram. But of course, Michael was right. One can co-direct one of one's old plays with one of one's old friends, as I'd done in Dallas with Stephen; one can direct while masquerading as the author, which I'd done to some extent at the Matrix, and twice comprehensively at the Long Wharf; but how, when it came down to it, did one co-direct with a co-director who actually wanted to co-direct? I refused to answer the question on the telephone at that time, and as a consequence had to address myself to it again at a crucial phase of rehearsals in New York, when I wasn't drunk, anxious, grieving or watching a bad film on television.

calls and letters from my side through Judy Daish; none at all from theirs. I finally withdrew the play and offered it to Duncan Weldon who is now producing it. It is called *Melon* and is in rehearsal as I write this.

† A thick-witted rip-off of *The Hustler*, with a climax that depends on the most unlikely event in the history of poker games – and in the history of the cinema – when one of the players (Edward G. Robinson) beats 'the kid' (Steve McQueen) with a straight flush against a full house. *That* isn't skill, that's luck. No. Worse. It isn't even luck, it's merely tawdry plotting, the writer working with a stacked deck, but calling it fate.

But Down There I Wasn't a Duck

Sunday, 7 September 1986

I flew to New York on Virgin Airlines, in their version of first class, which they call 'Upper', in contrast to their cheap seats, which they call, with refreshing frankness, 'Lower'.* From the glimpses of 'Lower' I treated myself to, the compartment resembled the hold of a nineteenth-century transport ship, people packed so closely together that they seemed to be sitting on top of each other, weeping or unconscious. 'Upper', on the other hand, is very spacious, and provides reasonable service – somewhere between the Super Club and First Class of the major airlines, though at less than Super Club prices. Virgin also hands out a free 'Lower' ticket to its 'Upper' customers, which you can either use yourself (fat chance!) or pass on to someone in feeble health, in whose life insurance you have an interest.

My old friend, Dena Hammerstein, and her son Simon (named, I modestly admit, after myself) were on the same plane. Simon is actually a bright and charming fellow, but as he's only eight years old, I had reached a pre-flight agreement with his mother that they would sit as far away from me as possible, meeting up by appointment only for a drink at the bar. This was not only mean-spirited but entirely sensible, as it would give me the chance to read a book, watch the film, eat my meal gravely by myself, un-molested. Simon, however, refusing to consider himself a party to this arrangement, quickly took to looming beside me, making all sorts of perfectly normal (i.e. nonsensical) eight-year-old requests; for example, could he have my book to read, could he occupy my

---

* They've since changed 'Lower' to 'Space', presumably on the grounds that what little there is should have attention drawn to it.

seat and listen to the in-flight music through my headphones, as
he was sure that it was better than the music to be heard through
his, what about giving him some money? In the end I turned a bit
uncley, and consented to show him my favourite, indeed my only,
card trick, which in loose outline consists of inviting someone to
choose in their head a card from the fifteen spread before them,
and then after a lot of flim-flammery, telling them which card
they've chosen. It's an absolute whizz of a trick, a jaw-dropper,
that has only one flaw – it depends for its success on the complete
integrity of the person you're showing it off to. Every time I flour-
ished Simon's card at him, he simply looked away with a bored
shake of the head, until I was forced to give up, sending Simon off
with a verbal message for the pilot, which he clearly didn't deliver,
as he returned unshackled and ungagged well before we reached
New York, almost at once in fact. Nevertheless Dena and I managed a few enjoyable gossips before we landed at Newark, the
most convenient international airport for New York, as it's sufficiently small for one to be able to pass rapidly through customs and
immigration – especially if you make it first to the desk as I did,
by means of some pretty ruthless sprinting and hustling, impeded
only by my overnight bag. I was in Manhattan a mere thirty
minutes after getting off the plane. This might be a record.*

When in New York I stay at the Algonquin, loving its eccentric
and animated lobby life, finding safety in the fact that most of the
bell-hops' faces are familiar, and feeling at ease in my suite. I
usually manage to get the same one, 310, which is comfortable,
pleasantly decorated with playbills of famous or poignantly long-
forgotten shows, and has three telephones, one of them in the
bathroom, beside the lavatory, which conjures up images of myself as Louis XIV, Lyndon Johnson, etc. In other words, for me the
Algonquin is home, never more so than now, when I'm not
staying in it. For once I've allowed economics to prevail over all
the really important instincts, and am in the Pankhurst,[†] which

---

* From the above I suppose I give the impression of exceptionally ungentlemanly
behaviour, even by my own low standards, but in fact Dena and Simon had a limo
waiting for them, as had I (Virgin provides a free limo to 'Upper' passengers), so
there was no point in jostling through customs and immigration together, only to
separate immediately afterwards.

† I have changed the name of the hotel for reasons that will become apparent.

gives you a special deal if you stay for a month, and pay in advance. As I've paid in advance, I'm stuck here for a month. It comes highly recommended by people in London whose judgement I shall make a point of ignoring in future. I can't remember what it is that they liked about it, although I think somebody connected with the National Theatre said it was 'wonderfully discreet', which should have been enough to put one off, as 'discreet' invariably means a dull lobby in which anything you do will be noticed, and possibly noted. And indeed the lobby is dull, or would be if it weren't actively depression-inducing, its atmosphere that of an antechamber to a funeral parlour, the only visible residents extremely old and sitting patiently about as if waiting their turn in the embalming room. I took an instant but for once not entirely irrational dislike to my suite, not least because its decor is an unattractive green, or rather variations on an unattractive green, and there are lots of those bogus classical-style lamps that one comes across in those hotels in the States that go in for being stylish, without any style. Not least I dislike the suite because it's not in the Algonquin, the doors of which my limo actually passed on the way here – I had to check a cry to the driver to stop, hold, this is where I get out. I wish I hadn't. I can't face unpacking. Unpacking will make my being here somehow definitive. By the way, the fridge in the closet-sized kitchen has a morose hum to it, from loneliness, I suppose.

Tuesday, 9 September, two nights later

Let me do a quick run-down on my dealings with the Pankhurst so far. The gays and other guys at the desk have been infuriatingly well mannered and helpful, easily frustrating my attempts to involve them in the kind of row that might lead them into paying me my money back, and letting me go. So far I've concentrated my attack on the curtains in my suite. They are heavy and brocaded (green within green on green) and hang at all the windows, four pairs in the sitting room, two in the bedroom, and have one redeeming feature – *they don't work!* When you undo the sash and tug and jerk at them, they neither move sideways to meet each other, nor fall down. They just hang there, inertly framing the windows it is their function to cover. I suppose, therefore, that they're ornamental curtains, but the joyous fact is that the blinds behind them are clearly inadequate either for privacy (there is a teeming office block opposite) or as protection against the light, and I therefore require curtains that curtain.

I saw at once that if I handled this properly, I might shortly be on my way out of the Pankhurst with a refund in my pocket, so phoning down to the desk I explained the situation, assuming the restrained manner of a man who means business. Before I could get into the inevitable repercussions – i.e. 'make up my cheque, please'* – I was told that the matter would be dealt with straight away, someone would be right up, sir. And right up came the housekeeper, a burly middle-aged woman of the kind you expect to find in a hotel in Moscow, who spoke English with the kind of accent you also expect to find in Moscow. She tugged futilely at the curtains, then said, 'Have to get man. Have to get man who do this,' and went. I was about to phone down again when man – a male version of the housekeeper, in that he was even burlier, so possibly a brother or husband, arrived with a toolbox and no English whatsoever, and set to work with screwdrivers and such, to no effect. I stood watching him with a drink in my hand, making discouraging exclamations of annoyance, clucking away at his failures. I was slightly drunk. I had, of course, been drinking on the plane but, as always happens with me – I've never quite understood the psychology – the moment I get into my hotel room I decide that it's about time for my first real drink of the day. When man had left scowling and muttering, I phoned down to the desk, and trying to keep the triumph out of my voice, reported on the situation. 'I can't stay here, you see,' I said, meaning the Pankhurst of course, but he took me to mean here in this particular room, and said he would send up a bell-hop to show me another one. I hesitated, thinking it was now or never, then deciding that it was better to clinch my case – there would almost certainly be something to object to in any room at the Pankhurst – I agreed. The bell-hop, a rather maternal middle-aged chap, with a reasonably fluent command of the language (he was Irish), took me down several floors to a suite that was noticeably different from mine

* As opposed to 'Make up my check, please'. The point being that *they* owed *me* money. Got it?

in that it was decorated in variations of an unattractive brown, nevertheless sticking to the main house style with classical lamps and non-meeting curtains. Back up I went, and down I phoned, to be told, with inflexible sympathy and courtesy, that the manager had just left, but when he came back in the morning he would surely sort my problem out. I gave it as my opinion, rather grimly, that he wouldn't, but decided to leave it at that for the evening, really quite pleased with the progress I'd made.

I stood at one of the sitting-room windows for a while, sipping further malt and watching the lights go out, the office workers departing, in the building opposite, then pulled down the blinds, a protracted and messy business as I can never work out which strings to pull, and invariably end up with one large corner of the blind tilted up and jammed. In fact I was wrestling with just such a corner when I was jolted upright by a sharp, savage ring, not from the telephone, possibly from the doorbell. But probably not from the doorbell either, as when I opened the door there was nobody there, and nobody hurrying down the corridor away from the door, either. This unexplained ring unnerved me. It hadn't sounded accidental, but peremptory, as if there were an urgent purpose behind it. I went out and did some shopping – toothpaste, razor blades, Nescafé, plums, sort of stuff – then had a meal in a nearby and cheerless hamburger joint where I went from brooding over my situation at the Pankhurst to brooding over the fact that so far I'd received no communication from my producer, Jack McQuiggan. When I'd made my way back along the drab and almost empty streets, through the dead man's lobby, up in the space-shuttle lift, into my greenish room, I set about trying to phone him. I had two numbers, home and office, but on both I got his answering service – the same answering service; in fact the same person on the same answering service, his voice cheerful, polite and indifferent, and therefore far more infuriating than a couple of answering machines. Most answering machines at least beg you to leave a message as if afraid of missing out on something. While I was dealing with the voice that I'd only just dealt with, there was another sharp ringing noise. I opened the door. Nobody there. I went to bed, pondering resentfully on the nature of producers,* but finally coasted calmly off on the thought that at least tomorrow, given that the curtain problem was quite unsolvable, I would be able to depart for the Algonquin. It even occurred to me that perhaps Jack, and possibly lots of other people as well, had left messages at the Algonquin, out of habit. I was woken at quarter to six by the sun bashing its way through the blinds, unresisted by the unmeeting curtains, just as I'd anticipated. New York blinds can't actually deal with the sun, which finds it perfectly easy to shoulder its way through their slats and get into your eyes.

So there I was at dawn, writing a long, argumentative letter to Harold about a recent anthology of poetry that he had co-edited. I went on for nine pages, questioning most of his inclusions and angrily challenging key omissions, breaking only to make some breakfast (hot-dog sausages, hot mustard and hot tomato sauce, which I'd purchased on my shopping spree the evening before – not perhaps a happy choice of early-morning fodder as it lingered around my intestines all day), until suddenly I realised it was nearly ten o'clock and time to get to the theatre to audition Peters. As I left my suite, I noticed for the first time a little pack of papers squeezed behind a specially fixed loop of metal on the door, which turned out to be telephone messages, most of them from Jack who had phoned before I arrived and then several times while I was out shopping, giving me various numbers at which I could reach him. This explained not only Jack's strange and insulting silence (what a waste of good resentment!) but also, presumably, those extraordinary rings, the bell-hop sticking the message on the door, ringing the bell, immediately departing, leaving me confronting an empty corridor – but how did he manage to do it all so quickly?[†]

---

* No doubt recalling the famous New York producer who was sitting at his desk one morning, when his phone rang. He answered, listened, went white, ran out of the office. His staff was astonished, as he'd never before left his office without letting them know where he was going, and how to get in touch with him. Three hours later he reappeared, sat down, began sorting through receipts. His staff entered *en masse*, convinced he'd been through some terrible experience, and asked him, with passionate concern, whether he was all right: 'Gee, Mr —, we were really worried about you, your rushing off like that, are you sure everything's OK?' Yes, yes,' he said irritably, he was fine, fine, somebody had rung up to say there was a bomb in the building, but it had turned out to be a hoax.

† By hurrying, of course. I subsequently discovered that the lift operator delivered the messages, and as he had to leave the lift door open when doing so, he had to get back to the lift as quickly as possible.

I went down to the lobby and moved into phase two of my escape plan, going to the desk and describing to the guy there what it had been like to be punched out of sleep by a fist of sunlight to the eyes, so to speak. 'Intolerable, quite intolerable,' I said. 'Really, really I can see no alternative but to leave. However much I like your hotel in so many other respects.' Instead of going on the defensive ('No one's ever complained before') or the offensive ('Go or stay, who cares as long as we got your money?') which I would have preferred, he went in for being deeply nice – obviously a show of deep niceness is the long-practised tactic at the Pankhurst desk – nodding gravely, and exclaiming, 'Oh, that's terrible!' he could *really* sympathise, he appreciated – that was the word he used – 'I appreciate what it's like to be woken so early in the morning with the light,' as if genuinely troubled on my behalf. Not on the hotel's behalf, on mine. Frustrated, I rocked off, still slightly hungover from the night before, more than nauseated by my hot-dog and mustard breakfast, and already exhausted from penning my long letter to Harold.*

When I finally got to the theatre – the Promenade, up on Broadway and 76; the Pankhurst down in the mid-fifties, off Park – I found my co-director, Michael McGuire, and my producer, Jack McQuiggan, already there, waiting for me. We had a brief talk about the cast we'd signed up, the chances of finding a good Peter from the auditions ahead, the problems David Jenkins would have reorganising his Long Wharf conception in the smaller, proscenium space of the Promenade, and then this and that, until I transferred the conversation to something important – i.e. my video machine. I had sent Jack urgent messages across the Atlantic, as I'd once sent them across the Pacific to Joe Stern, demanding that a video be installed in my room. I think I'd also sent urgent messages to Phyllis, my New York agent, making the same demand, so now I come to think of it, I probably have two videos on order. Jack said he'd put someone on to it straight away. I gave him the precise address of the Pankhurst to pass on to the proper party, forgetting that if luck went my way I'd no longer be staying there when the video arrived. I must at some time, when I have a great deal of leisure, examine this obsession I have with getting a video

---

* I never sent it, a cold-eyed reading revealing it to be befuddled in argument while rancorous in tone. There were also, in places, signs of illiteracy.

installed the moment I arrive in the States these days – or rather with trying to get it installed. Perhaps that's the point. That it's not the video itself I need, but the rigmarole of trying to get it installed.

Anyway, on from the furthering of my obsession to another bloody day in the theatre. The auditions for Peter seemed to go on for ever. We saw about twelve actors in the morning alone, of whom only one or two were even remotely appropriate. Of the inappropriate ones quite a few seemed not even to be particularly good actors. So there I sat in the stalls, chewing my nicotine chewing gum, watching actor after actor after actor after actor reading the same lines and failing to communicate any sense of the part, or communicating a perverse sense of the part, or just being desperately at sea. There was one lively moment when an enormous chap, about six foot four, very broad, looking like a college football player in fact, sauntered down the aisle, saying as he came that he was very much looking forward to my lecture in November. I said, 'What?' And he said, 'Yeah, well aren't you going to be there?' I suddenly remembered that I had long ago accepted an invitation to appear at the 92nd Street Y to discuss the process involved in turning a play into a film – the film in question being *Butley.* I said, 'God, yes, you're absolutely right, I'd completely forgotten,' adding, really just to say something while he was clambering on to the stage, 'I wonder if I get paid.' I heard his voice – his back was to me and I was very conscious of his enormous shoulders – drawling, 'Not by *me* you don't.'* This struck me as quite funny and I therefore felt well disposed until he began his reading. It was quite grotesque. There on the stage was this enormous and muscular man with a rather thick and bullish head, giving a pansified account-flouncing and mincing and virtu- ally lisping – of Peter, who is of course relentlessly and unchange-

* He must have known something. When I returned to New York in November, expecting a select gathering of devoted connoisseurs, I found myself in an enor- mous cinema – part of the vast 92nd Street Y complex – into which about a thousand people had been packed. After the film was shown I was first of all grilled by a critic from the *New York Times,* and then by quick-witted and erudite members of the audience. I don't remember any of the questions and the only answer I can recall involved my saying, apologetically, 'Well let's face it, two hours is a long time to spend with two guys in a room,' which brought a burst of sponta- neous but unwelcome applause from the house.

ably (I hope) heterosexual. So that was the end of that – a hopeless case. We finally settled for an actor called Dylan Baker, who is clearly very talented and has a lot of charm but is, I suspect, slightly too young for the part, even in such a young company, and possibly also too inexperienced. Not as an actor, I mean, but in life. His face is open and eager, and I'm not convinced it can ever register the exhausted cynicism that should mark Peter out towards the play's end. But it is always best to go for the talent.

We talked a bit, Jack, Michael and I, about rehearsal schedules. Seeing them together again, I was struck again by the contrast between them. Jack is always spruce, fresh-looking, rapid in everything he does, with bright round eyes and a cheerful, determined expression. Michael is lean, sunken-cheeked, somewhat theatrically dressed and haunted-looking, giving the impression that he's back on a short visit from Hades. Nevertheless they have three things in common. They're both Irish, they're both non-drinking alcoholics, they have both cut down from about sixty cigarettes a day to none at all. After we'd finished Michael and I arranged to meet in the evening before going on to have dinner with the cast. I came back to the Pankhurst for a bath while Michael, who's down on 48th and 8th where the sleaze is, went where I want to be – into the sleaze. That's another reason that I want to be at the Algonquin – to be able to step straight out of its sociable lobby into the sleaze. As other people like to step into the snow or the sunshine, I like to step into the sleaze. As far as I've been able to see there is no sleaze around the Pankhurst part of New York, it's just dull. A bit of Third Avenue, a bit of Madison and Park – all perfectly pleasant and respectable with office blocks, etc., and utterly dull.

Michael came over to the Pankhurst at about seven. After he'd expressed surprise and distaste at the complexion of the room, we had a long conversation during the course of which I got drunk, while he sat there sipping water, talking on and on about his lack of an ego problem – with reference of course to our being co-directors – until, drunker and therefore rasher, I said that people who don't have an ego problem don't have to keep saying that they don't have an ego problem, 'because the thing about an ego problem, Michael, is that it never occurs to you you've got one until you've got one and as soon as you've got one you spend your time denying that you've got one.' There was a long pause. He admitted that he did in fact have an ego problem about our co-directing. He was intensely worried about who was going to do what, we mustn't contradict each other in front of the actors, etc. I said, 'Listen, I'm co-director, you're co-director, we're after all both grown-up and both sort of human, intelligent, vulnerable. If we make mistakes, why pretend that we don't, and why be embarrassed in front of actors if we have disagreements?' He said, yeah, well he now saw that he did have a bit of a problem to do with his ego on this one and that he didn't really know how it was going to be resolved, he was beginning to find out about himself a little bit through this – the usual American stuff, except that he's an extremely charming and intelligent man, and his writhings were really only with himself – he wasn't trying to wrestle, so to speak, at a distance with me. As we had to go uptown for our dinner with the cast, the matter was left unconcluded.

I'd downed so many malts during the conversation with Michael that I was pretty gone when we arrived at the restaurant, which was up by the Promenade Theatre. Fortunately, or unfortunately, I'm really not sure which, I don't behave very differently when I'm drunk from when I'm sober. I don't fall over, throw up, sing sentimental songs, pick fights (although I admit I'm even quicker than usual to take offence, or start the kind of debate that could lead, but has only once led, to a fight – and then with someone drunker than I was), my speech remains comparatively unslurred, and my thought processes remain fairly uncluttered. To those who know me, I am genial, even affectionate, even *over*-affectionate, but not drunkenly so; to everyone else, and there were a lot of everybody elses this evening whose names and functions I couldn't quite grasp, but were probably mostly backers – one of the perks of being a backer is that you get to meet the company, possibly a greater perk for knowing that the company doesn't want to meet you – to all these I was uncommunicative, irritable, presenting them with a red and sweaty face, slightly unfocused eyes. I really have no memory at all of whom I talked to, or didn't talk to, apart from the actors and Michael and Jack, but I assume that I continued to drink, and I know that at about eleven, when the other guests were beginning to leave, I staggered to my feet with the intention of getting back to the Pankhurst, to discover that Nathan Lane, Kristoffer Tabori and Peter Friedman (our Humphry from the Long Wharf production) were going on to a bar in the neighbourhood, and that I felt an obligation (neither moral nor social) to join them. I had something more – something too much more – to drink. Finally achieving a conventionally and recognisably drunken state, I had myself put into a taxi, the driver of which must have been a man of considerable virtue as he could easily have mugged me at any traffic lights, tumbled me out into the gutter, without anyone, especially myself, being the wiser.

One of the many awful things about being at the Pankhurst is that it is miles from any part of New York you want to, or are likely to have to, be in. The trip back from anywhere you want or have to be is, even when drunk, a foul experience. For instance, from this restaurant near the Promenade we would have bowled rapidly down Broadway, about halfway to the Algonquin, then turned east, where all the streets are choked with traffic because the traffic lights never turn from red to green, or when they do, turn instantly back to red again, and the journey would therefore have taken twice as long as it would have taken to go to the Algonquin. Come to think of it, in terms of actual distance, the Promenade might well be closer to the Pankhurst than to the Algonquin.*

Back and swaying about in my room a salient and terrible fact swam into focus: somebody had been in while I was out and put up a whole new arrangement of curtains – of *working* curtains – thus snatching from me my plan for escape. Depressed, fatalistic and drunk, I clambered into bed, went out like a light.

Wednesday, 10 September

Woke at eight, made myself a heavy breakfast, went for a walk and then took a taxi to the theatre. First looked at the model of the set, talked to the designer, David Jenkins, and Michael McGuire about the stage furniture and its positioning, then settled down for the read-through, which went OK, the new young actor, Dylan Baker, doing well to keep up with the five actors who had done

---

* On rainy evenings it took a good twenty minutes longer, *after* I'd got a cab, which often took a bad twenty minutes.

the part before. Just before the read-through, a girl from Phyllis Wender's office had phoned to say that she'd arranged to have a video delivered whenever I wanted. Knowing that there was nothing but the usual video hassles ahead, I phoned her back after the read-through and said that I would return to the Pankhurst immediately to receive it. Back I went, settling down in my room for a long wait for a video that wasn't going to come, and if it came wouldn't work. Within half an hour there was a phone call from reception to say that the video man had just arrived. Although I'm on the seventeenth floor and it generally takes some time to get up from the lobby, I nevertheless – partly because I can't stand the sound of the bell – went straight to the door and opened it. To my disbelief – it seemed physically impossible – the video chap was coming along the hall towards me, carrying the box loosely and easily under his arm, almost as if it were empty. A slightly surreal figure, being a strange racial mix, even by New York standards – a combination of Filipino and West Indian, per-haps, quite young and almost certainly not too good at English. 'Look,' I said slowly, 'the one thing you've got to understand is that I'm immensely stupid and these machines never work for me, did you bring a tape' (I'd asked Phyllis's office to tell them to bring a tape) 'so you can give me a demonstration?' No, he said fluently but in a thick South American accent, he hadn't brought a tape, he'd just have to explain it to me. 'Look,' I said, 'it's no good, I won't understand anything without a tape.' It took him about three minutes to install the video. He then explained to me, with extraordinary rapidity, how to make it work. Actually my attention was fixed on his slightly simian gestures – among other things he was rubbing his thumb up and down under his left armpit. I knew I hadn't grasped anything he'd said and asked him to take me through it again. He said no, he was going. 'Come on,' I said, 'you can take me through it just once more.' 'Aw, is very simple,' he said, and departed, leaving his box on the floor. So the new video débâcle has begun.

I went out. I hadn't had any lunch actually because these hot-dog things I'd eaten at nine o'clock (the same breakfast as the day before) seemed to have swollen my stomach, making me feel rather flatulent. Out into the heat of New York. It's very odd how I've been in the heat in the States all through this year – in Los

Angeles in January, Dallas in February, and now here in September in New York, when it should be getting a little cooler. I trudged about looking for a video rental shop without luck, until finally, miles away, right down almost at the Algonquin, I came across one. It had taken me about forty-five minutes to get there. I felt faint. I joined their club and took out *Shane* – just the one video to test on a machine that wasn't after all going to work. I managed to get a taxi back, trembling with fatigue, came up into my room, put the tape into the video, turned on power, then did a kind of peculiar digital computorial thing to do with pressing buttons 3, 0 and 'entry' – how the video man had managed to feed this information into me subliminally, I really have no idea – put the tape in, sat listlessly down, and there, within a matter of seconds, was the title sequence of *Shane*. I watched to the end of the Alan Ladd–Jean Arthur dance scene, and then turned off the set, took out the tape, put it in again and played the scene through in slow motion – all this for practice, before settling down to think about the Gray–McGuire co-directing problem.

I came to the conclusion, out of a desire not to force the issue for the moment – i.e. cowardice – that I'd better stay away from rehearsals for a few days, my argument being that there's not much point my being there at this stage anyway. I've been through the play so often that I'm likely to become impatient, as I did in Los Angeles. The flaw in this argument is that five of the six other actors have also been through the play as well, and that I'm leaving them to be directed by someone who hasn't – so perhaps *they're* likely to become impatient if I'm not there, to help them to start from a fairly advanced stage. Of course there's no harm in Michael's doing some preliminary blocking, a rough sketch, so to speak, from which I can work subsequently. On the other hand, the longer I allow him to do that, the more difficult it will be to get my own grip on proceedings. And so backwards and forwards, facing up to, and not facing up to, the fact that I'm creating, have already created, a dodgy situation that could damage the company's morale before we've properly started. And facing up to a further, practical problem: what do I do instead of going to the theatre, if I don't go to the theatre? How do I find something sufficiently active to do, to keep my mind off rehearsals? Perhaps I should go out and hustle. Hustle what? Hustle myself, on the pavements of Eighth Avenue. But would anyone give five dollars for an hour with me?

Thursday, 11 September

My hair has felt foul all day. Hardly surprising as I forgot to bring any shampoo and haven't yet got around to buying any. So I went about conscious of this pad of rather unwholesome hair on my scalp. At one point in the day's rehearsals I found myself address-ing the problem of Peter's hair with Dylan Baker – Dylan has got a wonderful mop of blond, springy, positively exuberant hair informing him that one could tell a great deal about the ageing process from people's hair, which changed in some often quite subtle way, not just falling out or turning grey, but visibly losing life and energy. As I talked I could see him eyeing the lustreless pack of dead hair on my own scalp. He's obviously a bright young man who has to be watched very closely, with a view to putting down in him any irony or intelligence that threatens to surface.

After rehearsals I had a pleasant, relaxed and frequently jolly evening with Phyllis in spite of the restaurant, a small bistro-style dump on the East Side, with taped music. Although we arrived slightly late, the table wasn't ready so we had to stand about in the bar before being led to what, from the size of it, might have been a bedside table, one chair at which (mine) blocked the entrance to the wine cellars, thus allowing the waiters to push me backwards and forwards throughout the evening. I knew the food was going to be terrible, too, as all the dishes had chillingly simple names – for instance, crab fishcakes. When the waiter came and took our order – the waiters were ghastly, by the way, poncing about, with sun tans and empty grins, as if recently exported from Los Angeles – I decided to have the marinated swordfish, on the grounds that even this lot couldn't mess up something that is served raw, only to be informed that it was off. I said, 'But it's nine fifteen, how can it be off already?' He said jovially, 'Well, it's a very popular dish so it's off.' As the crab fishcakes were even worse than I'd assumed they'd be, there must be a rare talent at work in the kitchen. I tried to get a glimpse of the bill, peering nonchalantly down as Phyllis paid it. The sum that caught my eye was so monstrous that it must have been an optical illusion. I sometimes think that if you can't go to a *good* expensive restaurant, then you should go to a bad expensive one (as long as I'm not paying of course) – it's more fun. Perhaps that's what they've cottoned on to there.

Friday, 12 September

The theatre was immensely hot, but everything went OK, except for a minor discord between Michael McGuire and myself over the position of a chair, which had been placed right beside Stuart's desk – there's also a chair behind the desk of course. Stuart (Tabori) sat down behind the desk for the beginning of the very long conversation with Martin (Michael Countryman from the Long Wharf production), who immediately sat down beside the desk. So there were the two of them at the desk together, their elbows almost touching, and so it went for the whole fifteen minutes. I couldn't repress the old temper at the tedium, the *pointless* tedium of the experience. Granted that Michael McGuire had no idea what the scene was about and was trying to learn through having the actors sit down and chat their way through the text, I still didn't think it was correct or appropriate for Kris Tabori and Michael Countryman, both of whom have been through this scene endless times before, not to explore it on its feet, so to speak – anything would have been better than their sitting like two elderly clubmen gossiping about the stock market or X's divorce or Y's divorce or my divorce or your divorce. I said something rather tetchy to Michael McGuire, which led to a minor confrontation. He said he wanted to let the actors get to know each other. I said that they would best get to know each other by working through the scene properly, thus getting the scene on *its* feet. Nevertheless we had a quite pleasant lunch together.

In the afternoon things went on in a dull, achingly hot – it was so hot, one could scarcely breathe – achingly hot way until Marigold (Judy Geeson) came on at the end of Act One to announce her abortion. Whereupon Michael asked her what she felt about the abortion, how the fact of the abortion would show itself in her sense of the scene. I was almost beside myself with irritation. I have been through this conversation not once endlessly (in London), not twice endlessly (at the Long Wharf), not three times endlessly (in Los Angeles), but now for the fourth time, endlessly. I got up –

this was an hour before rehearsals were due to finish – swung my bag over my shoulder, made some very blurred apologies to Michael, and left the theatre. I knew that I couldn't sit solemnly on in an un-air-conditioned auditorium on a boilingly hot and airless day in New York, taking part in yet another discussion about what sort of state Marigold would be in when coming from her abortion.*

Came back to the Pankhurst, had a bath and then had dinner with Caroline Lagerfelt, who is extremely pregnant, as the consequence of an affair she'd had with an actor. She was buoyant, eyes sparkling, cheeks rosy, stomach bulging. I found myself feeling very emotional on her account.

Sunday, 14 September

Various members of the company have had to go off to do commercials, so Lois, the cheerful and rather portly stage manageress, has been reading variously the part of Nick, the part of Peter – every part in the play in fact except Stuart, Kris Tabori not having to go off to make a commercial, which I suppose is bad luck on him. But it's all going along as well as can be expected, given the fact that everyone, except Dylan, is far ahead of Michael McGuire, who so far is doing all the blocking and most of the talking. He shows his worry every time I intervene, so I suppose the old ego problem hasn't been disposed of after all. Actually I don't know quite how long we can go on like this, or at what point I shall have to do something about it. Thank God we have lots of time. Otherwise we get on very well, Michael and I.

I should mention that yesterday I damaged my back getting out of a chair in my hotel room. I knew even as I moved that I'd done something wrong. It's one of those chairs where your back can't meet the whole of the chair's back, which curves away from the base of your spine, leaving a gap that you have to be very careful about readjusting your body to when you move – which I

* What exasperation prevented me from making clear here is that in Los Angeles the actress concerned was also Judy Geeson. If we'd had a new actress in New York, I would of course have been prepared to go through the conversation again. At least I hope I would. Michael had no option but to go through the scene with Judy, as it was his first time round and he had still to learn how it worked.

wasn't. I spent most of the day in agony. Sitting down, getting up, bending, anything like that – getting into bed, getting into a bath – all painful. The prospect of picking up the *New York Sunday Times* from outside my door this morning was so depressing that I put it off until I'd lumbered about the room a bit. The sheer weight of the *New York Sunday Times*! I've heard that a small dog was actually crushed to death when a copy landed on it, thrown by what must have been a very muscular newspaper boy. The dog was found pasted to the underside of the front page, and shortly became news itself.

During a (physically) uncomfortable drink I had with Michael in the evening at a Parisian-like sidewalk café he told me he'd heard that Sam Weisman is going to sue Jack McQuiggan for breach of contract.* It seems to me astonishing that Weisman should want the world to know that the producer didn't have confidence in him as a director. He should surely have bowed gracefully out, using the usual 'artistic differences' as an explanation, which in this case would have been accurate, as there genuinely *was* an artistic difference – the difference being that Sam wanted to direct the play and Jack didn't want him to. We were in the middle of discussing this when a Russian lady, an actress that Michael knew, came past. He rose, embraced her, and insisted that she join us. She is one of those ladies that laughs an awful lot because – or so I like to think – she has absolutely no sense of humour, e.g. when Michael, suddenly remembering a Mickey Mouse joke I'd told him, asked me to repeat it. The Mickey Mouse story derives from a cartoon in the *New Yorker* I'd seen years ago. Mickey Mouse, with a five-day stubble on his face, is sitting on a stool in a bar, hunched over a drink, smoking. Two respectably dressed middle-aged men are watching him, one saying to the other, 'I don't know exactly. But they say he used to be big in Hollywood.' I told this joke – or rather described the cartoon – with considerable *élan*, I felt, to the Russian lady, who actually stopped laughing before I'd finished it. I mean she had laughed all the time before I began to tell the joke, and then partway through the joke, but went silent before the end of it, stayed silent, looking puzzled, then asked, 'That's the joke?' I got a cab to the Pankhurst

* To the tune of $3,000,000 I learnt later.

and went to bed, my back made worse by the journey. When I phoned home this morning, I got Ben, who told me that Beryl had pulled a muscle in her leg at approximately the same time, I worked it out, as I'd ricked my back.

Tuesday, 16 September

Yesterday was a day off. I spent most of it with my brother, Piers, who arrived on Sunday. We walked around New York. The only time I feel comfortable is when I'm up and walking.

Wednesday, 17 September

I'm waiting for Michael McGuire to turn up for what we call a showdown conversation. Yesterday at ten o'clock there was meant to be a run-through, which I'd decided not to attend because it seemed more important to find a chiropractor, my plan being to miss the run-through, which I didn't believe could be of much value at this stage, have my back fixed, and get to the theatre in time for rehearsals – the real day's work, as far as I was concerned. Also I had a particular reason for wanting to be at rehearsals as Michael McGuire had phoned me on Monday evening, to question me about the function and intention of Act One, Scene Two, which struck me as odd – surely it would be much simpler for me to address the actors directly, rather than going through him. Until it further struck me that perhaps he didn't want me to address the actors, the old ego problem again, in other words. Anyway, some time in the late morning I phoned the theatre to say that I hadn't been able to get hold of the chiropractor, at least the one that had been recommended to me, my back was extremely painful, how far along were they in the run-through, what time roughly would rehearsals begin, only to be told that they had been rehearsing all morning as the run-through had been cancelled – Judy Geeson not being well. They had been concentrating on Act One, Scene Two.

I phoned Jack McQuiggan and said we'd better talk, to thrash out once and for all the co-director question. We met in the hamburger joint around the corner from the Pankhurst, an appropriately seedy place where, in films, the cop gets his rake-off, the stoolie his bullet between the eyes. He told me what I already knew – that the actors were getting bewildered and fed up, why wasn't I running the show, why didn't I assume my proper role? I said I could see now that the co-directing idea had been a bad one, how did one apportion the work, we should have sorted it out before, to which he replied that he thought he had sorted it out – his understanding being that I'd do what he'd seen me do with the New York production of *Quartermaine's Terms*, concentrate on discovering all the details of the text with the actors, and help them to realise it, while Michael could deal with any problems on the technical side. He'd hoped that my being officially co-director would make my control of the production easier to achieve, not harder. How had I managed with Stephen Hollis in Dallas? I gave him a brief description, but said I didn't think anything could be learnt from it – Stephen had always assumed I'd take over completely after the second week, had indeed wanted me to, but I was pretty certain that the longer Michael went on doing what he was now doing, the harder it would be to take over from him. I wouldn't be able to insinuate myself into command as I'd done at the Long Wharf, because any move I made would be seen as a director's, a rival director's, move. In fact I had the worst of both worlds, unable to function either as playwright or as director. The situation had to be turned around, we both agreed, and as quickly as possible. But with proper respect for Michael, who was working hard and doing his best in an utterly false situation.

We cabbed down to the theatre, to find Michael running Dylan Baker in his big scene at the end of Act One. It was quite clear that they were both at a loss. At the end of it Michael proposed running the scene again. Dylan objected, asking to be allowed to stop whenever he was uncertain about the way a line should be played. Michael said no, don't stop, I don't think we should stop, let's run it. I stopped the scene almost at once, took Dylan back, discussed a line with him, started him again, stopped him again, every sentence or so. In fact I took over the direction in a manner that was not only high-handed, it was brutal, cutting across Michael whenever he showed signs of speaking, until he sat back impotent, no doubt humiliated. At the end Michael came over, unable to hide his distress, and said, 'Now we have a real problem. Who's going to direct? Who's going to talk to the actors?' We arranged to meet tomorrow at ten (now, in fact) before rehearsals, to answer this question after we'd both had a chance to think it through, but as far as I'm concerned the question is answered. It would not only be a nonsense, but an irresponsible nonsense, to let things go on as they've been going on. What makes it difficult, though, is that I know it's my fault: if I had acted decisively at the beginning, instead of passively waiting for my temper to erupt, as I sort of knew it would in the end, all this could have been avoided.

Late that night Michael came and we talked. A long and painful conversation, though its tone was civilised. He quite agreed that his attempting to direct a play that he knows far less well than I is preposterous. On the other hand, he certainly hadn't understood that Jack had always intended him to be in a subsidiary role, and if he had so understood, wasn't sure that he would have accepted the job. I said that I felt it would be subsidiary only during the next stretch of rehearsals, that once we were in the run-through and preview period, his eye, his ear and his judgement would be invaluable. He said his main problem would be how to deal with the actors. They would be aware of what had happened – Kristoffer Tabori had already given him a look, and he didn't think he could stand that sort of thing, especially as years ago he had been a sort of uncle figure to Kristoffer. I said that I didn't think he'd get that sort of thing from any of the other actors, and proposed that today he should go in as usual and do anything he wanted in the first two hours but before he began, he should say that I was going to come in later and do some very close work on the text, of the sort that I had done yesterday with Dylan Baker. Michael said that if I was going to take over he would prefer me to do it immediately, which left me with the prospect of five hours' rehearsal without a break – too much, really, given my back and the nature of the work. But we both agreed that from now on I would be running the rehearsals, which brought the conversation to an end. As it turned out I had enough stamina for only three hours, but they were three hours of intensely detailed work – the only sort of work I can do as a director. But then I don't think myself there is any other sort of work worth doing, as everything from the specific physical moves to the general shape of a scene grows out of it. I was absolutely exhausted by the end. As I didn't get much sleep last night, God knows how I'm going to cope with tomorrow's rehearsals.

Saturday, 20 September

The composer is young, bulky, bearded and on crutches, having snapped his ankle in a skiing accident, I suppose – it was never quite clear how he'd snapped his ankle, now I come to think of it. He lay, semi-recumbent on a sofa, outside the rehearsal hall, with his crutches beside him, telling me that, though my play was very 'neat', he planned to juice it up by slipping some music in under the dialogue. Music and dialogue to be going on at the same time, as in a movie. I tried to be polite, ordering him up a glass of champagne from the bottles I keep stored in the rehearsal-room fridge, and then decided to be dictatorial immediately about what I expected from him, in order not to have to be even more dictatorial later on. Music only where specified in the text – Bach, Wagner, etc. – and no music, by God, anywhere else, but particularly not under the dialogue. He lay there, his crutches beside him, a glass of champagne in his hand, shaking his head in bewildered disappointment. He has a habit of referring to himself by his surname, which I can't remember, but supposing it to be Plumbell (it was something like that), he would say, 'You mean it's going to be just Wagner and Bach and no Plumbell? Plumbell doesn't get a chance to use his own music. Is that what you mean?' I have an idea that this isn't going to be a happy collaboration, although I'm assured he's very talented. The trouble is we don't want a very talented Plumbell, we just want a good, solid, professional chap, who is modest about his own music and is anxious to serve the play with well-chosen passages from Bach and Wagner, etc.

Post Plumbell, Michael and I went and had a drink, as is becoming our habit. As least I have a true drink, an alcoholic drink, and he has club soda with a twist of lemon, or a Perrier with a twist of lemon. At the end of rehearsals I'm usually so tired that the first drink tips me over – when I say first, I'm not counting the champagne I sip very moderately while working. Anyway, the moment I get into my first Glenfiddich, I go plummeting into pleasant semi-oblivion. But Michael wanted to talk again about his position in the production. I said I needed him both as companion and friend, and as a highly intelligent and experienced man of the theatre to whom I could turn for some kind of judgement – on this move or that move, on this line or that. I also said that I needed his opinions on how the actors were progressing, and that he would certainly come into his own when we got to the preview stage. Besides, I said, it seemed to me extremely important that he should be present at every phase of the process so that he would be in full possession of it for any future productions, which he would be directing on his own. He said, yes, he understood all that but it was driving him crazy just sitting there not speaking. Furthermore, I'd got into a habit of doing something that he found particularly disturbing: talking to the actors without in any way referring to him, in fact going off with them, standing with my back to him, so that he couldn't even hear what I was saying. I apologised, explaining that I hadn't been aware even that I was doing it – that it was really just a matter of strolling with an actor as we talked and ending up where we happened to end up. He said that as far as he could see he had three options: either he could stay on as a co-director if he had an equal contribution to make to the production, but he didn't think he had; or he could withdraw entirely; or he could stay on as a consultant, in which case he would want his title changed, because he wasn't going to pass himself off as a co-director of a play he hadn't co-directed. I said I didn't give a damn what he was called as long as he was there for me to refer to on the terms that I've described. It was again an extremely civilised conversation. When we parted he said he'd go home and think about it. Fortunately, his young lady has arrived from Los Angeles, so he will have somebody to discuss it with.

Sunday, 21 September

They're putting the set into the Promenade, so we've moved rehearsals down to the Village, on the third floor of a tall building – tall, anyway, for the neighbourhood. It's a very spacious room, and would be a joy to work in if it weren't for one of the walls, which consists of two sliding doors. When they're closed, the room is almost unbearably hot. When they're opened, they lead you directly out on to the street. By way of a 60-foot plunge. A death plunge. As I suffer from both a fear of heights and a fear of death

I ordered the doors to be shut, and worked throughout the afternoon in suffocating heat. If the actors ever decide they want to exclude me from rehearsals, all they have to do is to demand that the doors are kept open. There is bound to be an Equity ruling that gives them the right to do so.

After rehearsals Michael McGuire and I had a drink at a nearby pub, the White Horse. It's a commodious and casual sort of place, with tables on the pavement outside, and inside lots of dark rooms, some small, some large. While I was downing my Glenfiddich I suddenly remembered that this was the bar in which – or rather, outside of which – Dylan Thomas pegged out after knocking off a dozen or so double shots of whatever it was he was drinking. Whisky, vodka. Perhaps both. He set them up in a line on the counter, threw them one after the other down his throat, lurched out of the main bar past the pavement tables, and collapsed into the gutter, from which he was removed to the hospital and death. At least so I've always understood. So I'll have to watch it at the White Horse – order my drinks one at a time, allow as long an interval as possible between each, confine myself to three doubles at the most. I don't want to end up in the White Horse gutter. Especially as I'm not that keen on Dylan Thomas's poetry. Not keen enough to be taken for a disciple, anyway.

Michael and I steered clear of the co-directing question. We mainly talked about New York, swapping stories about street encounters, most particularly about cab drivers. He told me what is apparently a famous story (i.e. probably untrue) about a yellow cab and a chequered cab, always in intense competition with each other. On one occasion, so this story goes, a chequered cab drew up beside a yellow cab at the traffic lights. The yellow cab driver looked across at the chequered cab, and seeing an extraordinarily fat woman sitting in the back, yelled out to the driver, 'Hey, that's some fat lady you got there! What a fat lady you got there!' The chequered cab driver shouted back: 'Listen, this lady is my passenger! She's a fine lady! Special! What do ya mean talking about this fine, fine lady like that? That's dreadful, you cunt, you shithead, you puke-maker *and* you fuck-all, you're talking here about an important passenger of mine!' The traffic lights changed. Driving off, he turned and said, 'How's that for telling 'em, fat lady?' Now I'd probably have forgotten this story, if it hadn't been for the

driver of the cab that took me from the White Horse to the Pankhurst. He was a Greek, and informed me, within minutes and very
quietly, that in his view New York was a zoo, yes, a zoo, he said,
and everyone in it was an animal. 'They call it Manhattan, but for
me it is a zoo.' Suddenly the cab in front did something with which
he disagreed, whereupon and still in thoughtful flow, he pulled
down the window, leaned out to scream, 'Hey, you fucking cunt,
you shithead, you big, big swine, what you doing there?' The
other taxi driver did whatever he was going to do anyway, and
my driver, calmly winding up the window, resumed his discourse
on Manhattan as a zoo. The thing is that Michael's story is a well-
known fiction, and mine is simply a report of something that happened a mere few hours ago, immediately after I'd heard Michael
retelling the fiction. And yet they tell almost exactly the same
story. Perhaps it repeats itself, in slightly different form, every few
minutes in New York.

Back at the Pankhurst I had a bath, then dinner with Piers in
what I have taken to be the hotel restaurant. Afterwards we came
up to my suite, and had a very nice time rocking about with glasses
of Glenfiddich in our hands until the Glenfiddich ran out. I phoned
down to the desk, and asked them to tell the bar or restaurant
to send up more. Neither could do it, I was told, as neither was
attached legally to the hotel. And the hotel couldn't do it, as it
didn't have a licence. Thus I discovered that the Pankhurst isn't
even a hotel, it's a kind of condominium. Which certainly explains
why I've never felt at home here. If we wanted a drink, I was told,
we'd have to come down to the bar. Where we wouldn't get one,
as the bar was already closed. How then had it come to pass, as I
was assured by someone or other that it had, that a famous actor
had drunk himself to death in the bar? With only a few hours at
his disposal, he must have been an even more impatient suicide
than Dylan Thomas, who could take his time at the White Horse,
open day and night.

Tuesday, 23 September

I'd just got back to the Pankhurst from rehearsals when Ronald
Harwood, in from London, phoned. We arranged to have dinner
in the restaurant downstairs. It was a very jolly evening, with lots

of laughter, decent wine, OK food, and an unbeatable, almost unpayable, bill. Ronnie was only staying the night, at a very splendid hotel, having been Concorded in (he was also being Concorded out) by a film company for a few conversations which, he said, could easily have taken place on the telephone. We wondered how it is that I never get involved in deals like his, Virgin 'Upper' being pretty well the limit to what people are prepared to offer me – and then I have to stay weeks and weeks to justify it. We agreed that Ronnie gets Concorde and big film deals because he is (a) handsomer, (b) more successful, (c) older, (d) shorter. After dinner I walked him down the street towards the Waldorf, then turned back to the hotel. I was, I must admit, rocking, swaying, in fact scarcely able to keep my balance, but I'd almost made it to the Pankhurst when this Jewish guy, with a rabbinical sort of hat on, swarmed up to me, gripped me by the shoulders and said he wanted twenty dollars. Otherwise he'd have to kill me. I said, no, there was no possibility of my giving him twenty dollars. He said, well, what about ten? I said no, not ten either. He said, 'Well what I'm going to do, I'm going to kill ya – I gotta kill ya,' he said. 'I gotta kill ya or I don't get home, what am I going to do?' So I said, 'Well listen, take this.' I poured all the change from my pockets – about 75 cents into his hands, and left him there. He was about six foot three, about twenty-five years old, and very Jewish with his Jewish skull cap on (I forget what they're called).* He stood there, where I'd left him, counting up the change.

Wednesday, 24 September

Arranged to meet Michael and Jack at the White Horse before rehearsals to discuss yet again the question of Michael's status in the production. Horrible ride, with the taxi driver masquerading as a sociologist – or, an even worse thought, a sociologist masquerading as a taxi driver – doing an in-depth analysis on the subject of the major change in New York life, viz. that some years back New York was a place where intelligent people gathered together to talk (he made the whole city sound rather like Les Deux Magots), but now it was just a place where people wanted to buy

---

* Yarmulkas.

condominiums.* That was it. That was his whole analysis, though he spun it out by repeating it endlessly.

Michael was already at the White Horse, at a pavement table. I think he's the only person I know who is more punctual than Harold – if, that is, punctual also includes being early. Jack was late of course. He is, I think, the *least* punctual man I know, always deflected on his way to meetings by meetings that give rise to further meetings. As I've said before, he is a very dapper dresser, with a well-knit figure and a neat-featured, wholesome, round face, and there he stood on the pavement of the White Horse, late, in his smart suit with highly polished shoes, his usual collar and tie, his hair slicked back, while around his chops was a five o'clock shadow at least three days old. Thick, grey-black stubble is what it was. I said, 'Jack, what's going on here?' He said, 'Well I just – I've decided not to shave until we've opened. You know, like baseball players or football players who don't shave until they've got through the championship. A superstition.' He was quite hard to take actually, because he looked simultaneously immaculate and sordid.† The conversation that then took place – on whether Michael should have a change of title or quit the production – followed the same course as the one Michael and I had already had, Jack's contribution being merely to support me in my determination to keep Michael with us, although he was strongly against a change of title on the grounds that it would cause unnecessary fuss in the press. It was once again friendly in tone, and once again ended with the matter unresolved. At least as far as I know. Jack and Michael stayed on, talking, while I rocked up to the West Beth Theatre Complex, or whatever it's called, to conduct rehearsals.

Afterwards, Nathan Lane, Michael Countryman, and I went back to the White Horse, and over drinks talked about the real nature of rehearsing and directing, the relationship between the director, the playwright and the actors, etc., all in very general terms. Bonhomous, philosophical, rambling, unproductive, except in the pleasure it gave us while it was going on. Then Michael Countryman got on his motorbike (though I've been begging him

---

* Perhaps he meant 'condoms', which would have made more sense.

† I'm glad to say that it was a short-lived combination, as the stubble came off next day. I like to think that it was the look on my face that did the trick.

not to ride it until after we've opened – or even better, after we've closed). Nathan and I went on talking and getting increasingly drunk, until first Dena and James turned up – we'd arranged to meet for dinner – and then Stephen Hollis, who was in town from Dallas to cast *A Streetcar Named Desire*. Nathan went rolling off into the night, his feet sort of skipping drunkenly across the pavement, while the remaining four of us crossed the road to a Chinese restaurant where the food was merely bad, while the drinks were positively appalling – Stephen receiving a glass of white wine which actually tasted like pear juice, though claiming to be a Chablis. Nevertheless we had quite a nice evening, just sort of relaxed and chatty. Stephen and I lingered on to talk about the triumphs and the horrors of the Dallas production of *Dog Days*. There were very few horrors, as we agreed, but then there were very few triumphs, we had also to agree. He went on to say that he was actually rather depressed about the situation at the New Arts, as since *Dog Days* every single member of the company apart from himself had been fired. We discussed the implications of this for his career* until, waving about from drink, I came back to the Pankhurst where I am now, reporting into the tape recorder. It's one in the morning, and though I've had quite a rough day and a far too sociable evening, I feel all right. A lot of good things are going on in rehearsal, the play seems to be becoming more vivid, breathing in a more relaxed way, and yet growing firmer and firmer. I am deeply tired, carrying on with this monologue because I'm convinced there's somebody out there somewhere that I need to communicate with – rather like E.T. trying to phone home, I suppose.

Tuesday, 30 September

Back on stage in the Promenade, with a major problem in the form of Kristoffer Tabori. During the last few run-throughs I'd noticed that he'd begun to regress, offering first a stale imitation of his best Los Angeles performances, rather as if he were doing it from

---

* About three months later the New Arts went bankrupt and the theatre was closed down. It was then that I discovered that I hadn't received any royalties, either as playwright or as co-director, and therefore ended up heavily out of pocket.

memory or that it was something he'd brought with him like a
suit, that he could just slip into when needed; and then through
that to his worst Los Angeles performances, his Lee J. Cobb
period, though with some extra mannerisms stuck on. It was a
heavy piece of impersonation, in fact, though I was never sure
who he was impersonating. Sometimes he reminded me of a
befuddled elderly academic; other times – this was a matter of the
voice – of Winston Churchill summoning the nation to war: in his
first speech of the play, which needs to be crisply thoughtful, we
get, 'I just don't *kn–o–ow* – I just don't *know* – there's a letter here
from *Le–e–e–avis*, full of *words* like *emba–a–attled* and *bele–e–eaguered.'*
For the most part, though, he was using voice to comment on
Stuart's language, elaborately stressing certain words and phrases
to indicate that here he was being ironic, there forceful. It became
impossible to judge what was going on in any scene in which he
appeared – he appears in almost every scene – because it was cluttered by his actorish gesticulations and his bizarre vocalizations.
No notes I gave him out in the open seemed to have any effect. He
didn't actually resist them, but – again – seemed to be impersonating an actor listening to a director.

The final straw came towards the end of today's rehearsal, during the long dialogue with Michael Countryman, a very difficult
passage, which works only if we can persuade the audience to
listen intently to every word, which in its turn can be achieved
only by having the actors listening intently to each other. During
one of Michael Countryman's speeches Tabori took off his spectacles, blew on them, wiped them, put them back on, fingered his
ears, stroked his chin, and stared down at his feet – he'd never
done any of this before but now he did all of it and all of it within
Michael Countryman's fairly short speech, which therefore went
for nothing. I decided the time had come to confront him directly,
but in such a way that I wouldn't seem to be making a big deal
of it. So, of course, in trying not to make a big deal of it, I succeeded
in making a big deal of it.

First, I chose a patch in the play, the beginning of the Epilogue,
in which every actor except Tabori appears, then telling Michael
what I planned, asked him to run it a few times, as often as necessary in fact, while I took Tabori out for a drink. We went to the bar
next door, where I ordered myself a large whisky, plugged a glass

of whatever he'd asked for into his hand, and began to tell him what he was doing. I employed my tentative smile and shy, uncertain voice technique, explaining the effect all his gesticulating and his mannerisms were having on his performance. He said but that was *him*, that was real life, he couldn't help it, that's what people did in life if they were naturally gesticulative people. I said yes, perhaps, but the trouble is that the character he's playing is intensely still and watchful, he was *written* that way. He made a vague gesture towards understanding this, and I recalled with a spasm of hope that we'd gone through almost exactly the same conversation in Los Angeles, to very good effect. I moved on with more confidence to discuss the question of his growing tendency to explain and comment on the text with his voice. I'd hardly got into it, in fact was in mid-sentence, when he said, 'Thank you very much for the drink, I don't want to hear any more, goodbye.' And, turning on his heel, walked out. I stood in the bar for about thirty seconds, thinking, ah yes, of course the Matrix strikes back* – the Matrix being the only theatre I've ever worked in where actors taking umbrage and flouncing off were likely punctuations in the day's work. I knocked off the rest of my drink and hurried after him, catching him as he was just about to turn into the theatre. Swallowing pride, bile, I said something oily along the lines that we really must continue this conversation, if offence had been given, none had been intended, etc. It was either that or *force majeure* (like a blow to his groin). But with the first public performance two days away, I realised it was wiser not to engage in a pavement brawl with my leading man. We went back to the bar for further drinks. After a preliminary and debasing conversation about his feelings and my feelings, our relationship in Los Angeles, when I was the playwright and he was first the director and then an actor, and now in New York where I was the director and he was again an actor, I manoeuvred the conversation around to the primary subject – his performance. I got most of the things said that I wanted to say – several times in fact – and he appeared to be taking it in, when we were interrupted by a member of the stage management, who said that Michael McGuire had finished

* I thought a number of other things too which are recorded on tape but don't sit prettily on the page.

running the scene. We went back to the theatre where Michael told me he had finished running the scene about eight times and didn't have the nerve to run it yet again.

Wednesday, 1 October

Rehearsals proceeded smoothly until there was another confrontation with Tabori. It came, as before, towards the end, when everybody was exhausted. He had obviously done his best to cut out as much of the distracting fussiness as he could but there were still lots of places where he was getting in the way of the play. I pointed them out to him as we came to them, with remorseless politeness and implacable good nature, though I could sense his smouldering resentment. When we returned to the top of Act One, Scene Two, I took him through his long conversation on the telephone, which he was concluding with a swivel in his swivel chair, as he simultaneously seized the datebook* and began to scan its pages with the telephone clamped under his ear, speaking into it as he made to jot something down. I knew that he was particularly fond of this piece of business as it had become more and more complicated, but having started on my road I was determined to keep going down it. 'Kris,' I said, with the air of a man about to move on to more important things, 'don't swivel in the chair and don't use the datebook.' Whereupon he asked to have a private word with me.

We went out into the foyer, where he launched into a feverish account of what he thought he was as an actor and what he thought acting was about. I found it very hard to listen to him because what I most of all noticed was that he was doing all the things he'd been doing on the stage, gesticulating, taking off his glasses, stepping forwards, stepping sideways, as if really bent on showing me that everything in his performance came directly from his personal observation of his own behaviour. Finally he allowed me to explain why he couldn't use the swivel and the datebook while speaking into the phone – that I wanted the audience to take in the significance of what he was saying, rather than admire his agility with props, although I put it more tactfully. He

* In England, known as a diary.

said I was stripping him down, stripping him down of everything he did as an actor, until there would be nothing left at all. He said that he really felt that if I went on doing this to him he would have no choice but to leave. He would open in the play of course, and then give his two weeks' notice immediately.* He didn't see he had any alternative, I was destroying him. I don't know whether I believed him or not and I don't know whether, at that moment, I cared or not, and I can't remember how we finished the conversation. But shortly afterwards we ended up back on the stage and went through the telephone conversation again, without swivel or datebook. He did it very well and it worked very well.

I then broke for the day, but before I could get off with Michael for a drink, Tabori somehow trapped me and began a curious debate about the principles of acting, he lying full length on stage, I standing in the aisle below him, my throat parched and full of yearning. Actually it wasn't a proper debate – I hadn't touched on the principles of acting, not knowing what they are. Nevertheless he claimed that he agreed with everything I'd said, he simply had a different approach. He was perfectly friendly and I suppose that, as the producer and the other actors were still hanging about the theatre listening, all he was really doing was showing that he and I were still talking to each other. Later, over my drink, I spoke to Michael in recuperating terms of my feelings – every other actor is doing so well, the rehearsals are in every other respect so harmonious and enjoyable. This drink, by the way, was taken at a bar-restaurant along 56th Street called Melon's, after the owner. The décor is all melons – drawings, watercolours, oil paintings, lithographs, photographs, everywhere you look there is a representation of this visually entertaining but otherwise rather dull fruit. As my new play is called *Melon*, after the central character, I find it slightly eerie. Certainly portentous. But of what?

---

* One of the serious disadvantages – perhaps the only serious disadvantage – of having a play done Off-Broadway rather than On-Broadway is that Equity allows actors the right to give two weeks' notice, thus jeopardising the stability and continuity of the production. The Equity argument is that actors are paid comparatively little Off-Broadway and should therefore be in a position to accept on the spot any work for which they might get paid more. In an Off-Broadway production of one of my plays some years back the leading lady did in fact give two weeks' notice just before we went into previews, which meant that she left the day after we'd opened.

Thursday, 2 October

Our first public performance, though not an official preview. In fact Jack had told us he'd merely invited a small group of friends. The auditorium, however, was packed and it turned out that almost everyone had paid for their tickets. This isn't a complaint, rather a little memorandum of admiration to Jack. I'd much rather play before a full house, whatever the circumstances, and so would the actors once they get going. And of course I'd always rather people paid for their tickets, especially when I get a percentage – two percentages in this case.

The show went OK for a first go. The nature of the work still to be done was pretty evident, mainly a matter of translating the rehearsal tempo into a theatrical tempo, eliminating irrelevant pauses, coming in far quicker on cue, re-examining a number of moves that now suddenly seemed redundant – the usual kind of stuff. And Kristoffer Tabori. He had in a sense proved his point. Now that he'd had everything stripped away he was nothing, or anyway gave us nothing, except a voice humanly hollow but nevertheless commenting and intoning. He allowed interminable pauses before speaking and made a point of not looking at the actors when they spoke to him, or indeed when he spoke to them. Instead he looked at the ground pointlessly, his shoulders slightly hunched. A particularly unfortunate posture in this lighting – the lighting clearly also requires a lot of work – as he invariably lowered his face into shadow, thus making himself look to the audience like a loser, a jerk and a loser. No, that's intemperate and not quite true. He has considerable physical charm on stage, so what he really looked like was a hounded schoolboy.

Friday, 3 October

I spent the morning rehearsing Tabori, trying to get some animation into his performance without allowing him to become a windmill. The worst aspect of this situation is that I've begun to neglect the other actors, all of whom need (or anyway *think* they need) attention. In the afternoon we had our first official preview. I would have been delighted by it, as would McQuiggan and McGuire, if it hadn't been for Tabori's performance. After the show the three of us proceeded to our table at Melon's, and over our respective drinks – two club sodas for them and a very large Glenfiddich for me – considered ways, some of them very sinister indeed, of dealing with our problem. Nothing in the end seemed feasible except the obvious one of my continuing to try to get from him what we all wanted – a live, quick-witted, uncommenting, ungesturing, fully expressed Stuart on the stage.

I went back to the Pankhurst, feeling dejected and defeated, had a bath, returned for the second preview. It went very much as the first had done. Michael McGuire and I went up to the dressing rooms to see the actors. The dressing rooms are actually one room divided into two sections. In the first section are Kristoffer Tabori and Judy Geeson, in the other section everybody else. But in order to get into the second dressing room you have to go through the first – a kind of rite of passage. The first person I saw was Tabori – he was taking off his make-up. Our eyes met in the mirror. I smiled at him with sickeningly cheerful intensity, gave his shoulder a half-squeeze which I tried not to make punitive, then turned to Judy and gave her a cuddle of real enthusiasm. I have come to admire her performance enormously – fresh, warm, uncomplicated and honest, which, given the fact that she spends almost all her time on stage telling lies, is a remarkable achievement. Then, liberated, through into the next dressing room, with heartfelt embraces and compliments for Michael Countryman, Nathan Lane, Peter Friedman and Dylan Baker. Dylan, having struggled far behind the others with the text in rehearsal and often quite clearly full of doubt, blossomed remarkably from the moment – it came very early – when he got his first laugh, and spent the rest of the evening joyfully garnering many more.*

Over a drink at Melon's Jack and I again debated the Tabori problem for a while, considering further alternatives. There *are* no alternatives, of course, but animated dismissals of impossible solutions somehow give one hope – or at least give one the illusion of doing *something*. We had to break off to go to a party, which was being held in the penthouse of the theatre. We were rather late – Michael McGuire and the cast had already gone up – and we

---

* Subsequently, in fact, he became so successful at laugh-garnering that he began to threaten the structure of the scenes and had to be held somewhat in check.

made ourselves even later by not being able to find any route from
the lobby to the penthouse, until we stumbled on a heavily dis-
guised lift that took us, not only up to the penthouse, but right
into the vast sitting room in which the party was under way. It
was a very lavish, beautifully appointed apartment, or at least so
I was told by several young men clustered about the place, whose
role I couldn't determine, but it was so dimly lit that I couldn't
make out much more than the essentials – i.e. where the sofas and
chairs, drinks and food were located. It did however command
a magnificent view of the river, though I sometimes think that
almost every apartment I've been into in New York commands a
magnificent view of the river – or, if not the river, of the park.
I wasn't sure who the apartment belonged to, but I suppose – logic
suggests – that it would be owned by the guy who owns the
theatre, but as I didn't know what he looked like (still don't)
I made a point of treating every rich-looking, unidentifiable male
as the host, issuing compliments on the food, the view, etc. Among
the people I talked to early on was Kristoffer Tabori's mother, the
actress Vivica Lindfors, and Holland Taylor, the actress who'd
played Anne Butley opposite Alan Bates on Broadway all those
years ago.

I gave neither of them full attention because all the time my
eyes were fixed on Michael McGuire and Kristoffer Tabori, who
were engaged in what looked like rather passionate conversation
on the other side of the room. Suddenly Tabori broke away, looking angry, distressed, something, and I remembered that at Melon's,
after the afternoon preview, Michael had offered to talk to Kristoffer as his old friend and mentor. So let's say that Tabori looked
exactly like a chap who's just been talked to by an old friend and
mentor. I slipped up to Michael, and asked him what had happened. He said he'd offered his services – anything he could do to
help improve Tabori's performance, talk, go through the scenes,
whatever. Tabori first went – or pretended to go – into a state of
shock, then asked why we were all ganging up on him, what was
the matter with his performance, he thought it was fine, everything had come together for him, he knew exactly what he was
doing, perfectly happy, why couldn't we leave him alone? This
deepened my depression. If Tabori really believes that he is ace in
the part, *and* is convinced that all criticism and offers to help are

merely part of a plan conceived by bullies to give him a bad time . . . I sought out Tabori, trying to look genial and yet impassive, but before I could start, he wanted to know what was going on, why we were all ganging up on him, etc., he thought he was doing just fine – after which I delivered a little pack of clichés, with an anchovy of a compliment on each, about the differences between the actor's view and the audience's, our need to develop, even change slightly, our perspective, and what harm could it do to talk to Michael, they were both intelligent men, after all Tabori could always discard anything that didn't seem to him useful, *such* a difficult part, as we all knew . . . In the end he agreed to talk to McGuire, although only on condition that he didn't have to listen to him. Reminiscent of the kind of arrangement I used to come to with Ben, my son, when he was having a dodgy time with the teachers at Highgate Primary School.

Sunday, 5 October

Yesterday afternoon I went into a bout of what I already recognise as uncontrolled paranoia (I like to think I live most of my life in a state of *controlled* paranoia). I sat through the matinee which, I think, went very well, and I know I took lots of notes, because I've still got them, on such technical things as pauses, looks that go astray, etc., but my only memory is of my eyes, mind, heart, soul being fixed in a kind of cold passion on Tabori, as he walked about the stage with the measured pace that no human being really walks with, *except* on stage, and certainly no *young* man should ever walk with, even on stage – walking in a stately way about the stage, and delivering his lines in a stately but strangled voice, then dropping his eyes to his feet, thus dropping whatever actor he was playing with (usually Michael Countryman) into the shit, as no other actor, however good he is, can play effectively on stage with someone who isn't there. But it was above all the lines, the way he delivered my lines. *My* lines. That was the point. So suddenly the playwright shouldered aside the director, crying out – how can this be allowed to happen? How could you let this guy maul my language? Real paranoia, or possibly schizophrenia in that there were suddenly two of me, one of whom was giving the other absolute hell.

I went to Melon's, spent most of the evening preview there, looking in on the theatre to glare at Tabori, before ducking back to Melon's. And did much the same during today's two performances, unable to stay longer than twenty minutes at a stretch during the matinee, making an occasional note, managing to go back and see the actors afterwards, grinning out compliments at Tabori in a tone as unnatural, I imagine, as his on stage. But really I was in a different world, a world of drink and anger. I spent almost all the evening peformance at Melon's, either by myself or with Jack and/or Michael – they kept darting back to see bits of the show, coming back to report on the lack of change in Tabori's performance. It must have been about halfway through the second act – anyway Jack was there and Michael wasn't – that I rose from the table and without even knowing I was going to do it, got some change at the counter, went to the cigarette machine and bought a packet of cigarettes. I smoked my way through them, one after the other and sometimes probably two simultaneously, and felt – I suppose this is the worst part – such joy, such release to have the murderous old friend swirling about in the lungs again. (Swirling about *now*, drifting through my nostrils, filling the room *now*, as I dictate this.) I won't say the paranoia leaked away on the spot, but I was able to discuss rationally with Jack, and then with Michael, how I intend to proceed with Tabori. I'll simply go on giving him notes, *all* the notes I make, closing him down in details, eliminating every pause, every look at his feet, force him to deal eyeball to eyeball with the other actors – in fact, assume that if we can't get him into the play as Stuart, we can get him out of its way as an imposter. Drill him into submissive service. That, it seems to me, is the director's duty to the playwright. Though I can't say I'm looking forward to performing it. It's now two in the morning. I have an overflowing ashtray and an almost empty cigarette packet beside me. If I smoke myself out, will I be able to start tomorrow afresh? *Afresh!* Hah!

Thursday, 9 October

Tomorrow I'll have done my time at the Pankhurst, and can move out. I've booked myself into the Algonquin, Suite 310, which they've assured me will be ready by lunchtime. I can't quite believe it, expecting at any moment to be summoned by a warder and taken down to see the Governor, a severe but compassionate man, who will break the news that there's been a hitch, the Parole Board have reviewed my case and come to the conclusion that I'm still not ready to be returned to society. If so, I'll make a run for it. On my desk, by the way, there's a cable from Joe Stern. It arrived this morning, to the accompaniment of the usual savage ring at the door. Catching his name before I took in the contents, I assumed it was a premature first night good-luck message. In fact, it's a short, angry statement to the effect that I'd given him my word that the name of the Matrix Theatre would appear on the title page of the Promenade programme. Obsessed as I've been with previews, I hadn't even looked at the programme. I did so immediately of course, and couldn't at first see any acknowledge-ment of the Matrix anywhere. Eventually I located it, in superfine print on a back page, squeezed into a paragraph of many other acknowledgements, one of them to a meat-packing company. (But what has a meat-packing company contributed to the production? Nobody eats meat in the course of the play. At least to my know-ledge.) I spoke to Jack, who's promised to move the Matrix to the title page, in large letters. What strikes me as a bit of a mystery, though, is how Joe got hold of the information about the Promen-ade programme? Somebody must either have sent him a copy or phoned him about it. But who? And why the coldly recriminatory cable, when he could easily have phoned? He can't really have believed that I, personally, put him down there with the meat-packers, can he? Or does he see me, since the *affaire* Weisman, as Perfidious Albion?

Anyway, at this moment – 11.30 p.m. – Perfidious Albion is lying on the green sofa of the all-green sitting room for what he hopes is the last time, a cigarette between his lips, a glass of malt in one hand, the tape recorder in the other, trying to get his mind back to tonight's preview. I haven't yet looked at my notes, but I have the general impression that it went OK, given that we're still nowhere very much with our leading man, though at least he's beginning to speed up, move the scenes along, and keep his eyes at eye-level. There was a great deal of applause at the end, which I chose to take as heartfelt, and even some 'bravos' – but then New Yorkers famously love to explode into 'bravos'. It's part of their idea of an evening out. It's part of my idea of their evening out, too, as a matter of fact.

In a few minutes I shall clamber to my feet, and make my way slowly and carefully a few hundred yards up the road to the Drake Hotel. I shall sit in the bar there and hope that the limp-wristed pianist who a few nights ago infuriated a large couple from Houston with a pansified version of 'The Yellow Rose of Texas' is on again tonight. If so I shall encourage him to have a go at pansifying 'Rule Britannia'.

Friday, 10 October

Came straight back from the matinee, packed my bags, and departed from the Pankhurst, shiftily announcing to everybody in earshot – which included the usual clutch of imminent ghosts – that I'd been very happy there *indeed*, would they please forward any mail to the Algonquin, to which I was having to move for convenience's sake, under-tipped the doorman from nerves (I usually do the reverse) and cabbed jauntily down here to the Algonquin, savouring the atmosphere of the familiar, much-missed lobby as I made my way to the desk, where I was informed that Suite 310 was not, after all, free, as its present occupant, some thoughtless swine of a senator, has postponed his departure until tomorrow morning. So I'm presently installed in 506, a pleasant enough suite which I took a violent dislike to moments before I saw it. As I'm only here overnight I haven't bothered to unpack my bag or the various carrier bags which I've used for transporting all the stuff – mainly unread paperbacks – that I've accumulated over the last four weeks. I've brought the video with me, too, of course, which I've insisted on having plugged in on the grounds, I suppose, that it will have to be unplugged and replugged in 310 tomorrow morning, and on the further grounds that I'll be too tired to watch anything on it tonight, when I get back from the theatre. Perhaps the need to be in possession of a functioning video has now passed beyond a neurosis into a kind of mono-mania. All I know is that now I've tested it with a few minutes of *Shane*, I feel much more comfortable, ready to descend to the lobby for a Glenfiddich and a couple of cigarettes before going on to the Promenade, for the evening preview. I probably won't even bother to pause at the desk, to make a further scene about being kept out of 310.

Later   Tonight's was our eighth preview. It was also the night on which Tabori made his breakthrough. Everything about him was simple, direct and focused. As a consequence he had authority, a real power, so that for the first time one understood why his friends look to him as a kind of standard-bearer. I don't know how he's managed it – though I noticed that he'd stopped straining for a characterising English accent, which must have helped him relax considerably.* I know I haven't given him any real help. From the moment he walked out on me in the bar I've found it impossible to talk to him except in very specific terms – 'Don't pause there,' 'Don't look down or away there,' 'Don't stress this word – and this – and this –' – all the steady drip, drip, drip of notes could do was limit his room for manoeuvre, not actually give him the kind of life he had tonight. Anyway, I was exhilarated, positively bounding up the stairs to the dressing room to salute him. He could tell – at least I hope he could – that for once I was paying him tributes from the heart, not simply flinging compliments around like confetti as a way of getting into the real business of dishing out notes. I gave Judy an extra dose of cuddles – I could see she knew something special had happened, and was thrilled by it – then went on into the second dressing room, where I found an extremely distressed Michael Countryman. Hardly surprising. He's got so into the habit of playing Martin as if he's alone on stage that suddenly finding himself confronted by a real human being who looked him in the eye and asked him questions threw him completely. He'd gone from floundering to sinking and now sat in the dressing room shaking slightly, scarcely able to speak.

I slipped along to Melon's, had a drink by myself, to toast the arrival in the play of a real Stuart at last, and then remembered that I was expected at a bar on Columbus Avenue, where Dylan

---

* I've always felt it far more important for American actors to worry about the intention of the text than to worry about how, precisely, to pronounce it. In my view dialect coaches are the bane of English plays in the American theatre, creating stress and self-consciousness over irrelevancies, and therefore undermining an actor's confidence in who and what he is. I don't mean one shouldn't try to get the accent right. Only that one shouldn't make an issue of it.

was celebrating his twenty-eighth birthday. I rambled along to it, revelling in my first anxiety-free half-hour since I'd arrived in New York. The bar, small, noisy and Irish, was called the Emerald Isle. Judy Geeson and Kristoffer Tabori had already left but Peter Friedman, Nathan Lane, Michael Countryman and his girlfriend, Dylan Baker and his girlfriend were there, all packed into one small booth. I squeezed on to the end of the banquette, which had room for only my right buttock, and talked a bit to Michael about what had happened tonight. And then, looking around at all these young faces, I suddenly decided to leave. I felt – I don't know quite what I felt exactly, perhaps just that I'd reached an age when both my buttocks require support, at least when sitting down. I came back to the Algonquin, lingered in the lobby, and over a drink or two and more than a cigarette or two, I thought about my smoking. At the Pankhurst, just before I started smoking again, I had a succession of nightmares. In the most vivid and disgusting of them I was staggering along, carrying in my arms an enormous block – a convict's load, in fact – of nicotine gum, out of which thick, black hairs were growing. So here I am, back on the weed, with all the old effects back too. The filth accumulating in my nose and lungs, the uncontrollable whistling wheeze, my voice enfeebled as I talk into this machine, up in 506. I shall leave a light on through the night, by the way. When the lights are out the blackness is impenetrable, but full of small noises. I've also got it into my head that somebody I know of died in 506. Was it Peter Lorre? I'm pretty sure he died in the Algonquin.

Saturday, 11 October

As soon as I awoke I phoned down to reception to arrange my move into 310. I was told that the bloat senator was going to stay on for another night. I got myself together very slowly, bathed, shaved, made a few phone calls, including one extremely long one home, then went down to the lobby for a glass of champagne, before plodding the hundred yards or so down 42nd to Un Deux Trois, the English papers under my arm. They get the English papers regularly at the Algonquin, only missing out on the days that really count – the report of the last day of a Test match, for instance, after you've been allowed to follow avidly the reports of the first four days. I ordered a businesslike cheese omelette and a glass of red wine, consumed all of the latter and about an eighth of the former. Not the fault of the omelette. I'm having a great deal of trouble eating at the moment. Glanced through the papers, fretting away about whether Tabori would keep what he'd found, or was it an accident? Or had I deceived myself? etc., then dragged myself out on to the pavement into a cab up to the Promenade for the matinee. When I went up to the dressing rooms to give some notes I kept my eye fixed casually on Tabori, looking for any significant change in his response. He took his own notes readily enough but without much show of interest. This depressed me. Neither the matinee nor the evening preview were quite up to last night. Tabori, while at least, and thank God, remaining real, had slowed down a fraction, especially in the second show. Hairline stuff, *just* a fraction, but a fraction on almost every line. Dangerous, as so many fractions spread the play out, imperceptibly, towards boredom. I talked it over with Michael and Jack at Melon's afterwards. Jack, who hadn't seen last night's performance, and therefore saw only the leap that Tabori had made, was elated. Michael, who saw the leap diminished, rather less so. I began to outline my plans for the next day's rehearsal, then gave up and got a taxi back to the Algonquin.

It was an extraordinary ride. The driver had his radio going, was jouncing his knee and singing as he ate either a hot dog or a hamburger, I couldn't see clearly which, while sucking on a can of Coke, while smoking a cigarette. He was quite clearly in charge of everything except the cab itself which swerved and dodged crazily in and out of the traffic, narrowly failing to smash up the cabs in front. But he had about him a kind of gaiety which communicated itself to me so that I actually enjoyed the ride almost as much as he did. It suddenly struck me that *The Common Pursuit* is precisely about this kind of gaiety, the gaiety of life, that every moment, however dreadful the surrounding circumstances, has its own inherent gaiety.*

I had a drink in the tumultuous, post-theatre Algonquin lobby, straining hard but unsuccessfully to overhear the conversation, at

---

* This is nonsense. There have been many moments in my life that have been entirely without gaiety – even the inherent kind. Whatever that is.

the next table between a gaunt but healthy-looking young man of about twenty-five with close-cropped yellow hair (dyed, I think) and a diminutive girl in slacks, dark, hollow-eyed, with ragged fingernails, which she kept gnawing at. It was a very intense conversation, the man seeming to be confessing something, the girl seeming to be confessing something back to him, but there was an impatience between them, as if they found it difficult to hear each other out. I couldn't pick up more than the occasional word, though I think I caught 'butter' and 'soufflé', so they might merely have been swapping recipes. But then I also caught, or thought I caught, 'groin'* from the girl. When I finally came up here I had a premonition that the unspeakably selfish or (politically more dangerous) indecisive senator in 310 was going to stay on and on, and decided to unpack my bag. I hung my few trousers in the closet, sorted out my dirty laundry, then settled at an angle to the video and allowed a fear to surface that I'd managed to suppress at the end of the preview: that the set, which I was sure I had seen falter during the second performance, might actually stick one night during the spectacular last change. Though it was a possibility too ghastly to contemplate, I contemplated it, until deciding that the stage-hands knew best and would certainly have alerted me,† and so slid my mind away to other aspects of the evening, discovering note after note, all of which I wrote down while trying not to smoke and smoking, keeping my eyes averted from the boxes of nicotine gum packed on top of the video. Ever since the nightmare about the hirsute block of gum, I've been unable to look at them without gagging. In fact, the mere memory of chewing the stuff makes me gag. Why do I keep it around then? Perhaps as a penance. Without it, I wouldn't even notice I'm smoking.

Monday, 13 October

Woke fairly late, phoned down to discover that the senator was about to depart from Suite 310, packed all my stuff and put it on

* This might have been 'loin', as in 'loin of lamb'.

† My inaction here has helped me to understand why ships and planes go down, trains crash, etc. The moral is not only to imagine the unimaginable, but to act accordingly. I hope, but don't assume, that I've learnt it.

the sofa to be moved down by the bell-hop, then went off to Melon's for brunch, which consisted of a glass or two of champagne, a mouthful of eggs Benedict, and some cigarettes. When Michael joined me we shuffled through our notes and then went into the matinee, for the best account of the play I've ever seen. Ever. Everything moving along at the right kind of pace, the first act fast, the second act not weighted down, as it has been from time to time, by being the *second act*. I burst out of the theatre, hurtled upstairs, flung open the door of the Geeson–Tabori dressing-room, to find not Geeson and Tabori, but the four chaps sitting with their backs to me, staring out at me from their various mirrors. They had changed dressing rooms before the performance because, apparently, the Taboris like it warm, and the chaps like it cold – although it could also be that the Taboris have more chance of getting away from my cigarette smoke in the second dressing room. I dished out a few notes, hurried back to Melon's, had a drink or two and a snack, then back to the evening show. It really is as quick as that – the matinee begins at three thirty on Sunday, the evening show at eight. By the time everyone is out of the theatre after the matinee it's nearly six o'clock, which leaves exactly an hour before the 'half'.* At seven I went back, gave them a few more notes, things I'd recalled over my drinks, went down and saw a fairly solid account of the play, though there wasn't the same intensity as in the afternoon. Far more disturbing was my sudden realisation – why has it taken me so long? – that there is something wrong with the first scene. Instead of being sprightly but serious, it is cutely charmless, and Tabori, who was fine everywhere else, looks like a bad actor badly directed. The fault is in the writing. Talked the scene over with Michael, had a few drinks and then further drinks, came back to the Algonquin, to find to my amazement that I was still in 506 because the utterly sordid senator in 310 had decided to stay on yet another night. So there I was with all my bags packed on the sofa, and nowhere to go, obliged to stay in 506, no alternative – well, what alternative did I have, actually?

Went to bed depressed and couldn't sleep, my mind busily melding together the injustices of Suite 506 with the inadequacies

* Actors have to be in the theatre half an hour before the performance starts.

of Scene One as I nursed whiskies, smoked cigarettes – right back to the old habits, which of course depressed me further. At one point I got up and lay on the sofa beside my bags, brooding drunkenly, the room full of smoke, my lungs full of smoke, on such large questions as 'Whither I?' and 'When?' Pretty soon, I guessed, if I went on like this. I must have made it across the room back to the bed, as I woke in it very late. I shambled frailly down to the desk, to register my matitudinal complaint about being in 506 instead of 310, while preparing myself for the news that the senator had decided to live out the rest of his life in 310. In fact he'd already gone. No doubt leaving behind him a trail of bad debts and broken promises.

I accompanied the bell-hop with my bags, a triumphal little procession, my heart soaring as I stepped into the familiar room, with the familiar playbills (some of them representing work by my rivals, none work by me) on the walls, then phoned down to reserve a bedroom off the suite, to make it a two-bedroom suite for Beryl's arrival, our policy being always to have an extra bedroom available, for one of us to retreat to when I snore, which I do fairly frequently, for reasons both obvious and shameful, and was told by the chap at the desk that there wasn't a bedroom off any longer. 'Nonsense,' I said, confident that my knowledge of the intricacies of 310 far surpassed his, 'there are two. I can see the doors. I'm looking at them now.' 'Doors, yes,' he said, 'but one door opens on to a bedroom that's been permanently booked, the other opens on to nothing, that room no longer exists, it's been removed.' I was so appalled by this news that I didn't get around to asking him *how* a room could be removed. The upshot of our exchange was that I could have Suite 510, which is identical to Suite 310, *and* has a bedroom off. He said he'd looked up the records and discovered that I've actually stayed in it quite a few times before. I began to protest that I've *always* stayed in 310, and then began to think that perhaps I haven't, that 310 and 510 have somehow become as one in my memory, so that whenever I've stayed in 510 I've just assumed, afterwards, that I'd stayed in 310. Anyway, up we went, the bell-hop and I, to 510. My immediate response, as I surveyed the playbills (also for the plays of rivals), was one of affection and nostalgia. So I settled in comfortably, unpacked my bags definitively, and arranged to have my video installed. Actually the only

447

advantage of 310 over 510 is that it's closer to the lobby, to and from which one can walk to one's rooms. One can walk down from 510, but not really, given one's habits, up. A nuisance, as the Algonquin elevator sometimes vanishes into a kind of Bermuda triangle somewhere between the seventh and tenth floors.* The advantage of 510, on the other hand, is that it has a fridge, in which I can store my champagne. And I've also worked out that Beryl and I must have occupied it for the successful New York opening of *Quartermaine's Terms*, so to complete my sense of comfort I've also decided that Fate has brought me, in its usual fussy and roundabout way, to the right place. 510 had been available all the time I was waiting in 506 for 310. Waiting patiently for me to be delivered into it. So I like to imagine.

I had a pleasant lunch with Phyllis at Un Deux Trois, then walked about, thinking of the first scene in the play, until somewhere up by the bookshop on 6th and 48th I had what I took to be a revelation – that I hadn't connected the Prologue properly to the Epilogue. In the Prologue Stuart is too lightweight and playful, opening the play on a jolly upbeat, whereas he ends it in a quite different spirit, an intensely serious young man. And yet the Epilogue is virtually a continuation of the Prologue. In previous productions we'd often rehearsed the two together, flowing from the Prologue into the Epilogue, leaving out all the text in between. What, I wondered, if we rehearsed it the other way around, running straight from the Epilogue into the Prologue, thus helping Tabori to continue the serious Stuart into the Prologue, and so (I hoped) eliminating all its present coyness? Highly excited by what I took to be a flash of directorial inspiration, I hurried back to 510 and phoned Tabori. I apologised for interrupting his rest day, did he mind? – 'Well,' (pause) 'no-o. Well,' (pause) 'go ahead.' I explained what I had in mind. He reacted as if I'd merely found a new and labyrinthine way of criticising him personally, embarking on a long defence of his acting, using truly ghastly words that I'd hoped never to hear again once I'd given up teaching – 'epiphany' was one of them. In the end, though, he agreed to give my little scheme a whirl. Actually he has no choice, given that I am

* Charles Laughton once said he'd spent twenty years of his life at the Algonquin, most of them waiting for the elevator.

the director and he the actor, but I suppose he doesn't want to be thought to be obeying me, merely to be agreeing with me. I believe C. S. Lewis had a dog like that.

Tuesday, 14 October

This day week I shall be fifty. Christ! But at least Beryl will be here to nurse me through it. And through the first night, the day before. Therefore we shall be reading the reviews together on my birthday. What better form of celebration?

Last night, drunk and chain-smoking, I furiously wrote down a synopsis of the characters in the play as I've come to understand them through this production. One of the things I'm wondering is whether, with the critics coming in throughout the rest of the week, I dare risk reading it out to the actors. On the whole I think I will, because it will give me a chance to slip in some important points about Stuart to Tabori, in the open, where all the other actors will hear them. The synopsis, by the way, includes an account of what I've come to believe is the right tone and dramatic direction of each scene, so that I won't simply be talking about the characters, but about the responsibilities of each actor in each scene.*

Wednesday, 15 October

It's just gone one thirty in the morning. A good preview – worryingly good, for the night before the critics come. The law that controls these things probably guarantees that tomorrow, when among others we have Clive Barnes of the *Post* coming in, it won't go as well. May not go at all. What I must remember to tell the actors is *not* to try to duplicate tonight's performance, but to come on stage as if it hadn't happened, to find their world afresh, *listening* to each other, *talking* to each other. Also I must fix a couple of blank moments in the first act. For instance, Tabori went right back to his Dullard's view of Hamlet, standing gazing down at his toes in order to avoid looking at the other actors, and on one occasion, after taking up an over-relaxed position by the banister,

---

* I read out an abbreviated form of the synopsis, then hurried on into notes.

suddenly slumping across it, and staying there, as if he'd fallen asleep. This doze, or whatever it was, seemed to refresh him as he then became hyperactive, laughing at Humphry's jokes when only smiles were in order (had in fact been ordered) and with such abandon that he swivelled violently in his chair, slopping his drink out of both his glass and his mouth, thus going a long way towards undermining the dramatically necessary idea that here was a chap in a state of considerable tension, an idea he expressed very well elsewhere in the act. It's true that he's honoured every note I've given him recently. Now I'll have to make sure that he doesn't start implementing a few of his own, on the side, or even worse, start improvising mid-performance. I'd thought that the improvising tradition was dead in New York. I'd *hoped* it was dead. But something closely resembling it twitched sporadically into unwanted life on the stage of the Promenade tonight. On the other hand – *on the other hand, don't forget* – he's cut out all the bogus gesturing, and is full of *wanted* life throughout most of the play. So on the whole we had a very good evening.

At the end of it, when I was scooting through the door that leads backstage, I was astonished to find an old colleague of mine from the English Department of Queen Mary College waiting to speak to me. He is an American, from New York, a specialist in eighteenth-century literature, who now occupies my old office – took it over in fact with rather unseemly haste, moving his books and self in slightly before I'd moved mine and self out. Anyway, there he stood, looking appreciative. Face red, but tone appreciative. I paused to appreciate the appreciative tone and even the face red – red from shyness, I flatter myself, as I know him to be of very abstemious habits. Or was, before he moved into my office. I have no idea what he's been getting up to since. He introduced me to his mother, who was also appreciative, with face pale. Buoyed by compliments I sped on up to the actors, to give out cuddles and congratulations all round, and some immediate notes all round too (i.e. Tabori's laughter), then on to the round table at Melon's, where I was joined by Dylan Baker and lovely old Nathan Lane, followed by Michael McGuire. We had a boisterous evening, making appalling jokes in abysmal taste on such subjects as ——.* After they'd gone I stayed on by myself, slumped pleasantly over the table in a posture reminiscent of Mickey Mouse in the cartoon, and then came back to old 510, went through the notes I'd made, added some more. Drinking, smoking, thinking, writing. Now here we are, at one twenty-seven in the morning, on Wednesday the 15th, with the critics-in phase of the production beginning tomorrow (today, come to think of it).†

Thursday, 16 October

Had lunch by myself at Un Deux Trois, where by sheer persistence I've become a welcome, or at any rate familiar, figure. I was hustled past a gratifyingly long queue to a quiet and comfortable corner. I love these long, solitary, meditative lunches, or breakfasts, I suppose they are, really, letting my mind drift around last night's performance, jotting down additional notes while my eyes float around the waiters, the waitresses, the clientele. After lunch I went to Melon's, where I met Michael McGuire, went through our notes with him, then went into the theatre to give them.

During these sessions I sit at the edge of the stage, the actors sit in the auditorium, near the front. On previous occasions the chaps and Judy Geeson have sat on one side of the aisle, Tabori has sat by himself on the other, creating yet another peculiar separation. Once, about a week ago, on one of the hottest afternoons, he sat not only apart, but in an overcoat, his collar turned up, looking haunted and poetical, with a touch, he said, of flu. Every time I wanted to speak to him I had to swing my head around, keeping my voice soothing and respectful, fearful of sending his tempera-ture soaring. But now, this afternoon, for the first time, Tabori was sitting among the cast. Consequently the atmosphere was con-genial, the note-giving what it should always be, relaxed and even funny, but concentrated. It occurred to me that Tabori might here have made a breakthrough as important, almost, as the one he's

---

* Shame prevents me from specifying the subjects.

† Checking back to the first sentence of this extract, I see that I appear to have begun it three minutes after I'd ended it. So either I'd misread my watch, or my watch had started going backwards, or it took me minus three minutes to make the report. Whichever I've decided to leave the error in. I distrust the *apparent* con-tinuity of time even more than I distrust my ability to record its obvious deceits. Besides there are Bergsonian, even Kantian, implications that will appeal to many readers, I know.

made on the stage, that will also help him on the stage.

Seizing the moment, I dismissed everyone except Tabori and Michael Countryman, and rehearsed the dreaded and treacherous Act One, Scene Two – the scene that I suspect I still haven't got quite right in the writing, and which the actors therefore have to get more than right in the acting. It was here that Tabori had threatened to send the audience into a doze by miming gloomy speculations before seeming actually to fall into a doze himself, over the banister. In fact I didn't rehearse the scene, I ran it, standing so close to it that I was very nearly in it, my eyes fixed pointedly on Tabori as he hunched his shoulders, dropped his eyes and lowered himself into the slough of despond. I stopped it about a quarter of the way through and said in a tone that I hoped was both affable and intense – it's the old question, Kris, I said, of not connecting. 'Your worry about the future has to be expressed as an active, inner tension, an *active* one. When people speak to you you've got to reply to them directly, not withdraw from them.' I pounded softly away at him, softly, softly, on and on, until neither of us could stand it a second longer.

I went back to Melon's, met McGuire, had a morale-enhancing Glenfiddich or two, and then into the theatre to sit amongst the first batch of critics and watch the show. I trained my eyes away from six or seven Clive Barnes look-alikes, at least one of whom must actually have been Clive Barnes, and kept my mind fixed on Tabori as if practising long-distance hypnosis. He was even better than on the night of his breakthrough. He is naturally so personable on stage that all he really has to do, in this part anyway, is to trust himself, concentrate, and never ever do anything that looks like *acting*. In fact if the evening hadn't been rather calamitous, I would now be prepared to consider myself a deeply satisfied chap, with nothing to fear from any conscientious and decent-minded critic except the usual slovenliness and ill-will.

Calamity Number One: the set, of course, which, having behaved normally since the evening when I'd thought I'd seen it nearly choke, now choked. The present began to glide off towards the wings, then stopped. The past began to glide forward from backstage, and also stopped. So there they were – Nathan, Dylan, Peter and Michael in one set, neither upstage nor down but in a kind of limbo, listening to Wagner; and there in the other set was Kristoffer Tabori, halfway to the wings, immobile on the stairs, looking like the captain of a ship that has perversely decided not to go down after all. I suppose this ghastly tableau lingered a mere fifteen seconds or so before the sets began to move again – I didn't time it precisely as I'd almost immediately run from my usual folding chair under the circle and out on to the stairs, shaking a fist and mouthing obscenities. What's called a diversionary tactic. It certainly diverted several people in the circle, among them the manager of the theatre, who was standing just inside the exit, but I doubt if anyone else, apart from Michael McGuire of course, would have realised that what had happened on stage was entirely God's fault and not simply another example of the director's bad timing.

Calamity Number Two: the audience. They were determined to laugh, even where laughter was positively (by me anyway) unwanted. Furthermore it was peculiar laughter, hysterical and undifferentiated, that inevitably bewildered and upset the actors, who equally inevitably began to lose their concentration. When I went backstage, pondering on the one hand on how to put it to God that I preferred him not to concern himself in my affairs, and pondering on the other the possibility of applying some kind of aptitude test to members of the audience before they were allowed into the theatre, I found an extremely emotional Jack McQuiggan, who told me that at the interval Peter Friedman had accused him of planting friends, or possibly even hirelings, among the audience – under orders, presumably, to laugh continuously and so persuade the critics that a terrific time was being had by all. Jack's eyes, usually round and clear from abstinence and ambition, were now moist, almost protuberant, from disbelief and fury – I've never seen him like this before. Not only would he never *want* to do a thing like that, he said, but he'd never be allowed to get away with it. People would find out in no time, he'd be finished as a producer in New York. I left him in the backstage lobby, went up to the dressing rooms, gathered them around, and said that there wasn't the slightest question of Jack's having rigged the audience, though yes, indeed, it had been an odd, undisciplined house and probably not the only one we'd get during the run. I suggested that as the play has already developed a reputation for smartness, some people would want to seize any opportunity, even the wrong one, to establish that they were pretty smart too. But they, the actors, I plonked, must never again allow themselves to be thrown by inappropriate responses. If every line they uttered were to be met by boos and jeers they were still to play their characters, play the play, etc. – the obvious kind of stuff in fact. Peter Friedman then issued a statement to the effect that he was mortified by his previous loss of control, now realised that Jack was innocent on all charges, and said he would apologise personally.

Someone – I think it was Nathan – then asked which critics had been in, had we had the 'biggie'? Yes, someone else – Michael Countryman, I believe – asked, had we had 'the crucial one, the big, big one'? What they really wanted to know, of course, was whether Frank Rich, of the *New York Times*, whose review would settle our fate, had been in. As a matter of fact he hadn't – he's coming in tomorrow night – but as they hadn't named him directly, I made a lightning decision to answer their questions literally. Yes, that's right, I said, tonight was the big one, the biggie, crucial. And so it was. Every night's a biggie as far as the playwright's concerned. There was a silence, almost of reverence, while they pondered the fact that the die was cast, there was no going back, we were already marked down as a success or a failure – though we wouldn't know which until the review was published after our official opening.* Someone, probably all of them, said what actors always say in these circumstances, viz. why did he have to come tonight, we were much better last night – and the audience – and the set! And so forth, until I stopped them with what I imagine directors always say in these circumstances, viz. that, well, actually, it was a very good evening, anyway no point in worrying about it, from now on you can relax, concentrate on your work, play the play. Let's have a drink.

On a note of rising conviviality, tension-free at last, we gamboiled down to Melon's, where Judy (Daish) was waiting, having flown in this afternoon. She had seen the show, and was very jolly.

---

* Theatrically, New York is a one-newspaper town. Thumbs-down in the *Times* usually closes a straight play within days. Thumbs-up usually guarantees a run. With my first play in New York, *Wise Child*, almost every review was favourable except the one in the *Times*. We closed after three performances. The reason for this peculiar, indeed dreadful, state of affairs is that New York theatregoers take the *Times*, and aren't going to risk quite a few dollars on the possibility that the reviewer has got it wrong.

Everybody was very jolly. Riotously jolly. By about half past midnight everyone but Nathan and myself had gone home. We stayed on, getting more riotously jolly by ourselves, until it was clear from my behaviour that the time had come to put me into a cab. I was in the middle of proclaiming the virtues of (a) the play and (b) this particular production, when I suddenly found myself out of control, my feet carrying me eagerly towards two men just emerging from a restaurant. Nathan grabbed my arm, swung me around, pulled me across the street – rather dangerously given the traffic – and ordered me to shut up. The two figures staring after us were, apparently, John Simon, theatre critic of *New York Magazine*, and Mel Gussow, theatre critic of the *New York Sunday Times*, who had been in to see the show. Nathan shovelled me into a cab and dispatched me to 510 via the lobby (a pause for refreshment) where I set about my late-night task of drinking and smoking myself into a stupor.

Friday, 17 October

Woke dully, clambered lethargically about my suite like a drugged ape, trying to keep my mind closed to the thought that in the evening we really would have the crucial one, the biggie, while keeping it open to the thought that in the evening Beryl would be arriving, possibly in time to share the anxiety. Or double it, depending on her view of the performance. I was on the point of falling down the stairs into the lobby for a glass of breakfast when Ian Hamilton rang. He's in town for a couple of days to deal with lawyers over his Salinger biography. Apparently Salinger is attempting to block publication on the grounds that he doesn't like being written about. We had lunch at Un Deux Trois at a series of tables, moving in little zigzags about the room, until we finally settled at one where I could both sit comfortably and hear almost everything he said. That's the only problem with Un Deux Trois – a lot of other people like it too, and furthermore insist on talking loudly over their meals – discussed the Salinger problem, then the Frank Rich/*New York Times* problem. He offered to sit in on the show tonight, in return I offered to sit in on his legal hearings – possibly posing as a surprise witness – and then, just before we left, he told me a rather touching story about a woman whose husband, a brigadier, had died recently. Wanting to make contact with him, she went to a medium for a seance. Eventually she succeeded in getting through. 'Well, what's it like up there?' she asked. 'Oh, it's wonderful,' he said. 'I sort of have a bit of sex and then I swim and then I have a meal and then I have a swim and then a bit of sex and then a meal and so it goes on. It's absolutely glorious.' And she said, 'Is that all you do?' He said, 'Yes, that's all I do really, swim, bit of sex, meal, swim, bit of sex, perfect.' She said, 'But you weren't very interested in sex as I remember when you were down here, in fact I remember very well that you weren't interested in sex. And you hated swimming.' 'Ah yes,' he said, 'but down there I wasn't a duck.' I have no idea why this lightened my spirits so much – perhaps simply the prospect of living through eternity on such straightforward terms. Especially as I'm extremely fond of swimming.

From Un Deux Trois straight to Melon's, where Michael told me that he had checked out the set, which seemed to be – he verbally crossed his fingers – OK. We picked over our notes from last night's performance, then went in and did a spot of rehearsing. I tried to make my manner cavalier, not wanting the cast to wonder why, if they'd got over the crucial one and were now to relax and enjoy the play, we were still rehearsing the production. 'Might as well get it *absolutely* right while we're at it,' I said jovially. 'Tighten it up. That sort of thing.' Then back to Melon's, of course, for an hour's jittery talk with Michael and Jack, then backstage for some bogusly carefree salutes and fraudulently casual injunctions to go out and *really* enjoy yourselves tonight, eh, and down to the auditorium. I sat on my folding chair, trying to spot Frank Rich. I'd got the idea from someone or other that he's a stripling of a mere three decades or so, who doesn't even look his age, and is a natty dresser, but all the youthful males I rested my eye on were hirsute, ill-dressed and looked old for their years – old and self-righteous. Possibly a pack of critics up from the *Village Voice*. Again there were several Clive Barnes look-alikes, not one of which was likely to *be* Clive Barnes this time around, unless he'd come back for seconds. The music rose, the lights went down, and we were off on our biggie.

I don't believe I've ever watched a show so intently in my life. Afterwards, on balance, weighing this against that and taking everything into account, I decided that it was perfect. Well, almost perfect. Furthermore, the set worked. If Rich didn't like it, then at least he didn't like what I wanted to be on offer. I went upstairs to the dressing rooms feeling – above all feeling a vast relief. The first person I saw was Kristoffer Tabori. I blurted out a heartfelt compliment, accompanying it with several emotional cuffs and strokes on his arm. He gave me an odd, shy look and muttered 'thank you' out of the side of his mouth. A real 'thank you' it seemed to me, in return for something done. I like to think that this was an acknowledgement of the whole stretch of misery, suppressed ill-temper and frustration we've experienced with each other, and also an acknowledgemeent that nevertheless we'd got it right in the end. But of course he might just have been thanking me for something very specific, like – I don't know – picking up one of his shoes. Although I can't remember actually picking up one of his shoes. When I went back into the other dressing room someone – I think it was Peter Friedman but it might have been Michael Countryman – asked if I knew who'd been in. 'Well, I said, smirking slightly, 'one or two. You know. Critics. Frank Rich, of course.' It took them a moment or two to rally from shock to outrage. They accused me of having lied, claimed that they were too relaxed to have given of their best, would have been more concentrated (i.e. tried harder – exactly what I'd wanted them to avoid) if they'd known. Nonsense, I said, nonsense. For one thing I hadn't lied, merely not told them the truth,* my decision had been totally justified by the performance they'd given, a much beter one than last night's, so why all the fuss, shut up, time for a drink. If Rich doesn't come through with the goods, they'll no doubt blame me. And I'll blame Michael McGuire. Or Jack. Or the audience. And of course Frank Rich.

Later, at Melon's, everyone was much calmer, if also much louder. Now they really can relax and enjoy playing the play. At least for as long as the reviews allow us to. I felt pretty good, very

---

* This position has been somewhat discredited by the head of the British Civil Service, Sir Robert Armstrong, when giving evidence on behalf of the British Government in Australia. But our situations were entirely different, as I hope Sir Robert would be the first to admit. He was not telling the whole truth merely to save the Government embarrassment. I was not telling the whole truth to a positive end – to keep the actors' morale high, and to unwind them for the crucial performance.

good really, and particularly enjoyed introducing Ian, who'd seen the show and was waiting for me in Melon's, to Tabori – the part of Stuart is based on Ian, or at least on his experiences when he was running a literary magazine in London, years ago. As I'd also introduced him to Nicholas Le Prevost, who'd played Stuart in London, on the critics-in first night at the Lyric, Hammersmith, I felt that Fate had pulled off a notable double here. I was just settling into a Glenfiddich or two and working on soliciting some compliments in the form of comments from Ian when Judy appeared, to announce that Beryl had arrived at the Algonquin, was safely ensconced in 510, was a mite exhausted from the flight (which had been preceded by a morning's teaching), wasn't quite up to coming down to Melon's, see me when she saw me. I scooted out of Melon's, into a taxi, but got here too late. Beryl was already deeply asleep. Is now deeply asleep. So here I am rollicking about on my own in the living room of Suite 510, in a state of high excitement at the realisation that at the very least I've done what I set out to do all those months ago in Los Angeles. The play is on the boards in New York, the die is cast, and there is my wife, for the first time it seems in years, asleep in a nearby room. Could a chap want more? Yes. He could want a clutch of good reviews, topped by a rave from F. Rich in the *New York Times*, to guarantee a decent run. That's what he could want. Along with another drink.

Sunday, 19 October

I went down to the lobby, had a glass of champagne, read the London papers until Beryl returned from her walk. There are very few things she likes better than roaming the streets of New York, unaccompanied, which I refuse to accept as evidence of a death wish. When she got back she took me straight out for my constitutional, i.e. the hundred-yard slog along 44th to Un Deux Trois. We had a long leisurely lunch, during which she slipped morsels of food into my mouth whenever she could take me by surprise. These attempts to save me from death by malnutrition nearly ended once or twice in death from choking. We talked mainly about the production, which she'd seen last night. She said she was keen on the new version of the play, liked all the actors but did find herself wondering whether here and there I hadn't allowed them to become physically trapped. I pointed out that the task, darling, had been to keep Tabori still and focused, and in doing that, my love, I'd perhaps inadvertently curtailed the freedom of the other actors, so yes, perhaps sweetie, now that the Tabori problem was solved I might find myself giving them some physical independence, though not too much, angel, given my almost pathological hatred of unmotivated stage movement. Thank you for the note, always my best critic. Thank you.*

We moved on to a discussion of how we would spend the afternoon – a walk, a film? Which would be best for keeping the prospect of the first night, and more consequentially, the prospect of the reviews out of our minds? – until I suddenly remembered that I hadn't got the cast and company any first-night presents, and as the performance started at half past six, we'd better get on with it. We zipped up to Scribner's, across and up a few blocks, my plan being to get seventeen copies of T. S. Eliot's *Collected Poems*. This isn't quite as pretentious as it sounds. Over the weeks I'd developed a peculiar habit of paraphrasing the Stetson lines from *The Waste Land* every time I chanced unexpectedly on an actor during rehearsals, clapping my hand to my forehead, reeling backwards, and crying out, 'What Nathan/Michael/Peter/Dylan/Judy *you* here!' I don't claim that this is a great joke. Come to think of it, I can't claim it's a joke at all. But repetition made it funny, and more importantly, made it comforting – one of those details of the rehearsal experience that years from now we'd probably all remember. Would *certainly* remember, if I underscored the relevant lines in the text. As it turned out Scribner's had only one copy. I'll repeat that. Scribner's had only *one* copy of *The Collected Poems of T. S. Eliot* in the shop. A large shop too. Pausing only to make a brief scene – time was getting too short for the comprehensive one that the situation deserved – we sped about plucking from the display stands all available copies of John Houseman's latest volume of autobiography, all available copies of Oliver Sachs's *The Man Who Mistook His Wife for a Hat*, all available copies of a collection of *New Yorker* cartoons – a bizarre assortment, the

---

* Beryl was quite right, of course. I did loosen the blocking before I left New York. On the other hand, I also cut out some moves.

collecting principle of which was merely panic. It was now four thirty. We would have to leave the Algonquin, showered and changed, by five forty-five at the latest. So we stood at the counter, Beryl passing the books to me and I scribbling into them love, gratitude, etc., before carrying them over to a highly intelligent young man who not only agreed to wrap them for us, but to mark on each wrapped copy the initials of the person to whom the book was going.

We dashed back to the hotel, showered and changed, got a cab, stopped off at the bookshop, picked up the books, proceeded to the theatre, arriving ten minutes before the show was due to start. The taxi driver, a West Indian hopelessly befuddled by the excitements of the last half an hour, not only couldn't break my twenty-dollar bill, but seemed unable to think of any scheme for doing so, and just sat shaking his head, fumbling with coins and bills, mumbling forlornly. Beryl took the twenty dollars, dashed to a news-stand, where an elderly and dignified gentleman gave her change, extracting for himself, as we subsequently discovered, a one-dollar commission. I escorted Beryl to the front of the theatre, got her her ticket, deposited her with James and Dena, then carried the books to Melon's, where, over a drink or two, I translated the initials into proper names. I dumped the books at the stage door, went round into the auditorium for the closing moments of the first act, returned to Melon's where I was joined by Michael McGuire and his girlfriend, back to my folding chair for the second act, upstairs to do my round of cuddles, back to Melon's to settle my long-running tab, then on to the party which was being given at Le Petit Bistro or was it Le Bistro Pathétique? Word had already got out that the *Times* review would appear at about ten thirty, leaving us with over an hour to get through.

One of the features of the party was that, although there were at least 350 souls – if souls is the appropriate word – there was no food, apart from a rarely sighted tray of canapés, while any real drink as opposed to cheap red and white wine, one had to pay for. It was hot, glum and crowded, in other words, its sole purpose being to give the investors a chance to tangle with the company. I was passed about from person to person, like a large, possibly contaminated parcel, waiting to be unwrapped by Frank Rich. The only encounter I can now remember was with Robert Vaughn, the

Man from U.N.C.L.E. We were presented to each other with great ceremony, and then stood facing each other in silence – each waiting for compliments or comments, I suppose. He was very eloquently dressed in dinner jacket, silk scarf, etc., but was otherwise mute. I was totally mute, sartorially as well as vocally. At least I hope I was mute sartorially, having come out of my tramp persona into humdrum and unnoticeable respectability for the occasion. Except for my shoes, of course. But nobody can see anyone's shoes at a crowded party. The silence lasted until we turned away from each other, he to a cluster of (I hope) admirers, I by a series of social ricochets to a table where James, Dena, Eduardo (Dena's co-playwright) and Judy (Daish) were sitting. We started a small, cheerful party of our own, fuelled by drinkable drinks that Judy and James had somehow conjured out of a bar they'd managed to locate, but remained invisible to me all evening. Beryl was on the far side of the room, by the way, having an excited, even dramatic-looking conversation with Caroline Lagerfelt, who was now very pregnant indeed. Suddenly there was a small tumult at the door.

The Frank Rich review had arrived, earlier than expected. One of the girls from Jack's office was carrying it urgently towards Jack, who stood in the centre of the room with some of his investors. There was a strange buzzing, or even droning noise from the guests, which sounded like the prelude to a tribal chant, as Jack received the review, began to read. Two members of his production team took up a position at each elbow and lowered their heads to read with him. Everyone within their immediate vicinity – top-ranking investors presumably – stood back, watching them warily. Eventually Jack lifted his head, and gazed around, as if confused. Ominous. He passed the review to someone else who read it rapidly, shook his head in confusion and handed it to someone else. More ominous. Beryl, blithely unaware of what was happening, hurried over in great excitement to tell me something about Caroline, then, seeing what my eyes were fixed on, fell silent. We stood watching as people skimmed through the review, handed it on. There were neither cries of joy nor moans of despair, just these small, imperceptible signs – head-shakings, shoulder-shruggings, muttered questions – of confusion. I was so transfixed – I've never seen a review have quite this effect before – that it would probably have passed through every hand in the party except mine if Beryl hadn't walked briskly over to the trio currently in possession and asked whether the playwright might be allowed a peek, please. We tucked into it together, James, Dena, Eduardo and Judy peering over our shoulders and around our arms.

One thing was immediately evident. The review was very long and carried a large photograph of Tabori and Judy Geeson. What was not immediately evident, as it took some deciphering, was that the review was not so much equivocal as actively equivocating, leading off with a string of vivid descriptive sentences that could have been compliments, followed by a small paragraph of reservations, followed by further and clear compliments punctuated, but not completely punctured by, further reservations. It didn't so much give with one hand and take with the other, as give with both hands simultaneously both praise and blame, sometimes within the same sentence. I also had a sense, in spite of the personal interest that I brought to it, that it amounted to a rather dull read – nothing like as dull as Dan O'Sullivan's,* of course, but dull by normal standards of readability, and far duller than anything I'd previously read by Frank Rich, whose style I usually found both perky and elegant. It was as if he weren't quite himself, assuming a tone he hoped might find favour with the characters in the play, rather than presenting his actual experience of the play to the readers. Could it be that a part of Frank Rich *wants* to live among the failed English literati, I wondered, be out there on the stage, so to speak, hobnobbing with the likes of Nick, Peter, Stuart? It hardly seems possible, given that in his present position in New York he has the power to ruin a celebration completely with one of his reviews, keep a celebration going for two days with another of his reviews, or bring a celebration to a baffled standstill, as he'd just done, with yet another of his reviews. A wizard's power, in fact. A few paragraphs on Monday conferring fame and fortune, a few paragraphs on Tuesday delivering failure and despair. Not just a wizard, when you come to think of it, but for many people (in New York anyway) the living embodiment of the Massy Wheel of Fortune.

* Of the Matrix production, in the *Los Angeles Times*.

Actually I doubt if these thoughts went clearly through my mind at the time. Instead I was listening with dunce-like intensity to Beryl, who was taking me through bits of the review, pointing out all the quotable quotes, and then listening with dunce-like intensity to Jack when he read some of them aloud, every now and then stating , emphatically that it was OK, this was a review he could build on, that he *would* build on, we were going to run, he'd see to it.*

Nathan came over, glanced quickly through the review, then embarked on a long, angry and very funny monologue on the nature of reviewers, their personal habits, sex lives, innate life-hatred, etc., a magnificent solo, full of riffs and variations, until he'd subdued himself through sheer vocal and emotional exhaustion. I passed about amongst the other actors, looking grimmer, Beryl told me subsequently, than was good for morale or than the review warranted, and then we – James, Dena, Eduardo, Beryl, Judy and I† – went down to the nearest restaurant for dinner. Either we ate outside (surely unlikely, at that hour) or we were surrounded by glass. At any rate we were obviously on public display, because Peter Friedman and his girlfriend dropped by for a few minutes, followed by Ben Sprecher, the theatre manager, who strolled insouciantly in, dropped the early-morning editions of the two other papers, the *Post* and the *News*, on our table, and strolled insouciantly out. The two reviews were raves, and if we preferred the Clive Barnes, it was only because it was the longer. A good note to end on, and for once I decided to end on it. On the way back here in the taxi Beryl told me what it was she'd come over to announce just as the Frank Rich review had arrived – that Caroline had left the party for the hospital, having gone into the preliminary phase of labour. Which brings something together very neatly, although I'm not sure what. It occurs to me now that as soon as the baby shows its face we should send Frank Rich over

* I believed him – with good reason, as he's the only New York producer I know of who's kept a production (*The Foreigner*) going for two years after it had been panned, not only by the *Times*, but by almost every other New York newspaper and magazine.

† Michael McGuire and his girlfriend were also at the party, but we never met up. He told me later that they were trapped in a corner table from which there was no exit.

to review it. You can't start coming to terms with the Massy Wheel
too early. As he's known to be a family man he should be favourably disposed. Or unfavourably, depending on the kind of family
he's got.

Monday, 20 October

Woke late, and lay in bed attempting to come to terms with the
fact that it's at last all over. No more rehearsals, no more previews,
no more notes, and today at least, as it's the rest day, no need even
to go to the theatre. I told my heart, therefore, to be still. And it *was*
still. Still enough for me to refuse to get up and join Beryl in a
shopping expedition for Caroline's baby. I clung on and on in bed,
not awake, not asleep, not dozing – mere, I suppose, inactivity,
until just after midday, when I finally managed to dress and
shave, then make it down to the bar where I quaffed back two
mimosas* with great rapidity, sedately ordering a third and pretending it was my first when I saw Beryl arriving with packages
of rattles, Babygros, etc. We went off to lunch at Un Deux Trois,
I leaning on her like a valetudinarian, trying to ignore the pint of
mimosa swishing around in my stomach. Over lunch Beryl and I
read, very cold-eyed, through Frank Rich's review and decided
that it really was OK, the first paragraph especially so, and that
most potential theatregoers wouldn't worry too much about the
subsequent equivocations, indeed probably wouldn't even get to
them. I phoned Jack from the restaurant to discuss what quotes to
use for the ad. He said that in fact Frank Rich had been on the
radio this morning in a follow-up review, in which he'd been more
openly complimentary, so we'd be able to synthesise both the
radio and newspaper reviews to what would amount to a rave,
almost.

When we got back to the hotel, Jack phoned and said quite
simply, 'It's a hit.' The box office had been immensely busy, we'd
taken an enormous amount of money and might even be on our
way to breaking a record or two. I phoned up each member of the
cast to let them know that all was very well indeed, the only ones

* Known in England as a Buck's Fizz – a combination of champagne (or if you're
unlucky, sparkling wine) and fresh (or if you're unlucky, packaged) orange juice.

I failed to contact being, somehow inevitably, the Taboris. Then I phoned Caroline Lagerfelt's hospital and was told that she'd been successfully delivered of a baby, although they seemed unable to give details, i.e. sex, weight, etc. We were going out to dinner with James and Dena to celebrate Dena's birthday, and I reflected, as I lay down on the bed to read the latest volume of John Houseman's memoirs (Beryl having dashed up to Saks in search of a sweater), on the life-enhancing coincidence that within twenty-four hours we'd had the first night, the birth of Caroline's baby, now Dena's birthday, with my own birthday turning up tomorrow. It was at about this point – anyway before I'd got properly into the Houseman – that Kristoffer Tabori phoned to say that he just wanted to apologise for having left the party early (actually I hadn't noticed). He'd found the heat, the lack of food and drink and the imminence of the Frank Rich review too much to take. I said I quite understood. There was an awkward pause and then he said, 'It's a wonderful production.' To which I didn't say, modestly, as I should have done, 'Oh, really, do you think so, I'm glad you think so,' whatever. I said, 'I'm very proud of what's on the stage.' There was a pause, and he said, 'Yes, right. OK. Well, before you go perhaps we could have a drink?' So perhaps there is some one further stage to go with Kristoffer Tabori.*

Tuesday, 21 October

One day into my fifty-first year. I failed to get out of bed in order to join Beryl on an expedition to the Frick, even though it's my favourite museum and contains my favourite painting, a Rembrandt self-portrait. Before she left Beryl phoned the hospital several times, and unsuccessfully, for news of Caroline and her baby, and after she'd gone I tried several times myself until finally discovering that the baby, far from having been born, was being delivered that very moment. There's no point in wondering how

* We never got around to the drink. The truth is, I didn't really want to, and I suspect he didn't either. For my part, I felt that the wounds hadn't yet become the kind of scars that we could reminisce over. His association with the production ended only a few months after we'd opened. While Judy Geeson was taking a break from the show, to organise their newly bought house in Los Angeles, Tabori had a disagreement with Jack, and left the show. Judy never came back.

the hospital could have made such a mistake. In my experience hospitals tend to get such matters as births and deaths hopelessly wrong.* Anyway if the baby gets a move on it should make it on my birthday which, as it's also Trafalgar Day, is an excellent day to he born on, carrying with it historic associations of triumph in glorious battle.

I met Beryl at Un Deux Trois for a long, lingering and chatty lunch, after which we strolled down to Grand Central Station, picking up *en route*, after trying about five news-stands, a copy of *Woman's Wear Daily*, which Jack had told me was both very influential and contained a highly favourable review. It was indeed favourable, and furthermore stood out on the centre page in astonishing black type. But what I don't understand is, if *Woman's Wear Daily* is so influential, how come you can only pick it up from one news-stand in six? Beryl decided not to come to the theatre, preferring, quite rightly, to lounge around 510 and watch television – she finds American television highly addictive, for about two or three days, and then ODs on it – but would join us all after the show for a birthday dinner with the cast at Melon's. I went straight to Melon's where Michael McGuire and I were interviewed by a rather nice man from the *Post*. I can't remember any of the questions, so suppose they must have been the usual questions, though he employed a charming, if practised, timidity when asking them. Michael left before me and I was a little late – about ten minutes late in fact – getting to the theatre. I was therefore somewhat surprised to discover Ken Frankel, the director of the Long Wharf production, negotiating for a ticket at the box office. He was wearing a very red sweater with words on it and a peculiar jacket.† He turned, saw me and behind his beard his face assumed an expression – actually I don't quite know how to describe it. Aghast. That was it. He looked aghast. Like an aghast sheep. He managed a strangled greeting, then asked me whether we could speak at the interval. I said no, I wouldn't be around at

* My father had just died, his three sons were grouped, weeping, around his bed in a classical tableau of grief, when a nurse entered, put his lunch down on the table beside him, with a cheerful admonition 'to eat up', and departed smiling.

† I can no longer remember in what respect the jacket was peculiar. I clearly have a blank spot about jackets. I can't remember the words on his sweater, either.

the interval because I always made a point of avoiding the audience, didn't he remember? OK, he said, then perhaps afterwards. We went in together, then separated, he up one set of stairs to the right-hand side of the theatre, I up the other set of stairs to the left-hand side of the theatre, to my folding chair. From there I watched him emerge into the auditorium, bustle down the aisle and push his way along a row, causing a lot of commotion in the audience and nearly as much on stage. Two of the actors from the Long Wharf production, Peter Friedman and Michael Countryman, became briefly paralysed, their eyes initially caught by the boisterous redness of the sweater, then by the thick beard which presumably reminded them of someone, then by the face behind it which they identified. They played the rest of the scene with too much consciousness. Who could blame them? Late entrances are bad enough without the late entrant also being the one-time director and then the rejected director of the play you are currently performing in. I suppose Ken Frankel's intention had been to slip surreptitiously in for a peek at the show, though it's hard to imagine how, short of yodelling too, he could have made a worse job of it.

I kept an eye trained on him – he sat impassively, arms folded – for the rest of the first act and the opening of the second act, until I became fairly absorbed, then at last completely absorbed in the play. A few seconds before the end I had one of those strange jolts, a prickling of the scalp, the sense of a familiar presence close by. I glanced to the right and there, sure enough, was Beryl standing at the exit. I got up and slipped out with her just as the lights went down and the applause started. We made it to the top of the stairs and then stopped dead. Frankel was bounding tumultuously down the stairs opposite, his face set in a peculiar kind of rage. He trampled across the lobby, through the backstage door, out of sight. I hurried after him, upstairs to the dressing rooms, where I found him already surrounding the three actors from the Long Wharf production, embracing them angrily with his arms, while he exclaimed in a voice throbbing with fury, 'It works beautifully, it works beautifully like this!' When he saw me he froze – had he wanted to be in *and* out before I arrived? – stepped dramatically close, and began a conversation that was only marginally longer than the one we'd had in the lobby. He said he was in a rush, I said

OK, give me a ring, let's have a drink, talk, I've written a new play, would like to give him a copy, he said he'd be interested to read it, maybe a drink, difficult, he was in the middle of a production himself, well, OK, gotta be off, goodbye. He made an ambiguous gesture with his arm, added another guttural farewell, and off he went, down the stairs, presumably into the night.*

Afterwards at Melon's, with Beryl, Michael McGuire and the cast, my birthday dinner. Lots of drink. Lots of laughter. A wonderful party. A real birthday party in fact. Marred only by the absence of Jack. He's made such a thing of my birthday, and then failed to turn up at the party. Not only at the party, he failed to turn up at the show, almost for the first time ever. Odd. Anyway Beryl and I are now back at the Algonquin. Beryl's asleep – she leaves tomorrow evening for a teaching commitment – and here I am, at ten to two in the morning, in the living room of old 510, pondering the implications, trying *not* to ponder the implications, of being fifty and a day.

Wednesday, 22 October

I hung about in bed while Beryl phoned the hospital and at last managed to speak to Caroline, whose unfortunate infant had failed by a mere hour or two to make it for my birthday. In all other respects, however, his prospects look pretty good. He weighs seven and a half pounds and is unbearably beautiful, luminously intelligent, with some hair. Beryl imparted this information while I was climbing out of bed and she was dashing out of the door on the way to see mother and son. I dressed very slowly, like a man palsied, and presented myself in the foyer for an interview with somebody or other – I don't know who he was, or even what

---

* When I was back in London I received a letter signed by Frankel and four of his colleagues at the Long Wharf, Edgar Rosenblum, John Tillinger, Arvin Brown and Anne Keefe, congratulating me on my success at the Promenade, and undertaking, in return for a credit and some money, not to expose me as a fraud who had stolen Ken Frankel's Long Wharf production. My reply, in which among other things I offered to discuss publicly the exact nature of Frankel's contribution to the Long Wharf productions of both *Quartermaine's Terms* and *The Common Pursuit*, and fuelled as it was by anger, contempt and downright disgust, is too long to publish here, and was probably not worth the writing. At least in as much as it is still unanswered eight months after it was posted.

publication he represented, but I do recall that he was short and plump, and was sitting contentedly in an armchair, a drink in his hand, with one eye gleaming and one eye dead. So whatever journalist in New York has a botched-up right eye, with an alert left eye, is probably the chap who interviewed me today at twelve noon. I sat down in an opposite armchair, but before we could get into any kind of stride we were interrupted by the production's press officer, an exceptionally devoted, hard-working and considerate chap, who clearly suspected that I was coming to the end of my tether and needed moral support. Or perhaps he just wanted company. Anyway he spread himself on the sofa that stretched between our two chairs, indeed lay so comfortably along it that I thought of summoning the bell-hop and ordering him up some blankets and a pillow, and began to engage interviewer and interviewee in lively conversation. Even when prone he exhibited an unnatural gift for converting my weedy, almost monosyllabic answers into an opportunity for a monologue – on the state of the theatre, on New York architecture, whatever – rendering me virtually redundant. I sat back, my eyes half closed as if in admiring attention, until it was time to make my way to Un Deux Trois, where I had arranged to meet Dena and Beryl for lunch.

I was almost out of the lobby when I was called back to the telephone. Jack, to say would I please be in the Algonquin in two hours' time for an extremely important interview. *Extremely* important. I said, oh come on, Jack, Beryl leaves this evening. He said, 'No, no, you must really. This is really the BIG time.' So I thought OK, I mean I'm all for the big time really when it comes to it, and said I'd talk to Beryl and find out how she felt about me and the big time. Then to Un Deux Trois where Dena was waiting. Beryl arrived a few minutes after me to report emotionally that Caroline's baby lives up to its reputation for intelligence, beauty and hair, and furthermore has a pointed head and is charmingly chubby. We toasted his achievements several times, then I went back to the Algonquin and presented myself to the interviewer, who, given his bulk, might have been described as Falstaffian except that his eyes didn't twinkle; his eyes were actually quite dead. Both of them. Which put him one ahead or one behind the pre-lunch interviewer, depending on which way you look at it.

After an hour of intense intellectual jousting, which left me feeling completely drained, he explained that he wasn't really doing an interview at all, merely hoping to pick up a useful quote or two for his review. I detached myself from him on the spot and went upstairs to 510 to collect Beryl.

We sauntered along to Grand Central Station, studied the walls and the roofs, watched the trains arriving and departing, had a drink in the Oyster Bar, and were just on our way out through the 42nd Street exit when we were stopped on the pavement by a bizarre drama. An elderly woman with a demented, wrinkled face but with lustrous, obviously much-shampooed red hair tumbling down her shoulders, was holding two dogs – Pomeranians, I think they were – on a lead. She was screaming abuse at a respectable-looking young man who was evidently some kind of Evangelist. They stood facing each other, he talking in a low, implacable, impersonal voice about the Church and its truth, she screaming back at him that *she* was the Church. 'I am the Church! I am the Church!' And while this was going on, he rigid talking, she screaming that she was the Church, the two Pomeranians were fucking at her feet. In a most peculiar way too, like humans. One of the Pomeranians lay on its back with its legs spread, the other Pomeranian lay on top of it, burrowed into it, and fornicated away, in a ghastly imitation of human sex. We watched them for a good ten minutes, then went back to the Algonquin. Beryl changed and packed. We went down to the lobby, out on to the street where her limo was waiting.

After she'd gone I sat in the lobby depressed, sipping Scotch, smoking, almost unable to move. Although in fact I did. Up here to 510 where, shaved and changed, I am dictating this. I have to be at the theatre by the end of the show as Jack is giving me a birthday party. He'd got the dates wrong which explains his absence last night. There is to be champagne and a cake on stage.

Later No second fiftieth birthday party after all. Jack had forgotten that the cast had agreed to have a discussion with the audience after the show. He was keen to wait until it was over, but feeling too depressed to go through the ritual of a party, especially of a party celebrating a birthday that was already over, and a fiftieth one at that, I suggested he pack the cake back into a box, put the champagne back into the fridge, and bring both out again on Friday, my last evening in New York.*

Michael McGuire and I went to Melon's, sat at the usual round table. He said that he was very tired, I said I was very tired, I said I was very depressed, he said he was very depressed, and so it went. We came back around midnight in a taxi. And here I am, back in my suite, still trying to understand how it's come about that on the occasion of my biggest success in New York I have no energy, and certainly no joy, no pleasure in what's taken place. I feel in a peculiar way completely defeated by the circumstances of life. Though what these circumstances are I don't know. No doubt I've demoralised myself by the intensity with which I've returned to smoking – back to between sixty and eighty a day. I sit slumped in bars, in corners of sofas or in armchairs, or at the corner of tables in restaurants, drinking, smoking, my stomach swelling, my head pounding slightly, not eating. I'm going to bed now. I hope tomorrow I shall feel much springier. I don't understand it.

Friday, 24 October, my last full day in New York

Lunch at the Players' Club. Over it, Michael McGuire, Ben Sprecher, the manager of the Promenade, and I agreed that we would resist any attempts – there's been considerable interest apparently – to move *The Common Pursuit* to Broadway. Came back to the Algonquin, 510. Thought of dictating into the machine, couldn't face it, tried to read, couldn't face that, lay on the bed and tried to sleep, couldn't manage that, then walked around and around the living room, still depressed, but also restless and irritable – a sign of reviving life, I hoped. At about five the phone rang. Nathan, down in the lobby, come around for a farewell drink. We sat in the lobby and chatted our way through our experiences from New Haven to New York by way of Los Angeles, then, in seemingly good time, hustled over to 8th Avenue where we somehow missed cab after cab, or cab after cab somehow decided to miss us, until – Nathan now desperate at the prospect of being late for the half – we got

---

* I never saw the cake or the champagne again. A relief actually, as I've never been particularly keen on cake and think of champagne as strictly a lunchtime beverage.

one to take us to the Promenade. Nathan hurtled up to the dressing room, I went on to Melon's, where Michael McGuire was waiting for me. We were both coming out of our depressions, beginning to laugh again. We whipped up to the dressing rooms, dished out a few notes to the actors, then down into the auditorium to a full house. I sat in my folding chair by the gangway, Michael took up his seat at the other end of the row. It went well.

Afterwards to Melon's where I'd reserved five adjoining tables for a farewell dinner. There was a young couple ensconced at the middle table, apparently embarking on what promised to be a long and complicated courtship. So there we were, one group of us crammed in on one side of this couple, the other group crammed in on the other side, and there *they* were, cutting us off as they reached across their table to touch fingers, whisper, sit bolt upright in excitement, crouch forward conspiratorially. Alone, in love, buggering up our evening. In spite of angry grimaces from me, constant polite attempts from the management to dispatch them by delivering their bill, taking it away, redelivering it, they would not *go* and they would *not* go. They did in the end, of course, allowing our two groups to join together at last. But it was too late. The impulse to celebrate, embrace and say goodbye had drained away. What remained of the evening passed in exhausted, humdrum affability. We split up early, and yet not early enough to do anything else with the night. Michael McGuire and I shared a last taxi together. I dropped him off at his rented apartment somewhere around 46th and 8th, and came on a few more blocks to the Algonquin. I packed my bags, arranged a morning call, ducked down for a Glenfiddich in the lobby, came back up and recorded this. Tomorrow midday I shall be boarding Concorde, heading for home.

Monday morning, 27 October, London

I got back late Saturday night, London time. Concorde was very cramped. Their idea, really, is to treat you as if you are a Strasburg goose, strapping you into your leather seat so that your knees rise fairly close to your chest while they stuff food down you. Alcohol too, I'm glad to say. Hated it, really.

I had a ragged night, starting out of my sleep fairly regularly to work out where I was, and why, then sinking back into a hotel room, but not my Algonquin suite, 510.

Yesterday I spent meandering woozily around the house, re-affirming contact with my family, the three cats and the garden, half looking for Hazel, whom I half expected to appear at any moment, blindly sniffing her way towards a loving presence. In the afternoon Beryl and I walked up to Highgate Cemetery and examined the grave of George Eliot, which Beryl is trying to get properly restored.

Tomorrow or the next day, some time soon anyway, I shall try to give up smoking.